HISTORY OF
HOCKEYTOWN®

Detroit Red Wings

YEARS

by Bob Duff

*Foreword by: Mr. Hockey® Gordie Howe®
and Steve Yzerman*

Detroit, MI

D0125766

Executive Editor – Michael Bayoff
Editorial Assistant – Michael Reed
Interior Design – Michelle Chmura & Kelly Nykanen
Archivist – Sharon Arend
Photo Coordinator – Kristy Wills

Production – North American Graphics
Detroit, Michigan

This book is dedicated to everyone who has been a part of Detroit Red Wing hockey over the first 75 years, and to the millions of fans around the world who have made **HOCKEYTOWN** *what it is today.*

AUTOGRAPHS

CONTENTS

ACKNOWLEDGMENTS

When Detroit Red Wings senior vice-president Jimmy Devellano called early in the summer of 2001 and asked whether it were feasible to assemble a Red Wings history book in time for the 2001-02 season, I answered in the affirmative.

For someone who grew up with a passion for the game and a dream of being the next Terry Sawchuk, it was truly an exciting opportunity.

Then reality set in. Hockey season was only two months away. Fortunately, I was able to draw upon a strong support staff. Like any sporting success, this book was a team effort. No work of this magnitude could ever be the product of merely one person's perspiration and inspiration. Many have contributed their efforts and are worthy of recognition. Kevin Allen, hockey writer for *USA Today* and a Hall of Fame author in his own right, was a vast wealth of information, having been weaned on Red Wings hockey at the Olympia. Paul Harris, editor of *Hockey Weekly* and author of *Heroes of Hockeytown*, was another native Detroiter who shared his memories, as well as the interviews and anecdotes he uncovered while working on his book. Red Wings statistician Greg Innis offered his time and insight into the team's history. Stan Fischler, the most prolific chronicler of the game and the man who gave me my first job in the business, was another whose cavern of knowledge was essential to the telling of the Red Wings story.

At home base, Mike Bayoff and Mike Reed of the Red Wings publications department were patient and understanding when I suggested changes and always willing to look at things from different points of view.

I'd also be remiss if I didn't thank my employer, The Windsor *Star*, for allowing me the time and providing the resources which greatly assisted in assembling such a demanding project. My family also deserves recognition for their patience during the production process, a time which saw me miss out on some family functions. Cori Prymak, the love of my life, was especially helpful, first as a sounding board and a second set of eyes to peruse my words, but most of all, for her understanding acceptance that I'd have fewer moments to spend with her for a couple of months. I hope she realizes how much she inspires me to be a better writer and, more significantly, a better person.

I must thank the players and staff of the Red Wings, both past and present, for sharing their memories of the last 75 seasons. And last but not least, all of us, players and writers alike, tip our hats to you, the fans of this team and the sport of hockey. Without your support, there would be no history to chronicle.

Bob Duff
September 18, 2001

FOREWORD by: Mr. Hockey® Gordie Howe®

From the moment I attended my first training camp at age 16 with the Red Wings, when I pulled that sweater over my head for the first time, I felt at home.

I got my first pair of skates through the kindness of a woman in our neighborhood and I wore those skates every day after school. Hockey was my first love affair and while you never really think you're going to be an NHLer, you dream. I remember going to the rink and asking for autographs and once I got the chance to play pro hockey, thinking, "Wouldn't it be great to get into one NHL game, so that I could brag that I was a big leaguer?"

To have been granted the honor of playing 32 pro seasons and skating 25 consecutive seasons in one NHL city where they truly care passionately about the game and its players is something I will never forget. I remember Jack Adams asking me in my first camp if I was related to Red Wings star Syd Howe. I wasn't, but he told me if I could have half the career Syd Howe had, I'd be lucky and he was right.

So many great players have worn this uniform. It was a privilege to follow the likes of Syd Howe, to skate alongside players like Sid Abel, Ted Lindsay, Bill Gadsby and Red Kelly and I have to tell you I really admire the way that No. 19 plays today and how he's carried on the Red Wings legacy.

I learned early about the love of the Wings fans when I suffered my head injury in the 1950 playoffs and was required to undergo a brain operation. I got boxes of get well cards from fans, beautiful letters. It was truly amazing to me how much they cared.

Detroit is where I met my wife Colleen and where we raised our children. It's where we got to enjoy the thrill of every parent, watching our son Mark pull on a Red Wings sweater and where the fans gave us a standing ovation when I started an NHL game on a line alongside my sons Mark and Marty, even though we were playing for Hartford, the visiting team. The biggest compliment I can give Detroit is that when the time came that I was through playing hockey, we said, "We're going back home," and returned to Michigan.

Detroit has always been home to me, because the fans have always made the Howes feel so much at home here. The passion you see every game at Joe Louis Arena, the sea of red paraphernalia you witness in the crowd, it's truly astonishing. Without fans, you don't have a game. That's why you've seen so many great games in Detroit, because Detroit has so many great fans. Detroit fans are the best in the world. They really are.

—Mr. Hockey® Gordie Howe®

FOREWORD by: Steve Yzerman

The history of the Red Wings is about tradition — tradition of the historic Winged Wheel crest, the tradition of excellence on the ice, the tradition of generations of the greatest hockey fans in the world at the Olympia Stadium and Joe Louis Arena.

It's been a thrill for me to carry on the legacy of the great players who came before me. And it has been a privilege to wear the captain's "C" on my chest. For as long as I can remember, I dreamed of lifting the Stanley Cup. You hold your dreams out there and wonder if you're ever going to get there. To accomplish that goal, to lift the Stanley Cup aloft in front of the home crowd at Joe Louis Arena, to share the moment together as our long-awaited dream came true, was truly a memory that I will always savor above all others.

Coming to Detroit to play for the Red Wings as an 18-year-old in 1983 was the culmination of a lifetime goal to become a hockey player. You hope as a young player to be able to establish yourself, to make a career for yourself at the NHL level. To have been able to spend that entire career with one team, in a city that has become my home and to perform in front of the best hockey fans in the world, is an honor I will never forget. I'm proud to have been a part of the great Red Wings tradition and you should, too. Because without the greatest hockey fans in the world, Hockeytown wouldn't be what it is today.

—Steve Yzerman

DETROIT COUGARS
Hockey is born in Detroit

Think it's difficult to imagine Hockeytown without a hockey team? Then ponder this — the NHL awarding a franchise to a city without a hockey rink.

That's exactly what happened May 15, 1926, when the league gave Detroit its team.

"Providing work has advanced far enough on the rinks to assure a home for the clubs to start schedules in November, Chicago and Detroit will have teams in the National Hockey League next season," reported the Canadian Press.

Detroit bought itself a complete team by purchasing the roster of the Western Hockey League's Victoria Cougars for $100,000, opting to maintain the Cougars moniker.

The Cougars defeated the Montreal Canadiens to win the Stanley Cup in 1924-25, losing to the Montreal Maroons in the 1925-26 final, so it appeared as if Detroit had landed itself instant contender status.

Certainly, the list of players was impressive. Goalie Hap Holmes owned four Stanley Cup titles and forwards Frank Foyston and Jack Walker were members of three Cup winners. All were teammates on the 1916-17 Seattle Metropolitans, the first American-based team to win the Stanley Cup.

Besides that trio, forward Harry Meeking was part of two Cup championship teams and defensemen Hobie Kitchen, Slim Halderson, Clem Loughlin and Gord Fraser and forwards Frank Fredrickson, Harold (Gizzy) Hart and Russ Oatman owned one Cup apiece.

Fredrickson was an interesting specimen, a World War I pilot who also played the violin and owned a degree from the Toronto Conservatory of Music. Returning from combat in Africa, Fredrickson's ship was sunk and he was found days later by a Japanese freighter, floating on a piece of wreckage, clutching his violin to his chest.

He and Halderson both won gold medals in hockey for Canada at the 1920 Olympics and after the Games, Fredrickson, who was of Icelandic descent, took a job assisting the country of Iceland to set up its first airline.

He bargained for his first pro contract between sets with a dance band at Winnipeg's Fort Garry Hotel and also set himself up with a sweet deal in Detroit. Too sweet, in fact.

Fredrickson negotiated his own pact for $6,500 when most players were earning between $2-3,000. Once word of Fredrickson's salary reached teammates, they stopped passing him the puck and the Cougars were forced to trade him to Boston, where he finished fourth in NHL scoring and helped the Bruins reach the Stanley Cup final.

When its 12,000-seat ice palace fell ninth months behind schedule, Detroit saved its NHL team by playing on the Canadian side of the Detroit River in Windsor's Border Cities Arena, making the Cougars the only franchise in North American pro sports history to play its entire home schedule for a season in a foreign country.

With so many obstacles to overcome, perhaps it's not surprising that the Cougars finished last in the NHL with a 12-28-4 record.

Hockey was officially born in Detroit, but it hadn't been an easy delivery.

BACK in TIME

• October 31, 1926
Master of Magic, Harry Houdini, died in Detroit.

• January 5th & 6th, 1927
In New York, Fox Studios exhibited Movietone, a new invention synchronizing sound and music making talking motion pictures possible.

• February 26, 1927
A new record for long distance telephone service was set when the president of Pacific Telephone in San Francisco and the president of AT&T in London clearly heard each other 7,287 miles apart.

• May 26, 1927
The 15 millionth Model T Ford, called the "Tin Lizzie" rolled off the assembly line at the River Rouge plant in Dearborn, Michigan.

quick cuts

Most Goals
Johnny Sheppard: 13

Most Assists
Johnny Sheppard: 8

Most Points
Johnny Sheppard: 21

Most Penalty Minutes
Johnny Sheppard: 60

Most Wins, Goaltender
Harry "Hap" Holmes: 11

Lowest Goals-Against Average
Harry "Hap" Holmes: 2.23

Most Shutouts
Harry "Hap" Holmes: 6

NHL Award Winners
None

FINAL STANDINGS

American Division	W	L	T	PTS	GF	GA
New York Rangers	25	13	6	56	95	72
Boston	21	20	3	45	97	89
Chicago	19	22	3	41	115	116
Pittsburgh	15	26	3	33	79	108
DETROIT	12	28	4	28	76	105

Canadian Division Winner - Ottawa Senators

Playoff Results
Did not qualify
Stanley Cup Champion
Ottawa Senators

1926-27 Season in Review

RED WINGS ARCHIVE

The moment they took the ice for their inaugural NHL game, the Detroit Cougars made history.

Without a major-league ice facility, the Cougars were forced to play all their home games on the Canadian side of the Detroit River at the 6,000-seat Border Cities Arena in Windsor, making them the only franchise in a North American major sport to play all of their home games in a foreign country. Many fans traveled by ferry across the border to witness their new NHL team in action.

An omen of the season to come was felt before that first contest even commenced. Goaltender Harry (Hap) Holmes was felled by flu on game day, forcing back-up Herb Stuart to don the pads for opening night, a 2-0 loss to the Boston Bruins.

Though blanked in their debut, the Cougars would quickly gather a few milestones. Slim Halderson got Detroit on the scoreboard in a 4-1 loss at Pittsburgh Nov. 20 and two nights later, Holmes made Frank Fredrickson's third-period goal stand up with 29 saves in a 1-0 win at Chicago.

Just like that, the first goal, win and shutout in franchise history were in the books.

Victories were few during a 12-28-4 campaign, but some were notable. Holmes stoned the reigning Stanley Cup champion Montreal Maroons 4-0 right at the Forum on Nov. 30. He had the whitewash brush at work again

Dec. 16 at Ottawa, stopping all 24 shots in a 5-0 victory over the Senators, who would win the Stanley Cup that spring.

The Toronto St. Patricks visited Windsor for a Feb. 15 date with the Cougars and were hammered 5-1. After the game, the Toronto squad changed its name to the Maple Leafs, dropping their green-and-white shamrock jersey for a blue-and-white one decorated with a maple leaf, in the process creating a traditional rivalry with Detroit which continues today.

Detroit's last home-ice victory of the season was a 7-1 rout of the Pittsburgh Pirates in which Keats fired the first hat trick in club history.

Duncan relinquished the coaching duties to Keats on Feb. 24, but the change didn't help. Detroit closed 2-7-2 under its new boss, finishing with the NHL's worst record. The financial books also showed red ink, with the club displaying operating losses of $84,000.

HOCKEYTOWN MOMENT
Detroit plays first season in the NHL

The coolest game on earth was the hottest thing on ice in 1926 and the Motor City was revving up its engines to get into the chase.

The NHL took on an American look in 1924 with the addition of the Boston Bruins and kept southward in motion by adding the Pittsburgh Pirates and New York Americans to the fold a year later.

By the midst of the 1925-26 NHL campaign, there were 11 bids from American cities for teams, including five from Detroit. "Detroit will have professional hockey, of that there is no doubt," guaranteed James Connor, spokesperson for the Detroit Hockey Club.

On May 15, 1926, that group, an outfit headed by Charles King, former public relations director for President Theodore Roosevelt and including such investors as Edsel Ford, S.S. Kresge, William Scripps and Hall of Fame goaltender Percy LeSueur, proved to be the successful bidder. The NHL had purchased the rights to all players of the Western Hockey League, a rival loop which competed with the NHL for the Stanley Cup and the owners of the new Detroit franchise acted quickly, acquiring the roster of the Victoria Cougars for $100,000.

In 1924-25, the Cougars were the last team from outside the NHL to win the Stanley Cup and were losing finalists in 1925-26. Sensing a winning tradition, the new owners opted to keep the nickname. That first Detroit team suited up five future Hall of Famers. Goaltender Hap Holmes was part of four Stanley Cup winners and left-winger Jack Walker owned three Cup titles. Eight others who skated for the Cougars that season - defenseman Slim Halderson, Hobie Kitchen and Clem Loughlin and forwards Frank Foyston, Jim Riley, Frank Fredrickson, Gizzy Hart and Harry Meeking - also had a Cup on their resumes. As well, Fredrickson and Halderson won gold medals for Canada at the 1920 Olympic Games in Antwerp, Belgium.

Captain Art Duncan, whose rights were acquired from Chicago, won a scoring title with Vancouver of the Pacific Coast Association in 1923-24, even though he played defense. He was named Detroit's first coach and manager.

On paper, the Cougars iced a great team. Unfortunately, the games are played on the ice and Detroit, with eight players 31 or older, no longer had the legs for the long haul.

"The fellow who called Detroit's hockey team the Cougars would name a troupe of trained fleas a herd of fire-breathing dragons," mocked the Chicago Tribune.

The Cougars stumbled home last in the NHL's American Division, 13 points out of a playoff spot.

Duke Keats

Among hockey's all-time greats, Duke Keats is often overlooked because he spent so little of his career - a paltry 82 games - performing in the NHL. But his contemporaries knew that Keats was a name which should be mentioned in the same breath as the likes of Gordie Howe, Wayne Gretzky and Howie Morenz.

"Gordon (Duke) Keats was the best player of all time," stated Lloyd McIntyre, a teammate of Keats with Edmonton of the Western Hockey League, where Keats once scored eight goals in a single game. "You would have thought he had a nail in the end of his stick, the way he could carry that puck around. He was that good."

Keats scored the first goal in a Cougars game and later, scored plenty of goals for the Cougars. He was toiling for Boston on Nov. 18, 1926 when he potted the game-winner in a 2-0 victory over the Cougars. Detroit obviously liked what they saw, because the Cougars moved Frank Fredrickson and Harry Meeking to acquire Keats and Archie Briden at mid-season.

His first tally for Detroit was an overtime winner in a 1-0 victory over the New York Americans. Keats netted 12 goals in 25 games for Detroit, including the club's first hat-trick in a 7-1 win over Pittsburgh on March 10, 1927.

"Duke is the possessor of more hockey grey matter than any man who ever played the game," noted Hall of Famer Frank Patrick. A fiery leader, once while playing for Toronto of the National Hockey Association during the 1916-17 season, Keats became so angered by the poor performance of goalie Billy Nicholson that he strapped on the pads and took over in net himself for the next period.

HOCKEY HALL OF FAME

That temper sometimes got Keats into hot water and it punched his ticket out of Detroit. During a game at Chicago early in the 1927-28 season, Keats swung his stick in the direction of taunting fans, nearly striking actress Irene Castle, the wife of Blackhawks owner Major Frederic McLaughlin.

The NHL suspended Keats indefinitely, a suspension which was lifted Dec. 16, 1927, when the Cougars traded him to of all teams, the Blackhawks, where he finished his NHL career the following season.

- **BORN:**
  Montreal, Que., March 1, 1895
- **ACQUIRED:**
  January 7, 1927 trade with Boston
- **BEST SEASON WITH RED WINGS:**
  1926-27 (12-1-13)
- **TOTALS WITH RED WINGS:**
  GP-30, G-12, A-3, PTS-15

- **HONORS:**
  Scored first hat trick in club history; Led team with three game-winning goals; Coached team for final 11 games of 1926-27 season; Elected to Hockey Hall of Fame in 1958

MOTOWN Classic

Holmes becomes Detroit's first goaltender

RED WINGS ARCHIVE

Mom and dad christened him Harry Holmes when he was born in Aurora, Ont. on Feb. 21, 1892, but everyone knew him as "Happy." And Hap Holmes had reason for his happiness.

Holmes holds the unique record of winning the Stanley Cup four times in four different leagues and each of the wins was unique. The 1913-14 Toronto Blueshirts of the National Hockey Association were the first team from that famous hockey city to win the Stanley Cup. The 1916-17 Seattle Metropolitans of the Pacific Coast Hockey Association were the first American Stanley Cup champs and the 1917-18 Toronto Arenas were the first NHL team to lift Lord Stanley's mug. In 1924-25 Holmes backstopped the Western Canada Hockey League's Victoria Cougars to the title, the last team from outside the NHL to capture the Cup.

Holmes wore his trademark hat in goal to protect his bald head from tobacco-spitting fans who often perched in the rail seats above him, looking to get in a little target practice. "I swear that some of those fellows used to load their tobacco with bird shot," Holmes said.

He often found himself in the midst of a shooting gallery in two seasons as the Cougars netminder. The limited margin of error Holmes was allowed in order to succeed is evidenced in that he posted 17 shutouts and just 30 victories in two seasons with Detroit.

Holmes left the Cougars in 1928 to accept a position as coach of the Cleveland franchise in the CanPro League. Elected to the Hockey Hall of Fame in 1972, the Harry (Hap) Holmes Trophy is presented annually to the AHL's leading goaltender.

ASSEMBLY LINE

In Detroit's first NHL game, a 2-0 loss to Boston, forwards Duke Keats and Archie Briden scored for the Bruins and must have impressed someone, because on Jan. 7, 1927, the Cougars dealt forwards Frank Fredrickson and Harry Meeking to the Bruins for Keats and Briden in one of the club's first major trades.

The Cougars also dealt defenseman Slim Halderson to the Toronto St. Patricks for Pete Bellefeuille, a speedy right-winger known as "The Fleeting French-

Frank Frederickson

RED WINGS ARCHIVE

man" and it looked like a good move when Bellefeuille scored six times in 18 games for Detroit.

In straight cash transactions, the Cougars sold the contracts of forward Gizzy Hart to the Montreal Canadiens and of forward Russ Oatman to the Montreal Maroons.

Red Wings Facts

Opening Night Roster

Detroit Cougars vs Boston Bruins

Border Cities Arena, Windsor
Thursday, November 18, 1926

Detroit		Boston
Hap Holmes	1	Sprague Cleghorn
Clem Loughlin	2	Eddie Shore
Slim Halderson	3	Lionel Hitchman
Harry Meeking	4	Jimmy Herberts
Frank Fredrickson	5	Duke Keats
Jack Walker	6	Perk Galbraith
Russ Oatman	7	Carson Cooper
Art Duncan	8	Archie Briden
(Manager and coach)		
Johnny Sheppard	9	Harry Oliver
Frank Foyston	10	Billy Coutu
Hobie Kitchen	11	Doc Stewart
Fred Gordon	12	Red Stuart
Gizzy Hart	13	
Herb Stuart	14	Chuck Cahill
		Hago Harrington
		Moe Roberts
		Art Ross
		(Manager and Coach)

5

THE RED BARN
Olympia Stadium

It was late arriving and mourned at its passing.

The Olympia was to Red Wings fans what Maple Leaf Gardens was to Toronto fans and Boston Garden to Bruins supporters.

It was home.

"It wasn't the bricks that gave the Olympia that feeling," former Red Wings trainer Lefty Wilson said. "It was the people."

Built at a cost of $2.15 million, when the Olympia first opened its doors, Detroit's NHL team wasn't even called the Red Wings yet.

A rodeo christened Detroit's new hockey home, but the NHL took over on Nov. 22, 1927.

"The scarlet-shirted cohorts of the Detroit Cougars, headed by Jack Adams, will swing into action at the Olympia tonight against the Ottawa Senators, professional puck-chasing champions of the universe," boasted the that day's editions of Windsor's Border Cities Star.

Twelve thousand fans, an NHL record, attended that night. The University of Michigan band played Hail To The Victors and Johnny Sheppard gave Detroit a 1-0 lead.

So much for fairy tale endings. Frank Nighbor and Frank Finnigan scored and the Senators won 2-1. It would be some time before great hockey was played by the team which resided at the corner of Grand River and McGraw.

Detroit's team became known as the Red Wings in the 1930s and the Olympia was known as a place to be feared by the opposition.

"The fans were right on top of the action," remembered longtime Red Wings broadcaster Bruce Martyn.

Detroit won the Cup-clinching games for five of its nine Stanley Cups on Olympia ice, including exciting Game 7 overtime decisions in 1950 and 1954.

"You got to where you'd expect anything there," said Sid Abel, who captained and coached the Wings in the Red Barn, as the Olympia was known. "The fans used to throw cigars on the ice whenever Toronto goalie Turk Broda allowed a goal. Turk loved cigars and he used to gather them up by the armful."

RED WINGS ARCHIVE

By the 1950s, Gordie Howe was tossing elbows and the fans were tossing octopi on the ice during the playoffs, feeling the eight tentacles represented the eight wins required in those days to capture the Stanley Cup.

"You'd come out of that tunnel, see Gordie Howe and Ted Lindsay and already feel like you were down 2-0," former Boston winger Willie O'Ree said.

The boards were egg-shaped and Detroit players learned exactly where to shoot the puck on dump-ins and where to go to retrieve it.

The Wings deteriorated in the 1970s and the old building also started to show its age. By the middle of the 1979-80 season, Joe Louis Arena was ready for the Red Wings and the last game at the Olympia was played Dec. 15, 1979. Detroit rallied from a 4-0 deficit for a 4-4 tie with the Quebec Nordiques on Greg Joly's goal at 18:35 of the third period.

"It's time to forget the past, for us to start a new dynasty," Joly said afterwards. "There were some great teams and players in the Olympia, but now it's time for this team to take off by itself."

The Olympia met the wrecking ball in July of 1986 and a United States Army armory was erected on the site.

BACK in TIME

- **October 6, 1927**

The first talking film, "The Jazz Singer," starring Russian-born actor Al Jolson debuted.

- **May 28, 1928**

Dodge Brothers, Inc. and the Chrysler Corporation merged, making the new consolidated firm the largest automobile company behind General Motors and Ford Motor.

- **June 3, 1928**

The first television set was placed on the market by Daven Corporation of Newark, New Jersey at a cost of $75.00.

quick cuts

Most Goals
George Hay: 22
Most Assists
George Hay: 13
Most Points
George Hay: 35
Most Penalty Minutes
Percy Traub: 78
Most Wins, Goaltender
Harry "Hap" Holmes: 19
Lowest Goals-Against Average
Harry "Hap" Holmes: 1.73
Most Shutouts
Harry "Hap" Holmes: 11
NHL Award Winners
None

FINAL STANDINGS

American Division	W	L	T	PTS	GF	GA
Boston	20	13	11	51	77	70
New York Rangers	19	16	9	47	94	79
Pittsburgh	19	17	8	46	67	76
DETROIT	19	19	6	44	88	79
Chicago	7	34	3	17	68	134

Canadian Division Winner - Montreal Canadiens

Playoff Results
Did not qualify
Stanley Cup Champion
New York Rangers

1927-28 Season in Review

Clearly disappointed with the lack of progress made during their first NHL season, ownership of the Detroit Cougars acted quickly to rectify the situation.

The first move was to hire NHL veteran Jack Adams as coach and manager. A center who'd won Stanley Cups with Toronto and Ottawa, Adams began to reshape the club almost immediately. Before the start of training camp, the new boss moved defenseman Art Duncan and forward Harry Meeking out of town, while acquiring defensemen Reg Noble, Bill Brydge and Stan Brown and forwards George Hay, Carson Cooper, Larry Aurie and Frank Sheppard, the younger brother of Detroit left-winger Johnny Sheppard, who was signed as a free agent.

By the time Adams was done wheeling and dealing, only Hap Holmes, Johnny Sheppard, Clem Loughlin and Jack Walker remained from the club's opening-night roster.

The newcomers displayed their mettle almost immediately. Hay led Detroit with 22 goals and 35 points, while Cooper tallied 15 times and the rookie Aurie potted 13 goals.

"The Cougars have a team that is 50 per cent stronger than the outfit of last year," noted Windsor's Border Cities Star, which was impressed with Detroit's new leader.

"Jack Adams not only has a stronger lineup, but he has his men in shape and he has perfect harmony throughout his squad."

A permanent farm team, the Detroit Olympics, was entered into the CanPro League and would also play at the Olympia, Detroit's new stadium, which was christened with a rodeo. Veteran Frank Foyston dropped down from the big club to serve as player-coach of the Olympics.

Detroit opened the season on the road, whipping Pitts-

RED WINGS ARCHIVE

burgh 6-0, with newcomers Hay (two goals), Cooper and Traub all scoring. The Olympia opener Nov. 22 before 16,000 saw Johnny Sheppard spot Detroit a 1-0 advantage before a pair of goals rallied the Stanley Cup champion Ottawa Senators to a 2-1 win.

By New Year's, Detroit was 8-6-1 and a serious playoff contender, so much so that Adams recalled Foyston from his minor-league coaching assignment to bolster the roster.

Battling to the wire for the third and final American Division playoff spot with the Pittsburgh Pirates, it all came down to a March 18 showdown at the Olympia, which the Pirates won 1-0 on Johnny McKinnon's second period goal. It was the only goal Holmes had allowed in three games, but it was enough to keep the Cougars out of post-season play.

A 7-2 home-ice victory over the Boston Bruins, Stanley Cup finalists the previous spring, closed out the season for Detroit two points shy of the playoffs, but at .500 for the season with a 19-19-6 slate, 16 points better than the Cougars' inaugural campaign.

HOCKEYTOWN MOMENT

Wings play first season at Olympia Stadium

No more border crossings would be necessary for Detroit fans to view NHL hockey. Though the Olympia was late in arriving (it was originally scheduled to open in February 1927), it proved worth the wait. Sixteen thousand excited fans packed the new state-of-the-art facility Nov. 22 to witness the Cougars do battle with the Stanley Cup champion Ottawa Senators.

"Occupying every seat in the huge arena and jamming all available standing room, the first nighters enthusiastically acclaimed hockey as a sport that has reached Detroit to stay," stated newspaper accounts of the opener.

Pomp and circumstance were everywhere to see. The University of Michigan's 100-piece band provided musical interludes during the intermissions and stoppages and world-famous Canadian fancy and trick skaters Norval Baptie and Gladys Lamb performed prior to the game and between periods.

The game itself was a splendid display of hockey. Johnny Sheppard put Detroit in front at 10:20 of the first period, jamming home the rebound of a Duke Keats shot. Frank Nighbor tied the count with Detroit playing two men short and set up Frank Finnigan for the game winner midway through the third frame.

Though they came out on the wrong side of the scoreboard, Detroit was truly a winner on this night that Hockeytown was officially christened.

RED WINGS ARCHIVE

Olympia Stadium

Johnny Sheppard

Firsts were foremost for Johnny Sheppard during his tenure with the Detroit Cougars.

The skilled left-winger was the first member of the Detroit organization to pull on the famous No. 9 jersey and with 13-8-21 totals in 1926-27, was the first player to lead the club in all three categories. He also led the team with 60 penalty minutes that inaugural campaign and he and Ted Lindsay are the only players in franchise history to top the club in scoring and penalty minutes in the same season.

The 1927-28 season saw Sheppard complete a famous Detroit first when he put a shot past Ottawa Senators goalie Alex Connell November 22, 1927 to score the first goal in the history of the Olympia. Another first was achieved in the season opener this season, November 15 at Pittsburgh, when Johnny and younger brother Frank Sheppard became the first brother combination to perform for the team.

Purchased from the Edmonton Eskimos of the Western Hockey League, the elder Sheppard was a bundle of speed, energy and courage. Called "Wee Johnny" due to his diminutive 5-foot-7, 165-pound frame, Sheppard was a rugged competitor who once worked as a trapper near the Arctic Circle. The deadly finisher possessed blazing speed on his skates.

Sheppard's talents also made him a marketable commodity and when new manager Jack Adams found he'd gathered an excess of offensive talent with newcomers George Hay, Carson Cooper and Larry Aurie all joining Sheppard in reaching double digits in the goal column in 1927-28, he moved the latter to the New York Americans prior to the following season,

RED WINGS ARCHIVE

acquiring center Bobby Connors, $12,500 and the rights to promising amateur Ebbie Goodfellow for Sheppard.

The deal seemed one-sided at the time, but Goodfellow would become a Hall of Fame performer for Detroit and won the club's first Hart Trophy in 1940.

Even in departure, Sheppard managed to engineer another first for the team.

- **BORN:**
  Montreal, Que., July 3, 1903
- **ACQUIRED:**
  Contract Purchased October 5, 1926 from Edmonton (WHL)
- **BEST SEASON WITH RED WINGS:**
  1926-27 (13-8-21)

- **TOTALS WITH RED WINGS:**
  GP-87, G-23, A-18, PTS-41
- **HONORS:**
  Led Detroit in goals, assists, points and penalty minutes in 1926-27; Scored the first goal at the Olympia

MOTOWN Classic

RED WINGS ARCHIVE

Adams begins his tenure in Hockeytown

Jack Adams sensed destiny was on his side when he met with Detroit Cougars president Charles Hughes to interview for the position as coach and manager. He'd been recommended for the job by NHL president Frank Calder and the Detroit brass was thrilled that a member of the Stanley Cup champion Ottawa Senators sought to work for them.

A skilled and rugged center, Adams won a Cup with the Senators and also with the Toronto Arenas in 1917-18. He'd had a brief fling at coaching with Toronto in 1922-23 and was seeking another chance. He knew Detroit was about to open a new ice palace and saw potential there.

He got the job, beginning a 35-year tenure with the franchise. A gruff man, his nickname - Jolly Jawn - was a misnomer, for Adams rarely smiled. "Jack was about

the crustiest individual that you'd ever want to meet," Hall of Fame broadcaster Budd Lynch said. "Part Army Colonel, but soft as putty if you got him at the right time."

A hard-nosed negotiator, Adams was reviled by players, but he was also the man who gave Hockeytown legitimacy as a hockey town. An innovator, he developed the farm system and convinced the NHL that flooding the ice between periods would improve the speed and quality of play.

ASSEMBLY LINE

Hired shortly after the conclusion of the 1926-27 Stanley Cup final, Jack Adams set out to build a foundation for Detroit, so naturally, one of his first trades sent Art Duncan to Toronto for defenseman Bill Brydge. He spent $15,000 to purchase left wing George Hay and defenseman Percy (Puss) Traub from Chicago and also purchased Stan Brown from the New York Rangers, while selecting Larry Aurie in the interleague draft.

Another move with the Blackhawks saw veteran Duke Keats go to Chicago for defenseman Gord Fraser and $5,000. It was actually Fraser's second tenure with Detroit, though his first opportunity to suit up. He'd been originally acquired when the club bought the Victoria (WHL) franchise in 1926, then dealt to Chicago for Duncan prior to the start of the 1926-27 season.

RED WINGS ARCHIVE

Bill Brydge

Red Wings Facts

Lady Byng Winners

Marty Barry	1936-37
Bill Quackenbush	1948-49
Red Kelly	1950-51,
	1952-53,
	1953-54
Dutch Reibel	1955-56
Alex Delvecchio	1958-59,
	1965-66,
	1968-69
Marcel Dionne	1974-75

Short Passes

 Defenseman Dr. Stan Brown was a dentist who had a practice in Windsor and was occasionally called upon to pull an injured teammate's tooth during games.

- 1928 • 1929 -

BACK in TIME

- **November 7, 1928**
The platform slogan of, "A chicken in every pot and a car in every garage", earned Herbert Clark Hoover the Presidential election in a landslide victory.

- **February 17, 1929**
Universal Air Line showed a 10-reel motion picture to its 12 passengers traveling from Minneapolis to St. Paul to Chicago in what is believed to be the first in flight movie showing.

- **June 27, 1929**
Bell Laboratories in New York developed a system for transmitting television in full color using three separate tubes for each primary color.

quick cuts

Most Goals
Carson Cooper: 18
Most Assists
Carson Cooper: 9
Most Points
Carson Cooper: 27
Most Penalty Minutes
Bobby Connors: 68
Most Wins, Goaltender
Dolly Dolson: 19
Lowest Goals-Against Average
Dolly Dolson: 1.37
Most Shutouts
Dolly Dolson: 10
NHL Award Winners
None

FINAL STANDINGS

American Division	W	L	T	PTS	GF	GA
Boston	26	13	5	57	89	52
New York Rangers	21	13	10	52	72	65
DETROIT	19	16	9	47	72	63
Pittsburgh	9	27	8	26	46	80
Chicago	7	29	8	22	33	85

Canadian Division Winner - Montreal Canadiens

Playoff Results
Lost to Toronto Maple Leafs (7 goals to 2)
Leading Playoff Scorers
George Hay (1G) & Larry Aurie (1G)
Stanley Cup Champion
Boston Bruins

1928-29 Season in Review

DETROIT COUGARS NATIONAL LEAGUE PLAYOFFS - 1928-1929
RED WINGS ARCHIVE

A break-even season which saw Detroit narrowly miss the playoffs in 1927-28 offered encouragement as the club began the 1928-29 campaign. And there was sound reason for such optimism.

Following a 2-0 season-opening loss to the Stanley Cup champion New York Rangers, Detroit rattled off wins over Pittsburgh and Boston, launching a seven-game (4-0-3) unbeaten streak and an 11-game unbeaten run (7-0-4) on Olympia ice. Detroit didn't lose a home contest until Jan. 27, a 2-1 setback to the New York Americans.

Changes implemented by coach-manager Jack Adams continued to pay dividends. Carson Cooper led the club with 18 goals and 27 points, while Bobby Connors (13 goals) and George Hay (11), also hit double digits. Rugged Bill Brydge rounded out a solid defensive corps and rookie Herbie Lewis tallied nine goals.

The struggles of Pittsburgh (9-27-8) and Chicago (7-29-8) assured playoff hockey for Detroit, which finished with its first winning record at 19-16-9, good for third in the NHL's American Division.

The Cougars were winning over Detroit fans, too. The team drew 178,447 for 24 home dates, an average of 7,436 per game, up almost 30 per cent from the previous season.

HOCKEYTOWN MOMENT

Detroit and Toronto commence historic Stanley Cup rivalry

Jack Adams appeared in three Stanley Cup finals as a player and in his playoff debut as a coach, boldly predicted his Detroit Cougars could go as far. "We've got a real chance to get into the finals," Adams said on the eve of Detroit's first playoff series against the Toronto Maple Leafs. "Everybody is keyed up for the Toronto series and we're not going to give up trying until the last dog is hung. And that last dog hanging act, by the way, may witness the crowning of the Cougars as champions."

The two-game, total goals quarter-final series began March 19 and an Olympia crowd was disappointed as Toronto won 3-1 behind the two-goal performance of Andy Blair. George Hay drew the honor of scoring first playoff goal in Detroit history, a third-period breakaway tally against Leafs goalie Lorne Chabot.

Now the Cougars were up against it, needing to make up a two-goal deficit at Toronto's Mutual Street Arena. Already minus Jimmy Herbert (shoulder injury), Adams lost Bobby Connors to a knee injury in Game 2, forcing him to employ defensemen Puss Traub and Reg Noble at center. The weakened Cougars fell 4-1, with Larry Aurie tallying the lone goal and 7-2 on the set.

The playoffs were over for Detroit, but a long-standing rivalry was launched. Detroit and Toronto have met 23 times in Stanley Cup play, second only to the 28 series between the Boston Bruins and Montreal Canadiens.

Carson Cooper

Carson Cooper seldom missed the mark during his NHL days and Detroit was well rewarded by Cooper's astute accuracy.

Purchased from Boston in 1927, Cooper led the Cougars in goals in each of his first three seasons with the team. He was Detroit's leading scorer with 18 goals and 27 points in 1928-29 and again in 1929-30, when he registered 18-18-36 totals.

He'd already displayed offensive prowess with the Bruins, scoring 28 times in 1925-26 and the credit for Cooper's touch around the net was given to his deadly accurate flip shot, a move which earned him the handle "Shovel Shot."

A star with the OHA senior Hamilton Tigers, Cooper was resistant to turning pro, mainly because he was being paid so handsomely under the table to remain an amateur. In 1924-25, the Bruins, struggling desperately to assemble a team prior to their first NHL season, used blackmail to get Cooper's name on a contract, gathering evidence of these illegal payments and threatening to take it to amateur hockey officials if he didn't turn pro with them.

After he left Detroit following the 1931-32 season, Cooper played three seasons in the minors, then made it his job to convince amateurs to turn pro, signing on as a scout with Detroit.

As Detroit's eastern scout, working in conjunction with western scout Fred Pinckney, the bird-dogging work of the two men turned Detroit into an NHL power in the 1940s and 1950s. Among Cooper's finds were Hall of Famers Ted Lindsay, Red Kelly and Harry Lumley.

Cooper finished his hockey days as he had begun them, playing a starring role in the amateur ranks.

DETROIT NEWS

- **BORN:**
  Cornwall, Ont., July 17, 1898
- **ACQUIRED:**
  Contract purchased May 22, 1927
  from Boston
- **BEST SEASON WITH RED WINGS:**
  1929-30 (18-18-36)

- **TOTALS WITH RED WINGS:**
  GP-222, G-68, A-48, PTS-116.
- **HONORS:**
  Led Detroit in goals and points in
  1928-29 and in goals, assists and
  points in 1929-30

MOTOWN Classic

Dolson ignites the Olympia crowd

Detroit coach-manager Jack Adams needed a goalie to replace veteran Hap Holmes, so he selected Clarence (Dolly) Dolson in the inter-league draft from the Stratford Nationals, CANPRO farm club of the Montreal Maroons.

An acrobatic netminder, Dolson, 31, immediately filled the bill, posting 10 shutouts and holding the opposition to a solitary goal on 18 other occasions during the 44-game schedule. The first Detroit goalie to post three consecutive shutouts, Dolson blanked the New York Rangers 1-0 on Feb. 21, then posted successive zeros versus the Chicago Blackhawks - a scoreless tie on Feb. 23 and a 3-0 triumph Feb. 26.

Serving with the Canadian infantry in France during World War I, Dolson was decorated for bravery on the battlefield. His eagle eye spotted a grenade sailing towards their trench. He positioned his body to block the shot, then cleared the rebound a split second before the grenade detonated.

ASSEMBLY LINE

Carson Cooper would go on to become a successful talent scout for Detroit, but his first player assessment didn't pan out. "If the Cougars get (Jimmy) Herbert," Cooper suggested, "that is all we need to win the league." Detroit followed his advice, acquiring Cooper's former Boston teammate from Toronto in exchange for Jack Arbour and $12,500, but Herbert produced just 10 goals in two seasons and was assigned to the minor leagues.

Herbie Lewis

Feisty center Bobby Connors came over from the New York Americans in the Johnny Sheppard trade and led the club with 68 penalty minutes. Defenseman Bill Brydge and winger Bernie Brophy were promoted from the CANPRO Detroit Olympics and for the second year in a row, manager Jack Adams successfully mined the minors, plucking goalie Clarence (Dolly) Dolson and winger Herbie Lewis through the inter-league draft.

Red Wings Facts

Single Season Shut-Out Leaders
(minimum 10 shut-outs)

1951-52	. .Terry Sawchuk	12
1953-54	. .Terry Sawchuk	12
1954-55	. .Terry Sawchuk	12
1955-56	. . . .Glenn Hall	12
1927-28	. . .Harry Holmes	11
1950-51	. .Terry Sawchuk	11
1928-29	. . .Dolly Dolson	10
1932-33	.John Ross Roach	. .10

Short Passes

Defenseman Percy (Puss) Traub played all 44 games without registering a point, the only non-goaltender to do so in franchise history.

15

- 1929  1930 -

BACK in TIME

• **October 24, 1929**
The Stock Market crashed on this "Black Tuesday" when financial uncertainty escalated into panic and investors ordered their brokers to sell at any price.

• **January 15, 1930**
The banning of alcohol under the 18th Amendment marked the 10th anniversary of prohibition.

• **May 30, 1930**
The winner of the 18th annual Indy 500, Billy Arnold, traveled at a speed of 100.4 mph in a Miller Hartz special racer.

quick cuts

Most Goals
Herbie Lewis: 20
Most Assists
Carson Cooper: 18
Most Points
Carson Cooper: 36
Most Penalty Minutes
Harvey Rockburn: 97
Most Wins, Goaltender
Bill Beveridge: 14
Lowest Goals-Against Average
Bill Beveridge: 2.71
Most Shutouts
Bill Beveridge: 2
NHL Award Winners
None

FINAL STANDINGS

American Division	W	L	T	PTS	GF	GA
Boston	38	5	1	77	179	98
Chicago	21	18	5	47	117	111
New York Rangers	17	17	10	44	136	143
DETROIT	14	24	6	34	117	133
Pittsburgh	5	36	3	13	102	185

Canadian Division Winner - Montreal Maroons

Playoff Results
Did Not Qualify
Stanley Cup Champion
Montreal Canadiens

1929-30 Season in Review

Just when the Detroit Cougars were beginning to make progress, dramatic NHL rule changes and the Great Depression combined to knock them back down again.

Looking to boost offense after a record 120 shutouts were posted the season before, the NHL began the 1929-30 season by allowing forward passing in all three zones on the ice and permitting players to kick the puck. Roster size was also increased from 12 to 15 players. These rule alterations had the desired effect, as NHL scoring jumped from 2.9 to 5.9 goals per game.

RED WINGS ARCHIVE

However, the changes had a detrimental effect on the Cougars, who didn't have the firepower to run and gun with the rest of the NHL. Detroit scored 117 goals, tied for sixth in the league with Chicago. The top three goal scorers in the NHL - Boston's Cooney Weiland (43) and Dit Clapper (41) and the Montreal Canadiens' Howie Morenz (40) - combined to outscore the Cougars. The 18-18-36 totals of Carson Cooper, Detroit's leading scorer, were only good enough for 16th overall in the NHL.

The season started in ominous fashion when defenseman Bill Brydge decided to test the negotiating prowess of manager Jack Adams, rejecting his contract offer. Adams suspended Brydge, then sold his contract to the New York Americans for $5,000.

Things didn't get much better from there. Minus Brydge and with three rookies patrolling the blueline of the now explosive NHL, Detroit broke from the starting gate 0-4-1. Goaltender Dolly Dolson was sent down and Bill Beveridge was borrowed from the Ottawa Senators to fill the void. The Cougars won three of their next four games, but were never able to right the ship, sinking to 14-24-6, fourth overall in the American Division and out of the playoff picture for the third time in four seasons.

Positive notes in an otherwise dismal season included a pair of rookies. Center Ebbie Goodfellow was second in team scoring with 17-17-34 totals. Meanwhile, hard rock defenseman Harvey Rockburn established a club mark with 97 penalty minutes. Second-year man Herbie Lewis scored 20 goals, garnering a team-record four of them in an 8-1 rout of Pittsburgh.

In the seats, the onset of the Depression made money tight and attendance dwindled, as people refused to spend their earnings to watch a mediocre team.

HOCKEYTOWN MOMENT

Detroit borrows goalie Beveridge from Ottawa

In its three NHL seasons, one constant for Detroit was solid goaltending. That changed in 1929-30. Second-year man Dolly Dolson struggled and was shipped to London of the International League after just five games, with the Cougars picking up Bill Beveridge on loan from the Ottawa Senators.

Beveridge was languishing behind the sensational Alex Connell in Ottawa, but got his first taste of NHL action in Detroit and his debut was a barn burner, a 7-6 victory over the Montreal Maroons. The new Detroit goaler won six of his first nine appearances and posted a shutout streak of 180 minutes and 20 seconds in January, including back-to-back 4-0 shutouts of the Montreal Canadiens and Chicago Blackhawks.

Beveridge finished with a 2.79 goals-against average in his only campaign with Detroit and was returned to Ottawa at season's end.

DWAYNE LaBAKAS

Bill Beveridge

17

Reg Noble

When Jack Adams sought to stabilize his lineup, one of the first moves he made was to spend $7,500 to add veteran Reg Noble in 1927, immediately naming him captain.

Adams was quite familiar with Noble's leadership qualities, having teamed with him for four seasons in Toronto. Adams was a rookie in 1917-18 when Noble led the Toronto Arenas to the Stanley Cup, scoring 30 goals in 18 games. Noble won a pair of Cups in Toronto, serving as both player-coach and captain and added a third with the Montreal Maroons in 1925-26, where his experience helped settle a young squad.

Off the ice, Noble was known to enjoy his bourbon and his fun. Once, when a power outage temporarily halted a Toronto-Ottawa game, he retrieved a pair of dice from the dressing room and entertained the fans by engaging teammate Harry Cameron and Ottawa's Frank Nighbor in a game of craps up against the boards at center ice.

A gritty competitor, Noble suffered a fractured skull when clipped by the stick of Ottawa's Hooley Smith in a 1925-26 game, but was back in the Maroons line-up after missing just four contests.

A fireplug of a player at 5-foot-8 and 180 pounds, Noble made the switch from left wing to defense with the Maroons and was a stabilizing influence on the back end. His ability to lend a helping hand was also evidenced on the score-sheet. Although he garnered only four assists for Detroit in 1929-30, it was enough to vault him past Nighbor into the NHL's career leadership in this category, with 93 helpers, making Noble the first of many players who would ascend to the all-time leadership of an NHL department while wearing a Detroit jersey.

Noble's last NHL season was 1932-33, allowing him to be one of a select few players to perform for Detroit under all three of its nicknames - Cougars, Falcons and Red Wings. He was also the last original NHLer to be an active player in the league. After his retirement from the game, he launched a career as an NHL referee and was elected to the Hockey Hall of Fame in 1962.

RED WINGS ARCHIVE

- **BORN:**
  Collingwood, Ont., June 23, 1896
- **ACQUIRED:**
  Contract purchased Oct. 4, 1927 from Montreal Maroons
- **BEST SEASON WITH RED WINGS:**
  1927-28 (6-8-14)

- **TOTALS WITH RED WINGS:**
  GP-270, G-23, A-24, PTS-47
- **HONORS:**
  Led Detroit in penalty minutes in 1927-28; Served as team captain from 1927-28 to 1929-30; Elected to Hockey Hall of Fame in 1962

18

Goodfellow records four assists in one period

Launching a 14-season career, it didn't take long for first-year center Ebbie Goodfellow to make his mark with Detroit. The rookie was especially helpful in a 7-3 win over the New York Rangers on Jan. 26, setting up four of the Cougars' goals.

Goodfellow wasted little time getting the lamp lit, setting up Stan McCabe for the game's first goal at 1:35 of the first period. He scored himself 1:05 later and by the end of the frame, had also made plays which resulted in a pair of goals by Carson Cooper.

Held off the scoresheet through the second period and well into the final stanza, Goodfellow completed his quartet of assists when he fed Herbie Lewis for the game's final goal with 2:52 to play.

Goodfellow's 17 assists were second on the team in 1929-30 and by the end of his first NHL campaign, he'd established himself as Detroit's No. 1 center.

RED WINGS ARCHIVE

ASSEMBLY LINE

The CANPRO League's leading scorer in 1928-29 while with the Detroit Olympics, Ebbie Goodfellow tallied 17 goals with the big club, setting a team record for rookies. Among other newcomers, left-winger Stan McCabe scored seven goals, while Hal Hicks, Harvey Rockburn and Rusty Hughes all took regular turns on defense. Goalie Bill Beveridge was added on loan from the Ottawa Senators.

RED WINGS ARCHIVE

Stan McCabe

Red Wings Facts

Fewest Road Loses in a Season

(7)
1951-52
& 1994-95

(9)
1927-28
1933-34
1936-37
1944-45
1947-48

Short Passes

Six of 17 players who suited up for Detroit in 1929-30 — Ebbie Goodfellow, Bill Beveridge, Stan McCabe, Roland Matte, Rusty Hughes and Harvey Rockburn — were NHL rookies.

BACK in TIME

- **June 12, 1930**

For the first time, a world heavyweight tittle was acquired on a foul when Max Schmeling was declared champion after opponent Jack Sharkey hit him below the belt.

- **September 1, 1930**

Thomas Edison tested the first United States electric passenger train between Hoboken and Montclair, New Jersey.

- **March 3, 1931**

President Hoover signed a bill making Frances Scott Key's "The Star Spangled Banner", sung to an old English drinking tune, the National Anthem.

quick cuts

Most Goals
Ebbie Goodfellow: 25

Most Assists
Ebbie Goodfellow: 23

Most Points
Ebbie Goodfellow: 48

Most Penalty Minutes
Harvey Rockburn: 118

Most Wins, Goaltender
Dolly Dolson: 16

Lowest Goals-Against Average
Dolly Dolson: 2.29

Most Shutouts
Dolly Dolson: 6

NHL Award Winners
None

FINAL STANDINGS

American Division	W	L	T	PTS	GF	GA
Boston	28	10	6	62	143	90
Chicago	24	17	3	51	108	78
New York Rangers	19	16	9	47	106	87
DETROIT	16	21	7	39	102	105
Philadelphia	4	36	4	12	76	184

Canadian Division Winner - Montreal Canadiens

Playoff Results
Did Not Qualify
Stanley Cup Champion
Montreal Canadiens

Coming off a disappointing 14-win season, Detroit entered the 1930-31 campaign with a new look, in more ways than one.

Eight new players were inserted into the lineup and the jerseys they pulled on were also new, as was the name on the front.

Four years as the Cougars led to mostly frustration, so it was decided to hold a newspaper contest to rename the team. A committee of newspaper people selected Falcons as the club's new handle. It was the most popular choice, being filled in on 93 of 2,000 ballots entered. The Falcons donned new uniforms with gold lettering, the only time in team history that the jersey was adorned with any shade other than red or white.

Detroit Falcons 1930-31

RED WINGS ARCHIVE

A 3-1-1 start to the season seemed to suggest the team was new and improved, but a 1-7 record in Detroit's first eight road games indicated otherwise. The playoffs would again be an event in which other teams participated and Detroit's struggles were punctuated by 2-0 and 7-5 setbacks against the woeful Philadelphia Quakers, who set an NHL futility mark by going 4-36-4.

Fans continued to stay away in droves and money was so tight that manager Jack Adams couldn't afford to sign a new practice goalie after Porky Levine landed a minor-league assignment, so Adams carved a wooden effigy of a goalie, outfitting it in full equipment, including skates. Detroit players pushed their plywood faux goalie into place in front of the net during practices and occasionally for pre-game warmups.

The bright spot for the Falcons was the performance of second-year center Ebbie Goodfellow, who set club scoring marks with 25-23-48 totals, finishing second in the NHL points race, three behind Howie Morenz of the Montreal Canadiens.

HOCKEYTOWN MOMENT
Detroit Scores 10 vs. Toronto

It arrived bereft of bows and ribbons and wasn't found under the tree, but Detroit fans couldn't have wished for a better Christmas present.

The Toronto Maple Leafs played the role of Christmas Day turkeys before 8,000 at the Olympia and were snowed under by a 10-1 count, as Detroit registered double digits in the goals column for the first time in franchise history.

The Falcons grabbed a 2-0 lead by the 1:04 mark of first period and owned a 5-0 advantage at the con-

clusion of the frame. Ebbie Goodfellow led the attack with four goals, equaling a club record. George Hay and Herbie Lewis scored two apiece, with Larry Aurie and Carson Cooper contributing singles.

Ace Bailey spoiled Dolly Dolson's shutout bid with 6:05 to play, but the Falcons spoiled more than that for Toronto goalie Ben Grant, who was shipped to the minors the next day.

George Hay

George Hay's pain was Detroit's gain.

The left-winger made his NHL debut with the Chicago Blackhawks in 1926-27, but was dealt to Detroit after producing just 22 points in 35 games.

Hay was hampered by torn shoulder ligaments that first season and by the time the 1927-28 campaign rolled around, was completely healed, as evidenced by his first game with Detroit, which saw him score twice and set up the game winner in a 6-0 shutout of Pittsburgh.

The 22-13-35 totals he put up that season led the team in scoring and were good enough to leave Hay fourth overall in the NHL scoring race. He was named to an unofficial NHL all-star team selected by NHL coaches and finished second to New York Rangers center Frank Boucher in voting for the Lady Byng Trophy.

Detroit's first 20-goal scorer was considered by many to

DETROIT NEWS

be the finest stickhandler in hockey. "Hay leaves all checks behind," noted one scouting report.

Hay turned pro with the Western Canada Hockey League's Regina Capitals in 1921-22 and posted 20-goal seasons in each of his first three pro campaigns. The gangly 5-foot-6, 155-pounder led the Western League in goals in 1925-26, potting 19 for the Portland Rosebuds.

It was Hay who was credited with the first playoff goal in Detroit history when he beat Toronto's Lorne Chabot in a 1929 Stanley Cup game.

Named captain this season, he appeared in all 44 games in 1930-31, but Hay's 18-point total was only good enough for fifth in team scoring. He was dropped to the minor-league Detroit Olympics in 1931-32, but returned to the big club for part of the next season and managed to appear in one game in 1933-34 before turning his focus to coaching Detroit's farm club.

Hay was elected to the Hockey Hall of Fame in 1958.

- **BORN:**
  Listowel, Ont., January 10, 1898
- **ACQUIRED:**
  Contract purchased April 11, 1927 from Chicago
- **BEST SEASON WITH RED WINGS:**
  1927-28 (22-13-35)

- **TOTALS WITH RED WINGS:**
  GP-204, G-60, A-52, PTS-112
- **HONORS:**
  Led Detroit in goals and points in 1927-28; Scored Detroit's first Stanley Cup playoff goal; Elected to Hockey Hall of Fame in 1958

MOTOWN Classic

Rockburn spends 118 minutes in the box

Detroit fans of this era knew the Rock not as a boastful WWF wrestler, but as the bad man of the Falcons blueline.

Rough around the edges and even rougher between the boards, Harvey Rockburn made his presence known this season, rollicking his way to 118 penalty minutes, a total which topped the NHL, making Rockburn the first single-season league leader in Detroit history.

Rockburn's energetic play and his collision-course style made him an instant hit with Detroit fans, but it also proved to be a detriment to his longevity. Too often caught out of position while in search of a hit, "Hard Rock," as he was known, was sent back to the minors by the Falcons after the 1930-31 season.

His career in Detroit was brief, but Rockburn's penalty-minute mark lasted as a club record until Ted Lindsay garnered 141 minutes in 1949-50.

When NHLers found themselves caught between the Hard Rock and a hard place, it was a painful experience.

RED WINGS ARCHIVE

ASSEMBLY LINE

After a year of minor-league seasoning, Dolly Dolson reclaimed his spot in Detroit's goal. Center Frank Fredrickson, a Detroit original in 1926-27, was signed as a free agent. Winger John Sorrell was purchased from London of the International League. Forwards Tom Filmore and Jimmy Creighton and defensemen Bert McInenly and Stew Evans were promoted from the minors.

RED WINGS ARCHIVE

"Dolly" Dolson

Red Wings Facts

All-Star Defensemen

Ebbie Goodfellow	1936, 1937, and 1940
Jack Stewart	1943, 1946, 1947, 1948, and 1949
Flash Hollett	1945
Bill Quackenbush	1947, 1948 and 1949
Leo Reise	1950 and 1951
Bob Goldham	1955
Red Kelly	1950, 1951, 1952, 1953, 1954, 1955, 1956, and 1957
Marcel Pronovost	1958, 1959, 1960 and 1961
Bill Gadsby	1965
Carl Brewer	1970
Paul Coffey	1995
Vladimir Konstantinov	1996
Nicklas Lidstrom	1998, 1999, 2000, 2001, 2002
Chris Chelios	2002

Short Passes

Detroit center Frank Fredrickson was a World War I flying ace who also played violin in a dance band and retired briefly from hockey to open a music store in Winnipeg, called "Frank Fredrickson's Melody Shop."

- 1931 1932 -

BACK in TIME

- **September 4, 1931**
Major James H. Doolittle set a new record for coast to coast travel when he flew from California to Newark in 11 hours, 16 minutes and 10 seconds at an average speed of 240 mph.

- **October 18, 1931**
One of the greatest inventors of all time, Thomas Alva Edison, died in his sleep at the age of 84.

- **March 31, 1932**
The nation was shocked after learning the 20-month old boy of Charles A. Lindbergh was kidnapped from his nursery while the parents were attending a dinner.

quick cuts

Most Goals
Ebbie Goodfellow: 14
Most Assists
Ebbie Goodfellow: 16
Most Points
Ebbie Goodfellow: 30
Most Penalty Minutes
Reg Noble: 72
Most Wins, Goaltender
Alex Connell: 18
Lowest Goals-Against Average
Alex Connell: 2.12
Most Shutouts
Alex Connell: 6
NHL Award Winners
None

FINAL STANDINGS

American Division	W	L	T	PTS	GF	GA
New York Rangers	23	17	8	54	134	112
Chicago	18	19	11	47	86	101
DETROIT	18	20	10	46	95	108
Boston	15	21	12	42	122	117

Canadian Division Winner - Montreal Canadiens

Playoff Results
Lost to Montreal Maroons (3-1)
Leading Playoff Scorers
Johnny Sorrell (1G, 1PT)
Stanley Cup Champion
Toronto Maple Leafs

24

1931-32 Season in Review

In all matters of historical chronology, there are watershed moments at which events can turn one way or another.

The 1931-32 season was such a point in the destiny of Detroit's NHL franchise.

On the ice, the team was struggling, missing the playoffs in each of the two previous seasons. In the boardroom, red ink flowed and the Falcons fell into receivership, in danger of disappearing from the NHL landscape.

Already the Philadelphia Quakers had folded and the Ottawa Senators took a leave of absence, reducing the NHL to an eight-team outfit. Ottawa's departure was actually a blessing for the Falcons, who landed five Senators - goalie Alex Connell, defenseman Alex Smith and forwards Art Gagne, Hec Kilrea and Dan Cox - in a dispersal draft of Ottawa talent.

Manager Jack Adams reshaped his squad and Detroit opened the season with nine new faces, possibly explaining why the club struggled to find consistency until mid-season.

Detroit's stumbling ways led to rumors that Adams was about to be dismissed, but with the club's bleak financial ledger, there was little he could do to rectify the situation. A chance to secure minor-league star Bill Thoms fell by the wayside when Adams couldn't scrape up the required $600 to complete the transaction.

"If Howie Morenz were available for $1.98, we still couldn't afford him," Adams said of the Montreal Canadiens superstar.

RED WINGS ARCHIVE

It didn't help that veterans Herbie Lewis (five goals) and Reg Noble (three goals), slumped badly, while Ebbie Goodfellow's 14-16-30 totals led the team, 18 points fewer than his club record of the season before.

Only Chicago (86) scored fewer goals than Detroit (95) and amazingly, only the Blackhawks (101) allowed fewer goals than the Falcons (108), thanks to the brilliant goalkeeping of Connell.

A club-record 18-game home unbeaten streak allowed Detroit, 18-20-10, to edge Boston for the third and final American Division playoff spot and the club's second playoff berth.

The Montreal Maroons downed Detroit 3-1 in a two-game, total goals series, but the playoff appearance saved Adams' job.

Little did he know that Detroit's biggest savior was about to arrive.

HOCKEYTOWN MOMENT
Falcons soar with Ottawa additions

The Falcons took on a serious Ottawa flavor, thanks to the acquisition of five players on season-loan from the idled Ottawa Senators.

Goaltender Alex Connell was a future Hall of Famer and he, left-winger Hec Kilrea and defenseman Alex Smith were teammates of Jack Adams on Ottawa's 1926-27 Stanley Cup winner. Right-winger

Art Gagne was originally Detroit property in 1926, but was traded to Chicago before playing a game. Left wing Dan Cox completed the quintet of borrowed Senators.

As well, leading scorer Ebbie Goodfellow was an Ottawa native who played all of his amateur hockey in Canada's national capitol.

Ebbie Goodfellow

Change is good for the heart and in Ebbie Goodfellow's case, it was great for Detroit.

A scorer from the time he first donned skates, Goodfellow led the Ottawa City Senior League in scoring in 1927-28 and after turning pro, finished as the CANPRO League's scoring leader in 1928-29.

Breaking into the NHL the following season, Goodfellow's second big-league campaign saw him set Detroit marks with 25-23-48 totals, good for second in the scoring race.

He also led the Falcons in scoring in 1931-32, so when manager Jack Adams approached Goodfellow at the commencement of the 1934-35 season and asked his veteran center to drop back and play defense, it would have been understandable were Goodfellow resistant to the idea.

Instead, he embraced the notion for the good of the team and with Goodfellow patrolling the blueline, Detroit won back-to-back Stanley Cups in 1935-36 and 1936-37. At six-feet and 180 pounds, he certainly owned a defenseman's physique. His ease in adjustment is evidenced in Goodfellow's three all-star selections at his adopted position, where he was also awarded the Hart Trophy as the NHL's most valuable player in 1939-40, the first Detroit player to be so honored.

Goodfellow served as Detroit captain for five seasons and played for three Stanley Cup winners, appearing in six finals.

Spending his entire 14-season career with Detroit, Goodfellow coached in the organization following his playing days and also served as president of the Red Wings Alumni Association. During the summer, he worked as caddie master at Detroit's prestigious Oakland Hills Country Club.

Goodfellow was elected to the Hockey Hall of Fame in 1963.

RED WINGS ARCHIVE

- **BORN:**
  Ottawa, Ont., April 9, 1907
- **ACQUIRED:**
  Oct. 14, 1928 trade with New York Americans
- **BEST SEASON WITH RED WINGS:**
  1930-31 (25-23-48)
- **TOTALS WITH RED WINGS:**
  GP-557, G-134, A-190, PTS-324

- **HONORS:**
  Won Hart Trophy in 1939-40; Selected to NHL First All-Star Team in 1936-37 and 1939-40; Selected to NHL Second All-Star Team in 1935-36; Played in NHL All-Star Game, 1936-37, 1939-40; Led Detroit in goals and points in 1930-31 and 1931-32; Served five seasons as team captain; Elected to Hockey Hall of Fame in 1963

MOTOWN Classic

Connell nearly meets his maker

Alex Connell set an NHL record with six consecutive shutouts for Ottawa in 1927-28, but it was his quick thinking with Detroit which may have saved his life.

Playing in overtime against the New York Americans at Madison Square Garden, a melee broke out when the Amerks' apparent winning goal was disallowed.

Connell got into it with the goal judge, punching the fellow in the nose. The Americans were owned by Bill Dwyer, well known to the authorities as a rum runner during prohibition and what Connell didn't realize was that he'd just slugged Dwyer's right-hand man.

The Detroit goalie received a police escort to the team hotel, but was accosted by some burly men while eating a late meal.

"Aren't you Alex Connell, goaltender for the Detroit Falcons?" one of the thugs demanded of him. "Not only do I not know who Alex Connell is, I've never heard of any Detroit Falcons," answered Connell.

The men bought his story and left, as Connell made perhaps the biggest save of his career.

ASSEMBLY LINE

Besides the five season-loan additions from the Senators, Detroit acquired defenseman Doug Young from the New York Americans and he netted 10 goals, a rookie mark for Detroit rearguards. The Falcons dealt Tom Filmore and Bert McInenly to the Amerks for left-winger Hap Emms and right-winger Frank Carson.

Doug Young

Red Wings Facts

Stanley Cup Winning Goals

1936	Pete Kelly
1937	Marty Barry
1943	Joe Carveth
1950	Pete Babando (OT)
1952	Metro Prystai
1954	Tony Leswick (OT)
1955	Gordie Howe
1997	Darren McCarty
1998	Martin Lapointe
2002	Brendan Shanahan

Short Passes

Frank Carson and Larry Aurie scored Jan. 23 as the Falcons won 2-0 at Boston, ending Detroit's 17-game losing streak in the city.

Gordie Howe was the heart and soul of the Red Wings and Jack Adams was as much a fixture in Detroit as the automobile.

Yet, without the backing of the Norris family, both would have likely been employed elsewhere.

Born in 1926, the Detroit Cougars floundered. Rechristened the Falcons in 1930, they didn't soar and were in receivership by 1932.

"Things were so bad, we didn't have enough money to buy a second set of uniforms," Adams said.

In the summer of 1932, that changed. Chicago grain millionaire James Norris (left) purchased the Detroit team and the Olympia for $100,000.

"When Mr. Norris came into the picture, it was a whole new ballgame," Adams said.

Norris renamed the team the Red Wings after the famed Montreal AAA, which had won the first Stanley Cup in 1893. He played defense for them in 1898 and the club's logo — a winged wheel— seemed perfect for America's automotive capital.

Two years later, the Wings were in the Stanley Cup final, capturing the storied mug in 1935-36 and 1936-37, the first American-based team to win consecutive Cups.

"Pop Norris was the bankroll and the boss and after he took over, Detroit hockey never looked back," Adams said.

A majority shareholder in Madison Square Garden and owner of Chicago Stadium, Norris was rebuked in his 1926 bid to acquire an NHL franchise for the Windy City. He also once considered purchasing baseball's Brooklyn Dodgers.

Inducted into the Hockey Hall of Fame in 1958, Norris Sr. died December 4, 1952 and the following season, the NHL introduced the Norris Trophy in his honor, to be presented annually to the league's top defenseman.

By this time, James Norris Jr., who was president of the International Boxing Club and Bruce Wirtz had purchased the Blackhawks, so Marguerite Norris (right), 27, daughter of James Norris Sr., took over as president of the Wings and in 1953-54, became the first woman to have her name inscribed

on the Stanley Cup when Detroit won a seven-game final from Montreal. After three years, she turned the handling of the team over to her brother Bruce Norris (left), 31.

Bruce was much more hands-on, sometimes skating with the team in practice and was the man who removed Adams from office in 1962 after 35 years with the team. In 1982, with the Norris Grain Company struggling financially, Bruce Norris sold the team for $8 million to Mike Ilitch, closing one legendary chapter of Red Wings ownership and launching another.

Bruce (1969) and James D. Norris Jr. (1962) joined their father in the Hockey Hall of Fame.

RED WINGS ARCHIVE

BACK in TIME

- **July 2, 1932**

  During the Depression, Franklin D. Roosevelt earned the Democratic Party's nomination for President by promising a "New Deal" for Americans.

- **January 30, 1933**

  After a month of secret negotiations, Nazi leader Adolf Hitler became Chancellor of Germany; also, the first concentration camp opened just outside Munich at Da Chau.

- **April 3, 1933**

  British pilots Clydesdale and MacIntyre performed the first flight over Mt. Everest.

quick cuts

Most Goals
Herbie Lewis: 20

Most Assists
Herbie Lewis: 14

Most Points
Herbie Lewis: 34

Most Penalty Minutes
Stu Evans: 74

Most Wins, Goaltender
John Ross Roach: 25

Lowest Goals-Against Average
John Ross Roach: 1.88

Most Shutouts
John Ross Roach: 10

NHL Award Winners
Carl Voss - Calder Trophy
(N.H.L. Rookie of the Year)
John Ross Roach - 1st Team All-Star

FINAL STANDINGS

American Division	W	L	T	PTS	GF	GA
Boston	25	15	8	58	124	88
DETROIT	25	15	8	58	111	93
New York Rangers	23	17	8	54	135	107
Chicago	16	20	12	44	88	101

Canadian Division Winner - Toronto

Playoff Results
Defeated the Montreal Maroons in Series "B" (5-2)
Lost to N.Y Rangers 6 goals to 3 in Series "D"
Leading Playoff Scorers
Johnny Sorrell (2G, 4PT)
Stanley Cup Champion
New York Rangers

1932-33 Season in Review

Manager Jack Adams arrived at the Detroit Falcons offices early in the spring of 1932 and was instantly flagged down by his secretary.

"There's a long-distance call for you," she excitedly told Adams. "The new owner wants to talk to you."

"New owner?" Adams asked with a puzzled look.

"Mr. James Norris, the grain millionaire," she responded.

Norris scheduled a meeting for the next day. A balding man with bushy eyebrows and round features centered around a stubby nose, Norris, who earned his millions as a Chicago grain broker, got right to the point.

"I'll give you a year's probation and we'll see how you make out," Norris told Adams.

Norris also gave Adams a new name for his team – the Red Wings – and handed him funds to begin improving their roster. Adams immediately invested $5,000 of it to acquire veteran goalie John Ross Roach from the New York Rangers.

Along with Norris' money, Detroit also received the roster of the Chicago (AHA) minor-league team he owned. Suddenly, Adams possessed two items he'd never before had at his disposal - cash and depth.

While Roach supplied all-star caliber netminding, captain Herbie Lewis returned to form, leading the Wings with 20 goals and 34 points. Four others hit double figures in goals.

RED WINGS ARCHIVE

Boston and Detroit finished deadlocked for top spot in the NHL's American Division at 25-15-8, but the Bruins were awarded first because they'd outscored Detroit 124-111.

The Wings opened the quarter-finals against the Montreal Maroons, the same team they'd played the spring before, only this time, Detroit would not be denied. After Roach posted a 2-0 shutout win in Montreal, the Wings edged the Maroons 3-2 at the Olympia and the first playoff series win in franchise history was secured.

Roach's old team provided the opposition in the semifinals and proved too worthy an opponent, winning the two-game, total goals set by a 6-3 count.

Nonetheless, Detroit served notice it was becoming a team to be reckoned with.

HOCKEYTOWN MOMENT

Falcons sold to James Norris Sr. and renamed the Red Wings

DETROIT NEWS

From the moment James Norris took hold of the Detroit franchise, it was apparent that the bleak days were over. He paid $100,000 for the team and Olympia Stadium, describing the expenditure as "loose change."

A shrewd businessman, Norris realized the Depression made economic times tough for everyone, so he implemented a monthly payment plan for season tickets. He scheduled weekend matinees to give children more opportunity to attend games. After his players earned a 1-0 victory over the Rangers, ending New York's 77-game scoring streak, Norris rewarded them with $50 bonuses.

Beyond his marketing savvy, the move for which Detroit hockey fans will be forever indebted to Norris is his decision to rename the team. He'd once played hockey for the famed Montreal Amateur Athletic Association, first winners of the Stanley Cup in 1893. They wore a winged wheel on the front of their jerseys, the same crest which was emblazoned on the floor at the club's entrance. "Our emblem will be a winged wheel, that's appropriate for Detroit," Norris said. "And we'll call the team the Wings - the Red Wings."

Wings of Legend
John Ross Roach

RED WINGS ARCHIVE

John Ross Roach was living proof of the theory, "If you can't beat 'em, join 'em." As a Detroit opponent with Toronto and the New York Rangers, Roach posted eight shutouts and a 1.70 goals-against average in 34 games. He once blocked 60 shots to preserve a 1-0 Rangers win over Detroit.

Those sort of performances led many hockey people to suggest Roach was the NHL's best goalie and few in Detroit would form an argument. The $5,000 used to purchase his contract from the Rangers was well spent. Roach posted 10 shutouts and his 25 wins were a club record, earning him selection to the NHL's First All-Star team. He was the first Detroit player to be placed on a post-season all-star unit.

He garnered the first playoff series win and first playoff shutout in team history, blanking the Maroons 2-0 at Montreal on March 25. Roach broke in with Toronto in 1921-22 and backstopped the St. Patricks to a Stanley Cup title as a rookie, defeating Jack Adams and the Vancouver Millionaires in the final. Though he stood 5-foot-5 and weighed just 130 pounds - earning him the nickname "Little Napoleon" - Roach was remarkably durable, missing only four games during his first 12 NHL campaigns. Once, in need of knee surgery, but with no other goalie available, Roach donned the pads for the Wings, basically playing on one leg, grabbing his crossbar with his glove hand at opportune moments to maintain his balance.

Known as a nervous goaltender, Roach was constantly in motion in front of his net and could often be seen clearing the snow from his crease and straightening his sweater whilst play was at the other end.

Roach spent three years with the Red Wings and successfully groomed Normie Smith as his replacement during the 1934-35 season. His 58 career shutouts rank Roach 12th on the NHL's all-time list.

- **BORN:**
  Port Perry, Ont., June 23, 1900
- **ACQUIRED:**
  Contract purchased Oct. 25, 1932
  from New York Rangers
- **BEST SEASON WITH RED WINGS:**
  1932-33 (25-15-8, 10 SO, 1.88 GAA)

- **TOTALS WITH RED WINGS:**
  GP-89, W-41, L-34, T-14, SO-15,
  GAA-2.20
- **HONORS:**
  Selected to NHL First All-Star Team,
  1932-33

MOTOWN Classic

Voss wins first NHL Rookie Award

DETROIT NEWS

The Canadian Press news gathering service instituted a new NHL award in 1932-33, to go to the NHL's top rookie. Simply titled "The NHL Rookie Award," it would be renamed the Calder Trophy in 1936-37 after NHL president Frank Calder.

The first winner of the trophy proved to be Detroit center Carl Voss, who exploded for 20 points in 38 games after he was acquired from the New York Rangers. It was a rare achievement for Voss, who toiled for eight teams in eight NHL seasons. He turned to officiating after his playing days ended and served as the NHL's referee-in-chief from 1950-65, a position which earned him enshrinement to the Hockey Hall of Fame as a builder in 1974.

ASSEMBLY LINE

Besides Roach and Voss from the Rangers, Adams also picked up winger John Gallagher from the Maroons. Forwards Leroy Goldsworthy (Two Harbors, Minn.) and Ron Moffatt (West Hope, N.D.), added from minor-league clubs, were the first American-born Red Wings. From the roster of new owner James Norris' Chicago (AHA) team, Adams plucked defenseman Walt Buswell and forwards Gus Marker, Eddie Wiseman, Jack Riley and Emil Hanson to play for the Red Wings.

RED WINGS ARCHIVE

Leroy Goldsworthy

Red Wings Facts

Wings Who Were A Part Of Four Or More Stanley Cup Teams

Gordie Howe - (4)
Ted Lindsay - (4)
Red Kelly - (4)
Marcel Pronovost - (4)
Marty Pavelich - (4)
Johnny Wilson - (4)

Short Passes

Detroit's new red uniforms clashed with those of the Montreal Canadiens, so the Red Wings donned white pullovers when playing the Habs. The next season, the NHL introduced a rule requiring visiting teams to wear white jerseys.

BACK in TIME

- **October 13, 1933**

Scientific genius Albert Einstein, in self exile from Germany, arrived in the United States to settle in Princeton, New Jersey.

- **December 5, 1933**

Following ratification of the 36th state, Utah, the 18th Amendment was repealed and prohibition came to an end in America.

- **May 29, 1934**

The United States ended its intervention in Cuban affairs when FDR signed a treaty annulling the Platt Amendment of 1903.

quick cuts

Most Goals
Johnny Sorrell: 21

Most Assists
Larry Aurie: 19

Most Points
Larry Aurie: 35

Most Penalty Minutes
"Hap" Emms: 51

Most Wins, Goaltender
Wilf Cude: 15

Lowest Goals-Against Average
Wilf Cude: 1.52

Most Shutouts
Wilf Cude: 4

NHL Award Winners
None

FINAL STANDINGS

American Division	W	L	T	PTS	GF	GA
DETROIT	24	14	10	58	113	98
Chicago	20	17	11	51	88	83
New York	21	19	8	50	120	113
Boston	18	25	5	41	111	130

Canadian Division Winner - Toronto Maple Leafs

Playoff Results
Defeated the Toronto Maple Leafs in Series "B" (3-2)
Lost to Chicago Blackhawks in finals (3-1)
Leading Playoff Scorers
Larry Aurie (5G), Herbie Lewis (10PTS)
Stanley Cup Champion
Chicago Blackhawks

1933-34 Season in Review

The indications of grandeur which accompanied Detroit following a successful 1932-33 campaign would not be denied, although the formula for success was not one you'd find in any manual.

Ten new faces dotted Detroit's roster during the season, as coach-manager Jack Adams employed 27 players in search for the right mix. The Wings reached New Year's Day with a mediocre 9-8-2 slate and without all-star goalie John Ross Roach, idled by facial injuries. Adams acquired goalie Wilf Cude on loan from the Montreal Canadiens and with him, the missing piece of the puzzle.

The Wings lost only two of Cude's first 20 games, racing to the top rung of the NHL ladder. Detroit captured the NHL's American Division title, finishing seven points ahead of Chicago.

In those days, the two first-place teams faced off in the opening round of the playoffs, with the winner advancing directly to the final and capturing the Prince of Wales Trophy as top first-place squad. Opening the best-of-five series on the road, Detroit won twice at Toronto's Maple Leaf Gardens, including a 2-1 over-time verdict which saw Herbie Lewis net the first Stanley Cup OT marker in Red Wings history just 1:33 into the extra session. Detroit then dropped two in a

RED WINGS ARCHIVE

row to the Leafs on home ice, but in the deciding game, Cude made Ebbie Goodfellow's goal stand up for a 1-0 verdict.

The Stanley Cup final match-up against Chicago seemed to favor the Wings, who went 4-1-1 against the Blackhawks during the regular season, but Chicago opened the best-of-five series with two wins at the Olympia. Before 17,700 at Chicago Stadium, the Wings staved off elimination, getting two goals from Larry Aurie in a 5-2 decision. But Mush March's goal after 30:05 of OT in Game 4 gave Chicago a 1-0 win and the Cup.

HOCKEYTOWN MOMENT
Red Wings Finish First

Doormats for years, Detroit and Chicago emerged as NHL powers in 1933-34, duking it out for supremacy in the NHL's American Division. As the race came down to the wire, a home-and-home series between the two teams would prove decisive.

The Red Wings opened the door for the Blackhawks, heading to Chicago Stadium for a March 8 date on a two-game losing streak, but Wilf Cude quickly closed it, posting a 3-0 road win which put Detroit back in the driver's seat.

Three nights later at the Olympia, Gord Pettinger's tally at 8:54 of overtime earned the Wings a 3-2 decision over the Blackhawks and for the first time, Detroit was the best of the bunch.

DETROIT NEWS

Frank Carson, Ebbie Goodfellow, Hap Emms

Wings of Legend

Wilf Cude

For one brief season, the NHL spotlight shone brightly on Wilf Cude's goal crease.

When December facial injuries felled John Ross Roach, Detroit's all-star goalie, Jack Adams sent out an S.O.S. for help between the pipes. He tried New York Americans farmhand Abbie Cox, then settled on Cude, acquired on a season loan basis from the Montreal Canadiens.

The move proved Adams was a man who paid attention.

Cude's only season as an NHL regular came in 1930-31 with the pitiful Philadelphia Quakers, where he went 2-25-3, posting a 5.77 goals-against average, but both wins came at the expense of Detroit. And his only game for Montreal in 1933-34 was a 3-0 shutout of the Wings.

Born in Barry, Wales and raised in Winnipeg, Cude was an acrobatic netminder and a fiery competitor. Once when Dave Trottier of the Montreal Maroons taunted him after scoring, Cude chased Trottier around the ice, attempting to club him with his goal stick. Another time, while eating dinner, Cude's wife wondered how he'd missed a shot in the previous game. He angrily fired his steak at her.

That competitive nature didn't take long to surface in Detroit. Cude went 10-2-8 in his first 20 games as a Red Wing, posting three shutouts. He finished the season with an NHL-leading 1.52 GAA and when he led Detroit to back-to-back wins over Chicago in March, it clinched first place in the American Division for the Red Wings.

"He is a high-class performer," Roach said of his replacement. Cude's 1-0 shutout victory over Toronto in the fifth and deciding game of the semifinals moved the Wings into their first Stanley Cup final, where Cude would oppose Chicago goaler and boyhood friend Charlie Gardiner.

HOCKEY HALL OF FAME

"He lived near my place on William Street (in Winnipeg)," Gardiner said. "For years, we went back and forth to school together."

Gardiner got the better of the best-of-five battle, which Chicago took in four games, two of them overtime decisions, including a 1-0 double OT contest in the Cup-clinching match.

It would be the last time the two men met on the ice. Cude was recalled by the Canadiens after the season, while Gardiner was dead six weeks later, the victim of a brain hemorrhage.

- **BORN:**
  Barry, Wales, July 4, 1910
- **ACQUIRED:**
  On loan Jan. 2, 1934 from Montreal Canadiens
- **BEST SEASON WITH RED WINGS:**
  1933-34 (15-6-8, 4 SO, 1.52 GAA)

- **TOTALS WITH RED WINGS:**
  GP-29, W-15, L-6, T-8, SO-4, GAA-1.52
- **HONORS:**
  Led NHL in goals-against average, 1933-34; Backstopped Detroit to first Stanley Cup final appearance, 1933-34

Sorrell nets four goals against New York Americans

The Montreal Canadiens gave up on John Sorrell without giving him a chance and the Red Wings were the beneficiaries.

In 1929, Detroit purchased Sorrell's contract from London of the International League, which had acquired him a year earlier from the Habs. Sorrell played his first of eight seasons with Detroit in 1930-31, but the 1933-34 campaign was his best as an NHLer. The left-winger tallied a career-high 21 goals and equaled a club record when he potted four of them Nov. 12 in a 5-2 victory over the New York Americans.

The Amerks must have liked what they saw, because four years later, they traded winger Hap Emms to Detroit to acquire Sorrell's services.

DWAYNE LaBAKAS

ASSEMBLY LINE

Jack Adams continued to reshape his Red Wings, purchasing forwards Gord Pettinger from the New York Rangers and Fred Robertson from Toronto. He traded 1932-33 NHL rookie of the year Carl Voss to Ottawa for former NHL scoring champ Cooney Weiland, added forward Lloyd Gross from Boston, defenseman Teddy Graham from the Montreal Maroons and borrowed goalie Wilf Cude from the Montreal Canadiens.

Ralph "Cooney" Weiland

DETROIT NEWS

Red Wings Facts

Longest Road Winning Streaks

(8) February 4 to March 9, 2002

(7) March 25 to April 14, 1995

(7) February 18 to March 20, 1996

Short Passes

When John Ross Roach left Detroit's Dec. 14, 1933 game at Chicago after stopping a shot with his face, defenseman Doug Young took over in net, allowing just one goal in 21 minutes of work in a 4-0 loss.

- 1934   1935 -

BACK in TIME

- **July 22, 1934**
Public enemy number one John Dillinger, wanted for bank holdups, prison breaks and 16 murders, was gunned down in front of a Chicago movie theatre.

- **February 22, 1935**
Plane flights were banned over the White House because they disturbed President Roosevelt's sleep.

- **August 16, 1935**
Popular humorist Will Rogers and famed aviator Wiley Post died in a plane crash while touring Alaska.

quick cuts

Most Goals
Syd Howe: 22
Most Assists
Larry Aurie: 29
Most Points
Syd Howe: 47
Most Penalty Minutes
Ebbie Goodfellow: 44
Most Wins, Goaltender
Normie Smith: 12
Lowest Goals-Against Average
Normie Smith: 2.01
Most Shutouts
John Ross Roach: 4
NHL Award Winners
Cooney Weiland - 2nd Team All-Star

FINAL STANDINGS

American Division	W	L	T	PTS	GF	GA
Boston	26	16	6	58	129	112
Chicago	26	17	5	57	118	88
New York	22	20	6	50	137	139
DETROIT	19	22	7	45	127	114

Canadian Division Winner - Toronto

Playoff Results
Did Not Qualify
Stanley Cup Champion
Montreal Maroons

1934-35 Season in Review

A first-place finish and a Stanley Cup final under their belt, the Detroit Red Wings felt bigger and better things were just around the corner.

They were right, but there was still one more serving of heartbreak to ingest before the glory days arrived.

The key man in Detroit's run to the final, goaltender Wilf Cude, was gone, recalled from loan by the Montreal Canadiens, who installed Cude as their No. 1 goalie.

Veteran John Ross Roach was back for his 13th NHL season and the club acquired youngster Normie Smith to serve as Roach's apprentice. Smith was one of nine newcomers to the Detroit roster, as manager Jack Adams continued his pattern of shuffling the deck.

Among the additions was forward Syd Howe, who was acquired from the St. Louis Eagles and led Detroit in scoring with 22-25-47 totals, good for second in the NHL scoring race. Teammate Larry Aurie (46 points) finished third and Detroit's Herbie Lewis (43) was sixth. John Sorrell also reached the 20-goal plateau and five other players - Aurie (17), Lewis (16), Cooney Weiland (13), Ebbie Goodfellow (12) and Eddie Wiseman (11) - managed to collect at least 10 goals. Weiland earned selection to the NHL's Second All-Star Team at center.

It was on defense where Detroit struggled. Doug Young was the only regular who could be counted on, though late-season call-up Bucko McDonald displayed promise, as did Ralph (Scotty) Bowman, acquired with Howe from St. Louis. Roach struggled in his final NHL season and was opted to the minors, leaving the goaltending in Smith's hands.

It wasn't so much that Detroit played poorly as it was the other teams in the American Division all played well. With a 19-22-7 slate, the Wings would have qualified for playoff hockey by a point were they in the Canadian Division.

There were a couple of impressive victories, including an 8-2 drubbing of the New York Rangers on Nov. 15 and an 11-2 rout of the Eagles Dec. 13, a game which saw Goodfellow score the first penalty shot goal in Red Wings history.

It was the pitiful Eagles, who brought up the NHL rear at 11-31-6, that proved to be Detroit's undoing, whipping the Wings three times. Those six lost points would have put Detroit into the post-season.

It was a disappointing turn of events just when it looked as if Detroit was on its way. But the depression would be short-lived.

HOCKEYTOWN MOMENT
Detroit's first Scotty Bowman

Ralph (Scotty) Bowman, a Detroit defenseman from 1935-40, is often confused with William (Scotty) Bowman, the coach of the Red Wings since 1993.

Bowman the defenseman was born June 20, 1911 in Winnipeg. Bowman the coach was born Sept. 18, 1933 in Montreal. But there are similarities. Each Bowman spent part of his NHL career in St. Louis and each came to Detroit and was a key part of Red Wings teams that won back-to-back Stanley Cups.

The Red Wings shipped $50,000 and defenseman Teddy Graham to the St. Louis Eagles Feb. 11, 1935 to acquire Bowman and forward Syd Howe. Howe was a flashy sniper who had several productive years while wearing the winged wheel, but Bowman was a stay-at-home defenseman who scored eight goals during his NHL career.

One of those was a historic tally, however. On Nov. 13, 1934, while with St. Louis, Bowman beat Montreal Maroons goalie Alex Connell for the first penalty shot goal in NHL history.

It's also a moment which adds to the Scotty Bowman confusion. "I get letters all the time, asking me about scoring that goal," Scotty Bowman the coach said. "They say, 'It must have been an amazing feat.'

"I always answer, 'Yes it was, considering I was a year old at the time.'"

Herbie Lewis

Long before he made the leap to the NHL, Herbie Lewis was a wanted man. The Montreal Maroons signed him in 1926, but the deal was voided by NHL president Frank Calder, since Lewis was already under contract to the American Hockey Association's Duluth Hornets.

Lewis was a star with the Hornets, leading the team in scoring in 1925-26, earning the nickname "The Duke of Duluth" in the process. He was the league's biggest drawing card and its highest-paid performer.

Detroit manager Jack Adams astutely scooped up this budding star through the 1928 inter-league draft and Lewis blossomed in the Motor City.

Lewis garnered a pair of 20-goal seasons and seven times collected at least 30 points during 11 NHL campaigns, all spent with Detroit. The 1934-35 season proved to be his most productive, as Lewis earned 43 points, good for sixth in NHL scoring. He was also reported to be the recipient of the NHL's top salary, an annual stipend of $8,000.

Lewis captained the Red Wings to their first Stanley Cup final appearance in 1933-34 and scored the first Stanley Cup final goal and first playoff overtime marker in club history. He finished as the leading goal scorer in that spring's post-season. It was also this season that Lewis and right-winger Larry Aurie, his regular linemate, represented Detroit in the first NHL All-Star Game, a benefit match for Toronto forward Ace Bailey, whose career was cut short by a head injury suffered in a game against Boston.

When Adams picked up Marty Barry from Boston to center Aurie and Lewis, the trio immediately clicked, sparking Detroit to successive Cup wins. Toronto manager Conn Smythe described the unit as, "The best line in hockey, coming and going."

RED WINGS ARCHIVE

A small, quick left-winger, Lewis possessed blazing speed on his blades and had a reputation as an accurate playmaker and a gentlemanly player.

He was inducted into the Hockey Hall of Fame in 1989.

- **BORN:**
  Calgary, Alberta, April 17, 1906
- **ACQUIRED:**
  Selected from Duluth (AHA) in May 14, 1928 inter-league draft
- **BEST SEASON WITH RED WINGS:**
  1933-34 (16-27-43)

- **TOTALS WITH RED WINGS:**
  GP-483, G-148, A-161, PTS-309
- **HONORS:**
  Served as team captain, 1933-34; Played in 1934 NHL All-Star Game; Elected to Hockey Hall of Fame in 1989

MOTOWN Classic

Weiland an All-Star Wing

When Jack Adams shipped Carl Voss to Ottawa in 1933 for Cooney Weiland, he was picking up one of the NHL's most explosive players. Weiland led the NHL in scoring with a record 73 points for Boston in 1929-30, skating on the Dynamite Line with Dit Clapper and Dutch Gainor. He played for two Stanley Cup winners with the Bruins and performed for the Red Wings in a losing effort in the 1934 final against Chicago.

Weiland finished second in club scoring with 32 points that season and was third with 13-25-38 totals in 1934-35, but his all-around play caught the attention of NHL All-Star voters, who placed Weiland at center on the second team, joining 1932-33 first-team goalie selection John Ross Roach as the only Wings to earn this honor.

DETROIT NEWS

ASSEMBLY LINE

Jack Adams liked to keep things moving and this season was no exception. He dealt Gus Marker to the Montreal Maroons for forward Wally Kilrea and sent Burr Williams to St. Louis for goalie Normie Smith before the season even started. Adams acquired brothers when he purchased the contracts of Des and Earl Roche from Buffalo of the International League on New Year's Day and unloaded a blockbuster Feb. 11, shipping Teddy Graham and $50,000 to St. Louis for forward Syd Howe and defenseman Ralph (Scotty) Bowman.

RED WINGS ARCHIVE

Wally Kilrea

Red Wings Facts

Players Who Played For The Cougars, Falcons And The Red Wings

Larry Aurie

Ebbie Goodfellow

George Hay

Herb Lewis

Reg Noble

Short Passes

Detroit's late-season trade with St. Louis and a quirk in the schedule allowed Syd Howe to participate in a record 50 games during the 48-game season.

 **BACK in TIME**

- **October 7, 1935**
The Detroit Tigers win their first World Series, defeating Chicago in six games.

- **June 22, 1936**
The U.S. Congress granted the Virgin Islands the right to elect their own legislature.

- **July 2, 1936**
The Pope ordered a world drive to raise the standards of motion pictures.

quick cuts

Most Goals
Marty Barry: 21
Most Assists
Herbie Lewis: 23
Most Points
Marty Barry: 40
Most Penalty Minutes
Ebbie Goodfellow: 69
Most Wins, Goaltender
Normie Smith: 24
Lowest Goals-Against Average
Normie Smith: 2.04
Most Shutouts
Normie Smith: 6
NHL Award Winners
Ebbie Goodfellow - 2nd Team All-Star

FINAL STANDINGS

American Division	W	L	T	PTS	GF	GA
DETROIT	24	16	8	56	124	103
Boston	22	20	6	50	92	83
Chicago	21	19	8	50	93	92
New York	19	17	12	50	91	96

Canadian Division Winner - Montreal Maroons

Playoff Results
Defeated the Montreal Maroons in Series "A" (3-0)
Defeated the Toronto Maple Leafs in finals (3-1)
Leading Playoff Scorers
Johnny Sorrell (3G, 7PTS)
Stanley Cup Champion
Detroit Red Wings

1935-36 Season in Review

Even though his team missed the playoffs in 1934-35, Jack Adams knew his recipe for success was nearing completion.

The Detroit Red Wings manager moved to add the final ingredients before the 1935-36 season commenced. His bold step to deal all-star center Cooney Weiland to Boston for Marty Barry, inserting Barry as his No. 1 pivot between Larry Aurie and Herbie Lewis, paid huge dividends when Barry's 21-19-40 totals left him second in NHL scoring. Linemate Lewis (14-23-37) finished ninth in the NHL points race.

Role players Hec Kilrea and Pete Kelly were also picked up and would make huge contributions. Ralph (Scotty) Bowman, a late-season acquisition in 1934-35 and heavy-hitting Bucko McDonald, who finished second in the voting for NHL rookie of the year, solidified the defense, while Normie Smith matured into a front-line NHL goalie.

The Wings finished atop the tough American Division, in which all four teams collected at least 50 points during the 48-game campaign. The Canadian Division champion Montreal Maroons provided opening-round playoff opposition, with the winner of this first-place showdown advancing directly to the Stanley Cup final.

The first game of that series is still talked about today. It lasted an NHL-record 176 minutes and 30 seconds on the game clock and nearly six hours in real time before rookie Mud Bruneteau tallied the only goal on a pass from Kilrea.

Detroit carried on to sweep the Maroons and took care of the Toronto Maple Leafs in four games to capture the Stanley Cup for the first time in history. Kelly's

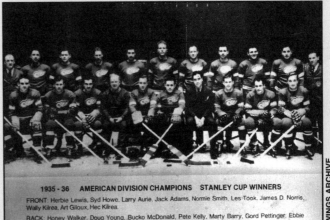

1935 - 36   AMERICAN DIVISION CHAMPIONS   STANLEY CUP WINNERS
FRONT: Herbie Lewis, Syd Howe, Larry Aurie, Jack Adams, Normie Smith, Les Took, James D. Norris, Wally Kilrea, Art Giloux, Hec Kilrea.
BACK: Honey Walker, Doug Young, Bucko McDonald, Pete Kelly, Marty Barry, Gord Pettinger, Ebbie Goodfellow, Johnny Sorrell, Scotty Bowman, Wilf Starr, Carl Mattson.

— *DETROIT RED WINGS* —

goal at 9:48 of the third period in Detroit's 3-2 win in Game 4 stood as the Wings' first Cup-winning tally. "Winning the Stanley Cup was the one ambition of my life," Wings owner James Norris said as he filled the mug's bowl with champagne. Everyone took a sip, including Adams, who had never before taken a drink of alcohol in his life.

An overflow crowd at Michigan Central Train Station greeted the team upon its return from Toronto the next day and a police escort helped Adams carry the Cup to safety through the revellers, but not before he promised them there would be more to celebrate next spring.

"Don't be surprised if the Wings make it two in a row," Adams boldly predicted. "I hope they make it a habit."

HOCKEYTOWN MOMENT
Wings win Stanley Cup

Detroit's first bid for Lord Stanley's mug ended in a disappointing four-game loss to Chicago in the 1934 final, but manager Jack Adams confidently stated that history would not repeat itself. "The Wings are a much stronger team than in 1934," he said.

Blasting their way to the final with a three-game sweep of the Montreal Maroons, only arch-rival Toronto stood in the way and Detroit set out to make short work of the Maple Leafs, whipping them 3-1 and 9-4 in the first two games at the Olympia. The nine goals were a single-game playoff record for the Wings.

Toronto rallied from a 3-0 deficit with 6:50 to play in regulation time in Game 4, winning 4-3 on Buzz Boll's overtime marker, but the setback was temporary. The Wings overcame a first-period goal by Leafs center Joe Primeau, racing to a 3-1 lead. They held on for a 3-2 verdict and the first championship in franchise history.

"Every player on the team has taken a turn at bringing the house down in these playoffs," Adams said. "I never saw anything like it."

43

Modere "Mud" Bruneteau

Working at the Norris Grain Factory in Winnipeg during the summer months of 1934, Modere (Mud) Bruneteau would often admire the photo of the 1933-34 Detroit Red Wings which hung in secretary C.E. Babbitt's office.

"I want to play for the Red Wings," Bruneteau told Babbitt.

Play for them? How about score one of the most memorable goals in team history?

The rookie right-winger took only one Stanley Cup game to cement his place in the archives of the battered mug's lore.

Detroit opened the 1935-36 playoffs March 24 at the Montreal Forum against the Maroons and it would be the first playoff exposure for the rookie Bruneteau, recalled from the International League's Detroit Olympics just two weeks earlier. The game went through regulation scoreless and carried on through five 20-minute overtime sessions without a decision. Used sparingly for much of the game, Bruneteau began to see more ice time as the sixth extra period commenced and he drove to the net as Hec Kilrea burst down the wing with the puck. Kilrea feathered a pass cross ice to Bruneteau, who lifted a high shot past sprawling Maroons goalie Lorne Chabot.

Hockey's longest game was over at 2:25 a.m. and Bruneteau's legend guaranteed.

"It was the funniest thing," Bruneteau recalled of his famous goal. "The puck just stuck there in the twine and didn't fall to the ice."

RED WINGS ARCHIVE

Bruneteau spent 11 productive seasons with the Red Wings, three times topping the 20-goal plateau, including a career-high 35 goals in 1943-44. He even scored another Stanley Cup OT winner, but it is his 1936 tally which ensured hockey fans will forever know the name Mud.

- **BORN:**
  St. Boniface, Manitoba, November 28, 1914
- **ACQUIRED:**
  Signed Oct. 25, 1934 as a free agent
- **BEST SEASON WITH RED WINGS:**
  1943-44 (35-18-53)

- **TOTALS WITH RED WINGS:**
  GP-411, G-139, A-138, PTS-277
- **HONORS:**
  Scored the overtime winner to end the NHL's longest game, March 24-25, 1936, after 176 minutes and 30 seconds

MOTOWN Classic

Smith sets playoff shutout mark

The Montreal Maroons gave up on Normie Smith, but he refused to give up anything to them. Smith's original team provided Detroit's opposition in the opening round of the 1936 playoffs and in Game 1 of the series, which lasted an NHL-record 176:30, the Detroit goalie threw a brick wall up in front of his cage, blocking 89 shots for a 1-0 win. He also blanked the Maroons 3-0 in Game 2 of the set and when Montreal finally slipped one past Smith in Detroit's 2-1 Game 3 verdict, he'd kept a clean sheet for a Stanley Cup record 248 minutes and 32 seconds, posting an 0.20 goals-against average for the series. Backstopping Detroit to a four-game decision over Toronto and the first Stanley Cup in club history, Smith led all goalies in wins (six) and shutouts (two) during the playoffs.

RED WINGS ARCHIVE

ASSEMBLY LINE

The moves Detroit manager Jack Adams made sealed the deal for Detroit's first Stanley Cup. He dealt Knucker Irvine and $7,000 to Toronto for left-winger Hec Kilrea and sent Cooney Weiland and Walt Buswell to Boston for center Marty Barry and right wing Art Giroux. Adams claimed former Wing Carl Voss in a dispersal draft of the defunct St. Louis franchise, then moved Voss to the New York Americans for right wing Pete Kelly.

RED WINGS ARCHIVE

Pete Kelly

Red Wings Facts

Wings who wore four different jersey numbers

Sid Abel - #4, #7, #9, #12, #14, #19, #20
Jimmy Rutherford - #1, #27, #29, #30
Howie Young - #2, #4, #20, #22
Marcel Pronovost - #2, #18, #21, #22, #23
Gary Bergman - #2, #3, #18, #23
Warren Godfrey - #2, #3, #5, #11, #18, #23, #25
Jack Stewart - #2, #3,#16, #18
Johnny Wilson - #8, #11, #16, #17, #23
Val Fonteyne - #8, #11, #12, #19, #21
Bob McCord - #2, #3, #24, #25
Bob Wall - #4, #5, #19, #23

Short Passes

Born in Calumet, John Sherf, a left-winger out of the University of Michigan, was the first native Michigander to play for the Red Wings.

45

- 1936 1937 -

BACK in TIME

- **December 30, 1936**

Seven General Motors Plants in Flint, Michigan were forced to close following sit down strikes idling 33,400 workers in a dispute over collective bargaining.

- **January 2, 1937**

Andrew W. Mellon gave his $19 million art collection to the American public along with a $19 million National Gallery to house it.

- **June 22, 1937**

Detroiter Joe Louis defeated James J. Braddock and became the second African American world heavyweight boxing champion.

quick cuts

Most Goals
Larry Aurie: 23
Most Assists
Marty Barry: 27
Most Points
Marty Barry: 44
Most Penalty Minutes
Ebbie Goodfellow: 43
Most Wins, Goaltender
Normie Smith: 25
Lowest Goals-Against Average
Normie Smith: 2.05
Most Shutouts
Normie Smith: 6
NHL Award Winners
Normie Smith - Vezina Trophy
Marty Barry - Lady Byng Trophy
Normie Smith, Ebbie Goodfellow,
Marty Barry, Larry Aurie and
Jack Adams - 1st Team All-Stars

FINAL STANDINGS

American Division	W	L	T	PTS	GF	GA
DETROIT	25	14	9	59	128	102
Boston	23	18	7	53	120	110
New York	19	20	9	47	117	106
Chicago	14	27	7	35	99	131

Canadian Division Winner - Montreal Canadiens

Playoff Results
Defeated the Montreal Canadiens in Series "A" (3-2)
Defeated the N.Y. Rangers in finals (3-2)
Leading Playoff Scorers
Marty Barry (4G, 11PTS)
Stanley Cup Champion
Detroit Red Wings

1936-37 Season in Review

If there were any doubts of Detroit's supremacy on the NHL scene, the Red Wings acted quickly to remove them.

They opened in fine fashion Nov. 5 with a 3-1 win over Toronto, as Syd Howe and Larry Aurie scored goals a club-record seven seconds apart. The Wings never looked back and won the American Division title for the third time in four seasons, posting a 25-14-9 mark.

As the season drew to a close, it was apparent the Red Wings would need to build an addition to the club's trophy case. Detroit won the Prince of Wales Trophy as the NHL's top first-place team for the third time in four years. Center Marty Barry was the first Red Wing to earn the Lady Byng Trophy as the NHL's best combination of ability and sportsmanship and goalie Normie Smith copped the Vezina Trophy as the league's leading netminder, another Detroit first.

Smith, Barry, left wing Aurie, defenseman Ebbie Goodfellow and coach Jack Adams were all selected to the NHL's First All-Star Team.

Barry finished second in the NHL scoring chase with 44 points, one better than Aurie, who led the NHL with 23 goals and was in the hunt for the scoring title when his season was ended by a broken leg. The Wings also lost defensemen Orville Roulston and Doug Young, the team captain, to leg fractures during the season and Smith went out with torn ankle ligaments early in the playoffs.

A lesser team might have folded, but Detroit's fortitude showed. Forced to go the distance in both of their playoff rounds, the Red Wings doused the Montreal Canadiens with a 2-1 Game 5 verdict on Hec Kilrea's goal at 11:49 of the third overtime period.

In the finals against the New York Rangers, the Wings trailed the best-of-five set 2-1, but minor-league call-up Earl Robertson posted 1-0 and 3-0 shutouts and Detroit retained the Cup.

Afterwards, the stress of defending the title showed on the undermanned Wings. Adams passed out while leading the cheers in the dressing room. Meanwhile, sudden hero Robertson slumped in his seat. "I'll get some sleep now," Robertson said. "I haven't had any for a long time."

HOCKEYTOWN MOMENT
Back-to-Back Cups

With all-stars Larry Aurie and Normie Smith, captain Doug Young and rookie defenseman Orville Roulston all injured, the Wings figured to be in tough against the New York Rangers in the Stanley Cup final, but Detroit's character carried the day.

Down 2-1 in the series, center Marty Barry stepped forward, scoring the only goal in Detroit's Game 4 win, then netting two goals, including the Cup winner, in a 3-0 Game 5 verdict.

"That's one goal for each of the broken-legged guys," Aurie suggested after the clinching win. He was joined on crutches by Young and Roulston, while an elbow injury idled Smith.

RED WINGS ARCHIVE

"With three all-stars out with injuries, we beat those high-flying Rangers," Wings manager Jack Adams boasted.

Detroit became the first American-based team to win successive Stanley Cups by edging the Rangers and joined the Ottawa Senators (1919-20, 1920-21) as the only NHL teams to finish first and win the Cup in back-to-back seasons.

Larry Aurie

DETROIT NEWS

A quiet superstar whose achievements were often overshadowed by others, left-winger Larry Aurie charged into the NHL spotlight in 1936-37 and only a broken leg could stop him.

Aurie scored his NHL-leading 23rd goal March 11 in a 4-2 win over the New York Rangers, but later in the game, fractured his leg in a collision with Rangers defenseman Art Coulter, ending his season. Aurie's performance earned him selection to the NHL's First All-Star Team, but simply confirmed what Detroit supporters knew from the moment Aurie broke in with the club - that the 5-foot-6, 148-pound right-winger was a special player.

"Aurie has a remarkable shot, almost always on the net," wrote H.G. Salsinger of the Detroit News. "He is quick, exceptionally fast and usually aggressive. There are few flashier gentlemen in hockey." Aurie's dedication to playing the game at both ends of the rink probably cost him more impressive offensive numbers, but it won him the respect of his peers. "Aurie's the hardest-checking right wing in the league," Toronto's Harvey (Busher) Jackson said.

A fitness freak who worked hard in the off-season to maintain his conditioning, Aurie's rugged style in combination with his diminutive stature earned him the nickname "Little Dempsey."

Twice during his career, Aurie led the Wings in assists and in 1933-34, his 35 points topped the club in scoring. He was third in NHL scoring with a career-high 46 points in 1934-35 and fourth overall in 1936-37 with 43 points.

Sadly, this was Aurie's last productive campaign. The lingering effects of his fractured leg and a decade in the NHL wars slowed him considerably. He slipped to 10 goals and 19 points in 1937-38 and was named player-coach of Detroit's AHL farm club in Pittsburgh the following season, making one last appearance for the Wings, scoring in a 3-0 shutout of Montreal.

As a tribute to Aurie's worth, manager Jack Adams deemed that no other player would don Aurie's No. 6 jersey.

"It wouldn't seem right for anyone else to wear it," Adams said.

Though the number was never officially retired, Cummy Burton, Aurie's nephew, is the only Detroit player to since wear No. 6.

- **BORN:**
  Sudbury, Ontario, February 8, 1905
- **ACQUIRED:**
  Selected from London (CANPRO) in Sept. 26, 1927 inter-league draft
- **BEST SEASON WITH RED WINGS:**
  1934-35 (17-29-46)

- **TOTALS WITH RED WINGS:**
  GP-489, G-147, A-129, PTS-276
- **HONORS:**
  Led NHL in goals in 1936-37; Named to NHL First All-Star Team, 1936-37; Played in NHL All-Star Game, 1933-34; Led Detroit in scoring, 1933-34; Served as team captain, 1932-33

Pinch-hitter Robertson wins Cup

RED WINGS ARCHIVE

When all-star goaltender Normie Smith went down with torn elbow ligaments in the Stanley Cup semifinals, Montreal Canadiens manager Cecil Hart was ready to dance a jig. "I don't see any reason why we shouldn't win it," Hart suggested. Earl Robertson saw things differently. Called up to make his NHL debut in Game 4 of the best-of-five set against the Habs, Robertson was a 3-1 loser that night, but posted a 2-1 win in Game 5, moving Detroit to the final against the New York Rangers.

In another five-game set, Robertson posted shutouts in Games 4 and 5 to clinch the title. "They could take me out and shoot me now," Robertson said. "I'd die happy."

ASSEMBLY LINE

Manager Jack Adams took a different tack this season. Trader Jack stood virtually pat with his Stanley Cup-winning line-up, adding only defense-man John Gallagher from the New York Americans. Gallagher did a previous tour with the Wings from 1932-34. Rookies Orville (Rolly) Roulston and Jimmy Orlando also broke in on the blueline.

DWAYNE LaBAKAS

Jack Adams

Red Wings Facts

Most victories
(pre -70 game season)

34 in 1948-49

31 in 1944-45

30 in 1947-48

Short Passes

Goaltender Earl Robertson, who backstopped Detroit to the 1936-37 Stanley Cup, never played a regular-season game for the Red Wings.

BACK in TIME

- **December 28, 1937**
President Roosevelt asked Congress for a larger U.S. Navy expressing "growing concerns for world events."

- **February 2, 1938**
Adolf Hitler named himself Supreme Commander of the German armed forces and seized direct control of foreign policy.

- **June 25, 1938**
The Fair Labor Standards Act was signed into law establishing a .40 per hour wage and a 44 hour work week for American businesses engaged in interstate commerce.

quick cuts

Most Goals
Carl Liscombe: 14
Most Assists
Marty Barry: 20
Most Points
Herbie Lewis: 31
Most Penalty Minutes
Marty Barry: 34
Most Wins, Goaltender
Normie Smith: 11
Lowest Goals-Against Average
Normie Smith: 2.66
Most Shutouts
Normie Smith: 3
NHL Award Winners
None

FINAL STANDINGS

American Division	W	L	T	PTS	GF	GA
Boston	30	11	7	67	142	89
New York	27	15	6	60	149	96
Chicago	14	25	9	37	97	139
DETROIT	12	25	11	35	99	133

Canadian Division Winner - Toronto

Playoff Results
Did Not Qualify
Stanley Cup Champion
Chicago Blackhawks

1937-38 Season in Review

Fresh off consecutive Stanley Cups, the Detroit Red Wings were about to find out about one of the harsh realities of sport. Those who stand still are easily surpassed.

When the 1937-38 NHL season opened, the Red Wings looked remarkably like the team which had won the previous two championships.

At least until the puck was dropped.

A 3-14-4 skid to begin the season included a nine-game winless slide from Dec. 9 through Jan. 2, which prompted Wings manager Jack Adams to announce, "We're out of it."

RED WINGS ARCHIVE

Thanks to the Chicago Blackhawks, they weren't. Chicago also stumbled, finishing at 14-25-9, but even that sad story was better than the one written by the Wings. A 12-25-11 mark equaled the club record for the fewest wins in a season, established in 1926-27, Detroit's first NHL campaign.

It was the sort of season where if something could go wrong, it did.

Winger Mud Bruneteau suffered a broken arm in a collision with teammate Red Beattie. Winger Larry Aurie, defensemen Doug Young and Rolly Roulston and goalie Normie Smith, all rebounding from serious injuries suffered the season before, were slow to recover. Aurie slumped from 43 to 19 points, while Marty Barry plummeted from 44 points to 29. Herbie Lewis, the third member of this veteran line, led the Wings with 31 points.

Even the rink attendants had a tough go of it. A mid-season decision to paint the Olympia boards for an ice show backfired when the weather suddenly

warmed. It didn't dry in time for the next game and white paint rubbed off all over the players and the puck.

Good news wasn't plentiful, but there was some to be found. Smith, Barry and Ebbie Goodfellow appeared in the second NHL All-Star Game, a benefit match in Montreal for the family of deceased Canadiens star Howie Morenz. Rookie left-winger Carl Liscombe led the club with 14 goals.

A 3-2 loss to the Canadiens Mach 15 officially eliminated Detroit from the playoffs, the first defending champion to miss post-season play since the 1925-26 Habs.

"Forget 1938, get ready for October," was the advice Detroit owner James Norris offered to Adams, who couldn't easily dismiss how standing pat cost his team so dearly.

"I'll never hesitate to bust up a champion again," Adams proclaimed.

HOCKEYTOWN MOMENT
Liscombe fires fastest hat trick

It was easy for Carl Liscombe to stand out in a crowd, since he was one of the few NHLers who wore a helmet. But on the night of March 13, 1938, Liscombe stood out for all the right reasons.

In a 5-1 victory over Chicago, the rookie left-winger tallied three goals in one minute and 52 seconds, beating Pit Lepine's NHL mark for the fastest three goals

by 1:05. He blasted a 10-footer past Chicago goalie Mike Karakas at 16:02 of the first period, then tallied at 17:31 and 17:54, both goals coming with Chicago's Earl Seibert in the penalty box.

Liscombe's performance remains a Detroit standard for the fastest three goals by one player.

Normie Smith

The beginning and end to Normie Smith's NHL days were nothing special, but what came in between was very special.

Smith broke in with the Montreal Maroons, playing 21 games in 1931-32, but didn't see NHL action again until he was acquired by Detroit in 1934.

During the 1935-36 and 1936-37 seasons, no NHL goalie was better than Smith. His 24 wins in 1935-36 and his 25 wins in 1936-37 were NHL bests. He topped the league in '36-37 with six shutouts and a 2.05 goals-against average, earning him First All-Star Team status and the Vezina Trophy. But it was the 1936 Stanley Cup playoffs where Smith's ultimate legacy was penned.

He blocked 89 shots for a 1-0 shutout over the Maroons in the NHL's longest game, a 176-minute, 30-second affair. "They fed us sugar dipped in brandy to keep us going," Smith said of that famous contest.

He stretched that shutout sequence to a Stanley Cup-record 248 minutes and 32 seconds, leading the playoffs with six wins and two shutouts as Detroit beat Toronto for its first of two straight Cups. "That bird Normie Smith robbed me more than any goaltender I ever fired at," Leafs left-winger Harvey (Busher) Jackson said.

Smith suffered torn elbow ligaments in the 1937 Cup semifinals against the Montreal Canadiens and never was the same after that. He slumped to a 2.66 GAA in 1937-38 and when he lost his first four starts of the 1938-39 campaign, Wings manager Jack Adams assigned Smith to their Pittsburgh AHL affiliate. Smith refused to report.

"I won't play minor-league hockey," Smith said. "I am either good enough to play for the Red Wings, or not at all."

His rights were traded to Boston for goalie Cecil (Tiny) Thompson, but Smith wouldn't go there, either and retired.

RED WINGS ARCHIVE

He made a brief comeback during World War II, when many players were unavailable to the NHL. Smith, who worked in a Detroit auto plant, suited up for five Red Wings games in 1943-44 and one more in 1944-45, all home games, ensuring he wouldn't miss a shift on the assembly line.

His time in the NHL was brief, but it was certainly notable.

- **BORN:**
  Toronto, Ontario, March 18, 1908
- **ACQUIRED:**
  Contract purchased Oct. 21, 1934 from St. Louis Eagles
- **BEST SEASON WITH RED WINGS:**
  1936-37 (25-14-9, 6 SO, 2.05 GAA)
- **TOTALS WITH RED WINGS:**
  GP-178, W-76, L-71, T-31, SO-17, GAA-2.26

- **HONORS:**
  Won Vezina Trophy, 1936-37; NHL First All-Star Team, 1936-37; Led NHL in wins, 1935-36; Led NHL in wins, shutouts and goals-against average in 1936-37; Holds Stanley Cup shutout mark of 248:32

RED WINGS ARCHIVE

MOTOWN Classic

Motter, Wings, caught in fog

The haze which engulfed Detroit in 1937-38 was not limited to game night, as rookie center Alex Motter discovered. Working on an all-rookie line between Carl Liscombe and Eddie Wares, Motter's 17 assists were good for fourth on the team, but he was the one in need of a helping hand the night of Feb. 12, 1938.

Visiting relatives in Flat Rock, Mich., Motter encountered heavy fog in the evening en route to Detroit. He picked out the taillight of a car in front of him to use as a guide, following it for more than 15 miles until the vehicle stopped abruptly. Motter couldn't react in time and crashed into its rear end. Jumping out to apologize, he was quickly overcome with pangs of embarrassment. He'd tailed the car right through the owner's own yard and collided with it at the entrance to the fellow's garage.

ASSEMBLY LINE

Quickly realizing his Stanley Cup machine would no longer function, Detroit manager Jack Adams set out to retool. He sold Earl Robertson and John Gallagher to the New York Americans and dealt John Sorrell to the Amerks for forward Hap Emms. Forward Red Beattie was picked up from Boston for Gord Pettinger, then sent to the Amerks for forward Joe Lamb. Right-winger Eddie Wares was acquired

RED WINGS ARCHIVE

Johnny Sherf

from the New York Rangers for John Sherf, NHL veteran winger Ken Doraty signed a free-agent deal and rookie forwards Alex Motter, Carl Liscombe and Ron Hudson were all given big-league shots.

Red Wings Facts

Most Goals Scored in a Road Game

11 December 13, 1934
at St. Louis (11-2 victory)

11 December 2, 1995
at Montreal (11-1 victory)

10 March 16, 1947
at Chicago (10-6 victory)

10 December 11, 1952
at Boston (10-1 victory)

10 January 6, 1994
at San Jose (10-3 victory)

Short Passes

Detroit's 1937-38 lineup included Mud Bruneteau and Ken Doraty, scorers of the goals which ended the NHL's two longest overtime games. Bruneteau scored his goal for Detroit in 1936 and Doraty tallied for Toronto in 1934.

- 1938   1939 -

BACK in TIME

• **November 12, 1938**

For the first time, popular singer Kate Smith sang Irving Berlin's "God Bless America", written in 1918, on her Armistice Eve Radio Show.

• **May 22, 1939**

With the objective of reorganizing Europe and creating a world peace, Italy and Germany signed a 10-year pact to bind them economically, politically and militarily.

• **August 18, 1939**

Frank L. Baum's children's classic, "The Wonderful Wizard of Oz" had its film premiere starring Judy Garland, Ray Bolger, Jack Haley and Bert Lahr.

quick cuts

Most Goals
Syd Howe: 16
Most Assists
Marty Barry: 28
Most Points
Marty Barry: 41
Most Penalty Minutes
Charlie Conacher: 39
Most Wins, Goaltender
Tiny Thompson: 16
Lowest Goals-Against Average
Tiny Thompson: 2.53
Most Shutouts
Tiny Thompson: 4
NHL Award Winners
None

FINAL STANDINGS

	W	L	T	PTS	GF	GA
Boston	36	10	2	74	156	76
New York	26	16	6	58	149	105
Toronto	19	20	9	47	114	107
NY Americans	17	21	10	44	119	157
DETROIT	18	24	6	42	107	128
Montreal	15	24	9	39	115	146
Chicago	12	28	8	32	91	132

Playoff Results
Defeated the Montreal Canadiens in Series "C" (2-1)
Lost to the Toronto Maple Leafs in Series "D" (2-1)
Leading Playoff Scorers
Charlie Conacher (7PTS)
Stanley Cup Champion
Boston Bruins

1938-39 Season in Review

DETROIT RED WINGS ~ 1938-39

RED WINGS ARCHIVE

Changes were afoot, both with the NHL and Detroit. The Montreal Maroons dropped out, leaving the NHL a seven-team loop. All teams were amalgamated into one division, with six of seven teams slated to qualify for post-season play. The NHL wouldn't see a two-division format again for another 29 years.

Jack Adams also decided it was time for a new look, so the manager of the Red Wings began making some hard decisions about his personnel. Veteran left-winger Larry Aurie, a Detroit player since 1927, was named player-coach of the club's Pittsburgh farm team in the AHL and Adams declared that no other player would ever don Aurie's No. 6 jersey. He'd play one last Wings game when he was recalled as an injury replacement for a Jan. 10 game with the Montreal Canadiens, scoring a goal in Detroit's 3-0 win.

The Wings purchased the contract of two-time NHL scoring champion Charlie Conacher. Rookie center Gus Giesebrecht produced 10 goals in 20 games, while defenseman Jack Stewart displayed a physical presence and left wing Sid Abel quickly made the jump to the big leagues after less than a year of seasoning with Pittsburgh.

The beginnings looked hauntingly familiar to the dismal 1937-38 campaign, as Detroit won only four of its first 18 games. After an 0-4 start, goaltender Normie Smith was shipped to Pittsburgh, but refused to report and was suspended. Rookie Harvey Teno posted wins in his first two NHL starts, but Adams sought veteran help in goal and found it in reigning Vezina Trophy winner Cecil (Tiny) Thompson of Boston, who was acquired Nov. 16 in exchange for Smith and $15,000.

Thompson provided stellar netminding for a team in transition, posting a 16-17-6 record as the Wings grabbed fifth place and a first-round meeting with the Canadiens, which would prove to be the first of 20 consecutive seasons of playoff hockey for Detroit.

Montreal swept to a 2-0 win in the opener of the best-of-three series, causing Habs manager Jules Dugal to declare, "We'll take the Wings in two straight."

He should have kept quiet, because the Wings rallied. Marty Barry's overtime marker in Game 3 produced a 1-0 triumph and a semifinal date with Toronto.

Six Detroit players - Abel, Syd Howe, (Ralph) Scotty Bowman, Hec Kilrea, John Sherf and Alex Motter - were hobbled with injuries as the Leafs captured the set on Gord Drillon's Game 3 OT goal, which garnered a 5-4 victory.

"Considering the injuries and other handicaps we had, the club has done much better than I expected," Adams said. "I've never had a gamer band of athletes and I'm just as proud of them as I would have been had they won."

HOCKEYTOWN MOMENT
Wings deal for two future Hall of Famers

Looking to buy time until his crop of promising youngsters matured, Detroit manager Jack Adams reached out for a pair of NHL legends, adding right-winger Charlie Conacher and goaltender Cecil (Tiny) Thompson to his roster.

Conacher, NHL scoring champ in 1933-34 and 1934-35 and a four-time 30-goal scorer who led the league in goals five times, was purchased from Toronto for $16,000. Limited by injury and illness to 40 games, Conacher sparkled in the playoffs, leading Detroit shooters with seven points.

Thompson owned four Vezina Trophies and when he was pushed out of his job in Boston by rookie Frank Brimsek, Adams gleefully dealt Normie Smith and $15,000 to get him. The four-time NHL all-star was a rock behind the rebuilding Wings, backstopping them to the Stanley Cup semifinals.

Thompson was enshrined in the Hockey Hall of Fame in 1959, while Conacher was inducted in 1961.

Marty Barry

A chance meeting between Detroit manager Jack Adams and Boston manager Art Ross in the lobby of Montreal's Windsor Hotel during the 1935 Stanley Cup final put the Wings on the path to back-to-back crowns in 1935-36 and 1936-37.

"If we had Cooney Weiland, we'd be here," Ross expressed of Detroit's all-star center. "If I had Marty Barry," Adams countered, referring to the Boston center, "we'd win the Stanley Cup."

The deal was consummated in June, with Barry and Art Giroux coming to Detroit for Weiland and Walt Buswell.

That April, Adams was proven a prophet. Barry finished second in NHL scoring with 40 points and the Wings whipped Toronto to win their first title. Barry was third in league scoring the following year and led all playoff snipers with 11 points as Detroit retained its crown.

The 1936-37 season was Barry's finest. He earned selection to the First All-Star Team, was awarded the Lady Byng Trophy and scored two goals in Detroit's 3-0 Cup-clinching victory over the New York Rangers, including the Cup winner.

"First, they award me the Lady Byng Trophy and then I score two goals tonight," Barry said after that game. "I guess I was celebrating."

RED WINGS ARCHIVE

Barry led the Wings in scoring in three of his four seasons with the club and the unit of Barry, Larry Aurie and Herbie Lewis was recognized as the NHL's most effective forward line.

"He was a very smooth centerman," teammate Carl Liscombe remembered of Barry. "He had the talent to get the puck by everyone. In that sense, Marty was one of the best."

When the Wings went for a youth movement, Barry was released following the 1938-39 season. He skated one season with the Montreal Canadiens, then turned to coaching in the minor leagues.

Barry was inducted into the Hockey Hall of Fame in 1965.

- **BORN:**
  Quebec City, Quebec, December 8, 1905
- **ACQUIRED:**
  June 30, 1935 trade with Boston
- **BEST SEASON WITH RED WINGS:**
  1936-37 (17-27-44)
- **TOTALS WITH RED WINGS:**
  GP-191, G-60, A-94, PTS-154

- **HONORS:**
  Won Lady Byng Trophy, 1936-37; Selected to NHL First All-Star Team, 1936-37; Played in NHL All-Star Game, 1937; Led Detroit in scoring 1935-36, 1936-37, 1938-39; Elected to Hockey Hall of Fame, 1965

MOTOWN Classic

Howe nets three power-play goals against Montreal

Down 1-0 in their best-of-three playoff series with the Canadiens, the Wings came back. And Howe.

Detroit center Syd Howe blasted a hat-trick as the Wings took Game 2 by a 7-3 count on March 23 and all three of his tallies were power-play markers.

In this era, teams played shorthanded for the entire duration of the penalty and Detroit capitalized on this factor.

Before 8,200 - the smallest crowd to witness a Stanley Cup game at Olympia Stadium - Marty Barry and Howe both scored power-play goals with Montreal's Paul Haynes off for cross-checking. With less than seven minutes to play in regulation time and the score tied 3-3, Montreal's Herbie Cain took a seat for tripping Herbie Lewis and Howe parked two more pucks behind Habs netminder Claude Bourque to seal the victory.

WORLD WIDE PHOTOS

ASSEMBLY LINE

Detroit manager Jack Adams dropped Larry Aurie and Normie Smith, stalwarts of his Stanley Cup teams, while acquiring right-winger Charlie Conacher from Toronto and goalie Cecil (Tiny) Thompson from Boston. Forward Dave Trottier came in from the defunct Montreal Maroons and Bucko McDonald was dealt to Toronto for forward Bill Thomson and $10,000. Right wing Charley Mason was picked up from the New York Rangers, then shipped to Chicago for right wing Phil Besler.

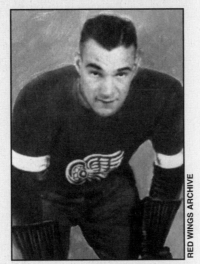

RED WINGS ARCHIVE

Charley Conacher

Red Wings Facts

Career Playoff Shut - Out Leaders

Terry Sawchuk - 11

Chris Osgood - 9

Harry Lumley - 6

Dominik Hasek - 6

Short Passes

Four Hall of Famers played goal for Toronto and Detroit – Hap Holmes, Terry Sawchuk, Harry Lumley and right-winger Charlie Conacher, who donned the pads in emergency situations three times for the Leafs and once for the Red Wings.

- 1939   1940 -

BACK in TIME

- **September 5, 1939**
President Roosevelt proclaimed U.S. neutrality in the war in Europe and issued an embargo on the shipment of military goods to those in a state of war.

- **May 10, 1940**
Prime Minister Winston Churchill gave his first speech to England's House of Commons and declared he had nothing to offer but "...blood, toil, tears and sweat."

- **October 29, 1940**
The first number was drawn in the United States peacetime military draft by Secretary of War Henry L. Stimson.

quick cuts

Most Goals
Syd Howe: 14
Most Assists
Syd Howe: 23
Most Points
Syd Howe: 37
Most Penalty Minutes
Jimmy Orlando: 54
Most Wins, Goaltender
Tiny Thompson: 16
Lowest Goals-Against Average
Tiny Thompson: 2.54
Most Shutouts
Tiny Thompson: 3
NHL Award Winners
Ebbie Goodfellow - Hart Trophy

FINAL STANDINGS

	W	L	T	PTS	GF	GA
Boston	31	12	5	67	170	98
New York	27	11	10	64	136	77
Toronto	25	17	6	56	134	110
Chicago	23	19	6	52	112	120
DETROIT	16	26	6	38	90	126
NY Americans	15	29	4	34	106	140
Montreal	10	33	5	25	90	167

Playoff Results
Defeated the N.Y. Americans in Series "C" (2-1)
Lost to the Toronto Maple Leafs in Series "D" (2-0)
Leading Playoff Scorers
"Mud" Bruneteau (3G, 5PTS)
Stanley Cup Champion
N.Y. Rangers

1939-40 Season in Review

Fresh off a semifinal playoff appearance, the Red Wings continued to restructure their team during the 1939-40 season.

The Wings switched from a finesse team to one with more grit, as veterans Marty Barry, Hec Kilrea, Scotty Bowman and Doug Young were fazed out, while youngsters like Don Grosso, Alex Motter, Kenny Kilrea, Sid Abel, Butch McDonald, Joe Fisher, Eddie Wares, Jack Stewart and Jimmy Orlando took on more prominent roles.

As with any team deep in youth, there were some difficult nights. Detroit suffered 10 shutouts and a 10-3 loss Feb. 13 at Boston, which was the most goals the club had ever surrendered in a single game. The few veterans who remained produced big years. Forward Syd Howe led the Wings with 14 goals and 37 points and old reliable Ebbie Goodfellow proved a calming influence on Detroit's kiddie corps of defensemen, becoming the first Red Wing to be awarded the Hart Trophy as NHL MVP.

Following the success he encountered moving Goodfellow from center to defense, Wings manager Jack Adams converted fifth-year man Motter from center to the blueline.

WORLD WIDE PHOTOS

A 16-26-6 mark was good for fifth place and Detroit swept the New York Americans in the quarter-finals, a set which saw Adams and Amerks manager Red Dutton scuffle behind the Detroit bench during a stoppage in play.

Toronto took care of the Wings in the minimum two games in the semifinals, with the two teams engaging in a bench-clearing brawl in Game 2.

HOCKEYTOWN MOMENT
Wings and Leafs duel in "Brawl of the Century"

What began as a rough night disintegrated into a donnybrook when the Wings and Toronto Maple Leafs clashed March 28 at Olympia Stadium in the deciding game of their Stanley Cup semifinal series.

During the first period, Toronto's Red Horner and Alex Motter duked it out in the penalty box, but Horner pulled his punch when a female fan clouted him over the head with her purse. Early in the third period, Detroit's Don Grosso launched Toronto's Hank Goldup completely over the boards with a bodycheck.

Then, all hell broke loose. Detroit's Sid Abel and Toronto's Gus Marker clashed at mid-ice and everyone on both sides dropped their mitts and paired off. Soon, both benches emptied. Toronto's Syl Apps and Detroit's Jimmy Orlando traded punches for five minutes. Orlando and Horner slugged it out twice. Toronto goalie Turk Broda tangled with Ebbie Goodfellow, Kenny Kilrea and Jack Stewart.

Described by The Windsor Star as, "The hockey fight of the century," when it was done, 17 players were fined $25 each.

By the way, Toronto won the game 3-1 to take the series.

Cecil (Tiny) Thompson

Detroit manager Jack Adams didn't mince words when he announced the Red Wings had acquired Cecil (Tiny) Thompson from the Boston Bruins early in the 1938-39 season.

"Tiny is the greatest goalie in the world," Adams said. "I'm sure this is what we have needed to give our team confidence."

Thompson certainly hauled an impressive resume over from Beantown, where he'd won four Vezina Trophies, been named an NHL All-Star a half-dozen times and backstopped the Bruins to the Stanley Cup as a rookie in 1928-29.

Thompson was being eased out in Boston in favor of rookie Frank Brimsek and saw his arrival in Detroit as a saving grace.

"As far as I am concerned, being traded by Boston to Detroit is a break for me," Thompson said. "I should last a few more years there than I would in Boston and I'll be among such friends as owner Jim Norris, manager Jack Adams and my old teammate Marty Barry."

Barry and Adams met Thompson at the train station, after Boston manager Art Ross sent Thompson on his way with a $1,000 bonus and his best wishes.

"He's good for at least five more seasons with Detroit," Ross predicted.

TINY THOMPSON

RED WINGS ARCHIVE

Not quite, but in the two seasons he did spend with the Red Wings before taking a coaching position with Buffalo of the AHL, Thompson proved a stabilizing influence while working behind a young defense.

His puckstopping skills allowed a team in transition to overachieve and reach the Stanley Cup semifinals in successive seasons after finishing as the NHL's worst team in 1937-38.

Voted the most popular Red Wing by Detroit fans during the 1939-40 season, Thompson was enshrined in the Hockey Hall of Fame in 1959.

- **BORN:**
  Sandon, Alberta, May 31, 1905
- **ACQUIRED:**
  November 16, 1938 trade with Boston
- **BEST SEASON WITH RED WINGS:**
  1938-39 (16-17-6, 4 SO, 2.53 GAA)
- **TOTALS WITH RED WINGS:**
  GP-85, W-32, L-41, T-12, SO-7, GAA-2.54

- **HONORS:**
  Led Detroit in wins, shutouts and goals-against average, 1938-39, 1939-40; Elected to Hockey Hall of Fame, 1959

Goodfellow first Wing to win Hart Trophy

There were whispers the year before that Ebbie Goodfellow was washed up, but the Detroit defenseman silenced his critics, finishing second on the team in scoring with 11-17-28 totals. That performance earned the 10-year veteran selection to the NHL's First All-Star Team and the Hart Trophy as the league's most valuable player. "He was the driving force for our club," Adams said of Goodfellow, who edged Toronto's Syl Apps and Boston's Aubrey (Dit) Clapper to become the first Red Wing to win the award.

RED WINGS ARCHIVE

ASSEMBLY LINE

The house-cleaning continued for Detroit manager Jack Adams, who released veterans Marty Barry and Doug Young, while purchasing goalie Alfie Moore from the New York Americans and right wing Cecil Dillon from the New York Rangers. Although they wouldn't be seen in Detroit this season, Adams signed three rookie free agents of note – goalie Johnny Mowers and forwards Adam Brown and Joe Carveth.

RED WINGS ARCHIVE

Marty Barry

Red Wings Facts

Playoff Record against Original - Six Teams

Boston Bruins - 14 wins 19 losses

Chicago Blackhawks - 31 wins 38 losses

Montreal Canadiens - 29 wins 33 losses

New York Rangers - 13 wins 10 losses

Toronto Maple Leafs - 59 wins 58 losses

Short Passes

Kenny Kilrea (1938-41, 1943-44) joined older siblings Hec (1931-32, 1935-40) and Wally (1934-38) as the only three-brother combination to play for the Red Wings.

BACK in TIME

• **November 11, 1940**
The Jeep, developed by the U.S. Army Quartermaster Corps and built by Willys, made its debut.

• **February 12, 1941**
Australian scientist Howard Florey, and German scientist Ernest Chain gave penicillin its first successful clinical trial at Oxford.

• **June 20, 1941**
In a move that affected 130,000 workers nationwide, Henry Ford signed a contract with the U.A.W. recognizing it as a C.I.O. union.

quick cuts

Most Goals
Syd Howe: 20

Most Assists
Syd Howe: 24

Most Points
Syd Howe: 44

Most Penalty Minutes
Jimmy Orlando: 99

Most Wins, Goaltender
Johnny Mowers: 21

Lowest Goals-Against Average
Johnny Mowers: 2.12

Most Shutouts
Johnny Mowers: 4

NHL Award Winners
None

FINAL STANDINGS

	W	L	T	PTS	GF	GA
Boston	27	8	13	67	168	102
Toronto	28	14	6	62	145	99
DETROIT	21	16	11	53	112	102
New York	21	19	8	50	143	125
Chicago	16	25	7	39	112	139
Montreal	16	26	6	38	121	147
NY Americans	8	29	11	27	99	186

Playoff Results
Defeated the N.Y. Rangers in Series "B" (2-1)
Defeated the Chicago Blackhawks in Series "D" (2-0)
Lost to Boston Bruins in Series "E" (4-0)

Leading Playoff Scorers
Syd Howe (8G) - Carl Liscombe (7PTS)

Stanley Cup Champion
Boston Bruins

1940-41 Season in Review

Steadily retooling his team from the disaster of 1937-38, Detroit manager Jack Adams would see vast improvement in his Red Wings in 1940-41.

Recording their first winning season since their 1936-37 Stanley Cup-winning campaign, the Wings' 21-16-11 mark was good for third spot in the seven-team NHL.

It was a performance built around defense and goaltending. Only the last-place Montreal Canadiens (99) scored fewer goals than the 112 netted by Detroit.

With old hand Ebbie Goodfellow and rugged young veterans (Black) Jack Stewart

RED WINGS ARCHIVE

and Jimmy Orlando anchoring a steady blueline crew, Adams gambled and promoted goalie Johnny Mowers from the minor leagues.

It was a stroke of genius. Mowers performed brilliantly, losing just once in his first nine starts and missing out on the Vezina Trophy by three goals. Adams was outraged when Montreal Canadiens forward Johnny Quilty edged Mowers in the Calder Trophy voting as NHL rookie of the year.

Seeking to boost his attack, Adams juggled his forwards, moving Sid Abel from center to left wing and returning Alex Motter to center from his 1939-40 experiment as a defenseman.

Heading into the playoffs, few gave Detroit much chance, but Boston manager Art Ross wasn't among the detractors. "Detroit is underrated," Ross said. "That Detroit club is a lot better than fans think. They're

rugged and capable and will be a mighty tough team to beat."

The New York Rangers and Chicago Blackhawks wouldn't argue. Detroit edged the Rangers in a three-game first-round series, then swept the Blackhawks 2-0 in the semifinals and readied to meet Boston for the Stanley Cup.

Entering the final series minus the injured Goodfellow, Detroit put up tough resistance, but fell in the minimum four games in the best-of-seven affair.

Afterwards, Adams talked only positively about the experience. "We did a lot better than anyone expected us to," he said. "I'm proud of the boys. I was greatly pleased by the improvement of fellows like Jack Stewart and Sid Abel and the way Johnny Mowers more than lived up to expectations.

"Next year, we should be stronger than ever."

HOCKEYTOWN MOMENT
Wings swept by Boston in finals

Back in the Stanley Cup finals for the first time since their 1936-37 triumph over the New York Rangers, the young Wings battled gamely, but were in over their heads against an experienced Boston Bruins team which had won the Cup two springs earlier. It didn't help that an elbow injury put veteran defenseman Ebbie Goodfellow on the shelf early in the playoffs.

The Bruins took 3-2 and 2-1 verdicts at Boston Garden, then went one goal better on Olympia ice, posting 4-2 and 3-1 decisions to sweep the best-of-seven set.

Despite the loss, Detroit manager Jack Adams bubbled with optimism.

"If we can get one or two more men that I have in mind, we'll be right back in there pitching again next winter," he boldly predicted.

Syd Howe

The first Detroit Red Wing named Howe to reign as the NHL's career scoring leader was Syd, not Gordie.

Steady and productive, Syd, a left wing who wasn't related to Gordie, toiled in the shadows of Detroit's other stars when the club won its two Stanley Cups in the 1930s. He led the team in scoring and finished second overall in NHL scoring in 1934-35, but no one seemed to notice because the Wings missed the playoffs.

The Wings thought so much of Howe they paid the St. Louis Eagles $50,000 and Teddy Graham to get him and defenseman Ralph (Scotty) Bowman and it was easy to see why. Howe was the ideal second-line forward, because he could do everything well.

The war years brought Howe into prominence. He led a young Wings club in scoring in 1940-41 with 44 points, providing a veteran example to Detroit's emerging crop of talented, young forwards.

He exploded for a club-record 55 points in 1942-43, and garnered 32 goals and 60 points in 1943-44, a season which saw him set a Red Wings record with a six-goal performance February 3, 1944 in a 12-2 decision over the New York Rangers. In NHL history, only a seven-goal game by Quebec's Joe Malone against Toronto on Jan. 31, 1920 surpassed Howe's effort.

The Rangers also provided the opposition March 8, 1945 when Howe set up a third-period goal by Joe Carveth to move past Nels Stewart (515 points) as the NHL's all-time points leader.

The record-breaking performance earned Howe selection to the NHL's Second All-Star Team.

He retired at the end of the 1945-46 season with 528 points, but Howe's record lasted less than a

RED WINGS ARCHIVE

season before his totals were overtaken by Boston's Bill Cowley.

Howe was inducted into the Hockey Hall of Fame in 1965.

- **BORN:**
  Ottawa, Ontario, September 18, 1911
- **ACQUIRED:**
  Feb. 11, 1935 trade with St. Louis Eagles
- **BEST SEASON WITH RED WINGS:**
  1943-44 (32-28-60)
- **TOTALS WITH RED WINGS:**
  GP-505, G-188, A-247, PTS-435

- **HONORS:**
  Selected to NHL Second All-Star Team, 1944-45; Led Detroit in scoring, 1934-35, 1940-41, 1943-44; Set club record with six goals in Feb. 3, 1944 game; Retired in 1945-46 as NHL's career scoring leader; Elected to Hockey Hall of Fame, 1965

MOTOWN Classic

RED WINGS ARCHIVE

Orlando leads NHL in penalty minutes

It was fitting that Wings defenseman Jimmy Orlando and Toronto rearguard Red Horner fought twice in Detroit's last play-off game of the 1939-40 season, because Orlando was about to ascend to Horner's throne as the NHL's toughest customer.

Horner's run of eight consecutive seasons as the NHL's penalty-minute leader ended when he retired after the 1939-40 campaign and Orlando took up his seat in the sin bin, leading the NHL in 1940-41 with 99 minutes. Toronto captain Syl Apps doffed his cap after dropping the mitts with Orlando. "As a fighter, kid, you're the best," Apps told Orlando.

Orlando and (Black) Jack Stewart formed the NHL's fiercest blueline tandem and anyone who got in their bombsights was in danger, including referee King Clancy, who was accidentally bodychecked into the boards by Orlando during the first game of the 1940-41 playoffs.

ASSEMBLY LINE

RED WINGS ARCHIVE

Hal Jackson

For once, Trader Jack Adams kept most of his cards to himself. His only deal of the season saw Eddie Bush and Cecil Dillon shipped to Providence (AHL) for defenseman Hal Jackson. Several rookies were promoted from the farm system, including goalie Johnny Mowers, defenseman Bob Whitelaw and forwards Joe Carveth, Art Herchenratter, Bill Jennings and Conny Brown.

Red Wings Facts

Most penalty shots by a Red Wings Player

10 - Ebbie Goodfellow

6 - Steve Yzerman

3 - John Sorrell

3 - Mud Bruneteau

3 - Petr Klima

Short Passes

The only two Stanley Cup goals ever scored by Detroit's Gus Giesebrecht were both overtime winners tallied during the 1940-41 playoffs.

- 1941   1942 -

BACK in TIME

• **October 10, 1941**
In Michigan, war tank output was crippled by inter-union struggles when the C.I.O. refused to handle parts made by the A.F.L.

• **December 7, 1941**
Three hundred and sixty Japanese warplanes attacked Pearl Harbor, pulling the United States into a war with Japan; four days later the U.S. declared war on Japan's fellow axis powers, Italy and Germany.

• **June 25, 1942**
Major General Dwight D. Eisenhower assumed command of the United States military forces in Europe.

quick cuts

Most Goals
Don Grosso: 23
Most Assists
Sid Abel: 31
Most Points
Don Grosso: 53
Most Penalty Minutes
Jimmy Orlando: 111
Most Wins, Goaltender
Johnny Mowers: 19
Lowest Goals-Against Average
Johnny Mowers: 3.06
Most Shutouts
Johnny Mowers: 5
NHL Award Winners
Sid Abel - 2nd Team All-Star

FINAL STANDINGS

American Division	W	L	T	PTS	GF	GA
New York	29	17	2	60	177	143
Toronto	27	18	3	57	156	138
Boston	25	17	6	56	160	118
Chicago	22	23	3	47	145	155
DETROIT	19	25	4	42	140	147
Montreal	18	27	3	39	134	173
Brooklyn	16	29	3	35	133	175

Playoff Results
Defeated the Montreal Canadiens in Series "C" (2-1)
Defeated the Boston Bruins in Series "D" (2-0)
Lost to the Toronto Maple Leafs in Series "E" (4-3)
Leading Playoff Scorers
Don Grosso (14PTS) - Carl Liscombe (13PTS)
Stanley Cup Champion
Toronto Maple Leafs

1941-42 Season in Review

Detroit entered the 1941-42 campaign with a good feeling. Its reshaped roster had battled to the Stanley Cup final the previous spring and there was cause for optimism.

When the Wings were slow out of the gate, starting the season 2-6-1, it was an indication that they'd struggle to find consistency all season long. Take the month of January, for example. On January 4, they blasted the Montreal Canadiens 10-0, with Syd Howe and Kenny Kilrea bagging five points each. Three weeks later on January 25, Detroit was handed the heaviest defeat in team history, an 11-2 shellacking by the New York Rangers.

Detroit's 19-25-4 slate was only good enough for fifth place, but this inconsistent team found its form as the playoffs commenced, edging Montreal in a three-game set, then sweeping Boston to advance to the Stanley Cup final for the second straight spring.

Detroit racked up three consecutive wins against the Toronto Maple Leafs in the final series, scoring 3-2, 4-2 and 5-2 decisions. In the third game, Detroit's Eddie Bush figured in all five goals, scoring once and assisting on the other four, to set a Stanley Cup record for points in a game by a defensemen which wasn't broken until 1985.

Then, almost as quickly, the consistency was gone. Toronto edged Detroit 4-3 in Game 4 and Detroit manager Jack Adams was suspended for the rest of the

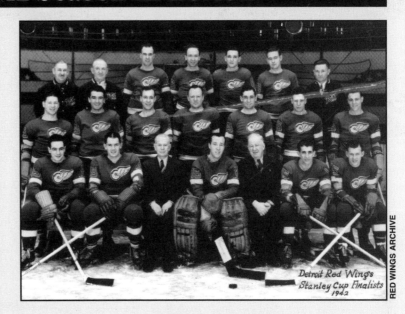

Detroit Red Wings
Stanley Cup Finalists
1942

RED WINGS ARCHIVE

playoffs after assaulting referee Mel Harwood. With defenseman Ebbie Goodfellow behind the bench, Detroit lost three straight and Toronto took the Cup in a most improbable comeback.

Amazingly, Detroit held third-period leads in two of four games it lost to the Leafs. Detroit center Sid Abel felt Toronto's depth eventually wore the Wings down, turning the tide.

"The Leafs had three strong lines, which wasn't always the case with us," Abel said.

A regular season of ups and downs had concluded with the most amazing up-and-down sequence in hockey history.

HOCKEYTOWN MOMENT

Detroit suffers stunning setback in Cup final

Everything, it seemed, was going in Detroit's favor in the 1942 Stanley Cup final. The Wings were up 3-0 in the best-of-seven series, but just like that, it all went horribly wrong.

Angered over penalties assessed to their team in a 4-3 loss to Toronto in Game 4, Wings players Eddie Wares and Don Grosso and manager Jack Adams went after referee Mel Harwood and a brouhaha ensued. When the dust settled, NHL president Frank Calder suspended Adams for the rest of the playoffs and fined Grosso and Wares.

Shaken up, Detroit lost the next game 9-3, then fell 3-0 in Game 6. At Toronto in Game 7, Detroit led 1-0 after two periods, but lost 3-1, becoming the only team to squander a 3-0 series lead in Stanley Cup final history.

"Someone had to lose," Detroit defenseman Jimmy Orlando said. "We just happened to be the unlucky ones."

Eddie Wares

What should have been the most memorable season in Eddie Wares' career came crashing to a halt on a night he'd never forget.

The sixth-year right-winger posted a career high with 38 points in 1941-42 and as Detroit raced to a 3-0 lead in its Stanley Cup final series with Toronto, Wares played a large part, setting up the winning goal in Detroit's 3-2 Game 2 victory.

He also played a huge role in the turnaround which saw Toronto win the last four games of the series to take the title. The Leafs were leading 4-3 late in Game 4 when Wares mouthed off to referee Mel Harwood. Harwood, insisting Wares used profanity, assessed the Detroit player a 10-minute misconduct. Denying the charge, Wares refused to go to the penalty box, standing instead by the Detroit bench.

Harwood assessed Detroit a bench minor and ordered forward Don Grosso to serve it. In protest, Grosso laid his stick and gloves at Harwood's feet.

When the game concluded, Grosso, Wares and Detroit manager Jack Adams beat a path towards Harwood and a brawl ensued.

Wares and Grosso were fined $100 each for their actions and Adams was suspended for the remainder of the post-season.

"I never said a thing to (Harwood)," Wares complained. "He said, 'You've got yourself a misconduct.' I asked, 'What for?' and he said, 'You don't know what for?'

"He never did tell me. That's why I refused to leave the ice."

It was a black mark on an otherwise solid career for Wares, a talented athlete who performed on Canada's schoolboy track and field team, winning the shot put competition at the 1934 British Empire Scholastic Games in Australia.

DWAYNE LaBAKAS

Wares was an instant hit with he arrived in Detroit during the 1937-38 season, scoring six goals and two assists in his first eight games. "Every once in a while, hockey produces one of those scoring opportunists, the kind that has a happy faculty for ringing the old gong just when a goal is needed," Adams said. "Wares is one of those birds."

Wares joined the Canadian Navy after the 1942-43 season and never played again for the Wings. His contract was sold to Chicago in 1945 and he spent two seasons with the Blackhawks, leaving the NHL for good in 1947.

- **BORN:**
  Calgary, Alberta, March 19, 1915
- **ACQUIRED:**
  January 17, 1938 trade with New York Rangers
- **BEST SEASON WITH RED WINGS:**
  1941-42 (9-29-38)

- **TOTALS WITH RED WINGS:**
  GP-214, G-50, A-84, PTS-134
- **HONORS:**
  Played for Detroit's 1942-43 Stanley Cup championship team

MOTOWN Classic

Grosso first Wing to reach 50-point mark

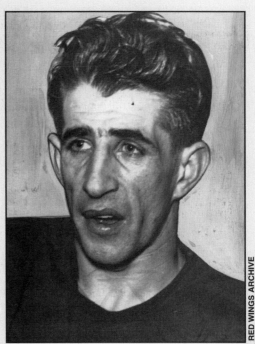

RED WINGS ARCHIVE

They called Don Grosso "The Count" and the left-winger certainly made his opportunities count during the 1941-42 season.

With 23 goals and 30 assists, Grosso led the Wings in scoring and became the first Detroit player to top the half-century mark in points for a single season.

Grosso was productive and he was quick. In a 6-4 win over Chicago in the regular-season finale on March 19, Grosso tallied two goals in eight seconds, a club record.

He kept up his record pace in the playoffs. Grosso's eight goals and 14 points led all scorers and were Stanley Cup records.

ASSEMBLY LINE

Left-winger Dutch Hiller was claimed on waivers from the New York Rangers, but lasted only seven games in Detroit before being traded to Boston for center Pat McReavy. Defenseman Eddie Bush was reacquired from Providence of the AHL, where he'd been traded the season before by Detroit manager Jack Adams.

RED WINGS ARCHIVE

Jack Adams

Red Wings Facts

Last Red Wings Successful Penalty Shot

Igor Larionov
(November 22, 1995 vs San Jose)

Short Passes

Detroit went three deep in Browns at forward in 1941-42 – second-year center Conny and rookie left-wingers Gerry and Adam – but none of them were related.

quick cuts

Most Goals
"Mud" Bruneteau: 23

Most Assists
Syd Howe: 35

Most Points
Syd Howe: 55

Most Penalty Minutes
Jimmy Orlando: 99

Most Wins, Goaltender
Johnny Mowers: 25

Lowest Goals-Against Average
Johnny Mowers: 2.48

Most Shutouts
Johnny Mowers: 6

NHL Award Winners
Johnny Mowers - Vezina Trophy
& 1st Team All-Star
Jack Stewart 1st Team All-Star

BACK in TIME

• **December 2, 1942**
The first controlled nuclear chain reaction was achieved by Enrico Fermi and his group of scientists, paving the way for nuclear energy and the creation of an atomic bomb.

• **February 7, 1943**
Shoe rationing began limiting American civilians to three pair per year, followed by the rationing of canned goods, which began March 1, 1943.

• **June 22, 1943**
Federal troops moved into Detroit to help restore order following a race riot in which 29 people were killed and hundreds injured.

FINAL STANDINGS

	W	L	T	PTS	GF	GA
DETROIT	25	14	11	61	169	124
Boston	24	17	9	57	195	176
Toronto	22	19	9	53	198	159
Montreal	19	19	12	50	181	191
Chicago	17	18	15	49	179	180
New York	11	31	8	30	161	253

Playoff Results
Defeated the Toronto Maple Leafs in Series "A" (4-2)
Defeated the Boston Bruins in Series "C" (4-0)
Leading Playoff Scorers
Carl Liscombe (14PTS) - Sid Abel (13PTS)
Stanley Cup Champion
Detroit Red Wings

1942-43 Season in Review

RED WINGS ARCHIVE

Two trips to the Stanley Cup finals which ended in heartbreak only served to fuel the fire inside the bellies of Red Wings players as they entered the dawning of the NHL's six-team era, created when the Brooklyn Americans ceased operations prior to the start of the 1942-43 season.

Signs of Detroit's single-minded determination emerged quickly, as the Wings rolled to a 25-14-11 first-place finish. In the season opener, goalie Johnny Mowers blanked Boston 3-0. Four nights later on Nov. 5, Detroit swamped the New York Rangers 12-5, establishing team and individual marks on several fronts.

The dozen goals were a Red Wings record and the most registered by an NHL team in a single game since the Montreal Canadiens blasted the Quebec Athletics 16-3 on March 3, 1920.

Left-winger Carlk Liscombe led the assault with three goals and four assists, establishing a club mark for points in a game which has never been bettered. At the time, it also tied the NHL standard in this category.

The Wings tallied six power-play goals in this contest, four of them in one period, to establish two more club records.

Detroit kept rolling and there were signs that this would be the year the Wings got the breaks. Take, for instance, a 2-2 tie Jan. 17 at Chicago, which saw Detroit captain Sid Abel net the tying goal at 19:59 of the third period.

In goal, Mowers was dominant. His six shutouts were one more than the other five NHL teams managed to gather collectively, helping the third-year netminder earn his first Vezina Trophy, as well as selection to the NHL's First All-Star Team. On defense, (Black)

Jack Stewart's preeminence as the NHL's most terrifying bodychecker was recognized when he was also made a First All-Star Team choice.

Offensively, balance was the story of Detroit's attack. No Detroit player cracked the top 10 in scoring, as only the Rangers (161) scored fewer goals than the 165 registered by the Wings. However, Detroit's Syd Howe set a club record with 55 points and eight players reached double-digits in goals. Familiar foes provided playoff opposition. Toronto was doused in a six-game semifinal series, with Adam Brown's overtime goal giving Detroit a 3-2 verdict in the deciding game.

Afterwards, Toronto captain Syl Apps criticized the Wings for playing scrambly hockey, insisting it was, "The only way they could beat clubs better than themselves."

NHL president Red Dutton took issue with Apps' criticism, describing Detroit as, "The best-coached team in hockey."

Boston, the team responsible for sweeping Detroit in the 1941 final, found itself on the business end of the broom this time, as the Wings swept to their first title since 1937.

HOCKEYTOWN MOMENT

Wings win their 3rd Stanley cup

Call it third-time lucky. Detroit finally found Stanley Cup success in its third consecutive trip to the finals, whipping Boston in the minimum four games.

Mud Bruneteau, always a strong playoff performer, fired a hat-trick in Detroit's 6-2 victory in the series opener. Don Grosso had a three-goal night and Mowers posted a shutout for a 4-0 verdict in Game 3. Mowers also kept a clean sheet in a 2-0 decision in Game 4. Joe Carveth tallied the Cup winner and Carl Liscombe's goal was his 14th point of the playoffs,

equaling the post-season scoring mark shared by Grosso and Boston's Bill Cowley.

The only disappointments came during the playoffs. Detroit defenseman Jimmy Orlando was arrested by the FBI and charged with draft evasion, accused of falsifying documents suggesting he held an essential war job and was therefore exempt from military service. Convicted, Orlando avoided jail time by enlisting in the Canadian armed forces.

Meanwhile, in the midst of Detroit's Stanley Cup celebration party, manager Jack Adams was informed that his mother had passed away.

Don Grosso

"The Count" was his nickname, which seemed appropriate, because Don Grosso was a guy Detroit could count on in the big games.

Signed away from the senior Kirkland Lake, Ont. Blue Devils late in the 1938-39 season, Grosso scored once and assisted on the game-winner in a 3-2 victory over Chicago.

"Gosh," Grosso exclaimed after the heady debut. "I'm so happy I can hardly speak."

The pesky left-winger's best years came while he skated with center Sid Abel and right-winger Eddie Wares on Detroit's "Liniment Line." "It was called that because one of us was always hurt," Grosso explained. "That's because we got so much ice time on our regular shift, killing penalties and on the power play."

Grosso's best regular-season performance came in 1941-42, when he registered 23-30-53 totals to finish third in NHL scoring and establish a new Detroit single-season mark for points. Three other times, he netted 15 goals and Grosso garnered 47 points in 1943-44.

Known as a money player, Grosso saved some of his best hockey for the playoffs. During the 1942 post-season, Grosso tallied a Stanley Cup-record 14 points, eight of them coming in Detroit's seven-game loss to Toronto in the finals.

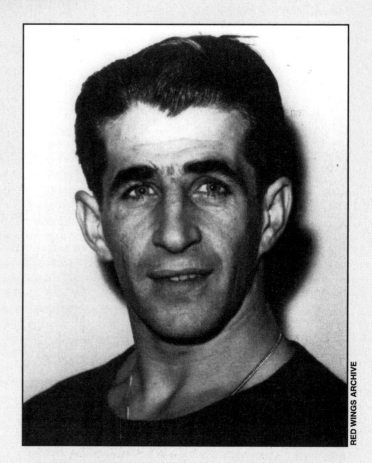

RED WINGS ARCHIVE

His hat-trick in Game 3 of the 1943 finals at Boston paved the way for Detroit's 4-0 win and left the Bruins down to their last gasp.

Grosso, whose colorful nickname was the result of his uncanny resemblance to Dracula, was finally counted out by the Wings in 1944-45, traded to Chicago in mid-season as part of a package which allowed Detroit to grab perennial all-star defenseman Earl Seibert.

- **BORN:**
  Sault Ste. Marie, Ontario, April 12, 1915
- **ACQUIRED:**
  Signed as a free agent, March 18, 1939
- **BEST SEASON WITH RED WINGS:**
  1941-42 (23-30-53)

- **TOTALS WITH RED WINGS:**
  GP-235, G-71, A-99, PTS-170
- **HONORS:**
  Led Detroit in scoring, 1941-42; Set a Stanley Cup scoring record with 14 points, 1914-42; Shares club record for points in a game with seven, 1943-44

MOTOWN Classic

Mowers captures the Vezina Trophy

The faith Jack Adams bestowed in Johnny Mowers when he installed the 23-year-old in the Red Wings' net in 1940 continued to pay dividends. Mowers backstopped Detroit to the Stanley Cup finals in each of his first three seasons and in 1942-43, pulled out all the stops.

Mowers led NHL goalies in wins (25), shutouts (six) and goals-against average (2.47), to win the Vezina Trophy. Selected to the NHL's First All-Star Team, Mowers continued to excel in the playoffs, posting back-to-back shutouts in Games 3 and 4 of the final series at Boston to clinch a Detroit sweep. "There's no doubt who won it for us," Wings forward Joe Carveth said. "Mowers did."

It would be the last hurrah for Mowers in a Detroit uniform. He joined the Royal Canadian Air Force before the start of the 1943-44 season and never won another game as a Red Wing.

RED WINGS ARCHIVE

ASSEMBLY LINE

Detroit selected forwards Harry Watson and Murray Armstrong and defenseman Pat Egan in a dispersal draft of the defunct Brooklyn Americans roster. Rookies making the grade included defenseman Cully Simon and forwards Les Douglas and Johnny Holota.

RED WINGS ARCHIVE

Pat Egan

Red Wings Facts

Last Two Successful Penalty Shots Against The Red Wings

Joe Nieuwendyk
(Dallas) February 18, 2001

Chris Drury
(Colorado) March 18, 2000

Short Passes

Detroit's Ebbie Goodfellow, who played his final season in 1942-43, was awarded 10 career penalty shots, but scored on just two of them.

- 1943 ![Red Wings logo] 1944 -

BACK in TIME

- **August 8, 1943**
  In the Pacific, Lieutenant John F. Kennedy saved his crew after a Japanese destroyer split his PT boat in half.

- **March 2, 1944**
  The Acadamy Award for the best picture of 1943 was presented to Casablanca, starring Humphrey Bogart and Ingrid Bergman.

- **June 6, 1944**
  Designated D-Day, Allied forces began the invasion of Normandy with landings on five beach-heads in Northern France.

quick cuts

Most Goals
Carl Liscombe: 36
Most Assists
Carl Liscombe: 37
Most Points
Carl Liscombe: 73
Most Penalty Minutes
Hal Jackson: 76
Most Wins, Goaltender
Connie Dion: 17
Lowest Goals-Against Average
Connie Dion: 3.08
Most Shutouts
Connie Dion & Jimmy Franks: 1
NHL Award Winners
None

FINAL STANDINGS

	W	L	T	PTS	GF	GA
Montreal	38	5	7	83	234	109
DETROIT	26	18	6	58	214	177
Toronto	23	23	4	50	214	174
Chicago	22	23	5	49	178	187
Boston	19	26	5	43	223	268
New York	6	39	5	17	162	310

Playoff Results
Lost to the Chicago Blackhawks in Series "B" (4-1)
Leading Playoff Scorers
Syd Howe (4PTS)
Stanley Cup Champion
Montreal Canadiens

No changes were made to the makeup of its six franchises, but the NHL wore a vastly different look in 1943-44.

The war effort deprived every NHL team of some of its stars and Detroit was no exception. Goalie Johnny Mowers, defensemen (Black) Jack Stewart and Jimmy Orlando and forwards Sid Abel, Harry Watson, Eddie Wares, Les Douglas, Conny Brown, Alex Motter and Johnny Holota all joined the military.

The patchwork lineups, along with the addition of the center red line, combined to send scoring skyrocketing and saw some outrageous numbers posted on NHL scoreboards. The pace was set early, when the Wings thrashed the New York Rangers 8-3 in the Oct. 31 season opener, but little did the Rangers know they were getting off easy.

Detroit pounded New York 15-0 on January 23, setting an NHL record for the largest shutout victory. Eleven days later on Feb. 3, Detroit's Syd Howe tallied a club-record six goals and Don Grosso equaled a team mark by collecting seven points in a 12-2 rout of the Rangers. In 10 meetings with New York, Detroit posted an 8-1-1 slate and outscored the Rangers 67-26.

DETROIT RED WINGS 1943-44

RED WINGS ARCHIVE

The Broadway Blueshirts weren't the only team entering shootouts with Detroit. In a March 16 game at the Olympia, the Wings outscored the Boston Bruins 10-9, establishing a Detroit mark for the highest total game score.

Carl Liscombe obliterated all of Detroit's season scoring marks by posting 36-37-73 totals, which in the inflated numbers of 1943-44 made Liscombe only the third-highest scoring left-winger in the league. Detroit topped the 200-goal plateau for the first time with 214, finishing second to Montreal with a 26-18-6 record.

Just like that, Detroit's offense dried up in the play-offs against Chicago. Held to eight goals, the Wings were knocked off in five games by the Blackhawks.

HOCKEYTOWN MOMENT
Wings defeat Rangers 15-0

Joe Carveth

RED WINGS ARCHIVE

The New York Rangers were Detroit's pet whipping boys in 1943-44 and never were they beaten as badly as the night of January 23.

Rangers goalie Ken McAuley fished 15 pucks out of his net, while Detroit's Connie Dion posted a shutout in the most lopsided score in NHL history.

The 15-0 verdict was the largest shutout win ever recorded in the NHL and the eight third-period goals gave Detroit another league mark which stood until 1980-81. Every player except Dion and defenseman Cully Simon figured in the Detroit scoring.

Detroit's Syd Howe fired a hat-trick and in the process, surpassed Herbie Lewis (148) for the Red Wings career lead in goals. Don Grosso and Carl Liscombe each scored twice and Joe Carveth collected club records for assists (four) and points (four) in a period.

Wings of Legend

Carl Liscombe

It didn't take Carl Liscombe long to make people notice him in a Red Wings uniform.

Called up to Detroit from Pittsburgh of the AHL early in the 1937-38 season, Liscombe set a club record for rookies by potting 14 goals. He collected an NHL-record three goals in 1:52 against Chicago for his first NHL hat trick and also showed everyone he couldn't be intimidated, scrapping with Toronto defenseman Red Horner, considered the NHL's toughest player.

The line of Eddie Wares, Alex Motter and Liscombe clicked that season, but in 1943-44, Liscombe skated alongside Syd Howe and they proved to be a potent pair.

Both players posted huge seasons. Howe tallied 32 goals and 60 points, while Liscombe tore apart the Detroit record book, finishing the season with 36 goals and 73 points, both club single-season standards. "He knew exactly where I was and I knew exactly where he was," Liscombe said of Howe, the center on the line. "I yelled only if I was open and if I was open, I got the puck."

Along with linemate Mud Bruneteau (35 goals), they became the first forward unit in NHL history to collect 100 goals in a season. Liscombe registered 12 points in the 1942 playoffs and the following season, as Detroit won the Stanley Cup, he gathered 14 points and a share of the Stanley Cup single-season scoring mark with Grosso and Boston's Bill Cowley. Liscombe posted a club-record seven points in a 12-5 win over the New York Rangers in 1942-43 and scored a record four goals in a 1944-45 playoff game against Boston, finishing his Detroit days with five hat tricks.

Growing up in the Ontario town of Galt, Liscombe worked at the local arena and skated sometimes up to five hours a day, honing the skills which would one day make him an NHLer.

"When there was no more skating for the night, I'd sling my skates over my shoulder and head for home," Liscombe said.

Liscombe's Detroit days ended in 1945-46, but he put up back-to-back 50-goal and 100-point seasons for the Providence Reds in the AHL, eventually hanging up his skates for good following the 1951-52 campaign.

RED WINGS ARCHIVE

- **BORN:**
  Perth, Ontario, May 17, 1915
- **ACQUIRED:**
  Signed as a free agent, September 24, 1935
- **BEST SEASON WITH RED WINGS:**
  1943-44 (36-37-73)

- **TOTALS WITH RED WINGS:**
  GP-373, G-137, A-140, PTS-277
- **HONORS:**
  Led Detroit in scoring, 1943-44; Shares club record for points in a game with seven, 1943-44

MOTOWN Classic

Howe scores six against New York

Syd Howe became Detroit's all-time goal-scoring leader in 1943-44 and he also became the club's single-game goal-scoring record holder, netting six in a 12-2 rout of the New York Rangers on February 3.

Howe scored two goals in each period and the goals were gathered in quick pairs. Howe scored twice in 18 seconds in the first period, twice in 62 seconds in the second frame and twice in 57 seconds in the third stanza.

"I just hit a hot night," Howe said. "I wonder what the boys in the shop will say now?"

Howe, like almost all wartime Red Wings, worked in the auto plants building military machinery.

"I'll be on the job at 7:10 a.m., just like I am six days a week," Howe said after his record goal outburst.

Howe finished the season with 32 goals, joining Carl Liscombe (36) and Mud Bruneteau (35) to make the 1943-44 Wings the first team in NHL history with three 30-goal men.

ASSEMBLY LINE

"Flash" Hollett

Major changes resulted from so many veteran players joining the armed forces. Critics began to refer to the NHL as the "Nursery Hockey League" because young players were so plentiful.

The Wings tried four different goaltenders, luring Normie Smith out of a five-year retirement and employing 17-year-old Harry Lumley. Connie Dion and Jimmy Franks also had stints between the pipes. Defenseman Flash Hollett was acquired from Boston for Pat Egan and Bill Quackenbush became a regular in the Detroit rearguard. Center Murray Armstrong joined the Wings after an army stint and impressed manager Jack Adams. "Haven't had one like him on the club in years," Adams said. "He doesn't smoke, doesn't drink and is strictly a team player."

Red Wings Facts

Fathers And Sons Who Have Played For The Wings

Sid and Gerry Abel

Adam and Andy Brown

Bill and Peter Dineen

Gordie and Mark Howe

Jim Peters Sr. and Jim Peters Jr.

Short Passes

Left-winger Vic Lynn, a Red Wing in 1943-44, is the only player to suit up for all of the so-called "Original Six" teams, also playing with the New York Rangers (1942-43), Montreal (1945-46), Toronto (1946-50), Boston (1950-52) and Chicago (1952-54) during an 11-season NHL career.

- 1944   1945 -

BACK in TIME

• **December 16, 1944**
The Battle of the Bulge, the last major German offensive of World War II, began as German forces broke through Allied defenses in the Ardennes.

• **May 8, 1945**
Known as VE-Day, for "Victory in Europe", the European phase of WWII came to an end with the unconditional surrender of Germany.

• **August 6, 1945**
The first atomic bomb used in war was dropped on Hiroshima, Japan. Three days later, Nagasaki was also destroyed by a second atomic bomb, bringing the war to an end.

quick cuts

Most Goals
Joe Carveth: 26
Most Assists
Syd Howe: 36
Most Points
Joe Carveth: 54
Most Penalty Minutes
Hal Jackson: 76
Most Wins, Goaltender
Harry Lumley: 20
Lowest Goals-Against Average
Harry Lumley: 3.22
Most Shutouts
Harry Lumley: 1
NHL Award Winners
"Flash" Hollett - 1st Team All-Star
Syd Howe & Jack Adams - 2nd Team All-Star

FINAL STANDINGS

	W	L	T	PTS	GF	GA
Montreal	38	8	4	80	228	121
DETROIT	31	14	5	67	218	161
Toronto	24	22	4	52	183	161
Boston	16	30	4	36	179	219
Chicago	13	30	7	33	141	194
New York	11	29	10	32	154	247

Playoff Results
Defeated the Boston Bruins in Series "B" (4-3)
Lost to the Toronto Maple Leafs in Series "C" (4-3)
Leading Playoff Scorers
Joe Carveth (11PTS) - Eddie Bruneteau & "Flash" Hollett (7PTS)
Stanley Cup Champion
Toronto Maple Leafs

1944-45 Season in Review

A record-setting season for the Red Wings saw some of Detroit's veterans grab places in NHL history and a few newcomers establish themselves as potential stars of tomorrow.

Detroit finished second in the standings with a 31-14-5 slate, pounding a club-record 218 goals past NHL netminders and several of those who turned on red lights reached previously-unattained levels.

RED WINGS ARCHIVE

At the top of that list was left-winger Syd Howe, whose assist in a 7-3 win over the New York Rangers was his 516th NHL point, moving him past Nels Stewart to become the league's all-time scoring leader. Howe was runner-up in the Lady Byng Trophy voting and named to the NHL's Second All-Star Team, as was coach Jack Adams. Howe finished 10th in NHL scoring with 53 points, one behind team leader Joe Carveth, who recorded his best season as an NHLer with 26-28-54 totals.

The same night that Howe etched his mark in the history books, right-winger Steve Wochy surpassed Ebbie Goodfellow's club points mark for rookies, finishing the season with 19-20-39 numbers, but it was another rookie who was turning heads in Detroit, a pit bull of a left-winger named Ted Lindsay, who tallied 17 goals and finished second on the club with 43 penalty minutes.

"He's going to be a real hockey player, or I miss my guess," Montreal defenseman Leo Lamoureux said of Lindsay.

Bill (Flash) Hollett was also producing goals at a record pace and when he put a shot past Toronto goalie Frank McCool on March 18, he became the first defenseman to score 20 goals in an NHL season, earning NHL First All-Star Team status via his seminal performance.

During an 8-4 win at Toronto's Maple Leaf Gardens on November 16, Detroit's Hal Jackson, Wochy and Don Grosso scored 28 seconds apart, setting a team standard for the fastest three goals, missing the NHL mark by four seconds.

The Leafs and Wings clashed in the Stanley Cup final, which looked hauntingly similar to the 1942 final between the two teams. Toronto won the first three games, all by shutout, then Detroit captured the next three, with 18-year-old rookie goalie Harry Lumley posting a pair of shutouts.

Toronto's Mel Hill and Detroit's Murray Armstrong traded goals in the decisive seventh game, but Toronto's Babe Pratt netted the Cup-winner at 12:14 of the third period and the Leafs narrowly avoided the embarrassment of blowing a 3-0 series lead.

Despite scoring at a record pace, the Wings came up one goal short.

HOCKEYTOWN MOMENT

Hollett becomes first defenseman to post 20-goal season

His blazing speed on skates earned Bill Hollett the nickname "Flash," but it was the goal lights he left flashing which made his name known to NHL fans in 1944-45.

The Detroit defenseman scored 20 times, erasing the league mark of 19 for defensemen, established by Toronto's Harry Cameron in 1921-22 and equaled by

Hollett in 1941-42. He also posted the first hat trick by a Detroit defenseman, scoring three times Dec. 21, 1944 in an 11-3 win over the New York Rangers.

The Wings acquired Hollett from Boston in 1944 and his mark stayed on the books for 24 seasons until Bobby Orr of the Bruins scored 21 times during the 1968-69 season.

Joe Carveth

The most potent season in Red Wings history proved to be one of the most productive campaigns of Joe Carveth's career.

Used to performing in the shadows behind other Wings stars, the fifth-year right-winger recorded a personal best with 26 goals and his 54 points led the Wings in scoring, leaving Carveth tied for fifth in NHL scoring with future Hall of Famers Teeder Kennedy of Toronto and Bill Mosienko of Chicago.

It was Carveth who sparked Detroit's attempt to rally from a 3-0 series deficit in the 1945 Stanley Cup final against Toronto. He potted the insurance marker in Detroit's 5-3 Game 4 triumph and had a goal and an assist as the Wings took Game 5 by a 2-0 count, finishing with 11 points to lead all playoff scorers.

Having a leg up on the competition was a completely different feeling for Carveth, whose early pro career was slowed by a pair of broken legs.

Carveth broke into the NHL with Detroit in 1940-41, but the season before with Indianapolis of the AHL, all he broke was his leg, ending his year after 11 games.

Detroit promoted the entire Indianapolis forward line of Carveth, Les Douglas and Arch Wilder for the following season, but a collision with Toronto's Hank Goldup ended Carveth's season with another leg fracture after 29 games.

Always willing to lend a helping hand, Carveth produced four assists in the third period of Detroit's record 15-0 shutout rout of the New York Rangers on January 23, 1944, setting Wings marks for assists and points in one frame.

Carveth figured in some pretty famous Detroit goals. Syd Howe's assist on March 8, 1945 which made him the NHL's all-time points king came on a goal by Carveth. And Carveth set up Steve Wochy for a goal and tallied on a pass from Wochy the same night to help Wochy set a points mark for Red Wings rookies.

Dealt to Boston in 1947, Carveth was reacquired by the Wings from Montreal early in the 1949-50 season, helping the club win the Cup that spring.

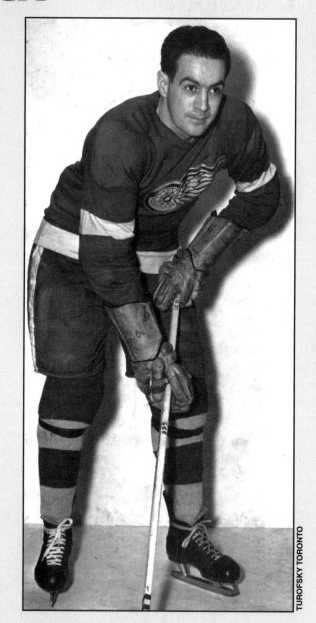

TUROFSKY TORONTO

- **BORN:**
  Regina, Saskatchewan, March 21, 1918
- **ACQUIRED:**
  Signed as a free agent, October 5, 1939
- **BEST SEASON WITH RED WINGS:**
  1943-44 (21-35-56)

- **TOTALS WITH RED WINGS:**
  GP-325, G-104, A-132, PTS-236
- **HONORS:**
  Led Detroit in scoring, 1944-45; Set single-game club records for assists (four) in a period, Jan. 23, 1944

MOTOWN Classic

Liscombe's four goals vault Wings into Cup final

The Wings were facing elimination and left-winger Carl Liscombe was facing up to frustration. "I had reached the stage where I was praying with every shot," Liscombe said after Game 7 of the 1945 Stanley Cup semifinals against Boston.

Liscombe had gone 10 games without a goal heading into the Boston tilt on April 3, but when the day was done, it was the Bruins who were gone, thanks to Liscombe.

Liscombe tallied once in each of the first two periods, but with 20 minutes left in regulation play, Boston held a 3-2 advantage.

Eddie Bruneteau tied the score, then Liscombe netted the game winner, icing a 5-3 verdict with an empty netter with six seconds to play.

His four-goal outburst has never been bettered in a Red Wings Stanley Cup game. Ted Lindsay also had a four-goal game for the Wings in the 1955 playoffs.

ASSEMBLY LINE

Earl Seibert

Looking to solidify his defense, Detroit manager Jack Adams dealt Cully Simon, Don Grosso and Byron McDonald to Chicago for 10-time NHL All-Star Earl Seibert. Adams also picked up right-winger Cliff (Fido) Purpur from the Blackhawks. Rookie forwards Ted Lindsay and Steve Wochy debuted and right-winger Eddie Bruneteau, younger brother of Mud, established himself as a regular.

Red Wings Facts

Red Wing goalies that wore uniform numbers other than 1, 30, 31, and 35

#20	Johnny Mowers	(1946 - 47)
#22	Glenn Hall	(1952 - 53)
#22	Roger Crozier	(1963 - 64)
#22	Harrison Gary	(1963 - 64)
#22	Pat Rupp	(1963 - 64)
#22	Bob Champoux	(1963 - 64)
#22	Carl Wetzel	(1964 - 65)
#25	Hank Bassen	(1963 - 64)
#27	Denis DeJordy	(1973 - 74)
#27	Jim Rutherford	(1973 - 74)
#29	Terry Sawchuk	(1968 - 69)
#29	Greg Stefan	(1981 - 82)
#29	Jim Rutherford	(1983 - 84 to 1986 - 87)
#29	Mike Vernon	(1995 to 1996 - 97)
#32	Sam St. Laurent	(1987 - 88)
#32	Tim Cheveldae	(1989 - 90 to 1993 - 94)
#34	Sam St. Laurent	(1986 - 87)
#34	Greg Millen	(1991 - 92)
#34	Norm Maracle	(1997 - 98)
#34	Manny Legace	(2000-01)
#37	Vince Riendeau	(1991 - 92 to 93 - 94)
#38	Scott King	(1990 - 91)
#39	Dominik Hasek	(2001 - 02)
#40	Rogie Vachon	(1978 - 79)
#41	Eddie Mio	(1983 - 84 to 1985 - 86)

Short Passes

Steve Wochy, who set Detroit rookie marks with 19 goals and 39 points in 1944-45, would never score another point in the NHL.

It was once said of Jack Adams that the only things he never did were drink, smoke and leave referees alone.

Known as a hard-driving taskmaster, Adams had a knack for unifying his team.

"When I played in Detroit, there was no dissension among the players," Wings forward Carl Liscombe said. "We all hated Jack Adams."

RED WINGS ARCHIVE

Such talk never fazed the man mockingly referred to as, "Jolly Jawn."

"General manager is not a job in which you win friends," Adams said.

"You do the best you can and if you satisfy your boss and sleep nights, you've done all right."

You could say that he did all right.

During his 20-season coaching tenure, the Wings played in six Stanley Cup finals, winning three of them. After focusing solely on his duties as GM, Detroit won four more Cups under his leadership.

"He ruled the team with an iron fist, but he was always honest and fair," Gordie Howe said. "He had more love and dedication for hockey than any man I knew."

An outstanding player who won Stanley Cups with Toronto and Ottawa, Adams came to Detroit in 1927 and literally did it all those early years — coached, managed, pondered playing, handled publicity and promotion and even sold tickets.

"I dug into my share of the playoff money one year to buy players," Adams remembered.

That wasn't necessary after millionaire James Norris purchased the team in 1932, providing the finances for the powerhouse teams Adams built.

Adams glowed with pride over his club in the 1940s and 1950s and when someone referred to the Red Wings as the New York Yankees of hockey, Adams snapped, "The Yankees are the Red Wings of baseball."

He developed a strong farm system and after watching the ice being resurfaced during a 1938 curling match in Paris, convinced NHL governors to adopt this idea.

"Our 1951-52 champions who won the playoffs in eight straight games was the greatest club ever assembled," Adams said. "My greatest satisfaction, though, was watching Gordie Howe develop into the all-time record pointmaker."

Adams listed goalie Terry Sawchuk, defensemen Ebbie Goodfellow and Jack Stewart and forwards Howe, Ted Lindsay and Syd Howe as his all-time Red Wings team.

Inducted into the Hockey Hall of Fame in 1959, seven years later, Adams was the first recipient of the Lester Patrick Trophy for contributions to hockey in the United States.

Wings owner Bruce Norris attempted to quietly retire Adams after the 1961-62 season, but the old curmudgeon would have none of it.

"I was fired," Adams complained.

Adams took over as president of the fledgling Central Professional Hockey League and was on the job at his desk May 2, 1968 when he died of a heart attack.

- 1945 1946 -

BACK in TIME

- **November 20, 1945**
The Nuremberg trials against Nazis accused of war crimes began with representatives of the United States, Great Britain, Russia and France sitting in judgement.

- **March 22, 1946**
The first U.S. built rocket to leave the Earth's atmosphere reached a height of 50 miles.

- **May 2, 1946**
The U.S. Marines landed at Alcatraz Penitentiary to battle armed convicts who were attempting a jail break.

quick cuts

Most Goals
Adam Brown: 20

Most Assists
Joe Carveth & Murray Armstrong: 18

Most Points
Joe Carveth: 35

Most Penalty Minutes
Jack Stewart: 73

Most Wins, Goaltender
Harry Lumley: 20

Lowest Goals-Against Average
Harry Lumley: 3.18

Most Shutouts
Harry Lumley: 2

NHL Award Winners
Jack Stewart - 2nd Team All-Star

FINAL STANDINGS

	W	L	T	PTS	GF	GA
Montreal	28	17	5	61	172	134
Boston	24	18	8	56	167	156
Chicago	23	20	7	53	200	178
DETROIT	20	20	10	50	146	159
Toronto	19	24	7	43	174	185
New York	13	28	9	35	144	191

Playoff Results
Lost to the Boston Bruins in Series "B" (4-1)
Leading Playoff Scorer
Fern Gauthier (3PTS)
Stanley Cup Champion
Montreal Canadiens

1945-46 Season in Review

RED WINGS ARCHIVE

"We'll have a pretty young team and without being overly optimistic, I think it will be a pretty good one," coach-GM Jack Adams said as the Red Wings readied for the 1945-46 season.

Several players returned from military service following the conclusion of World War II and suddenly left Detroit with a surplus of NHL-caliber talent. Among those back in town following war service were defensemen (Black) Jack Stewart and Doug McCaig and forwards Harry Watson, Adam Brown, Cliff Simpson, Jim Conacher and Johnny Holota.

"We're a little weak at center, but we've got a lot of material," Wings owner Jim Norris said. "If we had Sid Abel back, it would be different."

Still serving with the Royal Canadian Air Force in England, Abel made it back to Detroit for the final seven games of the regular season, returning to duty as Red Wings captain.

Detroit opened with a 7-0 rout of Boston and closed out the regular season with an 11-7 loss to Toronto, equaling the club mark for the most goals allowed in a game, Jekyll-Hyde bookend performances which were fitting. The Wings were an impressive 16-5-4 on Olympia ice and a dismal 4-15-6 away from home, grabbing the fourth and final playoff spot.

Joe Carveth led in scoring with 35 points, while Brown's 20 goals were a team high. Stewart banged his way to a league-leading 73 penalty minutes and a place on the NHL's Second All-Star Team. Tallying 11 points in his farewell campaign, Syd Howe retired as the NHL's career scoring leader with 528 points.

Second-year left-winger Ted Lindsay collected only 17 points and 14 penalty minutes, but garnered high praise from Adams.

"Lindsay, in many ways, reminds me of the best right-winger we ever had, Larry Aurie," Adams said. "Larry, despite his size, never backed down from anyone. Pound for pound, he was as good a hockey player as you ever saw. But Lindsay is further advanced after two seasons with us than Aurie was in three.

"Ted's still just a kid and has a long career ahead of him." The Wings weren't long for the Stanley Cup playoffs, though. Boston bounced them in five games.

HOCKEYTOWN MOMENT
Wings return from WWII

A number of Detroit players came back to the NHL during the 1945-46 season after surrendering a good chunk of their hockey days to the war effort, but it was a lesser name who made the ultimate sacrifice.

Joe Turner's NHL career amounted to one game - a 3-3 tie Feb. 5, 1942 against Toronto - but coach-GM Jack Adams often referred to Turner as, "The next Red Wings goalie."

The Windsor, Ontario-born netminder never got the chance to prove Adams right. A lieutenant in the U.S.

Army, Turner was killed in action in Holland in January of 1945.

The International Hockey League's championship trophy, the Turner Cup, was named in his honor.

Former Wing Hec Kilrea, a member of Detroit's first two Stanley Cup championship squads, suffered machine-gun and shrapnel wounds in France in December of 1944.

Adam Brown

One of the most productive months for Red Wings scouts came in October of 1939, when the club got the names of amateurs Adam Brown, goalie Johnny Mowers and forward Joe Carveth signed to pro contracts during the same week. All three were part of Detroit's 1942-43 Stanley Cup championship team. Mowers won the Vezina Trophy in 1942-43, Carveth was Detroit's leading scorer in 1944-45 and Brown's talents began to show when he potted a career-high 24 goals in 1943-44.

Heavier and faster following a year of trading his hockey stick for a rifle, the 5-foot-9, 175-pound left-winger returned to the Detroit lineup from military service and quickly established that 1945-46 was going to be another big year.

In a season-opening 7-0 whitewash of Boston, Brown led the way, firing three shots past Boston goalie Paul Bibeault. "I've never seen a club that looked better in its first game," bubbled Red Wings coach-GM Jack Adams after that opening-night performance.

Skating on a line with Murray Armstrong and Harry Watson, Brown continued to shine. His 20 goals paced Detroit shooters and with 31 points, he finished four behind Joe Carveth in the team's points race. During the playoffs, that unit was given the insurmountable task of holding Boston's formidable Kraut Line of Milt Schmidt, Woody Dumart and Bobby Bauer in check and for a brief time, got the job done.

They outscored the Krauts 2-1 through a split of the first two games, but the Boston trio figured in every goal in a 5-2 Game 3 verdict and the Bruins rolled to a five-game series victory.

Brown made his Detroit debut during the 1941-42 season and blossomed with Indianapolis of the AHL

RED WINGS ARCHIVE

the following season, where his 34-51-85 totals were good enough for second in league scoring.

That performance earned him permanent promotion to Detroit and by 1946-47, Brown was skating on the same line with a promising rookie right-winger named Gordie Howe.

Deciding to strike while the iron was hot, Adams dealt Brown and Ray Powell to Chicago in December of 1946 for left-winger Pete Horeck and defenseman Leo Reise.

It proved to be a shrewd move. Horeck replaced Brown's offense on the left side, while Reise was a solid defender on two Detroit Stanley Cup winners. Though Brown finished the 1946-47 campaign with 19 goals, he never again tallied more than 10 times in a season during a career which ended with Boston in 1951-52.

- **BORN:**
  Johnstone, Scotland, February 4, 1920
- **ACQUIRED:**
  Signed as a free agent October 3, 1939
- **BEST SEASON WITH RED WINGS:**
  1943-44 (24-18-42)

- **TOTALS WITH RED WINGS:**
  GP-148, G-58, A-43, PTS-101
- **HONORS:**
  Led Detroit in goals in 1945-46

MOTOWN Classic

Wings whip Wolverines in exhibition game

A sparse gathering of 1,354 watched October 30 as the Wings humbled the Michigan Wolverines 13-6 in an exhibition game at the Olympia. Employing three goalies - Harry Lumley, Harvey Jessiman and trainer Lefty Wilson - and seven minor-leaguers, including a 17-year-old right-winger destined from Omaha of the USHL named Gordie Howe, who scored once – the Wings got a hat trick from Carl Liscombe and two goals each from Syd Howe, Gerry Couture and Earl Seibert.

Michigan, which held first-period leads of 1-0 and 2-1, got two goals from Neil Ceeley. It was the first time the Wolverines ever faced NHL competition.

RED WINGS ARCHIVE

Syd Howe

ASSEMBLY LINE

Well-stocked with so many war returnees, the Wings made only one trade during the season, dealing Billy Reay to Montreal for forwards Roly Rossignol and Ray Getliffe. But when Getliffe retired instead of joining Detroit, the Habs gave the Wings forward Fern Gauthier as a replacement. Rookies who made an impact included right-winger Gerry Couture, left-winger Jim Conacher and center Pat Lundy, a late-season call-up who counted five points in four games.

RED WINGS ARCHIVE

Fern Gauthier

Red Wings Facts

Fewest Career Penalty Minutes
(200+ games played)

Val Fonteyne
375 Games - 18 Penalty Minutes

Billy Dea
210 games - 28 penalty minutes

Len Lunde
210 games - 39 penalty minutes

Jim McFadden
253 games - 40 penalty minutes

Joe Carveth
265 games - 44 penalty minutes

John Chabot
226 games - 44 penalty minutes

Bill Quackenbush
313 games - 49 penalty minutes

Gerry Couture
266 games - 49 penalty minutes

Dutch Reibel
306 games - 53 penalty minutes

Marcel Dionne
309 games - 59 penalty minutes

Short Passes

Total Olympia attendance for 25 home dates in 1945-46 was a record 326,397, breaking by 42,954 the team mark set in 1943-44.

87

- **1946** **1947** -

BACK in TIME

- **September 20, 1946**

The first film festival was held in Cannes on the French Riviera, bringing together film producers, directors, actors and critics from around the world.

- **October 2, 1946**

At a medical symposium at the University of Buffalo, scientists discussed the possible link between cigarette smoking and cancer.

- **April 7, 1947**

Henry Ford, the father of modern mass production utilizing assembly lines and conveyor built systems, as well as a believer in high wages and short hours, died.

quick cuts

Most Goals
Roy Conacher: 30
Most Assists
Billy Taylor: 46
Most Points
Billy Taylor: 63
Most Penalty Minutes
Jack Stewart: 83
Most Wins, Goaltender
Harry Lumley: 22
Lowest Goals-Against Average
Harry Lumley: 3.05
Most Shutouts
Harry Lumley: 3
NHL Award Winners
Jack Stewart & Bill Quackenbush
2nd Team All-Star

FINAL STANDINGS

	W	L	T	PTS	GF	GA
Montreal	34	16	10	78	189	138
Toronto	31	19	10	72	209	172
Boston	26	23	11	63	190	175
DETROIT	22	27	11	55	190	193
New York	22	32	6	50	167	186
Chicago	19	37	4	42	193	274

Playoff Results
Lost to the Toronto Maple Leafs in Series "B" (4-1)
Leading Playoff Scorers
Roy Conacher (8PTS), Billy Taylor (6PTS)
Stanley Cup Champion
Toronto Maple Leafs

It might have been recorded as an uneventful season, if not for the arrival of the sensation.

The Detroit Red Wings opened the 1946-47 campaign October 16 with a 3-3 home-ice tie against the Toronto Maple Leafs. One of the Detroit goals came when Sid Abel won a draw and rookie right-winger Gordie Howe, playing his first NHL game, snapped the puck past Toronto goalie Turk Broda. He also put Leafs captain Syl Apps out of the game with a solid check.

Two games later, the lanky Howe's mean streak emerged when Chicago goalie Paul Bibeault ventured from his net to play the puck and Howe steamrolled him to the ice, touching off a brawl.

Even though Howe would illuminate NHL goal lights another 800 times, his debut season didn't exactly leave a lasting impression on Detroit coach-GM Jack Adams, who often referred to the rookie as "Syd" Howe, the Detroit star who'd retired after the 1945-46 season.

Orignally ticketed to play with Indianapolis of the AHL, the ambidextrous 18-year-old Howe earned his NHL place ahead of schedule with his tremendous natural strength and ability. "He's the best prospect I've seen in 20 years," Adams said.

Howe finished the season with seven goals, as the scoring duties were left to a pair of off-season acquisitions. Center Billy Taylor, picked up from Toronto, led the team with 63 points, including a club-record 46

DETROIT NEWS

assists. Left-winger Roy Conacher, who wore the No. 9 jersey that Howe would later make famous, potted 30 goals after coming to Detroit in a trade with Boston. Third-year left-winger Ted Lindsay tallied 27 goals.

Defensemen (Black) Jack Stewart and Bill Quackenbush both earned selection to the NHL's Second All-Star Team, as the Wings finished fourth with a 22-27-11 slate.

It was another quick post-season for the Wings, who lost in five games to the Leafs. The lone highlight was a 9-1 win in Game 2 at Maple Leaf Gardens. The outburst equaled a club playoff record for goals in a game and when Jim Conacher, Roy Conacher and Eddie Bruneteau all scored in a span of 1:30 it set a Detroit Stanley Cup mark for the fastest three goals.

HOCKEYTOWN MOMENT
Jack Adams spends his final season as coach of the Red Wings

After two decades behind the Detroit bench, working through tough times as the Cougars and Falcons to the glory days of the Red Wings, Jack Adams finally decided he'd had enough of coaching.

Adams, 51, announced March 10, that the 1946-47 season would be his last as coach of the Red Wings. Tommy Ivan, coach of Detroit's AHL farm club in Indianapolis, would take over in the fall.

"It's a decision that has often been discussed by (owner Jim) Norris and myself," said Adams, who retained his position as general manager. His 20 years as coach of one team is an NHL record for longevity and the 964 games coached and 413 wins Adams posted remain Detroit marks.

Jack Stewart

Jack Stewart's theory of hockey was as straightforward as it was brutal.

"Hit 'em hard and hit 'em often," he'd say.

"Hockey was no tea party to Jack Stewart," New York Rangers coach Frank Boucher explained.

Stewart loved to bodycheck so much that opponents insisted you could see a smile forming on his face as he closed in for the kill.

"He wasn't dirty," Hall of Fame defenseman King Clancy said of Stewart. "But he was the roughest son of a gun you'd ever want to meet."

A mild-mannered sort off the ice, Stewart's power and strength were developed naturally, working the land as a farmer in his native Manitoba. His tremendous skating ability prevented enemy attackers from escaping his bombsights.

"He was one of the strongest guys I've ever seen in a hockey uniform," Detroit coach-GM Jack Adams said. "He worked hard on his farm all summer long and that probably accounted for it."

Stewart broke in with the Wings in 1938-39 and by 1942-43, established a presence on the NHL's First All-Star Team. A two-year stint with the Royal Canadian Air Force during World War II briefly interrupted his NHL career, but the rib-crunching rearguard returned with authority, leading the NHL in penalty minutes and earning Second All-Star Team status in 1945-46.

Originally paired with rock-hard Jimmy Orlando, Stewart later formed a tandem with Bill Quackenbush and both of them earned selection to the NHL's Second All-Star Team in 1946-47 and to the First Team in 1947-48 and 1948-49.

Complete opposites in style, Stewart struck fear into opponents, while Quackenbush finessed them off the puck.

"Jack did all the heavy work," Hall of Famer Lynn Patrick said. "He was always advising the other defensemen. And if they made an error, Jack was there to back them up."

Stewart detested his nickname of "Black Jack," feeling it implied he was a dirty player. Most of Stewart's

RED WINGS ARCHIVE

collision-course encounters were of the legal kind. He'd draw the assignment of battling the other team's top forward line and over the years, Stewart and Boston's all-star center Milt Schmidt attended more board meetings than the CEO of General Motors.

"Nice guy that Schmidt," Stewart recounted after one such rugged night. "But my goodness gracious, he does get in my way an awful lot." Stewart paid a price for his style, collecting over 50 scars and 200 stitches, once playing an entire season with a broken hand. Traded to Chicago in 1950, Stewart suffered a ruptured disc in his back. Doctors advised him to retire, fearing the possibility of spinal cord damage, but Stewart played one more season until a fractured skull ended his playing days in 1952.

He returned to Detroit and worked as a racing steward at Hazel Park Raceway and was enshrined in the Hockey Hall of Fame in 1964.

- **BORN:**
  Pilot Mound, Manitoba, May 6, 1917
- **ACQUIRED:**
  Signed as a free agent October 27, 1937
- **BEST SEASON WITH RED WINGS:**
  1947-48 (5-14-19)
- **TOTALS WITH RED WINGS:**
  GP-503, G-30, A-79, PTS-109

- **HONORS:**
  Selected to NHL First All-Star Team in 1942-43, 1947-48 and 1948-49; Selected to NHL Second All-Star Team in 1945-46 and 1946-47; Played in NHL All-Star Game, 1947-48, 1948-49, 1949-50; Led NHL in penalty minutes, 1945-46; Elected to Hockey Hall of Fame in 1964

MOTOWN Classic

Taylor leads NHL in assists

They called Billy Taylor "The Kid" and in his only season as a Red Wing, this kid was certainly all right. Acquired from Toronto in the summer of 1946, Taylor's slick playmaking skills saw him lead the NHL with a club-record 46 assists and his 63 points were good for third in the NHL scoring race.

His ability to lend a helping hand was especially evident March 16 in a 10-6 decision over Chicago, which saw Taylor assist on seven Detroit goals, setting a new NHL mark for assists in a game and gaining a share of Detroit's team standard for points in a game. Taylor's seven-assist night remains the standard for NHL competition and has been equaled only three times, all by Wayne Gretzky in the 1980s.

RED WINGS ARCHIVE

ASSEMBLY LINE

After scoring just 146 goals during the 1945-46 season, the Wings moved to improve their offense, dealing Joe Carveth to Boston for left-winger Roy Conacher and shipping Harry Watson to Toronto for center Billy Taylor. The changes paid off when Taylor and Conacher finished 1-2 in club scoring. Adam Brown and Ray Powell were sent to Chicago for defenseman Leo Reise and left-winger Pete Horeck, while rookie right-winger Gordie Howe was promoted to the NHL at the age of 18 after one season of minor pro hockey.

Adam Brown

RED WINGS ARCHIVE

Red Wings Facts

Red Wings Who Have Won Multiple NHL Awards

Gordie Howe
Art Ross, Hart, Lester Patrick

Sergei Fedorov
Hart, Selke, Lester Pearson

Steve Yzerman
Lester Pearson, Conn Smythe, Selke

Red Kelly
Norris, Lady Byng

Mike Vernon
Conn Smythe, Jennings

Terry Sawchuk
Vezina, Calder, Lester Patrick

Roger Crozier
Calder, Conn Smythe

Alex Delvecchio
Lady Byng, Lester Patrick

Nicklas Lidstrom
Norris, Conn Smythe

Short Passes

Two Red Dorans played in the NHL and both were members of the Red Wings. Center Lloyd (Red) Doran played for Detroit in 1946-47. Defenseman John (Red) Doran was with the Red Wings in 1937-38.

 **- 1947**  **1948 -**

 **BACK in TIME**

- **December 23, 1947**
President Truman granted pardons to 1,523 World War II draft dodgers.

- **May 14, 1948**
The state of Israel came into existence; the next day Egypt invaded and bombed Tel Aviv.

- **June 24, 1948**
A draft act, requiring men from 19-25 years of age to serve in the military for 21 months, was signed into law by president Truman.

quick cuts

Most Goals
Ted Lindsay: 33
Most Assists
Sid Abel: 30
Most Points
Ted Lindsay: 52
Most Penalty Minutes
Ted Lindsay: 95
Most Wins, Goaltender
Harry Lumley: 30
Lowest Goals-Against Average
Harry Lumley: 2.45
Most Shutouts
Harry Lumley: 7
NHL Award Winners
Jim McFadden - Calder Trophy
Ted Lindsay, Jack Stewart & Bill Quackenbush
1st Team All-Star

FINAL STANDINGS

	W	L	T	PTS	GF	GA
Toronto	32	15	13	77	182	143
DETROIT	30	18	12	72	187	148
Boston	23	24	13	59	167	168
New York	21	26	13	55	176	201
Montreal	20	29	11	51	147	169
Chicago	20	34	6	46	195	225

Playoff Results
Defeated the N.Y. Rangers in Series "B" (4-2)
Lost to the Toronto Maple Leafs in Series "C" (4-0)
Leading Playoff Scorers
Pete Horeck (10PTS), Jim McFadden (8PTS)
Stanley Cup Champion
Toronto Maple Leafs

1947-48 Season in Review

Leaving the bench after 20 seasons as coach of the Red Wings, Jack Adams insisted the timing was right.

"I promised I would give my successor the nucleus of another Stanley Cup champion before stepping aside and I feel that I have accomplished my task," Adams said in handing the coaching reigns to Tommy Ivan.

It was hard to argue with his logic. Players such as goalie Harry Lumley, defenseman Leo Reise and forwards Gordie Howe, Ted Lindsay, Gerry Couture and Pat Lundy were all 24 or younger and to this mix, they added defenseman Red Kelly and forwards Jim McFadden and Max McNab in 1947-48.

Adams touted McNab for the NHL's rookie award, but it was McFadden who captured the Calder Trophy, finishing second in team scoring with 24-24-48 totals. Howe produced 16 goals and 44 points in his second season, working on a new line with captain Sid Abel and left-winger Lindsay. People began to refer to the explosive unit as the "Production Line."

Lindsay, whose 33 goals led the NHL and defensemen (Black) Jack Stewart and Bill Quackenbush all earned selection to the NHL's First All-Star Team and all three were also selected to represent the Wings in the NHL All-Star Game, which became an annual affair commencing in 1947.

Toronto again proved to be the thorn in Detroit's side. A 6-0 loss to the Leafs November 9 before an Olympia regular-season record crowd of 14,746 saw Lumley suffer a rib injury and give way to practice

Jack Adams and Tommy Ivan

RED WINGS ARCHIVE

goalie Tommy McGrattan. A month later, the two clubs brawled in a 2-2 Olympia tie, which saw Howe tangle with Toronto's Bill Ezinicki and Lindsay duel in separate bouts with Gus Mortson, Jim Thomson and Leaf goalie Turk Broda.

While everyone on the ice scrapped, Leaf captain Syl Apps and Stewart paired off, but threw no punches. "Syl and I did a waltz," Stewart said. "It was much more artistic."

Back-to-back losses to Toronto to conclude the season left Detroit second behind the Leafs at 30-18-12. After handling the New York Rangers in a six-game semifinal, the Leafs awaited Detroit in the Stanley Cup final.

The Wings lost Stewart to a knee injury during the series and were swept in the final. "We were beaten and I haven't any alibis," Ivan said after the loss.

HOCKEYTOWN MOMENT
Tommy Ivan Replaces Jack Adams as coach of the Red Wings

The change from crusty, old Jack Adams to the more cerebral Tommy Ivan behind the Detroit bench sat well with the Red Wings players.

"Tommy was absolutely fantastic," Detroit forward Marty Pavelich said. "He was the type of guy who knew his personnel. Jack Adams would get mad at some guy and call for Tommy to bench him. We'd go on the road and Tommy would play him and play him and play him.

"Then Tommy would report back after the games and tell Jack how well that guy had played. By the time we were back in Detroit, Jack was waiting to see the guy play."

Ivan also knew how to run a hockey team, as his Detroit numbers indicate. During his seven Red Wings seasons, Ivan's squads finished first six times and captured three Stanley Cups.

Wings of Legend

Bill Quackenbush

The man Detroit fans simply knew as "Quack," provided living proof that nice guys don't always finish last.

A defenseman who used his head instead of hard bodychecks to halt the opposition, Quackenbush collected only 95 penalty minutes and one major infraction in 774 NHL games. He once played 131 consecutive games without visiting the sin bin.

"He wasn't a bodychecker, but he was a great standing pokechecker," teammate Marty Pavelich said of Quackenbush. "Defensively, he was as good as they come."

Quackenbush's ability to stop the other team without incurring infractions of the rules allowed him to make NHL history in 1948-49, when he became the first defenseman to be awarded the Lady Byng Trophy, which goes to the player who best combines gentlemanly conduct with outstanding performance. Quackenbush played the entire 60-game schedule without making a trip to the penalty box, gaining 52 of 54 first-place votes for the award.

"He taught me how to play the game without taking penalties," said Detroit's Red Kelly, who later won four Lady Byngs, beginning his NHL career in 1947-48 as Quackenbush's defense partner. Unfortunately, Quackenbush's quiet style often meant he was overlooked by fans.

"He was always there defensively, but kind of never heard from," Detroit forward Johnny Wilson said of the man called Gentleman Bill. "He'd come in close and get that stick out somehow. He was very productive in terms of getting the puck and getting it out of your end."

A three-time NHL All-Star selection while with Detroit, Quackenbush possessed excellent passing and puckhandling skills and an uncanny ability for reading the play.

"He analyzed players (to learn their tendencies)," Pavelich said. Opponents insisted the canny Quackenbush also had a few tricks up his sleeve. "He grabbed a lot of people and was very cagey at holding in the corners," Boston center Milt Schmidt said.

RED WINGS ARCHIVE

Slowed by a broken wrist in his rookie season of 1942-43, Quackenbush was established as a regular Red Wing by 1944-45, his first of seven straight 20-point seasons. Quackenbush was named the Red Wings' MVP in 1946-47.

He played in four Stanley Cup finals, but never finished on the winning side. Not everyone, it seemed, enjoyed the Quackenbush style of defense. After his Lady Byng win, Detroit GM Jack Adams shipped Quackenbush to Boston in a six-player deal on August 16, 1949.

Continuing his all-star ways there, Quackenbush appeared on two more post-season select squads and in a half-dozen NHL All-Star contests before retiring in 1956.

He was enshrined in the Hockey Hall of Fame in 1976.

- **BORN:**
  Toronto, Ontario, March 2, 1922
- **ACQUIRED:**
  Signed as a free agent October 19, 1942
- **BEST SEASON WITH RED WINGS:**
  1948-49 (6-17-23)
- **TOTALS WITH RED WINGS:**
  GP-313, G-40, A-89, PTS-129

- **HONORS:**
  Won Lady Byng Trophy, 1948-49; Selected to NHL First All-Star Team, 1947-48, 1948-49; Selected to NHL Second All-Star Team, 1946-47; Played in NHL All-Star Game, 1947-48, 1948-49; Elected to Hockey Hall of Fame, 1976

Lindsay leads NHL in goals

The greatness Jack Adams predicted for Ted Lindsay became apparent to the rest of the NHL when the rugged Detroit left-winger potted 33 goals to lead all of the NHL. Lindsay's 52 points topped the team, as did his 95 penalty minutes, making him the first Red Wing to lead in all three of these categories since Johnny Sheppard in 1926-27. Lindsay would lead Detroit in penalty minutes in nine of the next 10 seasons.

DETROIT NEWS

ASSEMBLY LINE

Both of Detroit's top two scorers from 1946-47 were gone early in the 1947-48 season. GM Jack Adams dealt Billy Taylor to Boston for left-winger Bep Guidolin. "We're building a young team," Adams explained. "Taylor is 28, Guidolin only 21." Money was the issue when Roy Conacher was dealt. Conacher sought a new contract for $8,500 a season, but Adams offered $7,000. At an impasse, he was dealt to the New York Rangers, but refused to report, voiding the deal. A few days later, Conacher's contract was sold to Chicago. Center Jim McFadden was acquired from Buffalo of the AHL, while forwards Marty Pavelich, Don Morrison, Rod Morrison and Max McNab made the jump from Detroit's deep farm system and defenseman Red Kelly moved into the NHL right from the junior ranks.

Bep Guidolin

RED WINGS ARCHIVE

Red Wings Facts

Red Wings who have played 200 regular - season games and no playoff games

Willie Huber	371 games
Walt McKechnie	321 games
Mickey Redmond	317 games
Guy Charron	316 games
Marcel Dionne	309 games
Red Berenson	283 games
Bill Collins	239 games
Bill Hogaboam	221 games
Larry Johnston	203 games

Short Passes

Detroit right-winger Gordie Howe switched from sweater No. 17 to his famous No. 9 in 1947-48 because in the days of train travel to road games, the players with single-digit numbers got to sleep in the larger lower berths.

- 1948 · 1949 -

BACK in TIME

- **December 10, 1948**
The United Nations adopted the Human Rights Declaration defining fundamental freedoms; it was drafted by former first lady, Eleanor Roosevelt.

- **January 10, 1949**
RCA demonstrated its new record system made of unbreakable vinylite with grooves revolving at 45 times per minute.

- **February 7, 1949**
The New York Yankees agreed to pay Joe DiMaggio $90,000 per year – the highest salary in baseball.

quick cuts

Most Goals
Sid Abel: 28
Most Assists
Ted Lindsay: 28
Most Points
Sid Abel & Ted Lindsay: 54
Most Penalty Minutes
Ted Lindsay: 97
Most Wins, Goaltender
Harry Lumley: 34
Lowest Goals-Against Average
Harry Lumley: 2.42
Most Shutouts
Harry Lumley: 6
NHL Award Winners
Sid Abel - Hart Trophy
Bill Quackenbush - Lady Byng Trophy
Sid Abel, Jack Stewart & Bill Quackenbush
1st Team All-Star
Gordie Howe & Ted Lindsay
2nd Team All-Star

FINAL STANDINGS

	W	L	T	PTS	GF	GA
DETROIT	34	19	7	75	195	145
Boston	29	23	8	66	178	163
Montreal	28	23	9	65	152	126
Toronto	22	25	13	57	147	161
Chcago	21	31	8	50	173	211
New York	18	31	11	47	133	172

Playoff Results
Defeated the Montreal Canadiens in Series "A" (4-3)
Lost to the Toronto Maple Leafs in Series "C" (4-0)
Leading Playoff Scorers
Gordie Howe (11PTS), Ted Lindsay (8PTS)
Stanley Cup Champion
Toronto Maple Leafs

RED WINGS ARCHIVE

Manager Jack Adams was confident his Detroit Red Wings were headed in the right direction and he'd be proven correct, as the Wings were about to embark upon an unprecedented run of success.

Looking for more balance in attack, Detroit began the season with Max McNab between Gordie Howe and Ted Lindsay, but it would be injury more than line juggling which broke up the Production Line. Lindsay missed time with a broken foot and torn shoulder ligaments, while Howe was idled for 20 games following knee surgery. Once reunited, Lindsay and captain Sid Abel both managed 54 points to share the club scoring lead. Detroit passed Boston to take over atop the standings in December and never looked back, clinching first place March 16 with a 6-2 rout of the New York Rangers.

The individual awards poured in. Abel won the Hart Trophy as MVP of the NHL and Bill Quackenbush, who didn't serve a penalty all season, became the first defenseman to garner the Lady Byng Trophy as the league's most gentlemanly player. Quackenbush, Abel and defenseman (Black) Jack Stewart earned selection to the NHL's First All-Star Team, while Howe and Lindsay were Second Team honorees. Howe, Lindsay, Quackenbush and Stewart represented Detroit in the NHL All-Star Game, the first of 23 times Howe would skate in the classic.

The playoffs brought clashes with the team which would serve as Detroit's fiercest rival over the next decade and the club which already was the Wings' arch rival.

A grueling, seven-game semifinal with Montreal saw the Wings file a $250,000 suit against Montreal Standard writer Andy O'Brien after he suggested in print that Stewart had deliberately injured Canadiens center Elmer Lach. Detroit fashioned its 3-1 victory in Game 7 when third-period goals by Leo Reise and Gerry Couture snapped a 1-1 tie. Ahead were the Leafs, as these teams met in the final for the second straight year and fourth time since 1942.

Howe scored eight goals in the semifinals, but Toronto's checking trio of Max Bentley, Ray Timgren and Joe Klukay shut down the Production Line, holding them to one goal and the Leafs, fourth-place finishers during the regular season, stunningly swept the Wings to capture the Stanley Cup for the third straight season.

Desperate to remove the Leafs' hex, the Wings made oxygen available to their players during Game 4, but still proved to be down to their last breath.

HOCKEYTOWN MOMENT
For the fifth time, the Red Wings finish first.

RED WINGS ARCHIVE

So many times the cause of pain to Detroit, the Toronto Maple Leafs were the source of great joy in Hockeytown the night of March 9, when the Wings plastered them 5-0 before an appreciative Olympia crowd. The victory locked up first place for the Red Wings, the first time they'd lifted the Prince of Wales Trophy as NHL regular-season champions since 1942-43.

They'd get used to the ritual, however, for Detroit would finish atop the standings seven consecutive times through the 1954-55 campaign, an NHL record.

Wings of Legend

Sid Abel

When the Detroit Red Wings once played an exhibition game in Saskatoon, a 12-year-boy knocked on Sid Abel's hotel-room door and asked if he could carry Abel's skates to the rink.

That young lad was Gordie Howe, who by 1948-49 was the most promising young star in the NHL and Abel's right-winger, but the story emphasized the sort of respect Abel carried in the hockey world.

The Red Wings captain was viewed far and wide as one of those players who possessed the hockey sense that only a few of the greats have and in 1948-49, everyone came to appreciate Abel's abilities.

Working as the pivot on Detroit's famous Production Line between Howe and left-winger Ted Lindsay, Abel and Lindsay tied for the club's scoring lead.

"I kept telling my wife Gloria to pinch me," Abel recalled of that magical season, which saw him earn the Hart Trophy as the NHL's most valuable player. "I felt sure I was going to wake up and find that I'd been having a wonderful dream."

Abel broke in with the Wings in 1938-39 and was named captain in 1942-43, the first of three seasons he led them to the Stanley Cup. "He was a great leader and a great player," teammate Marty Pavelich said. By 1948-49, Abel was one of the few veterans on a club emerging as the NHL's most dominant force and he appreciated every minute of it. "We've never had a club with so much spirit and ability," he said. "It's the best team I ever played with and I only hope I can stick around for a couple of more years, because it should be an outfit that keeps getting better."

Abel remained with the Wings through the 1951-52 season and during his career earned NHL All-Star status at both left wing and center. His winner in Game 6 of the 1950 finals helped the Wings rally from a 3-2 series deficit to beat the New York Rangers, as he led Detroit with six tallies that spring.

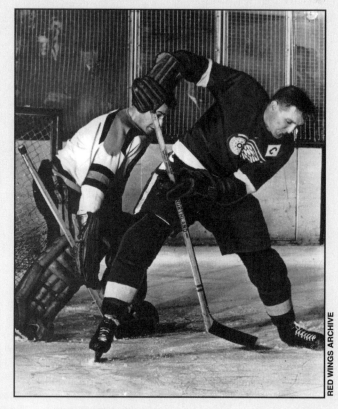

RED WINGS ARCHIVE

"He made you feel like every game was just another game and let's go have some fun," teammate Johnny Wilson said.

Abel took over as player-coach of Chicago in 1952-53, but returned to Detroit as coach in the midst of the 1957-58 campaign, leading them to four Stanley Cup final appearances in a 12-season tenure at the helm. He also served as GM of the Wings from 1963-71 and as a radio and television broadcaster.

Abel was enshrined in the Hockey Hall of Fame in 1969.

- **BORN:**
  Melville, Saskatchewan, February 22, 1918
- **ACQUIRED:**
  Signed as a free agent October 21, 1938
- **BEST SEASON WITH RED WINGS:**
  1949-50 (34-35-69)
- **TOTALS WITH RED WINGS:**
  GP-571, G-184, A-279, PTS-463

- **HONORS:**
  Won Hart Trophy, 1948-49; Selected to NHL First All-Star Team, 1948-49, 1949-50; Selected to NHL Second All-Star Team, 1941-42, 1950-51; Played in NHL All-Star Game, 1948-49, 1949-50, 1950-51; Served as team captain for eight seasons; Elected to Hockey Hall of Fame, 1969

MOTOWN Classic

Abel takes home the Hart Trophy

RED WINGS ARCHIVE

Jack Adams described the 1948-49 edition of the Red Wings as his "best team ever" and the catalyst for this group was the man who wore the "C," center Sid Abel.

Known as "Boot Nose" because of the odd shape of his oft-broken nose, Abel was awarded the Hart Trophy as the NHL's most valuable player in 1948-49, joining Ebbie Goodfellow (1939-40) as the only other Red Wing to have earned this prestigious honor.

Selected to the NHL's First All-Star Team, Abel shared the Detroit lead in goals (24), assists (30) and points (54) with Production Line teammate Ted Lindsay. In Detroit's first-place clinching win over Toronto, Abel scored twice, netting the game winner while the Wings were shorthanded.

ASSEMBLY LINE

RED WINGS ARCHIVE

In late October, Detroit GM Jack Adams dealt Bep Guidolin, Doug McCaig and Jim Conacher to Chicago for center George Gee and right-winger Bud Poile. Rookie forward Enio Sclisizzi and defenseman Lee Fogolin broke into the Red Wings lineup.

Norman "Bud" Poile

Red Wings Facts

First Round Playoff Exits

1929 vs Toronto (7 goals to 2)
1932 vs Montreal Maroons (3 goals to 1)
1944 vs Chicago (5 games)
1946 vs Boston (5 games)
1947 vs Toronto (5 games)
1951 vs Montreal Canadiens (6 games)
1953 vs Boston (6 games)
1957 vs Boston (5 games)
1958 vs Montreal Canadiens (4 games)
1960 vs Toronto (6 games)
1965 vs Chicago (7 games)
1970 vs Chicago (4 games)
1984 vs St. Louis (4 games)
1985 vs Chicago (3 games)
1989 vs Chicago (6 games)
1991 vs St. Louis (7 games)
1993 vs Toronto (7 games)
1994 vs San Jose (7 games)
2001 vs Los Angeles (6 games)

Short Passes

During a 13-7 win in a Jan. 13, 1949 charity game with the IHL All-Stars, Detroit goalie Harry Lumley switched sticks with defenseman Bill Quackenbush, charged down ice and scored a goal.

BACK in TIME

1926 1928 1947

• **August 29, 1949**
The USSR detonated its first atomic bomb in a secret test.

• **February 28, 1950**
Cadillac, the oldest auto manufacturer in Detroit, announced all of its car windshields would be built in one piece.

• **June 25, 1950**
North Korean forces crossed the 38th parrellel and invaded South Korea; two days later the United Nations and the United States agreed to send troops to aid Seoul.

quick cuts

Most Goals
Gordie Howe: 35

Most Assists
Ted Lindsay: 55

Most Points
Ted Lindsay: 78

Most Penalty Minutes
Ted Lindsay: 141

Most Wins, Goaltender
Harry Lumley: 33

Lowest Goals-Against Average
Harry Lumley: 2.35

Most Shutouts
Harry Lumley: 7

NHL Award Winners
Ted Lindsay - Art Ross Trophy
Ted Lindsay & Sid Abel - 1st Team All-Star
Gordie Howe & Leo Reise - 2nd Team All-Star

FINAL STANDINGS

	W	L	T	PTS	GF	GA
DETROIT	37	19	14	88	229	164
Montreal	29	22	19	77	172	150
Toronto	31	27	12	74	176	173
New York	28	31	11	67	170	189
Boston	22	32	16	60	198	228
Chicago	22	38	10	45	203	244

Playoff Results
Defeated the Toronto Maple Leafs in Series "A" (4-3)
Defeated the N.Y. Rangers in Series "C" (4-3)
Leading Playoff Scorers
Gerry Couture & George Gee (9PTS)
Stanley Cup Champion
Detroit Red Wings

1949-50 Season in Review

Captain Sid Abel simply gushed with enthusiasm at the future which presented itself to the Detroit Red Wings.

"Just think," Abel said. "Harry Lumley is 21; Gordie Howe is 20; Ted Lindsay is 23; Red Kelly is 21 and Marty Pavelich is 21.

"Why, they're just babies. Just wait until they grow up."

After two seasons of growing pains, that time had arrived.

Following successive heartbreaking losses to Toronto in the Stanley Cup final, Detroit GM Jack Adams decided to do what he did best - make a move.

In August, he sent all-star defenseman Bill Quackenbush to Boston in a six-player trade, the key acquisitions being forwards Pete Babando and Jim Peters.

The thinking was that Kelly had established himself, making Quackenbush expendable, while Peters and Babando would supply offensive depth. "I'm confident he'll score plenty of goals for us," coach Tommy Ivan said of Babando.

Detroit's Production Line of Lindsay, Abel and Howe finished 1-2-3 in league scoring. Lindsay took the Art Ross Trophy as NHL scoring champ and along with Abel, secured places on the NHL's First All-Star Team. Howe and defenseman Leo Reise were second-team selections. Detroit raced to first place with a 37-19-14 record, scoring a club-record 229 goals.

As the playoffs commenced, the Leafs again stood in the way. A seven-game semifinal saw triumph for Detroit following near tragedy.

In a mixup with Toronto captain Teeder Kennedy, Howe crashed into the boards, suffering a lacerated eyeball, fractures to his nose and right cheekbone and

DETROIT NEWS

severe head injuries which required a pair of surgeries to relieve pressure on the brain. Listed in critical condition, Howe's parents were summoned from Saskatoon, but the big right-winger pulled through, though he was done for the season.

Meanwhile, the Wings pulled together, rallying from 3-2 series disadvantages against the Leafs and the New York Rangers in the final to win the Stanley Cup, taking both Game 7 decisions on overtime goals - by Leo Reise in the semifinal and Babando in the final.

As the Olympia crowd chanted his name, Howe, in street clothes, joined the on-ice celebration, while Ivan marveled at the determination of his squad.

"They seemed to perk up when they were down," he said.

HOCKEYTOWN MOMENT
Wings capture their 4th Stanley Cup

The near-tragic loss of Gordie Howe in the first game of the playoffs could have easily subdued the Wings, but they persevered through this and several other challenges to earn their first Stanley Cup since 1942-43.

Detroit trailed arch-rival Toronto 3-2 in the semifinal, but rallied, winning Game 7 1-0 on defensemen Leo Reise's second overtime goal of the series.

"I never saw a team come back like this one did after Gordie Howe was hurt and we seemed like we were out of the series," Detroit coach Tommy Ivan said.

The New York Rangers got the jump on Detroit in the final, also grabbing a 3-2 series edge. Again Detroit rejuvenated and Pete Babando's goal after 28:21 of OT in Game 7 gave the Wings a 4-3 verdict and the title. "This is one of the great all-time hockey teams," proclaimed GM Jack Adams. "They still won the Cup, even with Gordie Howe out of the lineup. That's like taking a .400 hitter out of the World Series."

Wings of Legend

Harry Lumley

Harry Lumley seemed like a grizzled veteran in the Detroit Red Wings net, but that's only because he got such an early start.

Known as "Apple Cheeks" due to his ruddy complexion and full face, Lumley made his NHL debut during the 1943-44 season. At 17, he was the youngest goalie in NHL history.

"There was such a shortage of players (because of World War II) and I made it," said Lumley, who played three games that season, two for Detroit and one on loan to the New York Rangers, allowing 13 goals in the process.

He still qualified as an NHL rookie when he backstopped the Wings to a seven-game loss in the 1944-45 Stanley Cup final and was the first teenager in NHL history to tend goal in a Stanley Cup final game. A fiery netminder, Lumley once pummeled Montreal's Ken Reardon with punches when he invaded his crease and also went toe-to-toe with Toronto counterpart Turk Broda in a 1947 brawl between the Wings and Leafs. "The back of your legs had no padding and Lumley had the blade of his stick carving his initials in the calves of the opposition," remembered Red Wings announcer Budd Lynch.

Lumley's sensational goaltending lifted Detroit to the 1949-50 Stanley Cup. Down 3-2 in the semifinals against Toronto, Lumley posted consecutive shutouts to get the Wings to the final. He added another zero in the finals, as Detroit captured the championship with a seven-game verdict over the Rangers. Lumley's clutch nature is best exemplified by his 4-1 record with one shutout and a 1.60 goals-against average in seventh games of playoff series.

Lumley's only slip-up in 1949-50 was an injury which allowed hot prospect Terry Sawchuk to suit up for seven games, enough to show Detroit GM Jack Adams that he would be the team's goalie of the future. In July, Lumley was shipped to Chicago as part

DETROIT FREE PRESS

of a nine-player deal. His best season as a Red Wing turned out to be Lumley's last.

After leaving Detroit, Lumley also played for Toronto and Boston, establishing the Leafs' single-season shutout record of 13 in 1953-54, a season in which he earned the Vezina Trophy and the first of two consecutive NHL First All-Star Team nods.

Enshrined in the Hockey Hall of Fame in 1980, Lumley's competitive nature continued after hockey. He was partners with Jim Keeling in ownership of Orangeville Raceway and raced standardbreds, as well as driving the starting gate.

- **BORN:**
  Owen Sound, Ontario, November 11, 1926
- **ACQUIRED:**
  Signed as a free agent, October 13, 1943
- **BEST SEASON WITH RED WINGS:**
  1947-48 (30-18-12, 7 SO, 2.45 GAA)

- **TOTALS WITH RED WINGS:**
  GP-324, W-163, L-105, T-56, SO-7, GAA-2.75
- **HONORS:**
  Led NHL in shutouts, 1947-48; Elected to Hockey Hall of Fame, in 1980

MOTOWN Classic

"Terrible Ted" wins Art Ross Trophy

Left-winger Ted Lindsay nearly turned an astonishing hockey double when he won the Art Ross Trophy as Detroit's first NHL scoring champion. Lindsay set club records with 55 assists and 141 penalty minutes. His 78-point total earned him the scoring title ahead of Production Line mates Sid Abel (69) and Gordie Howe (68), the only time in NHL history three members of a Stanley Cup-winning team finished 1-2-3 in regular-season scoring.

Lindsay also finished three minutes behind Toronto's Bill Ezinicki for the penalty-minute crown. Lindsay did top the NHL penalty parade in 1958-59 and he and fellow Hall of Famer Nels Stewart are the only players to have led the league in scoring and penalty minutes during their careers.

Bill Quackenbush, Ted Lindsay, Jack Stewart

RED WINGS ARCHIVE

ASSEMBLY LINE

A busy season of moving saw Bill Quackenbush and Pete Horeck dealt to Boston for forwards Pete Durham, Pete Babando, Jim Peters and defenseman Clare Martin, while left-winger Steve Black was purchased from Buffalo of the AHL and Calum Mackay was shipped to Montreal for old Wing Joe Carveth. Rookie goalie Terry Sawchuk turned heads in a seven-game stint filling in for an injured Harry Lumley, recording the first of what would be an NHL-record 103 shutouts, while left wing Johnny Wilson and defenseman Marcel Pronovost came up from the minors during the playoffs to impact on Detroit's Cup run.

Pete Babando

RED WINGS ARCHIVE

Red Wings Facts

Fewest Road Victories in one Season

1980 - 81 (3)

1976 - 77 (4)

Short Passes

Doug McKay's only NHL game saw him play one shift for Detroit in Game 3 of the 1949-50 Stanley Cup finals against the New York Rangers. He's the only player to make his lone NHL appearance in the finals for a Stanley Cup champion.

HOCKEY

FICIAL PROGRAM AND GUID

OLYMPIA

IVER AVE. AT McGRAW, DETROIT

THE ALL-TIME RED WINGS TEAM:
FIRST ERA (1926-49)

CENTER — SID ABEL

"Boot Nose" joined the Red Wings in 1938 and earned NHL First All-Star Team status as a left-winger in 1941-42. Switching back to his natural position of center, he was a three-time all-star selection. Named Detroit captain in 1942-43, he resumed that position after returning from World War II in 1945-46 and led the Wings to three Stanley Cups. He shared the club scoring lead with Ted Lindsay in 1948-49, a season in which Abel won the Hart Trophy as NHL MVP. He was elected to the Hockey Hall of Fame in 1969.

LEFT WING — HERBIE LEWIS

Herbie Lewis joined Detroit in 1928-29 and had an immediate impact, leading the club with 20 goals in 1929-30. His 20-14-34 totals topped the team in 1932-33 and the following season, he captained the Wings to their first Stanley Cup final appearance. Lewis played all 11 of his NHL seasons in Detroit and upon retirement was the club's all-time goals leaders with 148. He was inducted into the Hockey Hall of Fame in 1989.

RIGHT WING — LARRY AURIE

Diminutive, but determined, Aurie could do it all — score, check, or play the physical game. Acquired in 1927, his game was similar to Ted Lindsay's — rugged and effective. Aurie was Detroit's leading scorer with 35 points in 1933-34 and his 23 goals led the NHL in 1936-37, a season in which he was selected to the NHL's First All-Star Team. Aurie served as team captain in 1932-33 and when he left the Wings in 1938-39, it was determined by Detroit manager Jack Adams that no other Detroit player would wear Aurie's No. 6 jersey.

DEFENSEMAN — BILL QUACKENBUSH

"Quack" played the game with cerebral stature. In 1948-49, he was the first NHL defenseman to win the Lady Byng Trophy as the league's most gentlemanly player, taking nary a penalty in 60 games. A precision puckhandler who registered more than 20 points in each of his last five seasons in Detroit, Quackenbush was a three-time all-star selection as a Red Wing. He was enshrined in the Hockey Hall of Fame in 1976.

DEFENSEMAN — JACK STEWART

Soft-spoken off the ice, Stewart was a one-man wrecking crew between the boards. His bodychecks reverberated throughout the league and enemy forwards knew they'd pay a dear price to venture into "Black Jack"'s territory. Five times Stewart was recognized as an NHL All-Star and his tenacious, fearless play earned him the respect of his peers. Stewart earned enshrinement to the Hockey Hall of Fame in 1964.

GOALTENDER — HARRY LUMLEY

Lumley turned pro at the tender age of 16 and was guarding an NHL net by the time he was 17, making him the youngest goalie in league history. He'd backstopped the Wings to four Stanley Cup finals by the time he was 24. Lumley led the NHL with seven shutouts in 1947-48 and was the league's leading winner in 1948-49 and 1949-50. He was inducted into the Hockey Hall of Fame in 1980.

quick cuts

Most Goals
Gordie Howe: 43

Most Assists
Gordie Howe: 43

Most Points
Gordie Howe: 86

Most Penalty Minutes
Ted Lindsay: 110

Most Wins, Goaltender
Terry Sawchuk: 44

Lowest Goals-Against Average
Terry Sawchuk: 1.98

Most Shutouts
Terry Sawchuk: 11

NHL Award Winners
Gordie Howe - Art Ross Trophy
Terry Sawchuk - Calder Trophy
Red Kelly - Lady Byng Trophy
Terry Sawchuk, Red Kelly, Ted Lindsay &
Gordie Howe - 1st All-Star Team
Leo Reise & Sid Abel - 2nd All-Star Team

BACK in TIME

• August 8, 1950
American Florence Chadwick swam the English
Channel in 13 hours, 20 minutes, breaking the
previous record set in 1926 by one hour.

• March 30, 1951
Julius and Ethel Rosenberg were the first
Americans to be sentenced to death for
espionage during peace time when they were
found guilty of stealing U.S. atomic bomb secrets
and giving them to the Soviet Union.

• July 17, 1951
In Michigan, General Motors displayed its
modernistic car of the future - the Le Sabre.

FINAL STANDINGS

	W	L	T	PTS	GF	GA
DETROIT	44	13	13	101	236	139
Toronto	41	16	13	95	212	138
Montreal	25	30	15	65	173	184
Boston	22	30	18	62	178	197
New York	20	29	21	61	169	201
Chicago	13	47	10	36	171	280

Playoff Results
Lost to the Montreal Canadiens in Series "A" (4-2)
Leading Playoff Scorers
Sid Abel & Gordie Howe (7PTS)
Stanley Cup Champion
Toronto Maple Leafs

1950-51 Season in Review

Gutting his Stanley Cup championship roster by making a nine-player trade with Chicago in July, some people thought Detroit GM Jack Adams had finally flipped his lid.

He wasn't in agreement.

"The Wings are stronger," said Adams, who kept just 10 of 18 players from the 1949-50 club. "Even a great team such as we had could be better and a better team is what we'll have now."

Debating the point was difficult, especially when the Wings whipped the NHL All-Stars 7-1 in the All-Star Game Oct. 8 at the Olympia, as Ted Lindsay collected a hat trick. Further arguments were silenced when the club set NHL records with 44 wins and 101 points.

Gordie Howe blossomed as the NHL's best player, winning his first scoring title with an NHL-record 86 points. Gentlemanly defenseman Red Kelly followed in the footsteps of his mentor, Bill Quackenbush, winning the Lady Byng Trophy. Kelly's 54 points were a record for a Detroit rearguard.

Goalie Terry Sawchuk lived up to his billing, posting 44 wins and 11 shutouts, earning the Calder Trophy as the NHL's rookie of the year and missing out on the Vezina Trophy by one goal.

Howe, Sawchuk, Kelly and Lindsay were all selected to the NHL's First All-Star Team, while defenseman Leo Reise and center Sid Abel earned Second Team honors.

RED WINGS ARCHIVE

Lindsay continued to run afoul of NHL lawmakers and was fined $300 after a gruesome fight with Boston's Bill Ezinicki in which Lindsay pummeled Ezinicki into unconsciousness. "I guess I'd better not bother dressing for the playoffs," Lindsay groused after one of his many fines. "It's liable to cost me too much money."

As amazing as their regular season performance was, it was the way in which the Wings exited the playoffs that left hockey fans gasping.

Heavily-favored in the semifinals against Montreal, a team which finished 36 points in arrears to Detroit, the Canadiens won the first two games at the Olympia, both on overtime goals by Maurice (Rocket) Richard.

Detroit rallied to take both games at Montreal's Forum, but blew a 2-0 lead and lost Game 5 on home ice by a 5-2 count. The shocking upset was completed with a 3-2 Habs victory back in Montreal.

HOCKEYTOWN MOMENT
Wings set NHL record with 44 Victories

Detroit's 88 points garnered in 1949-50 produced a new NHL mark, but one which didn't last long. The Wings established NHL standards for wins (44) and points (101) in 1950-51. Becoming the first team in NHL history to break the 100-point barrier, Detroit's total this season remained the benchmark for a 70-game campaign.

Included in the 44-win tally was a team-record nine-game winning streak, launched with a 3-1 victory March 3 at Montreal and continuing through a 4-1 decision March 21 over the New York Rangers at Madison Square Garden.

DETROIT NEWS

Wings of Legend
Leo Reise Jr.

An all-star defenseman who performed capably in the shadows of such Hall of Famers as (Black) Jack Stewart, Red Kelly, Bill Quackenbush and Marcel Pronovost, Leo Reise played a quietly effective game and owned a reputation for scoring clutch goals, especially during the Stanley Cup playoffs. Without Reise's sniping abilities, the Wings wouldn't have reached the finals in 1949 or 1950.

His third-period shorthanded goal in Game 7 of the 1949 semifinal against Montreal snapped a 1-1 tie and propelled the Wings to a 3-1 victory. Reise gathered the puck in his own zone and battled along the boards past all five Montreal skaters before driving a 40-foot shot past Canadiens goalie Bill Durnan.

"Leo Reise scored that goal that broke the tie because he absolutely refused to give up," Wings coach Tommy Ivan said. "He lost the puck twice and got it back because he kept fighting for it."

Down 2-1 to Toronto in the 1950 semi-finals, Reise whipped a backhand off the leg of Leafs defenseman Gus Mortson and behind goalie Turk Broda after 20:38 of overtime for a 2-1 victory. With the seventh game of the series scoreless and into the second OT session, Reise lifted a 35-foot backhander through a crowd past Broda and the Wings moved on to beat the New York Rangers in the final. "I never saw the puck until it hit the net and bounced out between my feet," Broda said. "I looked down and there it was."

Reise netted only four goals in 70 regular-season games, but the offensive outburst wasn't surprising. During his career, he averaged a goal every 18 games during regular-season play, but tallied once every six games in Stanley Cup competition.

"Those series were the ultimate," Reise said.

Acquired from Chicago in 1946, Reise was the son of an NHLer. His father Leo Reise Sr. played with the

DWAYNE LaBAKAS

Hamilton Tigers, New York Americans and New York Rangers from 1920-30.

A stay-at-home defenseman known for his fierce bodychecks, the younger Reise was named to the NHL's Second All-Star Team in 1949-50 and 1950-51 and was selected four times to play in the NHL All-Star Game.

"He was very businesslike and played his position very well," teammate Marty Pavelich said of the six-foot, 205-pound Reise.

Reise won another Stanley Cup with Detroit in 1951-52, but was dealt to the Rangers that summer, where he concluded his pro career in 1954.

- **BORN:**
  Stoney Creek, Ontario, June 7, 1922
- **ACQUIRED:**
  December 9, 1946 trade with Chicago
- **BEST SEASON WITH RED WINGS:**
  1950-51 (5-16-21)

- **TOTALS WITH RED WINGS:**
  GP-340, G-21, A-61, PTS-82
- **HONORS:**
  Selected to NHL Second All-Star Team, 1949-50, 1950-51; Played in NHL All-Star Game, 1949-50, 1950-51, 1951-52

MOTOWN Classic

A season full of "firsts" for Howe

Struggling with dizziness and headaches, a hangover from his head injuries suffered in the 1950 playoffs, Detroit right-winger Gordie Howe donned a helmet during the 1950-51 season. Goalies would have been well advised to erect barricades in front of their cages when Howe was coming in on them. Howe destroyed the NHL record book en route to his first of four consecutive Art Ross Trophies. With 43-43-86 totals, Howe established new Red Wings marks for goals and points, the latter number also being a new NHL single-season standard. Howe was the first player to lead the NHL in goals, assists and points in the same season since Howie Morenz in 1927-28.

Slowly taking over the mantle of the game's greatest player from Montreal's Maurice (Rocket) Richard, Howe stole the spotlight Feb. 17 at the Montreal Forum on "Rocket Richard Night" when he tallied the 100th goal of his NHL career to give Detroit a 2-1 win.

RED WINGS ARCHIVE

ASSEMBLY LINE

Trader Jack Adams even outdid himself in July 1950, uncorking an NHL-record nine-player deal by sending Harry Lumley, Jack Stewart, Al Dewsbury, Pete Babando and Don Morrison to Chicago for center Metro Prystai, left-winger Gaye Stewart, defenseman Bob Goldham and goalie (Sugar) Jim Henry. Lee Fogolin and Steve Black also went to the Blackhawks for left-wingers Vic Stasiuk and Bert Olmstead, then Olmstead was flipped to Montreal for right-winger Leo Gravelle. Versatile center/left-winger Glen Skov made the leap from Detroit's minor-league chain.

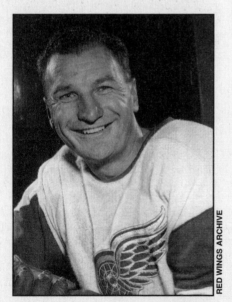

RED WINGS ARCHIVE

Vic Stasiuk

Red Wings Facts

Stanley Cup Winning Goals Against The Red Wings

1934	Mush March	(Chicago)
1941	Bobby Bauer	(Boston)
1942	Pete Langelle	(Toronto)
1945	Babe Pratt	(Toronto)
1948	Harry Watson	(Toronto)
1949	Cal Gardner	(Toronto)
1956	Maurice Richard	(Montreal Canadiens)
1961	Ab McDonald	(Chicago)
1963	Eddie Shack	(Toronto)
1964	Andy Bathgate	(Toronto)
1966	Henri Richard	(Montreal)
1995	Neal Broten	(New Jersey)

Short Passes

Detroit's 1950-51 roster had a real Father's Day feel to it. Five players – Gordie Howe, Sid Abel, Max McNab, Jimmy Peters and Lee Fogolin – would send sons to the NHL, while Leo Reise and Ted Lindsay were the sons of NHLers.

- 1951 1952 -

 BACK in TIME

• **October 16, 1951**

The first international television broadcast in the U.S. took place when Americans watched Princess Elizabeth during her Canadian visit.

• **April 15, 1952**

President Truman signed the Japanese Peace Treaty, granting Japan full sovereignty and officially ended WWII in the pacific region.

• **July 14, 1952**

General Motors perfected an air conditioning unit for cars using nontoxic Freon.

quick cuts

Most Goals
Gordie Howe: 47

Most Assists
Gordie Howe & Ted Lindsay: 39

Most Points
Gordie Howe: 86

Most Penalty Minutes
Ted Lindsay: 123

Most Wins, Goaltender
Terry Sawchuk: 44

Lowest Goals-Against Average
Terry Sawchuk: 1.94

Most Shutouts
Terry Sawchuk: 12

NHL Award Winners

Gordie Howe - Hart Trophy
Gordie Howe - Art Ross Trophy
Terry Sawchuk - Vezina Trophy
Terry Sawchuk, Red Kelly, Ted Lindsay &
Gordie Howe - 1st Team All-Star

FINAL STANDINGS

	W	L	T	PTS	GF	GA
DETROIT	44	14	12	100	215	133
Montreal	34	26	10	78	195	164
Toronto	29	25	16	74	168	157
Boston	25	29	16	66	162	176
New York	23	34	13	59	192	219
Chicago	17	44	9	43	158	241

Playoff Results
Defeated the Toronto Maple Leafs in Series "A" (4-0)
Defeated the Montreal Canadiens in Series "C" (4-0)

Leading Playoff Scorers
Ted Lindsay, Metro Prystai & Gordie Howe (7PTS)

Stanley Cup Champion
Detroit Red Wings

1951-52 Season in Review

Despite a stunning setback in the 1950-51 playoffs, excitement still buzzed in Detroit. The Red Wings owned the game's best player (Gordie Howe), its most determined competitor (Ted Lindsay) and the man ultimately rated as hockey's greatest goalkeeper (Terry Sawchuk). Soon, they would again lift the sport's ultimate prize.

This would be the last season for Detroit's legendary Production Line and once more, the trio of Howe, Lindsay and Sid Abel finished 1-2-3 in team scoring. Howe equaled his NHL mark with 86 points to retain the NHL scoring title, while his 47 goals set a club record, ranking Howe second in NHL history to the 50-goal performance of Montreal's Maurice (Rocket) Richard in 1944-45.

The Wings assembled a club-record 15-game unbeaten streak from November 27 through December 28, as well as a 10-0-5 record unbeaten run on the road from October 18 to December 20, losing consecutive games just once all season. "I always felt sorry for who we were going to play the next night after we lost, because we were going to kick the living hell out of them," forward Marty Pavelich said.

Finishing first, Detroit equaled its club record with 44 wins, posting a second straight 100-point campaign, the only franchise to accomplish this feat during the NHL's first 54 seasons.

Howe added his first Hart Trophy as NHL MVP to his second Art Ross Trophy, while Sawchuk hung up a

RED WINGS ARCHIVE

team-record 12 shutouts, earning the Vezina Trophy. Sawchuk, Howe, Lindsay and defenseman Red Kelly were selected to the NHL's First All-Star Team and all four, along with Abel, played in the NHL All-Star Game.

As outstanding as the regular-season was, the playoffs would prove to be the most dominant performance in Stanley Cup history.

The Wings swept to the championship in the minimum eight games, the first team ever to do so. Sawchuk posted four shutouts, as Detroit never allowed a post-season goal on Olympia ice. Lindsay scored in five straight playoff games, equaling a club standard established by Howe in 1948-49.

When it was over, GM Jack Adams described this group as the best Wings team ever assembled.

HOCKEYTOWN MOMENT

Wings sweep to their 5th cup

Detroit established there would be no letdown this spring, opening the semifinals with 3-0 and 1-0 whitewashes of Toronto. The Leafs were victimized 6-2 and 3-1 on home ice and the Wings were on their way to Montreal for the Stanley Cup final.

After posting 3-1 and 2-1 verdicts at the Forum, their return to the Olympia again saw Sawchuk close the door and a pair of 3-0 victories brought Lord Stanley's mug back to Hockeytown.

The Wings weren't the only ones flying on the ice that spring. So were mollusks, launched from the seats to commence a tradition which continues today.

When Detroit returned from Montreal up 2-0, Red Wings season-ticket holders Pete and Jerry Cusimano thought it would good luck to toss an octopus on the

Tommy Ivan

RED WINGS ARCHIVE

ice, since its eight tentacles represented the eight wins it took to attain the Stanley Cup.

Acquiring said mollusk would be easy, since the brothers were proprietors of an east-side Detroit fish market.

During the second period of Game 4 of the final, Pete reached under his seat and unleashed his flying octopus, changing Red Wings playoff hockey forever.

Terry Sawchuk

Hockey's most talented netminder was also the game's most tortured soul. No one stopped the puck better than Terry Sawchuk. And perhaps no hockey player endured as much tragedy.

Tragic circumstances caused Sawchuk to don the pads, taking over in net for a team in his Winnipeg home after the death of his brother, who was the goalie.

RED WINGS ARCHIVE

Once in goal, Sawchuk rapidly established his rare quality, advancing to the pro ranks at 17, winning rookie-of-the-year honors in the USHL, AHL and NHL. Three times he won the Vezina Trophy and seven times was named an NHL All-Star. Sawchuk established NHL records for games (971), minutes (57,194) and shutouts (103).

"You could throw a handful of corn at him and he'd catch every kernel," Ted Lindsay said.

Sawchuk garnered 56 shutouts, 195 wins and a 1.94 goals-against average during his first five full NHL campaigns, leading the league in victories each of those five seasons.

"He'd always say to the guys, 'Get me a couple and we'll win,'" former Detroit coach Jimmy Skinner remembered. "He didn't say it in a bragging kind of way. He was just that confident.

"I saw a lot of the greats, but to my mind, I haven't seen anyone better than Sawchuk. Reflexes, angles - he had it all and he also had a lot of guts. He was fearless in the net and extremely confident."

Consider Sawchuk's punishing legacy - punctured lungs, ruptured discs, a blocked intestine, a ruptured spleen, infectious mononucleosis, severed hand tendons, a broken instep, a dislocated elbow which never healed properly, leaving one arm shorter than the other, a twice-broken nose and 600 stitches. Sawchuk

once checked himself out of hospital to play a Stanley Cup game. The insecurity of his position - there were just six spots for NHL goalies - led Sawchuk to play through as much pain as he could endure, getting repaired when time permitted, once suggesting he spent summers "in the hospital." Dealt to Boston in 1955-56 after leading Detroit to its third Cup in four seasons, Glenn Hall took over in the Wings goal, but will refute any suggestion that he replaced Sawchuk.

"A lot of people think he was the greatest goalkeeper who ever played the game," Hall said. "I include myself in that group."

Sawchuk returned for two more stints with Detroit, won a Stanley Cup with Toronto in 1966-67 and played his last game for the 1969-70 New York Rangers. On May 31, 1970, at the age of 40, Sawchuk died from complications resulting from internal injuries suffered in a scuffle with teammate Ron Stewart.

The Hockey Hall of Fame waived its five-year waiting period, inducting Sawchuk in 1971.

- **BORN:**
  Winnipeg, Manitoba, December 28, 1929
- **ACQUIRED:**
  Signed to pro contract, November 5, 1947
- **BEST SEASON WITH RED WINGS:**
  1951-52 (44-14-12, 12 SO, 1.90 GAA)
- **TOTALS WITH RED WINGS:**
  GP-734, W-352, L-243, T-132, SO-85, GAA-2.45

- **HONORS:**
  Won Vezina Trophy, 1951-52, 1952-53, 1954-55; Won Calder Trophy 1950-51; Won Lester Patrick Trophy, 1971; Selected to NHL First All-Star Team, 1950-51, 1951-52, 1952-53; Selected to NHL Second All-Star Team, 1953-54, 1954-55, 1958-59, 1962-63; Elected to Hockey Hall of Fame, 1971

Sawchuk posts four shutouts in eight games

You can't win the Stanley Cup without great goaltending and with the type of goaltending Terry Sawchuk supplied in the 1951-52 playoffs, you couldn't lose. "Sawchuk performed as if he were triplets," Toronto writer Red Burnett suggested of his playoff performance.

Winning eight straight games, Sawchuk posted an astonishing 0.63 goals-against average and an amazing .977 save percentage. The red light never went on behind him in four games at the Olympia and his four shutouts tied a Stanley Cup record.

"I never had the idea the puck would get through," was Sawchuk's own assessment of his performance that spring.

Detroit GM Jack Adams embraced Sawchuk after the Cup-clinching win. "The greatest in hockey," he said of his goalie. "It sure helps when you've got a kid like that out there."

Harry Lumley and Terry Sawchuk

ASSEMBLY LINE

Gaye Stewart was dealt in the summer to the New York Rangers for Tony Leswick, who could play either wing. In a five-for-one deal with Chicago, Detroit GM Jack Adams shipped George Gee, Jim McFadden, Max McNab, Jimmy Peters and Clare Martin to the Blackhawks for $75,000 and defenseman Hugh Coflin. Center Alex Delvecchio, who set a rookie mark with six game-winning goals, center Fred Glover and defensemen Benny Woit and Larry Zeidel emerged from Detroit's farm system.

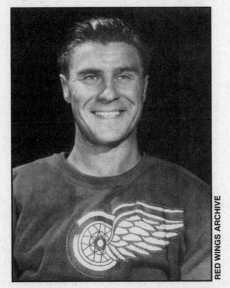

Tony Leswick

Red Wings Facts

Red Wing Captains who have coached the team

Art Duncan

Sid Abel

Ted Lindsay

Alex Delvecchio

Short Passes

Nine members of the 1951-52 Wings - Ted Lindsay, Alex Delvecchio, Sid Abel, Red Kelly, Fred Glover, Marcel Pronovost, Vic Stasiuk, Johnny Wilson and Larry Wilson - later served as NHL coaches or GMs.

- 1952 — 1953 -

BACK in TIME

- **July 25, 1952**

Puerto Rico was granted self rule, making it the first U.S. Commonwealth.

- **January 20, 1953**

For the first time, Americans from coast to coast were able to witness the inauguration of its President via television, as Dwight D. Eisenhower took the oath of office.

- **May 18, 1953**

One of America's leading fliers, Jacqueline Cochran, became the first woman to fly faster than the speed of sound.

quick cuts

Most Goals
Gordie Howe: 49
Most Assists
Gordie Howe: 46
Most Points
Gordie Howe: 95
Most Penalty Minutes
Ted Lindsay: 111
Most Wins, Goaltender
Terry Sawchuk: 32
Lowest Goals-Against Average
Terry Sawchuk: 1.90
Most Shutouts
Terry Sawchuk: 9
NHL Award Winners
Gordie Howe - Hart Trophy
Gordie Howe - Art Ross Trophy
Terry Sawchuk - Vezina Trophy
Red Kelly - Lady Byng Trophy
Terry Sawchuk, Ted Lindsay & Gordie Howe
1st Team All-Star
Alex Delvecchio - 2nd Team All-Star

FINAL STANDINGS

	W	L	T	PTS	GF	GA
DETROIT	36	16	18	90	222	133
Montreal	28	23	19	75	155	148
Boston	28	29	13	69	152	172
Chicago	27	28	15	69	169	175
Toronto	27	30	13	67	156	167
New York	17	37	16	50	152	211

Playoff Results
Lost to the Boston Bruins in Series "A" (4-2)
Leading Playoff Scorers
Ted Lindsay & Metro Prystai (8PTS)
Stanley Cup Champion
Montreal Canadiens

1952-53 Season in Review

Hockey's most coveted bauble was back in Detroit, but the game's most dangerous forward line was no more.

Sid Abel, center and linchpin on the Production Line and a Red Wing since 1938, moved to Chicago in the off-season to take over as player-coach of the Blackhawks. Ted Lindsay replaced Abel as Wings captain, but finding a suitable fit between Lindsay and Gordie Howe proved a far greater challenge. Alex Delvecchio, Metro Prystai, Reg Sinclair and Marty Pavelich all got work there.

The lack of a regular pivot certainly didn't hamper either winger. Howe came within one goal of the magical 50 mark and also equaled a Detroit mark with 46 assists, while his 95 points were an NHL record and earned Mr. Hockey® his third straight Art Ross Trophy and his second Hart Trophy in a row. Lindsay finished second in the NHL scoring race for the second year in a row with 71 points and became the first player to register 200 goals in a Detroit uniform.

Defenseman Red Kelly won the Lady Byng Trophy and goalie Terry Sawchuk retained the Vezina Trophy, as Detroit's 36-16-18 record left the Wings atop the NHL standings for the fifth consecutive season. Howe, Lindsay, Kelly and Sawchuk were NHL First Team All-Stars and Delvecchio earned Second Team status. One sad note during a productive regular season came December 4, when owner James Norris Sr., the man whose bankroll rescued Detroit from financial ruin in 1932 and turned the team into an NHL powerhouse,

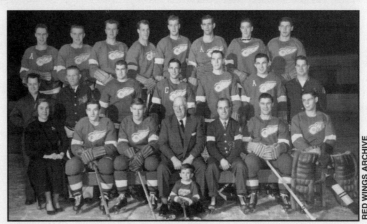

RED WINGS ARCHIVE

died of a heart attack. His daughter Marguerite Norris took over as president of the club.

Boston, 2-10-2 versus Detroit in the regular season, would provide playoff opposition and it certainly appeared to be a mismatch. Twice the Wings pounded 10 goals behind Boston netminder (Sugar) Jim Henry during the regular season and three times the Wings blanked the Bruins, so when Detroit rolled to a 7-0 triumph in Game 1, the rout looked to be on.

Then the tide suddenly turned. Using a veteran line of Milt Schmidt, 36, Woody Dumart, 35 and Joe Klukay, 30, to check Howe and Lindsay, Boston won the next three games, prevailing in six games.

Sawchuk, beaten 21 times in the series, blamed himself for the loss. "I had a poor season and I was lousy in the playoffs," he said. "But I'll be back next year and I'm going to have a big season."

HOCKEYTOWN MOMENT
Wings top NHL with most goals scored and fewest goals against

For the second straight season, the Red Wings were the NHL's most productive and stingiest team. Detroit led the NHL with 222 goals, while allowing a league-low 133 tallies.

Detroit's potency was evident when the Wings equaled a club mark set in 1944-45 by hitting double digits in three games. Chicago was victimized 10-1 on Nov. 22, while Boston fell 10-1 on Dec. 11 and 10-2 on March 2.

Meanwhile, Detroit blanked every NHL team at least once. Sawchuk, slimmed down from 208 to 174 pounds, garnered nine shutouts and rookie Glenn Hall posted one clean sheet in January while filling in for the injured Sawchuk.

DETROIT NEWS

Terry Sawchuk

Wings of Legend

Red Kelly

In there were a Hall of Fame for nice guys, Leonard (Red) Kelly would be a first-ballot inductee.

"Red Kelly is the greatest man I've ever met," longtime Detroit and Toronto teammate Marcel Pronovost said. "He's the most honest, most dedicated and possibly the most intelligent."

A welterweight boxer as a youth, Kelly eschewed fisticuffs at the rink, playing a more refined, controlled game. "He could stand up for himself when he had to," teammate Marty Pavelich said.

The Detroit defenseman was so chivalrous he refused to curse. "Hang it," was the strongest expression which passed through the redhead's lips. He neither drank nor smoked.

Between the boards, his effective, gentlemanly style earned Kelly four Lady Byng Trophies as the NHL's most sportsmanlike player. Evidence he could do the job without bending the rules was provided in 1953-54 when Kelly was the first recipient of the James Norris Trophy as the league's top defenseman.

Potent offensively, eight times Kelly led NHL defensemen in scoring and his 54-point total in 1950-51 stood as a Detroit record for rearguards until 1977-78. Eight straight seasons with the Wings, he was selected to the NHL All-Star Team. Detroit won four Stanley Cups with Kelly in the lineup.

Kelly often logged as much as 50 minutes of ice time in key games, but fell into disfavor with Detroit GM Jack Adams when he went public with a story that Adams asked him to play on a broken ankle while Detroit struggled in vain to qualify for the 1958-59 playoffs.

DETROIT NEWS

Adams traded Kelly and Billy McNeill to the New York Rangers for Bill Gadsby and Eddie Shack, but both players refused to report to the Rangers. The deal was voided. Undaunted, Adams shipped Kelly to Toronto for young defenseman Marc Reaume.

Leafs coach Punch Imlach converted Kelly to center and he was a big part of four Cup winners in Toronto, earning his fourth Lady Byng while performing at his new position.

While playing for Toronto, Kelly served as a member of Canadian Parliament from 1962-65 and after retiring in 1967, coached Los Angeles, Pittsburgh and the Leafs. He was inducted into the Hockey Hall of Fame in 1969.

- **BORN:**
  Simcoe, Ontario, July 9, 1927
- **ACQUIRED:**
  Signed to pro contract, September 9, 1947
- **BEST SEASON WITH RED WINGS:**
  1950-51 (17-37-54)
- **TOTALS WITH RED WINGS:**
  GP-846, G-162, A-310, PTS-472

- **HONORS:**
  Won Norris Trophy, 1953-54; Won Lady Byng Trophy 1950-51, 1952-53, 1953-54; Six-time NHL First All-Star Team selection; Two-time NHL Second All-Star Team selection; Played in nine NHL All-Star Games; Elected to Hockey Hall of Fame, 1969

MOTOWN Classic

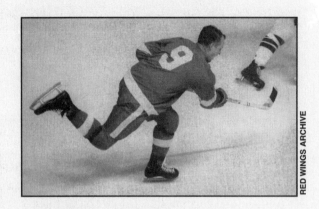

Howe comes close to fifty

With two games to play, Detroit right-winger Gordie Howe sat at 49 goals, one away from tying the NHL mark set in 1944-45 by Montreal's Maurice (Rocket) Richard.

Howe insisted the milestone was not a priority to him and his teammates did little to apply any more emphasis on this chance at history.

"We pulled for him silently," defenseman Marcel Pronovost said. "We just let him do his own thing. We didn't put any pressure on him."

After he was blanked by Chicago, Howe logged 32:33 of ice time in the season finale against Montreal, but had only one shot on goal and failed to register. Just to rub it in, Canadiens coach Dick Irvin raced out on the ice to raise Richard's arm like a champion prizefighter.

Actually, Howe had scored 50 goals, but in a magnanimous gesture, refused to take credit for a Red Kelly shot which he tipped during a March 12 game at Boston.

"I was going for my 200th goal as well as my 50th," Howe said. "Red was going for his 20th (which would have equaled the NHL record for defensemen). "Red shot, I deflected it and it hit (Boston defenseman) Hal Laycoe's skate and bounced in the net. Red knew that I was the last Detroit player to touch the puck, but he couldn't convince anyone of importance."

ASSEMBLY LINE

Captain Sid Abel left Detroit to take a position as player-coach in Chicago. Defenseman Leo Reise was dealt to the New York Rangers for center/right-winger Reg Sinclair and minor-leaguer John Morrison. Rookies who made the grade included goalie Glenn Hall, who had a six-game stint while Terry Sawchuk was injured, center/right wing Lou Jankowski, defenseman Jim (Red Eye) Hay and winger Marcel Bonin, who once held an off-season job as a bear wrestler.

John Morrison

Red Wings Facts

Red Wings who wore uniform #9

Johnny Sheppard, Herb Lewis, Harold Hicks, Roland Matte, Bert McInenly, Frank Carson, Tom Anderson, Ed Wiseman, Wally Kilrea, Pete Kelly, Mud Bruneteau, John Sorrell, Joe Lamb, John Sherf, Connie Brown, Ken Kilrea, Ed Bruneteau, Billy Thomson, Sid Abel, Roy Conacher, Gordie Howe.

Short Passes

Center Guyle Fielder, called up for the 1952-53 playoffs, played 10 games for Detroit without registering a point, but was the Gordie Howe of the Western Hockey League, leading that minor pro loop in scoring 13 times.

RED WINGS ARCHIVE

Adding up all the numbers, totaling the many records of a legendary, unparalleled career, there is one stat which tells the story of Gordie Howe's dominance better than all others.

He scored more NHL goals at the age of 52 (15), than he did at the age of 18 (seven).

"Gordie Howe is the best hockey player I have ever seen," said Montreal Canadiens Hall of Famer Jean Beliveau, who was a teammate of the great Maurice (Rocket) Richard, the man Howe surpassed as the NHL's career goals and points leader.

Even Richard conceded that Howe was the man.

"Howe was a better all-around player than I was," Richard said. "He could do everything."

Howe could skate, score, make plays and something that no other player was capable of doing, shoot with either hand.

Montreal's Bill Durnan was an ambidextrous goalie who had special gloves made which operated as both blocker and trapper. When an opponent got in the clear, Durnan switched his stick to that player's strong side.

Early in his career, Howe broke in on Durnan right-handed. Durnan switched hands, then Howe did, just before depositing the puck in the net.

At six feet and 205 pounds, Howe also took care of his own business and his sharp elbows and stick felled many opponents. He believed in what he called biblical hockey — that it was better to give than receive. Howe also believed in live and let live, but anyone foolish enough to mess with him got messed up pretty good.

"I'd wait to get even and tease them about what I was going to do, but they'd always know they were going to pay," Howe said. "After a few stitches in the head, they'd lay off."

Howe's numbers are astonishing. Thirty-two seasons in major-league hockey, 25 of them in a Red Wings uniform, where his 786 goals and 1,809 points figure to stand forever as club records. But more amazing than his ability on the ice is Howe's dedication as an ambassador for the game. He is to hockey what Babe Ruth was to baseball and Michael Jordan is to basketball. Simply the most recognizable player in the history of the sport.

"A lot of times, when you meet your idol, you come away disappointed," said Wayne Gretzky, who overtook Howe as hockey's all-time scoring leader.

"That wasn't the case with Gordie. He's such a kind, wonderful person to everyone he meets.

"My father (Walter) and Gordie Howe are probably the two men who have had the most profound effect on my life."

More than two decades after his final NHL game, Howe still gets mail from fans around the world and remains an icon in Detroit.

"There has always been a tremendous love affair between me and the fans here," Howe said. "Over the years, I never forgot Detroit. It's always been No. 1 in the hearts of the Howe family."

Likewise, we're sure.

MR. HOCKEY® Q & A

Q: Are you the greatest Red Wing of all-time?
A: "Someone asked me once, 'Who is the best in the league?' I answered, 'What city are we in?' The fans in Detroit have been very kind to the Howe family, and it's appreciated. Then the Ilitches came along, and have done a tremendous favor for Mark Howe. Am I the best Red Wing? It's a compliment to be chosen, because there were so many great ones."

Q: In hindsight, how did you characterize your relationship with Jack Adams?
A: "Let's put it this way: Jack Adams had a certain amount of meanness because he demanded respect. He'd say 'I don't care if I'm right or wrong, I'm the guy that signs the checks so that makes me right.' When I got seriously hurt, he took it upon himself to establish an open phone line to Saskatoon and the Howe family out there to give a commentary on how my surgery was going. That is not a bad man. Jack has also done some terrible things. When Marty, my oldest was born, he wanted to keep Colleen and Marty in the hospital until we finished our games. The doctor said 'There's no way! The child belongs with his father at home, with his mother!' Jack interfered sometimes."

RED WINGS ARCHIVE

Q: Were you immediately confident that the "Production Line" would be a hit?
A: "I learned so much being around Sid Abel. We traveled by train, and I was one of the quiet ones. I basically had nothing to say being around all of those veterans. I would just sit there and listen, and a question would be thrown at me now and again like, 'What did you do that for?' Later in life, my son Mark would do the same while I'd drive him in the car! Without saying anything, I learned a lot from Sid, and he saved my bacon by telling me two things: Don't drop your stick until the other man does, because you'll be wearing stitches if you do, and it takes two seconds when you jump over the boards to see who is against you and who is for you. These two statements helped my whole career."

Q: Your son Mark Howe told me that you were the meanest man he'd ever seen on skates.
A: "The only thing that ever hurt Gordie Howe was when I made the mistake that cost us a game. I never regretted hurting anyone else, but I regretted hurting my team. If a player is really hurt, you'll see both teams concerned. I think the biggest improvement in the game today is medical."

Q: You must have been pleased to see the Stanley Cup back in Detroit for two years.
A: "I remember a conversation with Sid Abel. He said, 'Isn't it wonderful? The fans haven't changed. They've always been really protective backers of the Red Wings.' The media has drawn so much more attention to the team than in my day. When I went to the 1998 Red Wing parade in downtown Detroit, I had never seen so many people. When I won four Cups, we'd come home by train and there would be only four cars there to greet us. The importance of the fan and media has been tremendous. When I played, the players had to sell the game. I wish I could have played under the Ilitches."

Q: Has expansion damaged some of the natural NHL rivalries?
A: "Stan Mikita cut my lip one time. I went to get him, but I saw the referee's whistle half-way to his lips and had to back off. In those days, you had 14 games, so you had ample time to get back. There was no reason to think I had to get to get him

right then. Now they do because they only have one game or two against an opponent. I waited four games and I got an opportunity. I threw the puck in and Ted Lindsay was going in on net all alone, so all 16,000 fans were watching him, and my fist made contact with Mikita's forehead. He woke up on the bench, and asked 'What happened?' The trainer told him 'Number nine!'"

Q: Is there a modern player that reminds you of yourself?
A: "I'd say Eric Lindros. When Mark Howe (who is the pro scout for the Wings) scouted him for the Stanley Cup Finals against the Philadelphia, they realized that Lindros thrived on being hit and hitting people. The scouts advised putting Draper and a few of the fast guys to bite at his ankles all night. They said it would drive him crazy, and it did. He didn't score a goal for the Flyers until the last minute of the last game. He'd almost given up because he was so frustrated. Eric's a big boy, but he's still very young."

Q: Would that tactic had worked on you?
A: "No. I like to find trouble. Our Red Wing teams could never get going until we got hit. If it took a hit or a fight to stimulate the play of the Red Wings, then one of us would have to step up and do it. Sometimes I wasn't too shy of that."

Q: What was your best intimidation tactic?
A: "Conversation, but I can't tell you what I said. I always referred to myself as bilingual: English and profanity. Lindsay used to call 'Rocket' (Richard) a lot of funny names and 'Rocket' would go red-faced the whole game. Most of it was threats. If I didn't like something, the first thing you'd hear after the crash is 'Look out!'"

Q:Any thoughts on the Russian impact on the NHL?
A: "Russians didn't like to be hit. We were playing an All-Star game, and one of the Russians was bothering Wayne Gretzky. I said to Wayne, 'You're smart enough. Flush him up the right side then when you hear me coming, get out of the way!' I walked over him and four or five minutes later he was getting up and I said, 'Oh, Wayne, we're in trouble. He's getting up!' They were tough! I met Vladimir Konstantinov for a picture after he won his first cup in 1997, and while he posed he pointed to himself and he pointed at me and said 'Dirty!' I love the way he played and the way he thought. The cold war is over, I love the Russians."

Q: Virtually everyone that played with you seems to have taken a turn behind the Detroit bench. Were you not interested in coaching?
A: "Yeah, but there was one hitch — nobody asked me, so it was a little difficult. I heard the rumor was that I had too much fun. My God, if you can't enjoy what you're doing then you ought to get out. Ulcers are made in those kinds of jobs."

Q: You're called "Mr. Hockey" and generally accepted as the greatest ever. How do the modern Red Wings compare to the legendary Hall-of-Fame loaded teams?
A: "The players today are bigger, stronger, and so much more talented. We actually had a player on one of my teams, Charlie Burns, who couldn't skate backward. Sid Abel would make him run drills and laugh at him. That wouldn't happen today. With the technical abilities and talent of the kids today, I would have to vote that the boys today are better hockey players than we were."

- 1953 1954 -

quick cuts

BACK in TIME

• **December 3, 1953**
University of Iowa scientists announced they had achieved the first human pregnancy using deep frozen sperms.

• **May 24, 1954**
IBM announced it would market an electronic calculator for business use.

• **June 22, 1954**
Automobile manufacturers Studebaker and Packard announced they would merge.

Most Goals
Gordie Howe: 33
Most Assists
Gordie Howe: 48
Most Points
Gordie Howe: 81
Most Penalty Minutes
Ted Lindsay: 110
Most Wins, Goaltender
Terry Sawchuk: 35
Lowest Goals-Against Average
Terry Sawchuk: 1.92
Most Shutouts
Terry Sawchuk: 9
NHL Award Winners
Gordie Howe - Art Ross Trophy
Red Kelly - Norris Trophy
Red Kelly- Lady Byng Trophy
Red Kelly, Ted Lindsay & Gordie Howe
1st Team All-Star
Terry Sawchuk - 2nd Team All-Star

FINAL STANDINGS

	W	L	T	PTS	GF	GA
DETROIT	37	19	14	88	191	132
Montreal	35	24	11	81	195	141
Toronto	32	24	14	78	152	131
Boston	32	28	10	74	177	181
New York	29	31	10	68	161	182
Chicago	12	51	7	31	133	242

Playoff Results
Defeated the Toronto Maple Leafs in Series "A" (4-1)
Defeated the Montreal Canadiens in Series "C" (4-3)
Leading Playoff Scorers
Gordie Howe & Alex Delvecchio (9PTS)
Stanley Cup Champion
Detroit Red Wings

1953-54 Season in Review

Angered by their stunning loss to Boston in the 1952-53 semifinals, the Wings set out in the fall on a mission.

Detroit opened the season against the New York Rangers looking as if they'd found a center to play with Gordie Howe and Ted Lindsay. Earl (Dutch) Reibel marked his NHL debut by setting up all four Wings goals in a 4-1 win, establishing an NHL mark for assists and a club record for points by a player in his first game. Reibel finished with 15-33-48 totals and as runner-up to New York's Camille Henry for NHL rookie-of-the-year honors. The victory improved Detroit's home opener record to 11-0-4 over the past 15 years.

Howe won his fourth straight Art Ross Trophy, registering 81 points. Defenseman Red Kelly captured his third Lady Byng Trophy and was the first recipient of the Norris Trophy as the NHL's top blueliner, an award christened to honor the memory of former Wings owner James Norris, who died in 1952. Lindsay surpassed Sid Abel to become Detroit's career scoring leader with 527 points.

Lindsay, Howe and Kelly were NHL First All-Star selections and goalie Terry Sawchuk was a Second Team choice. Sawchuk tied his club record with 12 shutouts and coupled with one zero posted by rookie Dave Gatherum, they set a new team record for whitewashes in a season.

DETROIT NEWS

With 88 points, the Wings grabbed first place and the Prince of Wales Trophy for the sixth straight season, easily bouncing Toronto in a five-game semifinal. Howe scored nine seconds into a 4-3 series-clinching win on April 1 to set a Wings playoff mark for the fastest goal from the start of a game. A thrilling, seven-game final with Montreal saw each team win twice in the other's rink and an Olympia-record crowd of 15,791 packed the building to the rafters for Game 7, a tilt which fell 2-1 in Detroit's favor on Tony Leswick's overtime goal.

"You little toad," captain Lindsay said as he hugged Leswick in the post-game celebration, before kissing him twice on the cheek.

HOCKEYTOWN MOMENT
Wings capture their sixth Stanley Cup

One of the most hard-fought finals in Stanley Cup history ended on one of the flukiest Cup-winning goals.

After splitting the first two games on Olympia ice, Detroit swept a pair of games at the Montreal Forum and seemed poised to make short work of the defending champion Canadiens. But Montreal had other ideas, winning Games 5 and 6 to send everyone back to the Olympia for a seventh and deciding match. Floyd Curry gave Montreal a first-period lead, but Red Kelly tied it in the second frame. After a scoreless third period, Tony Leswick's long shot in overtime eluded Montreal goalie Gerry McNeil and gave Detroit the Cup. "It seemed like an eternity before that red light went on," Wings coach Tommy Ivan said after the Cup-winning score.

The bitterness of the battle was emphasized when Montreal players left the ice before the traditional post-series handshake.

"Did you see how they shook hands?" Leswick said. "Not one of them came over." Gaye Stewart - the

DETROIT NEWS

player the Wings traded to New York to acquire Leswick in 1951 - was the only Montrealer to later offer congratulations.

"If I had shaken hands, I wouldn't have meant it and I refuse to be hypocritical," Canadiens coach Dick Irvin explained.

Marty Pavelich

A man who sacrificed the opportunity of individual productivity for the good of team success, Marty Pavelich was one of the unsung heroes of those powerhouse Red Wings squads of the 1950s.

Turning pro in 1947 after playing with Detroit's junior affiliate in Guelph, Ont., Pavelich needed only 26 games of minor-league seasoning before he was ready for his first taste of the big leagues.

He blossomed in 1948-49, collecting 10 goals and 26 points, one of four times in 10 NHL seasons that Pavelich would reach double digits in the goals column. The following spring, he scored four goals as Detroit captured its first Stanley Cup since 1942-43.

Pavelich produced career highs with 17-19-36 numbers in 1951-52, as Detroit won another Cup with what has been described as the greatest Red Wings team ever, a fact Pavelich chooses not to dispute.

"We had such chemistry on that team," he said. "I really think that team could have played all summer and we would have just kept winning."

His offensive output earned Pavelich the opportunity in 1952-53 to replace Sid Abel at center on the Production Line between Howe and Ted Lindsay, but when the Wings lost a six-game semifinal series to Boston, it was obvious his checking skills were sadly missed.

Pavelich normally drew the assignment of shadowing the other team's top players in playoff competition, which meant trying to stop the likes of Rocket Richard and Detroit coach Tommy Ivan realized Pavelich's value to the team in this area, so in 1953-54, put him in a checking role with Glen Skov.

Rookie Bill Dineen began the season as the third part of this unit, but eventually, Tony Leswick joined Skov and Pavelich and they did a masterful job of handling Montreal's powerful unit of Jean Beliveau, Bernie Geoffrion and Dickie Moore in a seven-game final series, surprising everyone by producing the Cup-winning goal. Skov started the play by digging the puck out of the corner, then feeding Leswick for the score.

RED WINGS ARCHIVE

Pavelich was part of another Detroit Cup winner in 1954-55. He was also a successful entrepreneur, owning a manufacturing business with Lindsay and rejected a 1958 contract which called for a minor-league option.

"I told him I could get him a $7,000 base salary in the minors, which is a good contract, but Marty said he'd retire first," Detroit GM Jack Adams said.

The man adept at keeping the opposition in check made certain he'd never long for one.

- **BORN:**
  Sault Ste. Marie, Ontario, November 6, 1927
- **ACQUIRED:**
  Signed to pro contract, September 9, 1947
- **BEST SEASON WITH RED WINGS:**
  1951-52 (17-19-36)

- **TOTALS WITH RED WINGS:**
  GP-634, G-93, A-159, PTS-252
- **HONORS:**
  Played in NHL All-Star Game, 1949-50, 1951-52, 1953-54, 1954-55

MOTOWN Classic

RED WINGS ARCHIVE

Leswick stars in Game 7

The "Mighty Mouse" of the Red Wings lineup came up mighty big. Tied 1-1 and playing overtime in Game 7 of the Stanley Cup final against Montreal, Tony Leswick launched a long shot towards Canadiens goalie Gerry McNeil. Montreal defenseman Doug Harvey attempted to pick the puck out of the air with his glove, but instead deflected it over the left shoulder of his netminder for the Cup-winning marker after 4:29 of the extra session. "I just shot as quickly as I could and it happened to go high," Leswick said of his famous tally.

At only 5-foot-6, Leswick was among the NHL's smallest players, but his Stanley Cup legacy was large. He and Pete Babando, scorer of Detroit's 1950 Cup winner, are the only players to settle a Stanley Cup with a Game 7 OT goal.

ASSEMBLY LINE

One of the quietest seasons of player movement in Red Wings history saw center Jimmy Peters, a member of Detroit's 1949-50 title-winning squad, reacquired from Chicago. Rookie center Earl (Dutch) Reibel shone as the pivot man between Gordie Howe and Ted Lindsay, while defenseman Al Arbour and Keith Allen and right-winger Bill Dineen were other first-year players who stepped up to the top rung of the Detroit chain. Trainer Lefty Wilson blanked Montreal for 16 minutes as an emergency replacement for an injured Terry Sawchuk and the next game, rookie Dave Gatherum blocked 24 shots for a 4-0 shutout of Toronto in his NHL debut.

Jimmy Peters

RED WINGS ARCHIVE

Red Wings Facts

Most Years Leading Wings In Goals

Gordie Howe (15)

Steve Yzerman (6)

John Ogrodnick (6)

Brendan Shanahan (5)

Syd Howe (4)

Short Passes

Marguerite Norris, who served as Red Wings president from 1952-55, was the first woman to have her name inscribed on the Stanley Cup.

- 1954  1955 -

BACK in TIME

- **July 19, 1954**

Nineteen-year-old Elvis Presley released his first record on the Sun Record label with "That's All Right Mama".

- **January 19, 1955**

President Dwight D. Eisenhower held the first televised Presidential news conference.

- **May 18, 1955**

The Warsaw Pact, militarily unifying the Eastern Bloc of nations - Czechoslovakia, Hungary, Romania, Bulgaria and Albania - was signed to abstain from the use of force in resolving international issues.

quick cuts

Most Goals
Gordie Howe: 29

Most Assists
Earl Reibel: 41

Most Points
Earl Reibel: 66

Most Penalty Minutes
Tony Leswick: 137

Most Wins, Goaltender
Terry Sawchuk: 40

Lowest Goals-Against Average
Terry Sawchuk: 1.94

Most Shutouts
Terry Sawchuk: 12

NHL Award Winners

Terry Sawchuk: Vezina Trophy
Red Kelly: 1st Team All-Star
Terry Sawchuk: & Bob Goldham:
2nd Team All-Stars

FINAL STANDINGS

	W	L	T	PTS	GF	GA
DETROIT	42	17	11	95	204	134
Montreal	41	18	11	93	228	157
Toronto	24	24	22	70	147	135
Boston	23	26	21	67	169	188
New York	17	35	18	52	150	210
Chicago	13	40	17	43	161	235

Playoff Results
Defeated the Toronto Maple Leafs in Series "A" (4-0)
Defeated the Montreal Canadiens in Series "C" (4-3)
Leading Playoff Scorers
Gordie Howe (20PTS) - Ted Lindsay (19PTS)
Stanley Cup Champion
Detroit Red Wings

1954-55 Season in Review

The Red Wings were welcomed to training camp by a new face. Jimmy Skinner assumed the coaching position when Tommy Ivan left to become GM of the Chicago Blackhawks.

He was new to the NHL, but Skinner knew his personnel. "We should win it all again," he announced. "We've got the best players, haven't we?" After battling to a 2-2 tie with the NHL All-Stars, Detroit opened the campaign 5-1, but then went 4-5-1 in the next 10 games.

To say the Wings struggled this season would be untrue, but things clearly weren't coming together as easily as in past years. Gordie Howe relinquished his four-year hold on the NHL scoring crown, finishing second on the team in scoring with 62 points, four fewer than teammate Earl (Dutch) Reibel. Howe endured one of the worst slumps of his career, scoring just four goals in a 17-game span.

Meanwhile, Ted Lindsay sat out a 10-day suspension after striking a Toronto fan with his stick and slumped to 38 points, his lowest totals since 1945-46.

Goalie Terry Sawchuk was stellar, winning the Vezina Trophy and earning an NHL Second Team All-Star berth along with defenseman Bob Goldham. Defenseman Red Kelly was Detroit's lone First Team selection.

Detroit trailed Montreal for first place most of the season, but Skinner never lost faith. "This team of ours can win anytime it wants to," he said. "It's all in their minds."

A 5-0 home-ice loss Dec. 19 to the Canadiens was symbolic, because it marked the last time Detroit would taste defeat on home ice the rest of the season. Closing out the regular season 13-0-5 at the Olympia,

they tied the team record for the longest home unbeaten streak, then went 5-0 at home in the playoffs. A club-record nine-game winning streak to conclude the regular campaign left Detroit in first for the seventh straight season, but not before surviving a scary situation.

Canadiens star Rocket Richard was suspended for the rest of the season after assaulting an official and the first game following the suspension saw the Wings visit Montreal on March 17.

With Detroit up 4-1, fans rioted during the first intermission and the game was forfeited to Detroit.

The infamous Richard Riot spilled into the streets, but it was all news to the Wings, who were ushered out a back exit and hurriedly taken to the train station.

"We missed the whole thing," defenseman Marcel Pronovost said. "We didn't know about the riot until the next day."

The Wings swept Toronto in the semifinal, then edged Montreal in a seven-game final to retain the Cup and prove Skinner prophetic.

HOCKEYTOWN MOMENT
Wings Win Seventh Cup

The Red Wings posted a perfect home slate in defending their Stanley Cup crown, sweeping Toronto in the semifinals, then taking Montreal in a seven-game final by winning all four games on Olympia ice.

They also established several post-season benchmarks. During a 7-1 rout of the Habs in Game 2, Ted Lindsay collected club records with four goals in the game and four points in one period. Gordie Howe posted his first Stanley Cup hat trick in Game 5 of the final and the line of Lindsay, Howe and Earl (Dutch) Reibel established a Detroit mark by combining for 51 post-season points. Howe's 20 points were a new Stanley Cup record and Lindsay's 12 assists tied the mark set by Montreal's Elmer Lach in the 1945-46 playoffs.

Combined with their nine-game win streak to conclude the regular season, Detroit won 15 consecutive games before succumbing 4-2 at Montreal in Game 3 of the finals.

Jimmy Skinner and Jack Adams

Ted Lindsay

Ted Lindsay arrived to the NHL wars in 1944 with a single-minded goal.

"I had the idea that I should beat up every player I tangled with and nothing ever convinced me it wasn't a good idea," explained the man who became known as Terrible Ted during his days with the Detroit Red Wings.

A left-winger, Lindsay stood only 5-foot-8 and weighed 163 pounds, but every ounce of that frame oozed competitiveness.

"Lindsay would not give an inch, regardless of what size anyone was," teammate Marcel Pronovost said.

Ten times, Lindsay led the Red Wings in penalty minutes, including a 173-minute effort in 1964-65, when he ended a four-year retirement to suit up for Detroit at the age of 39. Lindsay was NHL scoring champ in 1949-50 and the loop's penalty-minute leader in 1958-59. He and fellow Hall of Famer Nels Stewart are the only NHL players to turn this unique double.

The Wings scooped Lindsay up from the Toronto St. Michael's junior club, an affiliate of the rival Maple Leafs, who felt he wasn't a strong enough skater to make it as an NHLer.

He quickly proved otherwise and in 1947-48, led the NHL with 33 goals. Moving to the left side with Sid Abel and Gordie Howe on Detroit's famed Production Line, Lindsay became the league's best left-winger. Eight times, he was picked to the NHL's First All-Star Team. He captained Detroit to consecutive Stanley Cups in 1953-54 and 1954-55 and began a playoff tradition following that 1955 triumph, lifting the Cup over his head and leading a victory lap around the ice.

"Everyone's emotions were on high and I guess mine were a little higher," Lindsay said. "It was an impulsive sort of thing."

Lindsay proved to also be a pretty fair left-winger off the ice and in 1956, helped to organize the first NHL Players' Union, a fact which didn't sit well with Wings GM Jack Adams.

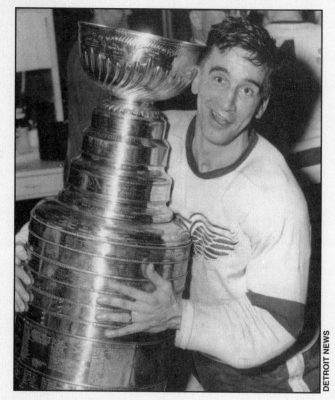

DETROIT NEWS

Adams dealt the fiery winger to Chicago following the 1956-57 season, even though Lindsay posted a career-high 85 points.

Lindsay felt Adams led a smear campaign against him.

"A series of rumors about my attitude, as well as derogatory remarks about myself and my family showed me that the personal resentment of the Detroit general manager toward me would make it impossible for me to continue playing hockey in Detroit," Lindsay said.

When Lindsay returned in 1964, Adams was no longer with the club.

- **BORN:**
  Renfrew, Ontario, July 29, 1925
- **ACQUIRED:**
  Signed as a free agent, Oct. 18, 1944
- **BEST SEASON WITH RED WINGS:**
  1956-57 (30-55-85)
- **TOTALS WITH RED WINGS:**
  GP-862, G-335, A-393, PTS-728

- **HONORS:**
  Won Art Ross Trophy, 1949-50;
  Selected to NHL First All-Star Team
  eight times; Selected to NHL Second
  All-Star Team, 1948-49; Played in 10
  NHL All-Star Games; Elected to
  Hockey Hall of Fame, 1966

MOTOWN *Classic*

Rookie coach wins the Cup

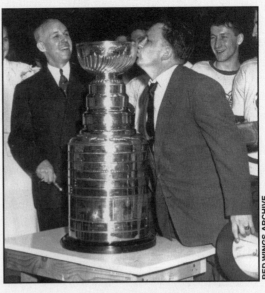

Few first-year NHL coaches can boast of the success that Jimmy Skinner enjoyed with the 1954-55 Red Wings.

Arriving from Hamilton of the Ontario Hockey Association without any pro coaching experience or NHL playing time, Skinner fell into a difficult position. The Wings were a complacent club who had won the Stanley Cup the spring before and trailed Montreal for first place for much of the season, until closing the campaign with a nine-game winning streak to nip the Habs for top spot.

Skinner showed he wasn't going to take any guff when, during a brawl with Montreal, he exchanged punches with Canadiens captain Butch Bouchard. Later in the season, he told off NHL president Clarence Campbell when Campbell approached the Detroit bench during a game to complain about the players using foul language.

Detroit jelled in the playoffs and after retaining the Cup, the rookie bench boss declined to accept the credit.

"It scares me to think of all the mistakes I made, right up to the end," Skinner said. "I've been plain lucky."

ASSEMBLY LINE

Lorne Davis

The biggest change in Detroit was behind the bench. Tommy Ivan left to become GM in Chicago and Jimmy Skinner was promoted from Detroit's Hamilton junior affiliate. On-ice changes were few. Center Metro Prystai was dealt November 9 to Chicago for right-winger Lorne Davis, while rookie defenseman Larry Hillman was re-called from the minors in time to play three playoff games and get his name on the Stanley Cup.

Red Wings Facts

Calder Trophy Winners

Carl Voss . . . . 1932 - 33
Jim McFadden . . . . . 1947 - 48
Terry Sawchuk . . . . . 1950 - 51
Glenn Hall . . . . 1955 - 56
Roger Crozier . . . . . 1964 - 65

Short Passes

Besides being linemates, Detroit's Glen Skov and Marty Pavelich both had brothers who worked in striped shirts. Art Skov was an NHL referee and Matt Pavelich was an NHL linesman who was inducted into the Hockey Hall of Fame in 1974.

127

- 1955   1956 -

BACK in TIME

• **September 30, 1955**
Teen Idol movie star James Dean was killed instantly in a car crash on his way to an auto rally.

• **December 5, 1955**
African-American Rosa Parks sat in the front of the Cleavland Avenue bus in Montgomery, Alabama and refused to give up her seat to a white man.

• **September 21, 1956**
Twelve-year-old Fred Safier of Berkley, California enrolled in Harvard University to study physics.

quick cuts

Most Goals
Gordie Howe: 38

Most Assists
Gordie Howe: 41

Most Points
Gordie Howe: 79

Most Penalty Minutes
Ted Lindsay: 161

Most Wins, Goaltender
Glenn Hall: 30

Lowest Goals-Against Average
Glenn Hall: 2.11

Most Shutouts
Glenn Hall: 12

NHL Award Winners
Glenn Hall - Calder Trophy
Dutch Reibel - Lady Byng Trophy
Ted Lindsay - 1st Team All-Star
Glenn Hall, Red Kelly & Gordie Howe
2nd Team All-Stars

FINAL STANDINGS

	W	L	T	PTS	GF	GA
Montreal	45	15	10	100	222	131
DETROIT	30	24	16	76	183	148
New York	32	28	10	74	204	203
Toronto	24	33	13	61	153	181
Boston	23	34	13	59	147	185
Chicago	19	39	12	50	155	216

Playoff Results
Defeated the Boston Bruins in Series "B" (4-1)
Lost to the Montreal Canadiens in Series "C" (4-1)
Leading Playoff Scorers
Gordie Howe (12PTS) - Alex Delvecchio (10PTS)
Stanley Cup Champion
Montreal Canadiens

1955-56 Season in Review

Jack Adams believed a hockey club held a shelf life of five seasons as a contender. He developed this theory after watching his consecutive Stanley Cups champs of 1935-36 and 1936-37 slump to the NHL basement in 1937-38, so a pair of titles in 1953-54 and 1954-55 weren't about to sway his judgment that it was time to shake things up.

By the time training camp opened, only Gordie Howe, Ted Lindsay, Earl (Dutch) Reibel, Alex Delvecchio, Red Kelly, Marty Pavelich, Bill Dineen, Bob Goldham, Marcel Pronovost and Larry Hillman remained from the 1954-55 Cup winners. "He definitely took the heart and character out of that team with those deals and he didn't get much in return," Pronovost said of Adams.

RED WINGS ARCHIVE

Gone were Vezina Trophy-winning goalie Terry Sawchuk and Glen Skov and Tony Leswick, two-thirds of Detroit's stellar checking unit. "It was unbelievable the way it happened," said Skov, dealt to Chicago in the flurry. "We couldn't believe Jack Adams would trade away eight players off a Stanley Cup team." Still, few were swayed from believing the Wings were the team to beat. In its season preview issue, The Hockey News announced that the Wings were, "Planning to imprison the Stanley Cup for all time."

The Wings opened 13-0-4 on Olympia ice, a new home unbeaten mark from the start of the season. Reibel won the Lady Byng Trophy, while rookie Glenn Hall proved an able replacement for Sawchuk, earning the Calder Trophy as the NHL's top rookie.

Lindsay was selected to the NHL's First All-Star Team and Howe, Hall and Kelly were Second Team choices. Howe ascended to the 300-goal plateau Feb. 7 in a 3-2 win over Chicago.

Detroit's seven-season run atop the NHL ended when the Wings finished second, 24 points behind Montreal. After Detroit blasted Toronto in a five-game semifinal, the Wings and Canadiens met in the Stanley Cup final for the third spring in succession.

The script was different this time, with Montreal winning handily in five games. "I am proud of my players," Detroit coach Jimmy Skinner said afterwards. "We have a lot of young fellows on our club and I think they did as well as we could expect."

HOCKEYTOWN MOMENT
Howe, Lindsay, receive death threats

Before Game 3 of Detroit's Stanley Cup semifinal series with the Maple Leafs, an anonymous caller to a Toronto newspaper boasted he would shoot Lindsay or Howe if either stepped on Maple Leaf Gardens ice that night. It was suggested in the Detroit dressing room that rookie Cummy Burton take the warm-up wearing Howe's No. 9 and Lindsay's No. 7, an idea everyone thought was brilliant except Burton.

It turned out no one shot either player, but they combined to shoot three goals in a 5-4 Detroit victory. After the game, Lindsay playfully pointed his stick like a gun and aimed it at the Toronto crowd.

"Ted and I hustled off the ice just a little faster than usual," Howe said. "If someone had set off a firecracker, I think we would have dug foxholes in the ice."

RED WINGS ARCHIVE

Gordie Howe & Ted Lindsay

Bob Goldham

It's often said that the posts are a goaltender's best friends. Except when Bob Goldham was on the ice, because he was truly the bosom buddy of all netminders.

A shot blocker supreme, this reliable defenseman laid down in front of more rubber than the asphalt on I-75. "Blocking shots in an art and he was the game's best practitioner," said Detroit teammate Al Arbour, who went on to develop his own qualities as a shot blocker. "I learned the right way to do it from Bob Goldham."

Early memories of Goldham would not be fond for Red Wings fans. He broke in with Toronto in 1941-42 and was part of the Leafs team which rallied from a 3-0 series deficit to defeat Detroit. Goldham scored in Games 5 and 6 of that series and set up Pete Langelle for the Cup-winning goal in Game 7. He won another Cup with Toronto in 1946-47, then was traded the next fall to Chicago in a move to acquire NHL scoring champion Max Bentley.

Goldham came to the Wings in a nine-player trans-action with Chicago on July 13, 1950 and provided a steadying, veteran influence on Detroit's younger players. "To this day, I can't understand why he's not in the Hall of Fame," former Detroit coach Jimmy Skinner said. "He was one of the best stay-at-home defense-men the game has ever seen."

Known as a jokester who used his sense of humor to crack dressing-room tension during crucial games, Goldham won three Cups with the Red Wings and played a big part in bowling over the opposition in 1954-55, helping to organize a team bowling league to promote camaraderie.

"The captains – Goldham, (Ted) Lindsay, (Red) Kelly and (Marty) Pavelich – they picked the teams and we put up $1,000 for the winning team," Skinner remembered. "It was a good way to get the boys away from the rink for a day."

DETROIT NEWS

Goldham earned his only NHL All-Star Team selec-tion that season, being picked to the Second Team. The following spring, after Detroit was dethroned by Montreal in the Stanley Cup final, he announced his retirement.

"It's quit being fun to play," he explained. "It's just work."

Detroit GM Jack Adams offered Goldham the job as coach of the Hamilton Ti-Cubs, a Red Wings junior affiliate, but Goldham made his name in another post-hockey career. The friendly, soft-spoken Goldham starred as an analyst on Hockey Night In Canada.

- **BORN:**
  Georgetown, Ontario, May 12, 1922
- **ACQUIRED:**
  July 13, 1950 trade with Chicago
- **BEST SEASON WITH RED WINGS:**
  1950-51 (5-18-23)

- **TOTALS WITH RED WINGS:**
  GP-406, G-11, A-92, PTS-103
- **HONORS:**
  Selected to NHL Second All-Star Team, 1954-55; Played in NHL All-Star Game, 1951-52, 1953-54, 1954-55

MOTOWN Classic

Hall named NHL Rookie-of-the-Year

Dealing away the man considered to be hockey's best goalie, Jack Adams was convinced he had a better one waiting for the Wings. "We had to make a decision between Terry Sawchuk and Glenn Hall," the Detroit GM explained. "Hall is more advanced now than Sawchuk when he joined us and all of the players insist Glenn has been NHL material for the past year."

Hall had an unusual superstition in which he felt he wouldn't play well unless he vomited before the game and some questioned whether he had the stomach to be an NHL regular. "He'll never be in Sawchuk's class," predicted New York Rangers GM Muzz Patrick.

Hall quickly silenced his critics and NHL shooters, setting a club mark for rookies and equaling the team standard by posting 12 shutouts, including a Wings-record three straight Dec. 11, 15 and 18. He also tied Sawchuk's rookie marks, playing every game (70) and minute (4,200) during the season, launching a Hall of Fame career.

No one blamed Hall when the Wings came up short in the Stanley Cup final. "Hall was very good all the way," Wings coach Jimmy Skinner said. "Terry Sawchuk couldn't have done better."

ASSEMBLY LINE

Real Chevrefils

The busiest trading season of Jack Adams' career left heads spinning throughout the NHL. Within 53 days of Detroit's 1954-55 Cup victory over Montreal, he'd moved Tony Leswick, Glen Skov, Johnny Wilson and Benny Woit to Chicago for defenseman Bucky Hollingworth, centers John McCormack and Dave Creighton and right-winger Jerry Toppazzini and shipped Terry Sawchuk, Vic Stasiuk, Marcel Bonin and Lorne Davis to Boston for goalie Gilles Boisvert, defenseman Warren Godfrey, center/right-winger Norm Corcoran, and left-wingers Ed Sandford and Real Chevrefils. He then dealt Sandford to Chicago for center Metro Prystai and sent Chevrefils and Toppazzini back to Boston for left-winger Lorne Ferguson and center Murray Costello. Center Norm Ullman and left-winger John Bucyk were two future Hall of Famers who broke in as rookies.

Red Wings Facts

Red Wing Coaches Who Never Played For The Team

Jack Adams
Tommy Ivan
Jimmy Skinner
Ned Harkness
Ted Garvin
Bobby Kromm
Wayne Maxner
Nick Polano
Harry Neale
Jacques Demers
Bryan Murray
Scotty Bowman

Short Passes

Right-winger Cummy Burton, a rookie in 1955-56, was the nephew of Detroit legend Larry Aurie and is the only Red Wing since Aurie to don Aurie's No. 6 jersey.

131

Before expansion diluted the NHL's talent pool, forward lines would remain intact for years.

In the early 1940s, Montreal's Punch Line of (Maurice) Rocket Richard, Elmer Lach and Toe Blake and Boston's Kraut Line of Milt Schmidt, Woody Dumart and Bobby Bauer were stars, but as those trios faded into the sunset, Detroit's sensational Production Line of Gordie Howe, Ted Lindsay and Sid Abel emerged to take over the mantle as hockey's greatest unit.

It was new Red Wings coach Tommy Ivan who first put the line together in the 1947-48 season and like a prospector striking gold, there was an instant gleam.

"We'll keep them together as long as they keep going," Ivan said.

Each man brought a uniquely distinctive game to the unit. Howe, on right wing, was the prototype for today's power forward. At six feet and 205 pounds, he was a hulk compared to most NHLers of his era. Howe could beat you with his skill and eschewed the slap-shot in favor of the wrist shot, feeling the latter's quicker release offered more potential to fool a netminder. Howe also policed his own territory and anyone who crossed him lived to regret it.

DETROIT NEWS

Left-winger Lindsay was the epitome of the non-conformist, a man who stood his ground and stood up for his beliefs. Someone who absolutely detested losing, he played the game like a Tasmanian Devil on skates and despite his slight 5-foot-8, 163-pound frame, was one of the NHL's most feared opponents and perhaps the most hated player in opposition rinks.

"He's the guy who holds us together," Abel said of Lindsay. "He keeps us at a high pitch."

Abel, the center, was the veteran of the line, coming to Detroit nearly a decade before the unit was put together. By the time the Production Line was formed, he'd already captained the Wings to one Stanley Cup and would lead them to two more flanked by his new wingers.

"We could all carry the puck, we could all skate and check and we could all make plays," was Howe's assessment of the Production Line. "Abel and Lindsay knew how to get into position for a pass."

The line jelled in 1948-49, combining for 66 goals, then took the NHL by storm in 1949-50, as Detroit won the Cup. Lindsay, Howe and Abel finished 1-2-3 in league scoring, combining for 215 points and producing at least one point in 58 of Detroit's 70 games.

Their last season as a unit saw Detroit sweep to the Cup in the minimum eight games in 1951-52. Abel took a job as player-coach in Chicago that summer and although Howe and Lindsay continued at their Hall of Fame pace for many more years, the Production Line was officially out of commission.

BACK in TIME

- **November 30, 1956**
The first use of video tape for television was utilized by CBS for "Douglas Edwards with the news."

- **July 6, 1957**
U.S. tennis star Althea Gibson became the first African-American to win a Wimbledon singles tittle.

- **October 20, 1957**
The New York Times Magazine listed oilman H.L. Hunt of Dallas as the richest American, with a fortune of $400-700 million.

quick cuts

Most Goals
Gordie Howe: 44

Most Assists
Ted Lindsay: 55

Most Points
Gordie Howe: 89

Most Penalty Minutes
Ted Lindsay & Warren Godfrey: 135

Most Wins, Goaltender
Glenn Hall: 38

Lowest Goals-Against Average
Glenn Hall: 2.24

Most Shutouts
Glenn Hall: 4

NHL Award Winners
Gordie Howe - Hart Trophy
Gordie Howe - Art Ross Trophy
Gordie Howe, Ted Lindsay, Red Kelly &
Glenn Hall - 1st Team All-Star

FINAL STANDINGS

	W	L	T	PTS	GF	GA
DETROIT	38	20	12	88	198	157
Montreal	35	23	12	82	210	155
Boston	34	24	12	80	195	174
New York	26	30	14	66	184	227
Toronto	21	34	15	57	174	194
Chicago	16	39	15	47	169	225

Playoff Results
Lost to the Boston Bruins in Series "A" (4-1)
Leading Playoff Scorers
Gordie Howe (7PTS)
Stanley Cup Champion
Montreal Canadiens

One year out of the NHL penthouse was enough for the Red Wings, who stormed back to the top of the standings to claim their eighth Prince of Wales Trophy in nine seasons.

With a 38-20-12 slate, Detroit finished six points ahead of the defending Stanley Cup champions from Montreal. Right-winger Gordie Howe also returned to form. His 44 goals and 89 points led the league, earning him his fifth Art Ross Trophy as scoring champ and third Hart Trophy as the NHL's most valuable player.

Ted Lindsay had a huge year, producing a career-high 85 points to place second in league scoring. He also collected his 300th career goal Nov. 18 in an 8-3 rout of Montreal. Second-year center Norm Ullman, the new pivot for this potent unit, collected 52 points and was 10th in scoring.

Goalie Glenn Hall, defenseman Red Kelly, center Alex Delvecchio and coach Jimmy Skinner represented Detroit in the NHL All-Star Game, a 1-1 tie with the Cup champ Montreal Canadiens which saw Lindsay net the All-Stars' goal.

Opening 5-0-2, Detroit never was far from the top all season long. Balance in attack was the key. Nine Wings reached double figures in goals.

In February, Lindsay was elected president of the NHL Players' Association, a movement to unionize NHL players. "We're not looking for any trouble," Lindsay said. "We just want to make playing in the league more attractive." Wings GM Jack Adams stripped Lindsay of his captaincy, awarding it to Red Kelly.

Oddsmakers listed Detroit as a 12-5 favorite to beat Boston in the semifinals. The Bruins won the opener, but the Wings smacked them 7-2 in Game 2. Just as quickly, Boston regained control, winning three straight to shuttle Detroit aside.

"We had our chances, but we lost through our errors," Adams said.

HOCKEYTOWN MOMENT
Wings place four players on the NHL's First All-Star Team

Returning to the top of the NHL standings for the eighth time in nine seasons, Detroit's dominance was recognized when four Red Wings were selected to the league's First All-Star Team.

Gordie Howe, who captured his fifth NHL scoring title in seven years, was the right-winger, while Ted Lindsay, whose career-high 85 points placed him second to Howe in the league points race, was the left-winger. Red Kelly, whose 10 goals led all NHL defenseman, earned a rearguard position and Glenn Hall, with a league-leading 38 wins, was the First All-Star Team's goaltender.

Wings of Legend

Gordie Howe

Young Gordon Howe knew he was destined for greatness, as evidenced by the day one of his brothers caught him practicing his autograph.

The signature for which he still gets countless requests.

"He was an all-around player," Detroit forward Carl Liscombe said. "He could do everything."

And Howe usually did.

Six times he won the NHL scoring title, earning a half-dozen nods as the NHL's most valuable player in a 26-season career which concluded with Howe, 52, skating alongside his sons Mark and Marty for the Hartford Whalers in 1979-80, his only NHL campaign in which Howe did not have the winged wheel on his chest.

Coming to the Red Wings training camp in 1945, Howe immediately turned heads, splitting the all-star defense tandem of Bill Quackenbush and Jack Stewart to score a goal.

"Even when he was 16 years old, you could tell he was going to be something special," Liscombe said.

Howe made the Wings in 1946-47 at age 18 and never left until he retired from the game in 1971, spending a quarter-century with Detroit. But he wasn't done and made a comeback with the WHA's Houston Aeros in 1973 to play on the same team as his sons.

Howe had it all going for him - longevity, durability, productivity and the ability to adjust to any style of game.

If a big goal was required, Howe would deliver, either by scoring it, or setting up a teammate. He could play defense in a pinch and even endured a brief stint in goal as a youngster. And if someone needed straightening out, Howe proved more effective than the chiropractor.

Howe's razor-sharp elbows were legendary and his fistic prowess so dominant that few messed with him.

"I remember my first NHL game against him," former Boston center Derek Sanderson said. "'Don't

RED WINGS ARCHIVE

mess with me, old man,' I told him. Next thing I remember was the smelling salts."

"If a guy slashed me, I'd grab his stick, pull him up alongside me and elbow him in the head," Howe explained.

No explanation is necessary of his talent. Turning a few pages of the NHL Guide and Record Book will suffice. Two decades after his last NHL game, he still maintains league career marks for seasons (26), games (1,767) and the most 20-goal seasons (22) - all consecutively, also a record. His goals (801), assists (1,049) and points (1,850) totals are all league records for a right-winger.

- **BORN:**
  Floral, Saskatchewan, March 31, 1928
- **ACQUIRED:**
  Signed to pro contract, November 1, 1945
- **BEST SEASON WITH RED WINGS:**
  1968-69 (44-59-103)
- **TOTALS WITH RED WINGS:**
  GP-1,687, G-786, A-1,023, PTS-1,809

- **HONORS:**
  Won six Hart Trophies; Won six Art Ross Trophies; Won Lester Patrick Trophy, 1967; Selected to 12 NHL First All-Star Teams; Selected to nine NHL Second All-Star Teams; Played in 22 NHL All-Star Games; Elected to Hockey Hall of Fame in 1972

MOTOWN Classic

Lindsay ties his own record

Leading the NHL with 55 assists, Ted Lindsay tied his own club record for assists originally set in 1949-50, the season he won the Art Ross Trophy as the NHL's leading scorer. His 55 helpers remain the seasonal standard for a Detroit left-winger.

His 85 points were a career high and Lindsay also set a Wings mark by appearing in the Stanley Cup playoffs for the 13th straight season. Unfortunately, 13 proved to be an unlucky number for him, as Lindsay was traded in the summer to the Chicago Blackhawks.

RED WINGS ARCHIVE

ASSEMBLY LINE

Left-winger Billy Dea and center Aggie Kukulowicz were acquired from the New York Rangers for Dave Creighton, Bronco Horvath and a sum of cash. Right-winger Bob Bailey's contract was purchased from Springfield of the AHL. Other Red Wings moves came from within. Right-winger Billy McNeill and defenseman Dale Anderson were promoted from the farm system.

RED WINGS ARCHIVE

Billy Dea

Red Wings Facts

All-Time Penalty-Minute Leaders

Bob Probert . . . . .2,090 minutes
Joey Kocur . . . . . .1,876 minutes
Gordie Howe . . . .1,643 minutes
Gerard Gallant . . .1,600 minutes
Ted Lindsay . . . . .1,423 minutes
Dennis Polonich . .1,242 minutes
Reed Larson . . . .1,127 minutes
Gary Bergman . . .1,101 minutes

Short Passes

Red Wings center Murray Costello served as director of the Canadian Amateur Hockey Association after his playing days concluded.

137

- 1957   1958 -

BACK in TIME

- **December 2, 1957**

The first full scale civilian atomic power plant, built by Westinghouse at a cost of $110 million, went into operation in Shippingport, Pennsylvania.

- **January 12, 1958**

The NCAA football league adopted the two-point conversion rule in the first substansive rule change in 45 years.

- **March 24, 1958**

Rock and roll singer Elvis Presley was inducted into the army, reducing his monthly earnings from more than $100,000 to $83.20.

quick cuts

Most Goals
Gordie Howe: 33

Most Assists
Gordie Howe: 44

Most Points
Gordie Howe: 77

Most Penalty Minutes
Forbes Kennedy: 135

Most Wins, Goaltender
Terry Sawchuk: 29

Lowest Goals-Against Average
Terry Sawchuk: 2.96

Most Shutouts
Terry Sawchuk: 3

NHL Award Winners
Gordie Howe - Hart Trophy
Gordie Howe - 1st Team All-Star
Marcel Pronovost - 2nd Team All-Star

FINAL STANDINGS

	W	L	T	PTS	GF	GA
Montreal	43	17	10	96	250	158
New York	32	25	13	77	195	188
DETROIT	29	29	12	70	176	207
Boston	27	28	15	69	199	194
Chicago	24	39	7	55	163	202
Toronto	21	38	11	53	192	226

Playoff Results
Lost to the Montreal Canadiens in Series "A" (4-0)
Leading Playoff Scorer
Johnny Wilson (3PTS)
Stanley Cup Champion
Montreal Canadiens

Everything old was new again, as far as the Detroit Red Wings were concerned. Well, a lot of it was.

Wings GM Jack Adams stunned the hockey world by dealing all-stars Ted Lindsay and Glenn Hall to Chicago, then he commenced gathering up some of the stars from Detroit's recent Cup-winning teams.

Left-winger Johnny Wilson came back in the Lindsay deal and left-winger Tony Leswick, scorer of the Cup-winning goal in 1953-54, also returned from Chicago. Three-time Vezina Trophy winner Terry Sawchuk was reacquired from Boston and couldn't have been happier.

"I have a natural preference for Detroit," Sawchuk said.

Adams denied the Lindsay deal was caused by his union activities. "All these wild rumors of personal differences between Lindsay and myself are without foundation," he said. "My job is to afford the hockey fans of Detroit and Michigan the best possible team."

Howe produced a team-leading 77 points and won the Hart Trophy as MVP of the NHL for the fourth time, earning First All-Star Team status. Defenseman Marcel Pronovost was a Second Team honoree. Howe, Pronovost, center Alex Delvecchio and defenseman

RED WINGS ARCHIVE

Red Kelly represented Detroit in the NHL All-Star Game. Wilson opened on the No. 1 line with Howe and center Guyle Fielder, but the unit never clicked and was quickly dismantled. Twenty-one new faces skated in Detroit colors, resulting in a 29-29-10 record and a third-place finish, the club's worst showing since 1946-47.

The playoffs weren't much better. Montreal swept aside the Wings in the minimum four games.

HOCKEYTOWN MOMENT
Sid Abel named new coach midway through season

RED WINGS ARCHIVE

For the first time since Duke Keats replaced Art Duncan in 1926-27, the Wings underwent a mid-season coaching change when Jimmy Skinner stepped down and former Production Line center Sid Abel was brought in as his replacement on January 2.

"I felt that I wasn't doing a very good job," Skinner said. "I wasn't giving it my best. The club wasn't backchecking. I've had these migraine headaches for some time and it got to the point where I couldn't bring myself to bawl them out anymore.

"I'm sure the change will be good for the Red Wings."

Abel had two seasons of coaching experience in Chicago and was working in the sheet metal business when called into action with Detroit slumping at 13-17-7. "I know the personnel of the entire team and will give everything I have to help them make the playoffs and become a threat for the Stanley Cup," Abel said.

Detroit rallied for a record of 16-12-5 under Abel, improving from fourth to third spot in the final standings.

Wings of Legend

Johnny Wilson

Johnny Wilson's memories of the glory days of the Detroit Red Wings start with the Olympia dressing-room entrance.

"There was a sign on the locker-room door," Wilson recalled. "It said, 'We'll supply everything but guts.'"

That was okay with him, because Wilson already had enough guts to go around. The NHL iron man of his era, Wilson played a record 580 consecutive games, shattering Murray Murdoch's league mark of 509 on March 21, 1959 against the New York Rangers.

"I think it's sort of ingrained in you as a kid," Wilson said of his durability. "I never missed a day of school.

"In hockey, I was fortunate because I never had a major injury like a broken bone, or anything where I had to sit out. As a young player, I remember Ted Lindsay telling me to play through hurts, because there's another guy sitting out there, waiting to take your job.

"I guess I must have listened."

A scorer as a junior, Wilson switched to a defensive role in the pros. "When I came to Detroit, Jack Adams told me they had enough scorers," Wilson said. "He wanted guys who could go up and down the ice and backcheck, so that's what I did."

Wilson was shuttled twice in the many moves of Detroit GM Adams during the mid 1950s — leaving shortly after the 1955 Cup win, then returning in the 1957 Lindsay deal. He's of the opinion that Adams tinkered too much and sidetracked a good thing.

"Jack certainly knew his hockey, but I think he made a big mistake in making such wholesale changes," Wilson said. "It was still a young team. Most of us were 27 or 28 and we had a few more years of good hockey left."

RED WINGS ARCHIVE

Wilson was moved again in 1959, dealt to the Toronto Maple Leafs and he finished his playing days with the Rangers in 1961-62.

Returning to Detroit as coach of the Wings from 1971-73, Wilson still makes his home in the area and maintains a regular presence with the Red Wings Alumni team.

- **BORN:**
  Kincardine, Ontario, June 14, 1929
- **ACQUIRED:**
  Signed to pro contract, September 9, 1949
- **BEST SEASON WITH RED WINGS:**
  1952-53 (23-19-42)

- **TOTALS WITH RED WINGS:**
  GP-379, G-79, A-100, PTS-179
- **HONORS:**
  Played in NHL All-Star Game, 1954-55; Set NHL record by playing 580 consecutive games

MOTOWN Classic

Howe wins fourth Hart Trophy

Winning the Hart Trophy as the NHL's most valuable player for the second season in succession and the fourth time in his career, Gordie Howe joined select company. At the time, former Boston defenseman Eddie Shore was the only other four-time Hart Trophy winner.

He led the club in scoring for the seventh time in eight seasons and Howe also became the NHL's all-time assist leader, surpassing Elmer Lach (408) by setting up two Red Kelly goals in a 3-1 win Nov. 30 at New York. He finished the campaign with 440 helpers.

ASSEMBLY LINE

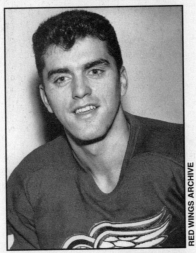

Hec Lalande

Angered by Ted Lindsay's union activity, GM Jack Adams shipped the veteran left-winger and goalie Glenn Hall to Chicago for center Forbes Kennedy, goalie Hank Bassen, left-winger Johnny Wilson and minor-leaguer Bill Preston. Goalie Terry Sawchuk returned to Detroit from Boston for Johnny Bucyk. Right-winger Bob Bailey was lost to Chicago in the NHL intra-league draft, then reacquired from the Blackhawks with defenseman Jack McIntyre, left-winger Nick Mickoski and center Hec Lalande for Billy Dea, Earl (Dutch) Reibel, Lorne Ferguson and Bill Dineen. Right-winger Tony Leswick was purchased from Chicago, while rookie defensemen Pete Goegan and Gord Strate and forwards Tom McCarthy and Don Poile became regulars.

Red Wings Facts

Most Seasons Leading the Wings in Points

Gordie Howe - 17

Steve Yzerman - 11

Syd Howe - 4

Short Passes

Rookies Dave Amadio and Brian Kilrea debuted with Detroit in 1957-58 and neither would play in the NHL again until they were teammates with the 1967-68 Los Angeles Kings.

- 1958   1959 -

BACK in TIME

• **October 28, 1958**

Following the death of Pope Pius XII, a liberal cardinal was chosen as the new Pope and named John XXIII.

• **January 1, 1959**

Rebel leader Fidel Castro and his forces seized control of Havana, Cuba and on January 16th named Manuel Urrutia as provincial president.

• **August 21, 1959**

Hawaii became the 50th state and a new 50 star flag was unfurled - the 20th design since the United States was formed.

quick cuts

Most Goals
Gordie Howe: 32
Most Assists
Gordie Howe: 46
Most Points
Gordie Howe: 78
Most Penalty Minutes
Pete Goegan: 111
Most Wins, Goaltender
Terry Sawchuk: 23
Lowest Goals-Against Average
Terry Sawchuk: 3.12
Most Shutouts
Terry Sawchuk: 5
NHL Award Winners
Alex Delvecchio - Lady Byng Trophy
Terry Sawchuk, Marcel Pronovost,
Alex Delvecchio & Gordie Howe
2nd Team All-Stars

FINAL STANDINGS

	W	L	T	PTS	GF	GA
Montreal	39	18	13	91	258	158
Boston	32	29	9	73	205	215
Chicago	28	29	13	69	197	208
Toronto	27	32	11	65	189	201
New York	26	32	12	64	201	217
DETROIT	25	37	8	58	167	218

Playoff Results
Did Not Qualify
Stanley Cup Champion
Montreal Canadiens

142

1958-59 Season in Review

RED WINGS ARCHIVE

The struggles of the 1957-58 campaign frustrated the once-mighty Red Wings, but they would pale in comparison to the ailments about to strike them down.

Sid Abel's first full season behind the Wings bench started out promising enough. Detroit was situated in second place at mid-season, but by that time was already in the midst of a 1-10-4 skid from December 13 to January 18 which plummeted the Wings out of the playoff picture.

There were some highlights along the way. Alex Delvecchio, playing left wing instead of his usual center position this season, won the Lady Byng Trophy and Delvecchio, defenseman Marcel Pronovost, goalie Terry Sawchuk and right-winger Gordie Howe were selected to the NHL's Second All-Star Team. Delvecchio, Howe, Pronovost and defenseman Red Kelly participated in the NHL All-Star Game.

Howe, now the Wings' captain, shook the Richter Scale and the face of New York Rangers tough guy Lou Fontinato in a February 1 fight. Fontinato came to the defense of Rangers rookie Eddie Shack, who was getting worked over by Howe and paid the price, taking several stiff uppercuts and suffering broken blood vessels and a badly fractured nose, which listed severely towards his right ear after the bout.

"His nose looked like the subway had hit it," Rangers coach Phil Watson said. LIFE magazine ran a three-page photo spread of the carnage. Howe didn't come away unscathed. He broke his right pinky finger on Fontinato's face.

Gordie Howe Night was held March 3 at the Olympia and the legendary Red Wing was given a new station wagon and showered with $10,000 in gifts from admirers during the first intermission of a 2-2 tie with Boston.

Johnny Wilson became the NHL's official iron man March 21 against the Rangers when he played his 509th consecutive game, shattering the mark of former Ranger Murray Murdoch.

All of these milestones couldn't alter the reality that the Wings finished the season last overall for the first time since 1926-27, Detroit's inaugural NHL campaign, missing the playoffs for the first time in two decades.

HOCKEYTOWN MOMENT
Wings miss playoffs for the first time since 1938

For the first time since the 1937-38 season, the Wings found themselves watching other NHL teams contest the playoffs.

A 2-7-2 slide in March, ending with back-to-back losses home-ice losses to the Rangers and Toronto, assured there would be no playoff hockey in Detroit for the first time in 20 years.

A particularly feeble effort February 5 in a 5-0 loss to the New York Rangers saw coach Sid Abel fine 14 players $100 each for playing what he described as, "The worst game of hockey I've seen in 20 years."

Right-winger Gordie Howe felt the series of moves engineered by GM Jack Adams since 1955 finally caught up with the Wings.

"They just devastated the team with trades," Howe said.

RED WINGS ARCHIVE

Sid Abel

Wings of Legend

Alex Delvecchio

If not for the looming shadow of Gordie Howe, Alex Delvecchio's accomplishments as a Red Wing would have made front-page news.

"Alex wasn't a flashy player," noted teammate Johnny Wilson. "He operated under control."

Certainly not as potent offensively as Howe, Delvecchio was nonetheless a consistent contributor, as his 17 seasons with at least 50 points testify. His forte was the soft, accurate pass, a tool he utilized to collect 825 career assists.

"I'd say he and (Montreal's Jean) Beliveau had the softest hands of anyone I've ever seen," Detroit defenseman Marcel Pronovost said. "He could find you in the crowd with an aspirin. That's how accurate his passes were."

Not an athletic-looking sort, Delvecchio's nickname was "Fats," but to believe he wasn't a great player was to be deceived.

"He wasn't like a Henri Richard or a (Stan) Mikita or a Beliveau who would just bust down the ice," Wilson said. "He methodically got down there and knew what the hell he was doing.

"He never got himself in a bind, always kept the puck going and always knew where to move it."

RED WINGS ARCHIVE

The six-foot, 195-pound center required only six games of minor-pro seasoning, jumping into the Detroit lineup late in the 1950-51 season and not leaving until he accepted the position as coach of the club on November 9, 1973. Switching from center to left wing to play on Detroit's No. 1 forward unit with right-winger Howe and center Norm Ullman in 1958-59, Delvecchio earned the first of three Lady Byng Trophies he'd win in his career and was also an NHL Second All-Star Team choice at his new position. He'd been a second-team choice at center in 1952-53.

Besides versatility, Delvecchio also displayed durability, missing only 43 games in 24 seasons, all of them spent with Detroit. He holds the NHL record for seasons and games played (1,549) by a player who toiled for just one team his entire career.

Consistency was another Delvecchio forte. He posted 13 seasons of at least 20 goals and 11 times finished in the NHL's top 10 scorers. He still rates 21st on the league's all-time points list and he and Carolina's Ron Francis are the only members of the NHL's 400-goal club who never posted a 40-goal campaign. Leadership was perhaps Delvecchio's strongest quality. He served as Wings captain from 1962-63 until he retired to become coach, later adding the duties of GM to his resume.

Delvecchio was inducted into the Hockey Hall of Fame in 1977.

- **BORN:**
  Fort William, Ontario, December 4, 1932
- **ACQUIRED:**
  Signed to pro contract, March 24, 1951
- **BEST SEASON WITH RED WINGS:**
  1968-69 (25-58-83)
- **TOTALS WITH RED WINGS:**
  GP-1,549, G-456, A-825, PTS-1,281

- **HONORS:**
  Won Lady Byng Trophy, 1958-59, 1965-66, 1968-69; Won Lester Patrick Trophy, 1974; Selected to NHL Second All-Star Team, 1952-53, 1958-59; Played in 13 NHL All-Star Games; Elected to Hockey Hall of Fame, 1977

144

MOTOWN Classic

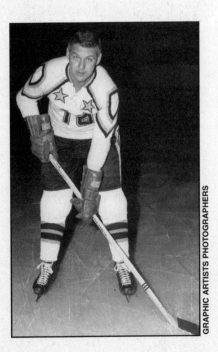

Gentleman Delvecchio wins Lady Byng

Continuing a Red Wings tradition, Alex Delvecchio skated away with the Lady Byng Trophy as the NHL's best combination of sportsmanship and ability.

He was the sixth Red Wing to win the award in the last 11 seasons.

A center who switched to left wing this season to skate on Detroit's top line with Gordie Howe and Norm Ullman, Delvecchio garnered just 383 penalty minutes in 1,549 NHL games.

"I think I had maybe five fights my whole career," Delvecchio said. Teammate Johnny Wilson felt Delvecchio's ability made it unnecessary for him to commit fouls.

"Alex was the toughest guy to knock off his feet," Wilson said. "He had tremendous balance. They could push him, but he'd never hit the ice."

ASSEMBLY LINE

Veteran defenseman Gus Mortson, who led the NHL in penalty minutes four times during his career, was acquired from Chicago. Gene Achtymichuk was dealt to Montreal for left-winger Claude Laforge. Detroit-born center Charlie Burns was signed as a free agent and right-winger Chuck Holmes and center Len Lunde were promoted from the farm system.

Charlie Burns

Red Wings Facts

Best Record vs Opponent One Season "Minimum 6 Games"

1950-51
vs Chicago 13 wins 1 loss

1951-52
vs Chicago 12 wins 2 losses

1944-45
vs Boston 9 wins 0 losses 1 tie

Short Passes

Working an off-season job as a lifeguard in Charlottetown, P.E.I., Red Wings center Forbes Kennedy saved a young girl from drowning in August of 1959.

DETROIT NEWS

When Glenn Hall was an up-and-coming Red Wings goalie prospect, playing across the Detroit River for the club's junior affiliate in Windsor, there was nothing he liked better than to come to the Olympia and watch Terry Sawchuk play goal for the Wings.

"I tried to copy his style, to use that low crouch he played," said Hall, like Sawchuk, a Hall of Fame netminder.

Every goalie wished they could stop the puck like Sawchuk.

Jimmy Skinner remembers coaching a young Sawchuk with the Windsor Spitfires during the 1947-48 season. Actually, make that 1947. Sawchuk was long gone before New Year's Day.

"He was only 17, but even then, he was outstanding," Skinner said. "A few games into the season, (Detroit GM) Jack Adams called me and said, 'I've got some bad news Jim, we've got to move Sawchuk to Omaha (of the minor pro USHL).'

"I wasn't surprised, though, because I figured he should have been there in the first place."

Marcel Pronovost was another who first encountered Sawchuk with that Windsor Spitfires team and he quickly discovered both Sawchuk's on-ice ability and his icy demeanor.

"He was aloof and distant," said Pronovost, who would grow to become Sawchuk's closest friend in hockey through their lengthy stints as teammates with Detroit and Toronto.

Sawchuk's 103 shutouts will never be matched by another NHL goaltender.

His 971 games played and 57,194 minutes logged in front of the cage are also league records.

"He was a great competitor and someone with a lot of passion for the game," said Colorado Avalanche goalie Patrick Roy, who surpassed Sawchuk's career wins mark of 447 in 2000-01.

Everyone who played with Sawchuk on their team eventually experienced a sampling of his mean streak.

"He was a very low-key guy," said Skinner, who coached Detroit's 1954-55 Cup winner with Sawchuk in goal. "And he could be very moody and surly when he was playing. He didn't talk much. You really had to know him to get him to talk."

Pronovost is convinced this side of Sawchuk's persona was fueled by his personal demons. "He got himself in trouble through his insecurities," Pronovost said. "He was always worried about how he would take care of his family when he was done playing. He worried about whether he would be able to give them all he could."

Sawchuk served three tours in Detroit — from 1949-55, 1957-64 and 1968-69. He died tragically on May 31 1970 from internal injuries suffered in a scuffle with New York Rangers teammate Ron Stewart.

"I had tears in my eyes when I heard," Pronovost said, while admitting the tragedy didn't come as a complete surprise.

"The way he lived his life, it seemed like he was asking for it."

 **- 1959** **1960 -**

 **BACK in TIME**

- **November 19, 1959**
Ford Motor Company announced the end of production of the Edsel automobile, which had lost the automaker $350 million.

- **May 1, 1960**
A U.S. reconnaissance plane taking pictures of Soviet military installations and piloted by Frances Gary Powers was shot down over Russia.

- **September 26, 1960**
Millions watched the first ever television debate between Presidential candidates Richard M. Nixon and John F. Kennedy.

quick cuts

Most Goals
Gordie Howe: 28
Most Assists
Gordie Howe: 45
Most Points
Gordie Howe: 73
Most Penalty Minutes
Jim Morrison: 62
Most Wins, Goaltender
Terry Sawchuk: 24
Lowest Goals-Against Average
Terry Sawchuk: 2.69
Most Shutouts
Terry Sawchuk: 5
NHL Award Winners
Gordie Howe - Hart Trophy
Marcel Pronovost & Gordie Howe
1st Team All-Star

FINAL STANDINGS

	W	L	T	PTS	GF	GA
Montreal	40	18	12	92	255	178
Toronto	35	26	9	79	199	195
Chicago	28	29	13	69	191	180
DETROIT	26	29	15	67	186	197
Boston	28	34	8	64	220	241
New York	17	38	15	49	187	247

Playoff Results
Lost to the Toronto Maple Leafs in Series "B" (4-2)
Leading Playoff Scorers
Alex Delvecchio (8PTS) - Gordie Howe (6PTS)
Stanley Cup Champion
Montreal Canadiens

148

1959-60 Season in Review

Revamping a team which had missed the playoffs the season before, Detroit GM Jack Adams brought in 15 new faces over the course of the 1959-60 season.

A quick 5-0-1 start saw Detroit residing in first place, but that was followed by a four-game winless skid. At the mid-season mark, the Wings, 16-12-8 and Toronto Maple Leafs were deadlocked for second place, a distant 11 points behind the Montreal Canadiens.

Then things turned ugly and Detroit won just six of its last 25 games, but one of those wins, a 6-3 decision March 19 over the New York Rangers in the second-last game of the season, clinched the fourth and final playoff spot by three points over the Boston Bruins.

Meanwhile, NHL fans were glued to another race, that for the NHL's career scoring lead. When Detroit right-winger Gordie Howe picked up an assist Jan. 13 in a 5-2 loss at Chicago, it left him and Montreal's Maurice (Rocket) Richard deadlocked at 945 points. Richard reclaimed his lead a night later with an assist against Toronto, but January 16 at the Olympia, Howe netted a goal and an assist as the Wings edged Toronto 4-3. With 947 points, Howe left Richard in the

RED WINGS ARCHIVE

rear-view mirror forever and would reign as NHL points king until being dethroned by Wayne Gretzky in 1989.

Howe won his record fifth Hart Trophy as league MVP, while he and defenseman Marcel Pronovost earned NHL First All-Star Team recognition. Howe, Pronovost, center Alex Delvecchio and goalie Terry Sawchuk played in the NHL All-Star Game.

The Leafs and Wings were opponents in the semi-finals and the series was deadlocked after four games. Gerry Melnyk's overtime goal, the last playoff OT marker scored by a Wing on home ice for 35 years, gave Detroit a 2-1 decision in Game 4, but the Leafs won the next two games and the series was over.

HOCKEYTOWN MOMENT
Kelly dealt twice in five days

RED WINGS ARCHIVE

When a magazine article appeared in which Red Wings defenseman Red Kelly suggested he was asked to play down the stretch of the 1958-59 season with a broken ankle, Detroit GM Jack Adams was outraged, terming the accusation "ridiculous."

A few days later on February 5, Kelly and right-winger Billy McNeill were dealt to the New York Rangers for defenseman Bill Gadsby and left-winger Eddie Shack, but both Detroit players announced they'd retire and the deal was voided.

Undaunted, five days later, Adams sent Kelly to the Toronto Maple Leafs for defenseman Marc Reaume.

"This is a tough business and sometimes, there's no room for sentiment," Adams said. "You can't make progress by standing still."

It was the Leafs who would make progress, though. Switching Kelly to center, they won four Stanley Cups in the next eight seasons. Meanwhile, Reaume played only 47 games as a Red Wing and never scored a goal.

Marcel Pronovost

Often overshadowed by the many great Detroit players of the 1950s, some fans don't realize what an outstanding player Marcel Pronovost was.

Pronovost could skate, score, make plays, check and defend his end of the ice as well as any NHLer.

A forward as a youngster, Pronovost displayed his selflessness by switching to his club's blueline brigade.

"One year, we didn't have enough defensemen on our team, so since I was the biggest kid on the team, they asked me to play defense," Pronovost said. "By the time I got to (Detroit's junior affiliate in) Windsor, I'd already played two years at defense."

He turned pro in 1949 and his big break came when Gordie Howe's near-fatal head injury in the 1950 playoffs forced Detroit coach Tommy Ivan to move Red Kelly up to the forward line. Pronovost was called up from Omaha of the USHL to fill the void on defense.

He played so well in Detroit's Stanley Cup win that veteran Jack Stewart was dealt to Chicago in the summer.

With his skill, Pronovost easily might have attained more points, but chose to play within Detroit's defense-first team concept.

"He could've been a helluva a lot more productive," recalled teammate Johnny Wilson, who marveled at Pronovost's knack for the open-ice hit.

"Marcel, he'd hit anything in sight. He hit guys coming through that center-ice zone. Man, he would rock them. If he hit a guy head-on, that guy was gone. I saw him put some guys out of commission."

A four-time NHL All-Star selection, Pronovost was runner-up in the Norris Trophy voting in 1960-61. Swiped by Detroit from Montreal's backyard in Shawinigan Falls, Quebec, Pronovost was presented with a car by his French-Canadian supporters on March 5, 1960, when Marcel Pronovost Night was held as the Wings visited the Montreal Forum. His Detroit teammates gave Pronovost the gift of a diamond ring.

A member of four Detroit Cup winners, Pronovost was traded to Toronto in 1964 and helped the Leafs to a Cup in 1967.

DETROIT NEWS

Inducted into the Hockey Hall of Fame in 1978, Pronovost coached the Wings for nine games during the 1979-80 season and continues to win Stanley Cups as an amateur scout for the New Jersey Devils.

- **BORN:**
  Shawinigan Falls, Quebec, June 15, 1930
- **ACQUIRED:**
  Signed to pro contract, September 9, 1949
- **BEST SEASON WITH RED WINGS:**
  1954-55 (9-25-34)

- **TOTALS WITH RED WINGS:**
  GP-983, G-80, A-217, PTS-297
- **HONORS:**
  Selected to NHL First All-Star Team, 1959-60, 1960-61; Selected to NHL Second All-Star Team, 1957-58, 1958-59; Elected to Hockey Hall of Fame, 1978

MOTOWN Classic

Adams enters Hockey Hall of Fame

An NHLer from 1917-18, the league's first season, the long and illustrious contribution of Jack Adams to the game was recognized when he was inducted into the Hockey Hall of Fame in 1960.

Detroit's coach from 1927-47, Adams still holds franchise marks for games coached (964) and wins (413). He also served as GM of the club from 1927-62, but it wasn't only his work in guiding the Wings to seven Stanley Cups which earned Adams this honor.

A feisty center, he won two Stanley Cups as a player, with the Toronto Arenas (1917-18) and Ottawa Senators (1926-27). Playing for Vancouver of the Pacific Coast Hockey Association, Adams led that league in penalty minutes in 1920-21 and in scoring in 1921-22.

RED WINGS ARCHIVE

ASSEMBLY LINE

After a season absent of playoff hockey, Detroit GM Jack Adams went to work to rectify the problem. Johnny Wilson and Frank Roggeveen were dealt to Toronto for right-winger Barry Cullen and left-winger Gary Aldcorn. Nick Mickoski went to Boston for defenseman Jim Morrison and Red Kelly was traded to Toronto for defenseman Marc Reaume. Charlie Burns was lost to Boston in the NHL intra-league draft, while right-winger John McKenzie was claimed from Chicago. Left-winger Val Fonteyne was purchased from Seattle of the WHL. Dennis Riggin, whose son Pat would also be an NHL goalie, put in a nine-game stint while Terry Sawchuk was idled with a leg injury. Center Murray Oliver, right-winger Len Haley, left-winger Brian Smith and center Gerry Melnyk also graduated from the minor leagues.

RED WINGS ARCHIVE

Barry Cullen

Red Wings Facts

Brothers Who Have Played For The Red Wings

Eddie & Mud Bruneteau
Charlie & Roy Conacher
Barry & Ray Cullen
Fred & Howie Glover
Bryan & Dennis Hextall
Hec, Ken & Wally Kilrea
Frank & Pete Mahovlich
Basil & Chris McRae
Don & Rod Morrison
Bud & Don Poile
Desse & Earl Roche
Frank & Johnny Sheppard
Carl & Nakina Dalton Smith
Cully & Thain Simon
Johnny & Larry Wilson

Short Passes

Left-winger Val Fonteyne, who broke into the NHL with Detroit in 1959-60, set an NHL record by playing 185 consecutive games without incurring a penalty from March 3, 1965, through Dec. 3, 1968.

- 1960   1961 -

BACK in TIME

- ### November 18, 1960
Chrysler Corporation discontinued the production of the DeSoto automobile, which had been manufactured since 1928.

- ### January 20, 1961
President Kennedy stirred the nation and world during his inaugural address with the words "Ask not what your country can do for you; ask what you can do for your country."

- ### February 15, 1961
The entire U.S. figure skating team was killed in a plane crash on the way to the World Championships in Prague.

quick cuts

Most Goals
Norm Ullman: 28
Most Assists
Gordie Howe: 49
Most Points
Gordie Howe: 72
Most Penalty Minutes
Howie Young: 108
Most Wins, Goaltender
Hank Bassen: 13
Lowest Goals-Against Average
Hank Bassen: 2.89
Most Shutouts
Terry Sawchuk: 2
NHL Award Winners
Marcel Pronovost - 1st Team All-Star
Gordie Howe - 2nd Team All-Star

FINAL STANDINGS

	W	L	T	PTS	GF	GA
Montreal	41	19	10	92	254	188
Toronto	39	19	12	90	234	176
Chicago	29	24	17	75	195	180
DETROIT	25	29	16	66	195	215
New York	22	38	10	54	204	248
Boston	15	42	13	43	176	254

Playoff Results
Defeated the Toronto Maple Leafs in Series "B" (4-1)
Lost to the Chicago Blackhawks in Stanley Cup Finals (4-2)
Leading Playoff Scorers
Gordie Howe (15PTS) - Alex Delvecchio (9PTS)
Stanley Cup Champion
Chicago Blackhawks

1960-61 Season in Review

The progress made by the Red Wings during the 1959-60 season left GM Jack Adams bursting with pride.

"They wrote us off," Adams said. "I said when we hit bottom that we'd be back and we're on our way. The road ahead should be much brighter."

He was right. The Wings were ready to return to status as legitimate contenders, although their appearance in the 1960-61 Stanley Cup finals would be a bit of a surprise.

As long as Gordie Howe patrolled right wing, Detroit was always going to have a chance. Howe finished fifth in NHL scoring with a team-leading 72 points, despite missing nine games through injury — two after hurting his knee in the NHL All-Star Game and seven more following a concussion after being victimized by a high stick from Toronto's Eddie Shack.

Howe, who returned from the injury wearing a helmet, scored his 450th NHL goal November 9 against the New York Rangers. On November 24, an Olympia-record crowd of 15,859 watched the Wings down the Stanley Cup champion Montreal Canadiens 3-1.

Howe was an NHL Second All-Star Team selection, while defenseman Marcel Pronovost was picked to the First Team. Those two, along with center Norm Ullman, skated for Detroit in the NHL All-Star Game. Ullman scored four goals March 14 in a 5-2 win over the Rangers.

RED WINGS ARCHIVE

Sitting third at mid-season, the Wings came home fourth overall at 25-29-16, but after losing the opener of their semifinal series with Toronto, they swept the next four games, upsetting a team which had finished 24 points ahead of them in the standings.

Detroit and Chicago met in the first all-American Stanley Cup final since the Rangers and Wings battled in 1949-50. The series was even after four games, but a shoulder injury hampered Detroit goalie Terry Sawchuk and the Blackhawks won in six games.

HOCKEYTOWN MOMENT
Wings and Blackhawks battle in finals for the first time since 1934

The first time Detroit ventured into the Stanley Cup final, it was the Chicago Blackhawks who offered opposition. The Blackhawks won that 1933-34 best-of-five series in four games and would again emerge victorious this spring.

Detroit lost goalie Terry Sawchuk (shoulder injury) and defenseman Marcel Pronovost (ankle injury) in the opening game, a 3-2 Chicago victory. Detroit split the next two games without either player, then won 2-

1 on rookie Bruce MacGregor's first NHL goal when both returned for Game 4.

It was clear that Sawchuk's ailing shoulder was still bothering him in a 6-3 loss in Game 5 and back-up Hank Bassen was back between the pipes for Game 6. Parker MacDonald gave Detroit a 1-0 first-period lead, then the Blackhawks rattled home five unanswered goals and lifted the Cup.

Howie Young

It could be said that Howie Young was Bob Probert before Probert was ever born.

A reckless performer as a young player both on and off the ice, Young fought battles with opponents and alcohol, but later cleaned up his act and went on to live a healthy and productive life, much like Probert has done.

Acquired from Hershey of the AHL, Young's impact as a rules offender was apparent when he led Detroit with 108 penalty minutes in 1960-61, even though he didn't crack the lineup until mid-January.

"Rookie defensemen are often untamed at first," Detroit GM Jack Adams said, comparing Young's style to old-time hockey paragon Eddie Shore. "Young has fine potential. He has color. The crowds love him."

Adams also suggested NHL referees picked on Young.

"He's not vicious or crude and he never pops off when he gets a penalty," Adams said. "If he did those things, we'd be the first to get rid of him."

In 1962-63, Young established a new NHL single-season penalty-minute mark of 273 minutes, averaging more than four minutes per game, obliterating Lou Fontinato's previous standard of 202 minutes.

Young was also enduring his share of run-ins off the ice, both with the law and team officials. It wasn't unusual for him to miss practice and he was frequently fined and suspended by the club for rules vio-

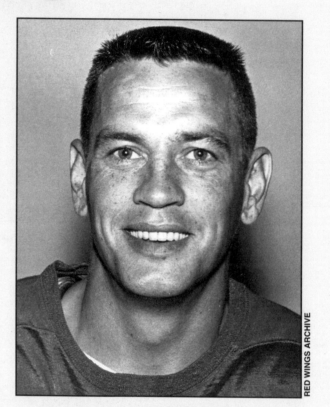

RED WINGS ARCHIVE

lations. "He's had a rough go of things and he thought the world was against him," Adams said. The Wings finally ran out of patience with Young and dealt him to Chicago in 1963.

Assignment to Los Angeles of the WHL in 1963-64 offered Young the opportunity to boast he was the only man to work alongside Gordie Howe and Frank Sinatra. While playing for the WHL's Los Angeles Blades in the mid-1960s, Young launched an acting career and appeared as Private Waller in the 1965 World War II film None But The Brave, which starred and was directed and produced by Sinatra.

Los Angeles was where Young reformed his wild ways, a fact acknowledged by Detroit coach-GM Sid Abel, who moved to reacquire the pugnacious blueliner, trading three players to L.A. for Young on December 20, 1966.

Young spent two more seasons with the Wings and moved on to again play with Chicago and later for the Vancouver Canucks.

He left the NHL in 1971, but wasn't done. Young played in the WHA and in 1985 at the age of 48, made a comeback with Flint of the IHL.

"I'm glad I lived through it," Young said of his battles with the bottle. "A lot of people don't. I was very fortunate."

- **BORN:**
  Toronto, Ontario, August 2, 1937
- **ACQUIRED:**
  January 12, 1961 trade with Hershey (AHL)
- **BEST SEASON WITH RED WINGS:**
  1967-68 (2-17-19)

- **TOTALS WITH RED WINGS:**
  GP-229, G-9, A-46, PTS-55
- **HONORS:**
  Set NHL record with league-leading 273 penalty minutes in 1962-63; Led Detroit in penalty minutes 1960-61, 1962-63

Howe becomes first to reach 1,000 points

RED WINGS ARCHIVE

As he continued to produce season after season, Gordie Howe was steadily turning the NHL record book into his autobiography.

The Detroit right-winger rewrote a few more chapters this season. With two assists in a 3-2 loss December 1 at Boston, Howe moved his combined regular-season and playoff points totals to 1,093, two better than Maurice (Rocket) Richard's NHL mark of 1,091.

"He's an inspiring leader," Montreal GM Frank Selke said. "His big assets are his almost super-human strength, powerful wrists, passing, playmaking, shooting and stickhandling. There doesn't seem to be a thing Gordie Howe can't do except sit on the bench."

Howe was already the NHL's all-time regular-season scoring leader and on November 27, 1960, he became the league's first four-digit regular-season scorer, setting up a goal in a 2-0 win over Toronto to register his 1,000th regular-season point.

With two assists in Game 2 of the Stanley Cup final against Chicago, Howe surpassed Doug Harvey (59) to become the NHL playoff leader in this department.

ASSEMBLY LINE

RED WINGS ARCHIVE

Howie Glover

There were personnel changes galore again in Hockeytown, as Trader Jack Adams continued to shuffle the deck. Tom McCarthy, Murray Oliver and Gary Aldcorn were dealt to Boston for right-winger Leo Labine and left-winger Vic Stasiuk, a former Wing. Center/right-winger Al Johnson was purchased from Montreal. Center Parker MacDonald (New York Rangers) and goalie Hank Bassen (Chicago) were selected in the NHL intra-league draft and Jim Morrison was dealt to Chicago for right-winger Howie Glover. Pete Conacher, Jack McIntyre and Marc Reaume were traded to Hershey (AHL) for Howie Young. Center Bruce MacGregor, left-winger Ed Diachuk and defenseman Gerry Odrowski came up through the Detroit chain.

Red Wings Facts

Wings Who Served Two-or-more Tenures With Detroit.

Ralph Almas	Pete Mahovlich
Thommie Bergman	Ab McDonald
Joe Carveth	Walt McKechnie
Bart Crashley	John Ogrodnick
Billy Dea	Jim Peters Sr.
Gary Doak	Doug Roberts
Roy Edwards	Jimmy Rutherford
Guyle Fielder	Andre St. Laurent
Val Fonteyne	Terry Sawchuk
Todd Gill	John Sherf
Warren Godfrey	Vic Stasiuk
Doug Houda	Billy Thomson
Petr Klima	Bob Wall
Joe Kocur	Bryan Watson
Igor Larionov	Tom Webster
Tony Leswick	Johnny Wilson
Ted Lindsay	Howie Young

Short Passes

Chicago's triumph over Detroit in the 1960-61 Stanley Cup final marked the only time during a span commencing with the 1941-42 season and ending with the 1968-69 campaign that one of Detroit, Montreal, or Toronto did not win the Cup.

BACK in TIME

- **August 13, 1961**

Insoluble problems between East and West Germany caused East Germany to close its borders with West Berlin and construction of the Berlin Wall began.

- **February 20, 1962**

In the spacecraft Friendship 7, Lieutenant Colonel John H. Glenn Jr. became the first American to orbit the Earth in a three orbit flight.

- **July 12, 1962**

The first broadcasts from Europe to America via the space satellite Telstar, developed by AT&T, took place.

quick cuts

Most Goals
Gordie Howe: 33

Most Assists
Gordie Howe: 44

Most Points
Gordie Howe: 77

Most Penalty Minutes
Bill Gadsby: 88

Most Wins, Goaltender
Terry Sawchuk: 14

Lowest Goals-Against Average
Hank Bassen: 2.81

Most Shutouts
Terry Sawchuk: 5

NHL Award Winners
Gordie Howe - 2nd Team All-Star

FINAL STANDINGS

	W	L	T	PTS	GF	GA
Montreal	42	14	14	98	259	166
Toronto	37	22	11	85	232	180
Chicago	31	26	13	77	217	186
New York	26	32	12	64	195	207
DETROIT	23	33	14	60	184	219
Boston	15	47	8	38	177	306

Playoff Results
Did Not Qualify
Stanley Cup Champion
Toronto Maple Leafs

1961-62 Season in Review

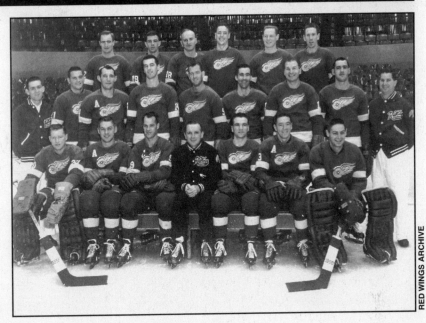

RED WINGS ARCHIVE

Fresh off a surprise appearance in the Stanley Cup final, logic suggested the Wings were on their way back to the top of the standings. Reality spelled out an entirely different story.

A 2-5-2 October identified that it would be a long, dreary winter in Hockeytown. Like a golfer continually coming up one club short, the Wings played all season on the fringe of the playoff picture, but never seemed to find a groove. A frustrating 6-22-7 road slate spelled doom for Detroit, which slumped to three points behind the New York Rangers March 6 after a 5-4 loss. A 2-2 tie with the Toronto Maple Leafs on March 23 certified that the Wings would miss the play-offs for the second time in four seasons.

Hidden within the disappointment was the splendid play of Detroit's top forward line, which consisted of right-winger Gordie Howe, center Alex Delvecchio and Norm Ullman, who made the switch from center to left wing for the season.

All three players finished amidst the NHL's top 10 scorers with more than 60 points apiece, Howe leading the way with 77 points, including his 1,000th point in NHL regular-season play. This season also saw him become the NHL's first 1,000-game man, while earning Second All-Star Team status.

That trio, along with defenseman Marcel Pronovost, were the Detroit players picked to play in the NHL All-Star Game.

While Howe's aura continued to grow, another Detroit legend was at the end of the line. Shortly after the Wings failed to make the playoffs, it was announced on April 25, 1962 that Jack Adams, 66, would retire as GM of the club, a position he'd held since 1927.

"This has been a surprise to all of us," Wings owner Bruce Norris said. Adams stated for public consumption that retirement was, "Pretty much my own decision," but later suggested, "I wasn't retired. I was fired."

HOCKEYTOWN MOMENT

Wings miss the playoffs for the second time since 1938

For 20 seasons between 1938-39 and 1957-58, Detroit was ever-present in the Stanley Cup playoffs, but 1961-62's 60-point performance left the Wings fifth, four points shy of a playoff position and out of post-season play for the second time in four seasons.

Veteran right-winger Gordie Howe cited an ongoing deterioration from within, caused by the numerous trades of the 1950s, most of which turned out poorly for the Wings.

"They gambled on young defensemen who didn't develop," Howe said. "They got mad at Red Kelly and traded him (to Toronto). Glenn Hall was another great one they let go and Boston's whole Uke Line (of John Bucyk, Vic Stasiuk and Bronco Horvath), they all used to be with Detroit."

Norm Ullman

Norm Ullman, it seemed, had everything going for him except good timing.

The slick, playmaking center arrived in Detroit in 1955-56, the year after Detroit's Stanley Cup win. In 1967-68, his Detroit days ended when the Wings dealt him to Toronto, one season after the most recent Cup win by the Maple Leafs.

Ullman skated in the NHL for two decades without winning the Stanley Cup, but it is the only item missing from his impressive resume. He posted 20 goals in 16 of his 20 NHL seasons, leading the league with 42 goals in 1964-65 after a taking a tip from linemate Gordie Howe to increase his shooting.

"Normie always tried to move past one too many men, so he could make the perfect pass," Howe said. "Once he started to shoot, he started scoring more goals."

So quiet was Ullman that teammates often lost track of him off the ice. "You'd ask, 'Is Normie around?'" teammate Johnny Wilson recalled, "'And someone would say, 'Yeah, he's sitting next to you.'"

Finding him on the ice was never a problem. Seven times, Ullman finished among the NHL's top 10 scorers, including a second-place finish in 1964-65, when he registered a career-high 83 points. Chicago center Stan Mikita won the scoring title, but Ullman was named pivot on the First All-Star Team, one of two times he earned NHL All-Star recognition.

RED WINGS ARCHIVE

Ullman employed his skating speed as an effective weapon. "He was the greatest forechecker in hockey," noted New York Rangers coach Emile Francis. That fierce forechecking helped him produce a Detroit playoff record two goals in five seconds in an April 11, 1965 game with Chicago. Ullman was Chicago's personal nightmare in post-season play. He collected two hat-tricks and 13 points versus the Blackhawks in the 1964 semifinals and had a pair of five-point games against them in Stanley Cup play - on April 7, 1963 and again on April 7, 1964.

Ullman finished third in NHL scoring with 70 points in 1966-67, but was dealt to Toronto in a seven-player trade the following season in which Detroit landed Frank Mahovlich.

He toiled for the Leafs through the 1974-75 season and spent two years with Edmonton of the WHA before retiring in 1977.

The Hockey Hall of Fame welcomed Ullman as a member in 1982.

- **BORN:**
  Edmonton, Alberta, December 26, 1935
- **ACQUIRED:**
  Signed to pro contract, March 19, 1954
- **BEST SEASON WITH RED WINGS:**
  1964-65 (42-41-83)

- **TOTALS WITH RED WINGS:**
  GP-875, G-324, A-434, PTS-758
- **HONORS:**
  Selected to NHL First All-Star Team, 1964-65; Selected to NHL Second All-Star Team, 1966-67; Played in eight NHL All-Star Games; Elected to Hockey Hall of Fame, 1982

Red Wings Owners

James "Pop" Norris

When James "Pop" Norris purchased the Detroit franchise and Olympia Stadium in 1932, he resurrected a failing team and saved hockey in the city of Detroit. The successful owner of the Norris Grain Company, James would run the Wings until his death in 1952.

James Norris Jr.

While "Pop" Norris maintained his home base in Chicago, James Jr. worked closely with head coach Jack Adams to turn a once lackluster franchise into a hockey dynasty. After his father's death, Norris moved on to become majority stockholder in the Chicago Blackhawks, leaving the reigns to his 27-year-old sister Marguerite Norris.

Bruce Norris

Just 31 when he took over control of the Red Wings from his sister Marguerite in 1955, Bruce Norris was a college hockey player at Yale who would sometimes skate with the Wings in practice. The team reached the Stanley final five times under his ownership and it was Bruce who engineered a $2.5 million expansion to the Olympia in the mid 1960s.

Mike & Marian Ilitch

Already respected business owners around the city of Detroit, Mike and Marian Ilitch further invested in the city when they purchased the Red Wings from the Norris family in 1982. Through intense commitment and persistence, the Ilitches helped restore Hockeytown to glory with back-to-back Stanley Cup Championships in 1997 and 1998.

Red Wings General Managers

Jack Adams

Throughout his 35-year career in Detroit, Jack Adams played a major role as head coach, general manager, public relations director and promoter. His innovative tactics drew huge crowds to Olympia Stadium, while his aggressive style as general manager drew many critics, but also led the Wings to seven Stanley Cups and during his tenor.

Sid Abel

One of the most popular and productive players in Red Wings history, Abel added the duties of GM to his coaching responsibilities in 1962 from Jack Adams and the club reached the Stanley Cup final in three of his first four seasons in the position. Abel, Art Duncan, Ted Lindsay and Alex Delvecchio are the only men to serve the franchise as captain, coach and GM.

Jimmy Devellano

Already a proven and well-respected NHL scout, Jim Devellano got his first chance to be a general manager when the Ilitches hired him in 1982. He is credited for building the franchise back into the shape of its glory days with the drafting of players like Steve Yzerman, Chris Osgood, Sergei Fedorov, Nicklas Lidstrom and Darren McCarty.

Ken Holland

Holland took over as general manager in 1997 after deftly handling several different front-office duties for the club over a 15-year period. With Holland's innovative style, he has quickly established himself as one of the more aggressive GM's in the NHL.

Red Wings Coaches

Jack Adams

Adams spent 20 years behind the bench for the Red Wings from 1927-1947 before focusing all of his attention on the role of general manager in 1948. He is the team's all-time leader in games coached (964), wins (413), losses (390) and ties (161).

Sid Abel

Taking over duties midway through the 1957-58 season, Abel compiled the second-longest run behind the bench in Red Wings history. In 811 games coached, the former Red Wings All-Star posted a 340-339-132 record over 11 seasons.

Tommy Ivan

Ivan became the fourth coach in Red Wings history after Jack Adams turned over the reigns to him at the beginning of the 1947-48 season. For the next seven seasons, Ivan guided the Wings to three Stanley Cup Championships while compiling a record of 262-118-90.

Jacques Demers

For four seasons Jacques Demers turned around a slumping Red Wings team and led them to back-to-back Norris Division crowns between 1987 and 1989, compiling a 137-136-47 record.

Scotty Bowman

Already the NHL's all-time winningest coach, Scotty Bowman came to Detroit in 1993 to help complete Detroit's recipe for a Stanley Cup. With over 400 wins in only nine seasons, Bowman ranks second among Detroit coaches in all-time victories.

1996-1997 DETROIT RED WINGS
Stanley Cup Champions

Front, from left: Mike Vernon, Brendan Shanahan, Assistant General Manager Ken Holland, Senior Vice-President/Hockey Operations Jim Devellano (Conn Smythe Trophy), Vice-President Atanas Ilitch, Owner/Secretary-Treasurer Marian Ilitch, Owner Mike Ilitch, Captain Steve Yzerman (Stanley Cup), Director of Player Personnel/Head Coach Scotty Bowman, Associate Coach Barry Smith (Clarence Campbell Trophy), Associate Coach Dave Lewis, Associate Coach Mike Krushelnyski, Chris Osgood, Kevin Hodson.

Middle, from left: Dressing Room Asst. Wally Crossman, Masseur Sergei Mnatsakanov, Athletic Trainer John Wharton, NHL Scout Dan Belisle, Joe Kocur, Vladimir Konstantinov, Viacheslav Fetisov, Doug Brown, Martin Lapointe, Kris Draper, Sergei Fedorov, Igor Larionov, Tomas Holmstrom, Darren McCarty, Kirk Maltby, Vyacheslav Kozlov, Equipment Manager Paul Boyer, Asst. Equipment Manager Tim Abbott, Dressing Room Asst. Mike Vella, Dressing Room Asst. Johnny Remejes.

Rear, from left: Nicklas Lidstrom, Tomas Sandstrom, Mike Knuble, Jamie Pushor, Bob Rouse, Larry Murphy, Mathieu Dandenault, Aaron Ward, Tim Taylor.

1997-1998 Detroit Red Wings
Stanley Cup Champions

First Row, from left: Chris Osgood, Kevin Hodson, Sergei Mnatsakanov, Senior Vice-President Jim Devellano, General Manager Ken Holland, Vice-President Atanas Ilitch (Conn Smythe Trophy), Owner/Secretary-Treasurer Marian Ilitch, Owner Mike Ilitch, Captain Steve Yzerman (Stanley Cup), Head Coach Scotty Bowman, Associate Coach Barry Smith, Associate Coach Dave Lewis (Clarence Campbell Bowl), Asst. General Manager Don Waddell, Vladimir Konstantinov, Brendan Shanahan, Norm Maracle.

Second Row, from left: Dressing Room Asst. Wally Crossman, Athletic Trainer John Wharton, Masseur Bob Huddleston, Dressing Room Asst. Art Mnatsakanov, Goaltending Consultant Jim Bedard, Darryl Laplante, Brent Gilchrist, Martin Lapointe, Tomas Holmstrom, Darren McCarty, Joe Kocur, Kris Draper, Kirk Maltby, Doug Brown, Igor Larionov, Vyacheslav Kozlov, Viacheslav Fetisov, NHL Scout Dan Belisle, Equipment Manager Paul Boyer, Asst. Equipment Manager Tim Abbott, Dressing Room Asst. Mike Vella, Dressing Room Asst. Johnny Remejes.

Third Row, from left: Dmitri Mironov, Mike Knuble, Mathieu Dandenault, Anders Eriksson, Bob Rouse, Nicklas Lidstrom, Sergei Fedorov, Larry Murphy, Aaron Ward, Jamie Macoun.

Homes Of The Detroit Red Wings

Border Cities Arena

Though it only lasted for one season, this 6,000-seat rink in Windsor, Ontario played host to the first season of hockey in Detroit history. Construction delays on the team's home rink in Detroit forced the team to move across the Detroit River for all 22 of their home games during the 1926-27 season.

Olympia Stadium

On the evening of Nov. 22, 1927, a state-of-the-art arena was introduced to Detroit fans as 11,000 people packed in to see the first Detroit Cougars game at Olympia Stadium. The million-dollar arena, known as the "Old Red Barn" would be home to the team for the next 52 years.

Joe Louis Arena

Named after legendary Detroit heavyweight champion Joe Louis, this arena opened midway through the 1979 hockey season. Without a bad seat in the house, "The Joe" continues to provide over a20,000 fans an up close and personal look at the action on the ice.

MOTOWN Classic

Howe becomes second to reach 500 goals

A 3-2 loss to the New York Rangers on March 14 put Detroit out of the playoff picture in fifth spot, but added another page to Gordie Howe's record book.

With Detroit playing shorthanded, Howe deked around Norris Trophy-winning defenseman Doug Harvey and fired a low shot past goalie Gump Worsley for his 500th NHL goal.

After his accomplishment, Howe talked about his hopes to equal Dit Clapper's NHL mark of 20 seasons.

"There isn't another club in hockey that depends on one player so much," Montreal GM Frank Selke said of Howe. "I don't know what the Wings would do without him."

Earlier in the season, on November 26 against Chicago, Howe became the first NHLer to skate in 1,000 games.

RED WINGS ARCHIVE

ASSEMBLY LINE

Jack Adams' last season as GM of the Red Wings was not unlike his first 34. Players were coming and going all year long. Bill Gadsby, the defenseman he'd tried to get two seasons earlier in the failed Red Kelly trade, was acquired from the New York Rangers for Les Hunt. Center/right-winger Ed Litzenberger, who captained Chicago to the 1960-61 Stanley Cup over Detroit, was picked up for Brian Smith and Gerry Melnyk, but lost to Toronto on waivers in December. Pete Goegan was dealt to the Rangers for defenseman Noel Price. Centers Bob Dillabough and Marc Boileau and left-winger Larry Jeffrey moved up to the big club from the farm system.

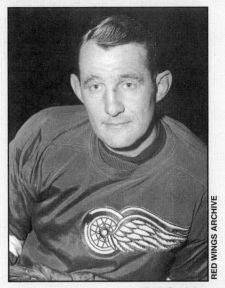

RED WINGS ARCHIVE

Bill Gadsby

Red Wings Facts

**Red Wing Goalies
On NHL's All-Time
Shutout List:**

Terry Sawchuk		
(1st)	103	85 with Det.
Glenn Hall		
(3rd)	84	17 with Det.
Tiny Thompson		
(5th)	81	7 with Det.
Alex Connell		
(5th)	81	6 with Det.
Harry Lumley		
(9th)	71	26 with Det.
Dominik Hasek		
(11th)	61	5 with Det.

Short Passes

Claude Laforge, a left-winger, was the first Red Wing to wear a goalie mask in a game. Laforge suffered a fractured cheekbone in his last minor-league game before a recall from Hershey (AHL), playing Dec. 28, 1961 wearing the mask.

BACK in TIME

- **October 14, 1962**

The United States discovered Soviet offensive missiles in Cuba and issued an ultimatum demanding their removal. After several days of tense confrontation, the Soviets removed their missiles on October 18th.

- **January 7, 1963**

The United States postal service raised the postage for first class mail to 5 cents.

- **May 2, 1963**

Five hundred individuals were arrested in Birmingham, Alabama following protests against the state's segregation policies. On May 18th, President Kennedy sent Federal troops in to establish order.

quick cuts

Most Goals
Gordie Howe: 38
Most Assists
Gordie Howe: 48
Most Points
Gordie Howe: 86
Most Penalty Minutes
Howie Young: 273
Most Wins, Goaltender
Terry Sawchuk: 23
Lowest Goals-Against Average
Terry Sawchuk: 2.48
Most Shutouts
Terry Sawchuk: 3
NHL Award Winners
Gordie Howe - Hart Trophy
Gordie Howe - Art Ross Trophy
Gordie Howe - 1st Team All-Star
Terry Sawchuk - 2nd Team All-Star

FINAL STANDINGS

	W	L	T	PTS	GF	GA
Toronto	35	23	12	82	221	180
Chicago	32	21	17	81	194	178
Montreal	28	19	23	79	225	183
DETROIT	32	25	13	77	200	194
New York	22	36	12	56	211	233
Boston	14	39	17	45	198	281

Playoff Results
Defeated the Chicago Blackhawks in Series "B" (4-2)
Lost to the Toronto Maple Leafs in Finals (4-1)
Leading Playoff Scorers
Gordie Howe & Norm Ullman (16PTS each)
Stanley Cup Champion
Toronto Maple Leafs

1962-63 Season in Review

The Wings couldn't mask their disappointment at missing the playoffs in 1961-62, but goaltender Terry Sawchuk finally decided he could mask his face from the cutting blows of vulcanized rubber.

Sawchuk donned a mask for the 1962-63 season, becoming the first Detroit goalie to wear facial protection and it appeared to make a huge difference.

The Wings began the season with a record 8-0-2 unbeaten run, as Sawchuk, who won a training-camp battle with Hank Bassen and Dennis Riggin to retain his job, allowed one goal or fewer in six of those 10 games, posting three shutouts.

"After camp, there was no question that Terry was the best," Detroit coach-GM Sid Abel said.

The record start also included six straight home-ice wins to commence the campaign, another club mark.

A series of injuries, including a bruised shoulder and instep and two severed hand tendons, slowed Sawchuk and the Wings slumped to fourth by mid-season, which was where they'd finish the season.

Gordie Howe was a big reason why Detroit returned to the playoffs. Howe won the Art Ross and Hart Trophies for the sixth time each, both NHL records, as his 86 points led the NHL in scoring. Howe was selected to the NHL's First All-Star Team, while Sawchuk's strong campaign earned him Second Team

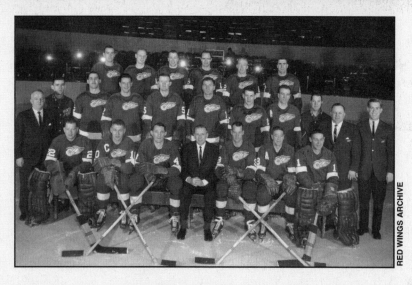

RED WINGS ARCHIVE

recognition. Howe and centers Alex Delvecchio and Norm Ullman were NHL All-Star Game participants. It was Howe's record 14th appearance in the game.

The Wings fell behind 2-0 in their semifinal series with Chicago, but a Bruce MacGregor slash broke Chicago star Bobby Hull's nose late in Game 2 and the tide turned for Detroit, which won four straight. Ullman set a playoff record with five points in Detroit's 7-4 series-clinching win on April 7.

The defending champion Toronto Maple Leafs were next on the agenda in the Stanley Cup final and once again, Detroit fell behind, losing the first two games on the road. This time, there would be no rally and Toronto captured the Cup in five games.

HOCKEYTOWN MOMENT
Goal scoring on the rise

While Terry Sawchuk's return to form solidified Detroit defensively, the offense lit the lamp regularly at the other end, as the Wings reached the 200-goal plateau for the first time since 1954-55.

The usual suspects contributed mightily. Gordie Howe potted a league-high 38 goals, while Norm Ullman, back again at his natural center position, netted 26 and Alex Delvecchio registered 20.

The surprise of the season was left-winger Parker MacDonald. Playing on a line with Howe and Delvecchio, the journeyman produced career highs with 33 goals and 61 points. Center Alex Faulkner, the first Newfoundlander to skate in the NHL, potted 10 goals, which would prove to be his career best. Andre Pronovost (13 goals) and Bruce MacGregor (11) were other hearty contributors. Bill Gadsby led Wings defensemen with 28 points, becoming the first rearguard in NHL history to crack the 500-point barrier.

Parker MacDonald

If the NHL presented an award for its most improved player, Parker MacDonald would have been a worthy recipient for the 1962-63 season. There was no reason other than a hunch for Red Wings coach-GM Sid Abel to give MacDonald a shot on the left wing of Detroit's No. 1 forward line with right-winger Gordie Howe and center Alex Delvecchio.

After an unimpressive training camp, Abel was set to ship MacDonald to the minor leagues, when as a last resort, he threw him on the big line, which was in desperate need of left-side production.

Almost immediately, the trio clicked. MacDonald garnered four goals and seven points in Detroit's first eight games. By early November, he was leading the NHL in scoring.

The trio combined to top all NHL forward lines with 193 points. Howe won his sixth NHL scoring title with 86 points, while Delvecchio (64 points) finished seventh overall and MacDonald's career-high 33-28-61 numbers left him tied for 11th-best.

As a chemistry experiment, it was a huge success.

"On another line, Parker may be less than ordinary," Abel admitted. "But the three of them together is a happy marriage."

MacDonald posted a 90-point season as a junior with the Toronto Marlboros, but

RED WINGS ARCHIVE

following failed attempts to make it with Toronto and the New York Rangers, came to the Wings via the NHL intra-league draft. He scored 14 goals his first season with Detroit, but spent much of the 1961-62 campaign in the minors.

Almost as quickly as it arrived, MacDonald's punch disappeared. He scored 21 goals in 1963-64, then slumped to 13 and was dealt to Boston in 1965, only to be reacquired and reunited with his old linemates through a December 30, 1965 trade with the Bruins.

"The only reason I let him go in the first place is because the fans were getting on his back," Abel said.

This time, the mix didn't work. MacDonald scored eight goals in two seasons and was lost to Minnesota in the 1967 NHL expansion draft. He finished his playing days with the North Stars in 1968-69 and later coached them and the Los Angeles Kings.

- **BORN:**
  Sydney, Nova Scotia, June 14, 1933
- **ACQUIRED:**
  Selected from New York Rangers in June 7, 1960 NHL intra-league draft
- **BEST SEASON WITH RED WINGS:**
  1962-63 (33-28-61)

- **TOTALS WITH RED WINGS:**
  GP-361, G-94, A-122, PTS-216
- **HONORS:**
  Won Stu Evans Trophy (most sportsmanlike Red Wing), 1962-63

Delvecchio takes over as captain

Accepting an assistant's position to coach Sid Abel, NHL regulations forced Gordie Howe to relinquish his captaincy, since no player could hold both a coaching and captain's position.

Alex Delvecchio was given the "C" and "Fats" proved a wise choice. His laid-back style of leadership had a calming influence on the club. Red Wings broadcaster Bruce Martyn recalled a particular moment that displayed the easy manner through which Delvecchio could diffuse a touchy situation.

After a one-sided loss at Toronto, the Wings' bus ride to the airport was as morbid as a funeral procession.

"You could have heard a pin drop in there, it was so quiet," Martyn said. "All of a sudden, Alex calls to Budd Lynch." Lynch, Martyn's broadcast partner, lost his right arm in combat during World War II. "We've got a question back here that maybe you can answer," Delvecchio said to Lynch. "How in the heck do you wind your watch?"

Delvecchio served as captain until his retirement in 1973 and only Steve Yzerman (16 seasons and counting) has worn the "C" longer in Red Wings history.

RED WINGS ARCHIVE

ASSEMBLY LINE

Sid Abel's first season as GM showed he'd learned a few things from Jack Adams. Abel traded Len Lunde and John McKenzie to Chicago for defenseman Doug Barkley and dealt Forbes Kennedy to Boston for left-winger Andre Pronovost. He selected center Alex Faulkner from Toronto and right-winger Floyd Smith from the New York Rangers in the NHL intra-league draft,

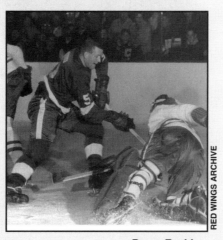

Doug Barkley

RED WINGS ARCHIVE

while Warren Godfrey was lost to Boston. Defenseman Ron Harris, center Eddie Joyal and left-winger Lowell MacDonald moved up the ladder from the farm system. In the NHL's first amateur draft, center Pete Mahovlich was Detroit's top pick.

Red Wings Facts

Norris Trophy Winners
(with scoring totals)

Red Kelly
1953-54 - 16 goals, 33 assists, 49 pts
1st Team All-Star

Paul Coffey
1995-96 - 14 goals, 44 assists, 58 pts
1st Team All-Starr

Nicklas Lidstrom
2000-01 - 15 goals, 56 assists, 71 pts
1st Team All-Star

Nicklas Lidstrom
2001-02 - 9 goals, 50 assists, 59 pts
1st Team All-Star

Short Passes

Detroit traded defenseman Pete Goegan to the New York Rangers for defenseman Noel Price on February 6, 1962. The Wings traded Price to the Rangers for Goegan on Oct. 8, 1962.

- 1963   1964 -

BACK in TIME

• November 22, 1963
President Kennedy was hit by an assassin's bullet while riding in a Dallas motorcade and died 30 minutes later without regaining consciousness.

• April 13, 1964
Sidney Poitier won an Oscar for Best Actor for "Lilies of the Field", the first African American to win a major Oscar since Hattie McDaniel won for Best Supporting Actress in "Gone with the Wind."

• July 11, 1964
"Where Did Our Love Go" by Motown favorites The Supremes, hit the top 40 chart.

quick cuts

Most Goals
Gordie Howe: 26
Most Assists
Gordie Howe: 47
Most Points
Gordie Howe: 73
Most Penalty Minutes
Doug Barkley: 115
Most Wins, Goaltender
Terry Sawchuk: 24
Lowest Goals-Against Average
Terry Sawchuk: 2.68
Most Shutouts
Terry Sawchuk: 5
NHL Award Winners
Gordie Howe - 2nd Team All-Star

FINAL STANDINGS

	W	L	T	PTS	GF	GA
Montreal	36	21	13	85	209	167
Chicago	36	22	12	84	218	169
Toronto	33	25	12	78	192	172
DETROIT	30	29	11	71	191	204
New York	22	38	10	54	186	242
Boston	18	40	12	48	170	212

Playoff Results
Defeated the Chicago Blackhawks in Series "B" (4-3)
Lost to the Toronto Maple Leafs in Finals (4-3)
Leading Playoff Scorers
Gordie Howe (19PTS) - Norm Ullman (17PTS)
Stanley Cup Champion
Toronto Maple Leafs

1963-64 Season in Review

It certainly didn't appear as if a legitimate shot at glory was within the grasp of the 1963-64 edition of the Red Wings. The regular-season campaign was anything but smooth.

Shuffling due to injuries and the constant search for a successful formula, coach-GM Sid Abel employed 33 skaters and a record six goaltenders.

A back injury put Terry Sawchuk on the sidelines and gave Wings fans their first glimpse of the acrobatic Roger Crozier, being groomed as Sawchuk's heir apparent. Crozier played well until a slapshot fractured his cheekbone.

Hank Bassen, Bob Champoux, Pat Rupp and Harrison Gray all saw stints filling in for the injured Sawchuk and Crozier.

Sawchuk and Gordie Howe provided the individual highlights of the season. Howe led the team with 26 goals and 73 points and one of those goals, coming November 10 in a 3-0 victory over Montreal, was the 545th for Howe in regular-season play, moving him past Maurice (Rocket) Richard into top spot on the NHL's all-time goals list.

Sawchuk's shutout the same night was his 94th, tying George Hainsworth's NHL record. He broke that mark January 18 with a 2-0 verdict over the Canadiens and on February 8, Sawchuk played his 804th game, surpassing Harry Lumley's NHL standard for netminders.

RED WINGS ARCHIVE

Sawchuk, Howe, defenseman Marcel Pronovost and centers Alex Delvecchio and Norm Ullman were Detroit's picks to the NHL All-Star Game. Right-winger Howe was selected to the NHL's Second All-Star Team.

Earning the fourth and final playoff spot at 30-29-10, the Wings rallied from a 3-2 series deficit to down Chicago in the semifinals, thanks to center Norm Ullman, who had two hat tricks and a club-record five-point game during the series.

Moving to the finals, the tables turned. Detroit squandered a 3-2 series lead, losing to Toronto for the second spring in succession.

HOCKEYTOWN MOMENT
Wings come ever so close to winning the Cup

The breaks which didn't go Detroit's way during the regular season started falling the Wings' way in the playoffs and for a while, it appeared that destiny might be on their side.

Detroit trailed Chicago three times in the semifinals, but a different hero emerged whenever one was required. Goalie Terry Sawchuk went out with a shoulder injury four minutes after the opening faceoff of Game 2, but Bob Champoux stepped into the breach to lead the Wings to a 5-4 win in his NHL debut.

Sawchuk checked himself out of hospital to post a 3-0 shutout in Game 3, but was reinjured and returned to hospital during Game 4.

Norm Ullman took over the hero role in Game 6, collecting three goals and five points in a 7-2 Wings win to stave off elimination. The comeback was completed with a 4-2 verdict in Game 7.

The Wings maintained control for much of the final series with Toronto, possessing 2-1 and 3-2 series advantages, Leading 3-2 in Game 6, Detroit was 2:12 away from lifting the Cup when Toronto's Billy Harris scored. Leaf defenseman Bobby Baun, skating on a hairline ankle fracture, won it 2:43 into overtime.

Back on home ice for Game 7, Toronto was an easy 4-0 winner.

Doug Barkley

Among the many moves made by the Red Wings during the 1960s, the acquisition of Doug Barkley from Chicago would have stood out, if not for the intervention of tragic circumstances.

The 25-year-old defenseman was already a six-year veteran of the minor leagues when Detroit shipped forwards Len Lunde and John McKenzie to the Blackhawks for Barkley.

He emerged as a prominent player during the 1963-64 season, when Barkley's 11 goals led all NHL defensemen and were the most tallied by a Red Wings blueliner since Marcel Pronovost also counted 11 times in 1958-59. Barkley's 115 penalty minutes that season were also a team high.

Barkley garnered 25 points as Detroit finished first overall in 1964-65 and was going strong again during the 1965-66 season, with 20 points in 43 games, when tragedy struck.

During the second period of a January 30, 1966 game at the Olympia against the Blackhawks, Barkley was clipped in the right eye by the stick of Chicago's Doug Mohns.

"He was in great pain and couldn't see out of the eye when he came into the dressing room," Red Wings team physician Dr. Milton Kosley said after the accident.

RED WINGS ARCHIVE

"I brought my stick up under his to try and lift it off the puck, but he moved his stick and mine came right up and hit him," Mohns said. "It wasn't intentional. I'm sorry it's so serious."

Specialist Dr. Patrick Murray performed emergency surgery that night at Detroit Osteopathic Hospital to stop hemorrhaging and to repair a tear to the lunis of Barkley's right eye. Doctors speculated Barkley would be out at least a month, while cautioning that it would be several days before they could determine whether there was any permanent damage.

The worst fears were realized. Barkley underwent several more operations in attempts to repair a detached retina, but on June 7, 1966, it was announced he'd lost the sight in his right eye. Barkley was done as a player.

"Losing Doug Barkley was a real blow to the team," Gordie Howe said. "He was developing into an all-star defenseman."

Moving into coaching, Barkley served two stints behind the Red Wings bench. He coached them for the last half of the 1970-71 season, stepping down a month into the 1971-72 campaign. Barkley's second tour of duty behind the Wings bench came during the 1975-76 season.

You can still find Barkley's smiling face whenever the Calgary Flames visit Joe Louis Arena. The Lethbridge, Alberta-born Barkley works as a radio analyst on their broadcasts.

- **BORN:**
  Lethbridge, Alberta, January 6, 1937
- **ACQUIRED:**
  June 5, 1962 trade with Chicago
- **BEST SEASON WITH RED WINGS:**
  1963-64 (11-21-32)

- **TOTALS WITH RED WINGS:**
  GP-247, G-24, A-80, PTS-104
- **HONORS:**
  Led NHL defensemen in goals, 1963-64; Led Detroit in penalty minutes, 1963-64

MOTOWN Classic

Howe becomes NHL's career goals leader

Netting his 544th goal to tie Maurice (Rocket) Richard's NHL record on October 27, Gordie Howe endured a five-game wait for the record breaker and felt the pressure mounting.

"Since I tied the record, everything just seemed so much harder to do," Howe said. "I must have lost 10 pounds in that stretch."

The waiting period ended, oddly enough, while the Wings were killing off a high-sticking major to Alex Faulkner during a 3-0 win November 10 over the Habs. Marcel Pronovost started the play, passing it to Howe in the Detroit zone, who in turn fed Billy McNeill at center. Bill Gadsby joined them on a three-on-two break. Howe took a pass from McNeill and drove a low shot past Montreal goalie Charlie Hodge for No. 545. "I knew that one was in," Howe said. "I saw it all the way and I also saw it bounce out."

Howe continued his record-setting ways in the playoffs. He registered a point in a club-record 12 consecutive games and on April 5, collected his 127th point in Stanley Cup competition, becoming the career leader in that category.

RED WINGS ARCHIVE

ASSEMBLY LINE

John MacMillan

RED WINGS ARCHIVE

The Wings dealt the troubled Howie Young to Chicago for goalie Roger Crozier and defenseman Ron Ingram, then shipped Ingram to the New York Rangers for defenseman Junior Langlois. Rightwinger John MacMillan was claimed on waivers from Toronto. Defenseman Irv Spencer (Boston), center Ted Hampson (Rangers) and center/left-winger Art Stratton (Rangers) were claimed in the NHL intra-league draft, while Val Fonteyne was lost to the New York Rangers. Gerry Odrowski was dealt to Boston for defenseman Warren Godfrey. Defenseman John Miszuk and right-winger Paul Henderson graduated from the farm system.

Red Wings Facts

Most Playoff Wins By A Coach

Scotty Bowman	81
Jack Adams	52
Tommy Ivan	36
Sid Abel	29
Jacques Demers	20

Short Passes

Ian Cushenan, a Detroit defenseman in 1963-64, played only 129 NHL games, but can boast that he was a teammate of Gordie Howe, Bobby Hull and Maurice (Rocket) Richard.

167

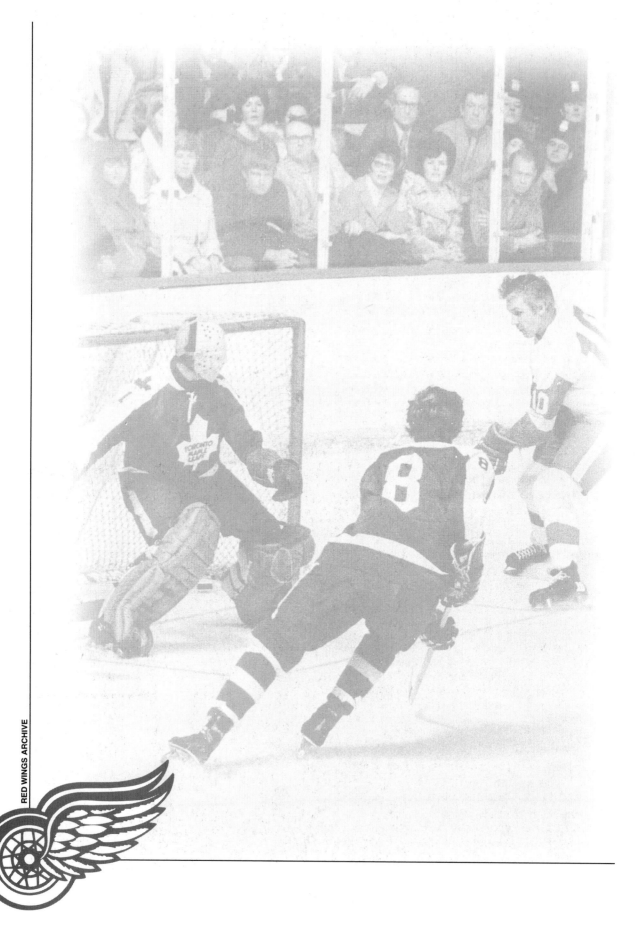

WINGS vs. LEAFS
The Detroit-Toronto Rivalry

Growing up in the Southwestern Ontario town of Leamington, about 30 miles from Detroit, Darren McCarty experienced first-hand the pulling effect of divided loyalties.

"I was always a Red Wings fan, because I idolized guys like Steve Yzerman and Bob Probert," McCarty said. "But when I was a little kid, back in the days when they had Darryl Sittler, I was a big Toronto fan."

Until the Buffalo Sabres joined the NHL in 1970, no NHL team could boast the unique geographic location of the Red Wings and the resulting conflicts which resulted.

You can see Canada from Joe Louis Arena, leaving those who live on the Canadian side of the Detroit River facing a difficult decision.

Do they cheer for the Red Wings, the team they can see? Or the Leafs, the team they see on television, who play in their home province of Ontario?

"You're drawn towards the Wings, because they're right across the river and you can go to the games," McCarty said. "But at the same time, Hockey Night In Canada is on every Saturday and there's the Leafs."

Michiganders who didn't want to root for the Red Wings naturally adopted the Leafs as their team, since they could watch them on television.

It didn't hurt that the two clubs grew to despise each other.

"Montreal-Toronto was the traditional rival," former Leaf Bob Nevin said. "Detroit-Toronto was the bitter rivalry.

"We had some pretty good battles over the years."

The first time Detroit reached the playoffs, as the Cougars in 1928-29, Toronto bounced them in the first round. Seven years later, now known as the Red Wings, Detroit whipped the Leafs in the final to capture the franchise's first Stanley Cup.

It was the first of seven Stanley Cup final meetings between the two teams and the only time the Wings came out on the winning side.

In the 1942 final, underdog Detroit raced to a 3-0 series lead, only to see Toronto rally to take the set in seven games. Three years

later, the Leafs won the first three games of the 1945 final, then the Wings took the next three. The Leafs rallied for a 2-1 decision in Game 7 to avoid Detroit's 1942 embarrassment.

Twice in their history, the Leafs captured three consecutive Stanley Cups, earning the latter two victories of each hat trick — in 1947-48 and 1948-49 and in 1962-63 and 1963-64 — at the expense of the Red Wings.

Naturally, some acrimony emerged on both sides.

"They paid us to play the other teams," Wings captain Sid Abel once remarked. "We played the Leafs for free."

In 23 playoff series between the two clubs, the Leafs hold a slight 12-11 edge. Even more amazingly, the all-time regular-season series between the two teams stood at 270-270-93 entering the 2001-02 season.

"People talk about Toronto-Montreal, but Toronto-Detroit was just as intense a rivalry," said Hall of Fame defenseman Marcel Pronovost, who experienced the pitched battles as both a Leaf and Wing.

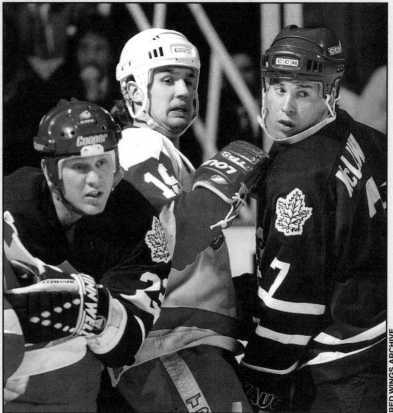

RED WINGS ARCHIVE

169

- 1964   1965 -

BACK in TIME

- **November 19, 1964**

South Vietnamese forces, supported by 105 U.S. Army Helicopters, initiated the largest attack of the war, striking a Communist guerrilla stronghold 40 miles north of Saigon.

- **January 1, 1965**

The University of Michigan won the Rose Bowl in Pasadena, California by beating Oregon State with a score of 34-7.

- **June 3, 1965**

Astronaut Edward White left his spacecraft Gemini 4 to take a 20 minute untethered stroll in space 100 miles above the Earth.

quick cuts

Most Goals
Norm Ullman: 42
Most Assists
Gordie Howe: 47
Most Points
Norm Ullman: 83
Most Penalty Minutes
Ted Lindsay: 173
Most Wins, Goaltender
Roger Crozier: 40
Lowest Goals-Against Average
Roger Crozier: 2.42
Most Shutouts
Roger Crozier: 6
NHL Award Winners
Roger Crozier - Calder Trophy
Roger Crozier & Norm Ullman
1st Team All-Stars
Bill Gadsby & Gordie Howe
2nd Team All-Stars

FINAL STANDINGS

	W	L	T	PTS	GF	GA
DETROIT	40	23	7	87	224	175
Montreal	36	23	11	83	211	185
Chicago	34	28	8	76	224	176
Toronto	30	26	14	74	204	173
New York	20	38	12	52	179	246
Boston	21	43	6	48	166	253

Playoff Results
Lost to the Chicago Blackhawks in Series "A" (4-3)
Leading Playoff Scorers
Norm Ullman (10PTS) - Gordie Howe (6PTS)
Stanley Cup Champion
Montreal Canadiens

1964-65 Season in Review

A season which started with a pair of big gambles resulted in great rewards for the Red Wings.

Positive Roger Crozier was his goalie of the future, Detroit coach-GM Sid Abel left Terry Sawchuk unprotected during the NHL's intra-league draft, losing him to Toronto.

While one veteran left, another unpacked. Left-winger Ted Lindsay, 39, ended a four-year retirement, earning a spot in training camp.

It was clear Lindsay had lost none of his fire. He scored 19 goals, led the Wings with 173 penalty minutes and earned the wrath of NHL president Campbell after refusing to pay $100 in fines he received in a January 2 game at Toronto.

"I'm not going to sit for Campbell's kangaroo court," said Lindsay, who later apologized and paid up.

Gordie Howe achieved another NHL milestone November 14 when he scored at Montreal, moving Howe past Maurice (Rocket) Richard for the career lead in combined regular-season and Stanley Cup goals with 627. A 7-3 rout of the New York Rangers December 16 was the 1,000th victory in Red Wings history.

It was a 7-4 pasting of the Rangers March 25 which clinched the Prince of Wales Trophy for the Wings. The regular-season title was the 13th earned by Detroit in 39 NHL seasons, but its first since 1956-57.

Crozier claimed the Calder Trophy as rookie of the year and was joined on the NHL First All-Star Team by center Norm Ullman, who led the NHL with 42 goals. Howe and defenseman Bill Gadsby were second-team choices.

A familiar foe awaited in the playoffs, as the Wings and Chicago met for the fourth time in five seasons. Home ice held through the first six games. Detroit posted a thrilling 4-2 win in Game 5, when Ullman scored twice in a Stanley Cup-record five seconds.

The Wings owned a 2-0 advantage after one period of Game 7, but Chicago scored four unanswered goals for a 4-2 verdict.

Despite the upset, Abel was optimistic. "Ullman, Delvecchio and (Marcel) Pronovost should have several good years left," he said. "Gadsby's near the end and we don't know how long Howe will go. But some of our younger men are maturing."

Abel was right. This team had one more great run left in the tank.

RED WINGS ARCHIVE

HOCKEYTOWN MOMENT
Wings finish first in regular season

When Detroit wrapped up top spot with a 40-23-7 slate, Sid Abel was chortling. "No one picked us for first place before the season started," the Red Wings coach-GM said. "In fact, only one person picked us for second place in a preseason poll. We were given a lot of votes for fourth and fifth place, though."

Credit for the success was given to Abel's system of employing four forward lines, allowing more rest for veterans like Gordie Howe, Ted Lindsay, Alex Delvecchio and Norm Ullman.

Abel had to admit that his team didn't figure they were first-place contenders until late in the season. "They had beaten Canadiens on Montreal ice a couple of times and were winning on the road," he said.

"They sort of looked around then and said to themselves, 'Who's any better?'"

Bill Gadsby

Bill Gadsby's on-ice outcomes changed dramatically in June of 1961, when he was finally afforded the opportunity to don the winged wheel.

A seven-time NHL All-Star, Gadsby's first 15 seasons were split between the New York Rangers and Chicago Blackhawks. In those 15 campaigns, he skated in four playoff series, never on the winning side.

"Coming to Detroit, I thought it was going to be a chance to win it all," Gadsby said. "We had some tremendous teams."

Red Wings GM Jack Adams worked diligently to make Gadsby part of those teams. His first attempt to acquire the skilled defender came on February 5, 1960, when Adams dealt Red Kelly and Billy McNeill to the Rangers for Gadsby and Eddie Shack. When both Kelly and McNeill refused to report, the deal was voided.

JOHN BUTSICARIS

Following the 1960-61 season, Adams finally got his man, sending prospect Les Hunt to Broadway for Gadsby, who brought an impressive resume to Hockeytown.

A power-play specialist who registered at least 20 points in 12 seasons, Gadsby was an outstanding puckhandler and quite comfortable joining the rush. He finished 10th in NHL scoring with 51 points for the Rangers in 1955-56 and equaled that total in 1957-58, when his 46 assists established an NHL record for rearguards which stood until Boston's Bobby Orr collected 87 helpers in 1969-70.

As a Red Wing, Gadsby reached several more milestones. On November 4, 1962, he became the first NHL defenseman to record 500 career points. February 5, 1966, Gadsby became the first player in NHL history to play 300 games for three different teams. That same season, he and teammate Gordie Howe joined former Boston star Dit Clapper as the NHL's only 20-year men.

"It had been a goal of mine to play 20 seasons," said Gadsby, who never grabbed hockey's ultimate prize.

Three times, the Wings reached the Stanley Cup final during his tenure - losing to Toronto in 1962-63 and 1963-64 and Montreal in 1965-66. After that six-game loss to the Habs, Gadsby called it quits.

"You can't dwell on the disappointment," Gadsby said of never lifting Lord Stanley's mug. "I had a wonderful career and got to play with some great players."

He coached the Wings to a 33-31-12 mark in 1968-69, but was unceremoniously dumped after winning the first two games of the 1969-70 campaign. "I must have been the first coach batting 1.000 to get canned," Gadsby said.

Gadsby still makes his home in the Detroit suburbs and was inducted into the Hockey Hall of Fame in 1970. He's also a member of both the Michigan and Alberta Sports Halls of Fame.

- **BORN:**
  Calgary, Alberta, August 8, 1927
- **ACQUIRED:**
  June 13, 1961 trade with New York Rangers
- **BEST SEASON WITH RED WINGS:**
  1961-62 (7-30-37)

- **TOTALS WITH RED WINGS:**
  GP-323, G-18, A-94, PTS-112
- **HONORS:**
  Selected to NHL Second All-Star Team, 1964-65; Played in NHL All-Star Game, 1964-65; Elected to Hockey Hall of Fame, 1970

MOTOWN Classic

Crozier shines during rookie season

Leaving three-time Vezina Trophy winner Terry Sawchuk unprotected in the NHL intra-league draft was a big gamble for Detroit coach-GM Sid Abel, who put his faith in the acrobatic Roger Crozier. Crozier didn't let him down, posting an NHL-leading 40 wins and six shutouts to carry Detroit to the Prince of Wales Trophy and earn himself the Calder Trophy as the NHL's top rookie performer.

In 1963-64, Crozier had posted the AHL's lowest goal-against average (2.34) and was voted that loop's rookie of the year, earning a 15-game stint with the Red Wings and giving Abel the idea Crozier was ready for the big leagues.

"When you analyze any hockey team, you have to start with the goalie," Abel said. "Roger was sensational for us. I said at the start of the year I thought he'd be a great one. Now I'm sure of it."

ASSEMBLY LINE

Ted Lindsay

The stirring comeback of Ted Lindsay after seven years out of a Red Wings uniform was Detroit's most notable addition. Lindsay's contract was purchased from Chicago in October. Left-winger Ron Murphy and defenseman Autry Erickson, who was named after actor Gene Autry, were also added from the Blackhawks in exchange for Art Stratton, John Miszuk and Ian Cushenan. Defenseman Gary Bergman (Montreal) and right-winger Murray Hall (Chicago) were selected in the NHL intra-league draft, while Terry Sawchuk was lost to Toronto during the draft process. Left-winger Val Fonteyne was claimed on waivers from the New York Rangers for a second tour of duty with Detroit. Center Pit Martin came up from Pittsburgh of the AHL.

Red Wings Facts

Most Goals By A Red Wing In One Game

6 Syd Howe (Feb. 3, 1944)
vs New York Rangers

5 Sergei Fedorov (Dec. 26, 1996)
vs Washington Capitals

Short Passes

Called up for a one game stint on November 11, 1964, Jim Peters centered a line of Ted Lindsay and Gordie Howe - just as his father Jim Peters Sr. did briefly in the 1950s.

- 1965   1966 -

BACK in TIME

• July 30, 1965

President Johnson signed the Medicare Social Security Bill into law at the Harry S. Truman Library in front of the former President, who had first proposed a federal program of health insurance.

• March 22, 1966

The president of General Motors apologized before a congressional committee for the company investigation into the private life of Ralph Nader, the crusader for safe cars.

• July 19, 1966

After being identified by the sole survivor of the mass slaying of eight student nurses, ex-convict Richard F. Speck was arrested for the brutal killings.

quick cuts

Most Goals
Norm Ullman & Alex Delvecchio: 31
Most Assists
Gordie Howe: 46
Most Points
Gordie Howe: 75
Most Penalty Minutes
Bryan Watson: 133
Most Wins, Goaltender
Roger Crozier: 28
Lowest Goals-Against Average
Roger Crozier: 2.78
Most Shutouts
Roger Crozier: 7
NHL Award Winners
Alex Delvecchio - Lady Byng Trophy
Jack Adams - Lester Patrick Trophy
Roger Crozier - Conn Smythe Trophy
Gordie Howe - 1st Team All-Star

FINAL STANDINGS

	W	L	T	PTS	GF	GA
Montreal	41	21	8	90	239	173
Chicago	37	25	8	82	240	187
Toronto	34	25	11	79	208	187
DETROIT	31	27	12	74	221	194
Boston	21	43	6	48	174	274
New York	18	41	11	47	195	261

Playoff Results
Defeated the Chicago Blackhawks in Series "B" (4-2)
Lost to the Montreal Canadiens in the Finals (4-2)
Leading Playoff Scorers
Alex Delvecchio (11PTS) - Norm Ullman (10PTS)
Stanley Cup Champion
Montreal Canadiens

174

1965-66 Season in Review

After a semifinal loss to Chicago in the 1964-65 playoffs, reconstruction was plentiful in Detroit.

Off-season moves brought seven new players to the Red Wings, while old guard Marcel Pronovost was traded to Toronto and Ted Lindsay retired after being claimed by the Leafs in the NHL's intra-league draft.

Meanwhile, summer work on the Olympia, which involved the knocking down of one wall, increased seating capacity from 11,700 to 14,200.

Speaking of foundations, right-winger Gordie Howe and defenseman Bill Gadsby achieved milestones simply by stepping on the ice. It was the 20th NHL campaign for both Red Wings.

Howe led the team with 75 points and earned NHL First All-Star Team status. He was also the MVP of the NHL All-Star Game after a record four-point performance in a 5-2 win over Montreal. Captain Alex Delvecchio won the Lady Byng Trophy for the second time and former Wings GM Jack Adams was the first recipient of the Lester Patrick Trophy, which recognized meritorious service to hockey in the United States. Tragedy struck the Wings January 30 when defenseman Doug Barkley lost the sight in his right eye after being clipped by the stick of Chicago's Doug Mohns.

More deals during the season garnered a pair of future Hall of Famers - defenseman Leo Boivin from Boston and center Andy Bathgate from Toronto. Bathgate, a former Hart and Art Ross Trophy winner, was impressed at how the Wings ran their show.

RED WINGS ARCHIVE

"This is the most harmonious club I've ever played for," he said. Coming home in fourth spot at 31-27-12, the Wings fell 2-1 to Chicago in the opener of the best-of-seven semifinal, then ripped the Blackhawks 7-0 in Game 2 at Chicago Stadium before a national television audience. Getting six powerplay goals from Bathgate, the Wings won the set in six games.

That momentum carried into the final and Detroit grabbed a 2-0 series lead over the Canadiens at Montreal. The defending champs regrouped to capture the next four games to retain the Stanley Cup.

"I feel sorry for them," Montreal GM Sam Pollock said of the Wings. "They played so hard and so well."

Despite finishing on the losing side, Wings goalie Roger Crozier was presented with the Conn Smythe Trophy as MVP of the playoffs.

HOCKEYTOWN MOMENT
Wings face Canadiens in finals

Opening with 3-2 and 5-2 wins on Forum ice at Montreal, the Stanley Cup looked set to come to Hockeytown for the first time in 11 seasons, but the Canadiens had other ideas. They won Games 3 and 4 at Detroit and caught a break when Wings goalie Roger Crozier suffered a knee injury in Game 4. With Crozier playing on his injured leg and defenseman Bill Gadsby laboring on a broken toe, Montreal were easy 5-1 winners in Game 5 and took the series 4-3 on

Henri Richard's controversial overtime goal just 2:20 in the extra period of Game 6.

To this day, Detroit players are convinced the goal should have been disallowed.

"Richard crashed into Roger Crozier and pushed the puck in the net with his glove," Gadsby said. "If they'd had replay back then, it could have changed the outcome."

Wings of Legend
Roger Crozier

So certain was Detroit coach-GM Sid Abel that Roger Crozier was a budding NHL superstar, he didn't protect veteran Terry Sawchuk for the 1964 NHL intra-league draft, losing his three-time Vezina Trophy winner to Toronto.

"If he doesn't do the job, I'll be sitting out there in the stands like everyone else, wondering what the devil went wrong," Abel said of Crozier, "but I have the utmost confidence in him. He's going to be a star. He's quick and he's got fast hands."

Abel's faith was rewarded. Detroit finished first and the acrobatic, 5-foot-8 Crozier led NHL netminders in wins (40) and shutouts (six), earning the Calder Trophy as NHL rookie of the year.

The joy was short-lived. That August, at his home in Bracebridge, Ont., Crozier woke up in agony with severe stomach pains.

Rushed to hospital, he was diagnosed with pancreatitis, a pancreas inflammation which poisons the blood. Infection set in and Crozier was given a 50-50 chance of survival, hovering near death for four days before pulling through.

He reported to training camp that fall down 12 pounds from his playing weight of 170 pounds, his skin a yellowish hue. The illness would plague him the remainder of his career.

Despite his ailment, Crozier backstopped Detroit to the Stanley Cup finals in 1965-66. Although the Wings lost to Montreal in a six-game set, Crozier was awarded the Conn Smythe Trophy as playoff MVP.

The Wings sent Crozier and his wife Arlene on a three-day Florida holiday during the 1965-66 season to help him recharge his batteries, but he'd call for his own time off in 1967-68.

The Wings were struggling and so was Crozier, who announced his retirement November 5, 1967. "We were winning 4-1 (against Los Angeles) after two periods and they scored five in the third to win," Crozier said. "The illness was getting to me, the moodiness and the depression were getting to me. I had to get out."

"He told me he'd lost his confidence and forgot how to play goal," Abel said. "His hair was falling out. He felt he was headed for a nervous breakdown."

RED WINGS ARCHIVE

Abel predicted Crozier would be back and the goalie returned to Detroit two months later. The Wings returned to the playoffs in 1969-70, but Crozier was dealt to the expansion Buffalo Sabres the following spring. "We felt he was no longer the goaltender he once was," Abel said.

Crozier helped Buffalo reach the Stanley Cup finals in 1974-75 and hung up his pads for good in 1977, frequently battling the effects of his illness, averaging about three attacks a season.

"All goaltenders are going to heaven," Crozier once said, "because we know all about hell."

- **BORN:**
  Bracebridge, Ontario, March 16, 1942
- **ACQUIRED:**
  June 5, 1963 trade with Chicago
- **BEST SEASON WITH RED WINGS:**
  1964-65 (40-22-7, 6 SO, 2.42 GAA)
- **TOTALS WITH RED WINGS:**
  GP-313, W-131, L-123, T-41, SO-20, GAA-2.93

- **HONORS:**
  Won Calder Trophy, 1964-65; Won Conn Smythe Trophy, 1965-66; Selected to NHL First All-Star Team, 1964-65; Selected to play in NHL All-Star Game, 1965-66

MOTOWN Classic

RED WINGS ARCHIVE

Bugsy stings the Golden Jet

His Detroit teammates knew him as "Bugsy" and "Superpest" and Bobby Hull probably called Bryan Watson plenty worse during the 1965-66 semifinal series between the Wings and Hull's Chicago Blackhawks.

Hull had won the NHL scoring title with a record 54 goals and 97 points and someone was going to have to stop him if Detroit were to advance. Wings coach Sid Abel determined Watson, normally a defenseman, was his man.

Bugsy followed Hull all over the ice, doing whatever he could to get under the Golden Jet's skin.

"My job is to keep Hull off the scoresheet and that's what I intend to do," Watson said. "Maybe he'll beat the hell out of me, I don't know. I'm not afraid of him."

Performing his task effectively, Watson held Hull to a pair of goals, while scoring twice himself as the Wings took the series in six games. Afterwards, Hull refused to talk about Watson's work. "He's gained too much publicity at my expense," the Chicago star reasoned.

ASSEMBLY LINE

Two blockbuster deals in May, 1965 sent Marcel Pronovost, Autry Erickson, Larry Jeffrey, Eddie Joyal and Lowell MacDonald to Toronto for center Andy Bathgate, right-winger Billy Harris and left-winger Gary Jarrett and Junior Langlois, Parker MacDonald, Ron Harris and Bob Dillabough to Boston for left-winger Ab McDonald and defenseman Bob McCord. Center Don McKenney was claimed on waivers from Toronto and defenseman Bryan Watson was selected from Chicago in the NHL intra-league draft. Two late-season trades with Boston saw defenseman Leo Boivin come to the Wings for Gary Doak, Steve Atkinson and Bill Lesuk and left-winger Dean Prentice arrive in exchange for Ron Murphy. Center/left-winger Parker MacDonald returned to Detroit from Boston for Pit Martin and defensemen Bob Wall and Bert Marshall were promoted from the minors.

RED WINGS ARCHIVE

Andy Bathgate

Red Wings Facts

Most 1st-Team All-Star Selections

12 - Gordie Howe
8 - Ted Lindsay
6 - Red Kelly
5 - Nicklas Lidstrom
3 - Terry Sawchuk
3 - Jack Stewart
2 - Ebbie Goodfellow
2 - Bill Quackenbush
2 - Marcel Pronovost
2 - Sid Abel
2 - Jack Adams

Short Passes

Dean Prentice, Bill Gadsby and Norm Ullman, members of Detroit's 1965-66 Stanley Cup finalist squad, all played 20 NHL seasons and never won a Cup.

BACK in TIME

- **November 8, 1966**

In his first bid for public office, Ronald Reagan, movie star turned politician, was elected governor of California.

- **January 27, 1967**

In the first tragedy of the space program, astronauts Virgil I. Grissom, Edward H. White, and Roger B. Chaffee were killed in a ground flash fire that engulfed their Apollo 1 spacecraft.

- **April 30, 1967**

Cassius Clay, known as Muhammad Ali, was stripped of his world heavyweight boxing title for refusing to be inducted into military service.

quick cuts

Most Goals
Bruce MacGregor: 28

Most Assists
Norm Ullman: 44

Most Points
Norm Ullman: 70

Most Penalty Minutes
Gary Bergman: 129

Most Wins, Goaltender
Roger Crozier: 22

Lowest Goals-Against Average
Roger Crozier: 3.35

Most Shutouts
Roger Crozier: 4

NHL Award Winners
Gordie Howe - Lester Patrick Trophy
Gordie Howe - 2nd Team All-Star

FINAL STANDINGS

	W	L	T	PTS	GF	GA
Chicago	41	17	12	94	264	170
Montreal	32	25	13	77	252	188
Toronto	32	27	11	75	204	211
New York	30	28	12	72	188	189
DETROIT	27	39	4	58	212	241
Boston	17	43	10	44	182	253

Playoff Results
Did Not Qualify
Stanley Cup Champion
Toronto Maple Leafs

1966-67 Season in Review

Coming off a Stanley Cup final appearance, the Wings acted quickly to secure Conn Smythe Trophy-winning goalie Roger Crozier, signing him to a four-year contract, the longest in Red Wings history. "I'm a pioneer," Crozier joked. "I'm just sorry that it doesn't include a Florida vacation."

Sent with his wife Arlene to Florida in January of 1966 for some rest and relaxation, by mid-season, Crozier could have used another such rest.

The loss of Doug Barkley (career-ending eye injury) and Bill Gadsby (retirement) left Leo Boivin as the only Wings rearguard with more than three seasons experience. Rookies Bob Wall and Bart Crashley, sophomore Bert Marshall and third-year man Gary Bergman completed the unit. "When Bobby Hull, Jean Beliveau and Frank Mahovlich come at the rookies, I don't know whether they'll faint or fall down," Detroit coach-GM Sid Abel lamented.

The concern was warranted. Only Chicago (264) and Montreal (252) scored more goals than the 212 netted by the Wings, but only last-place Boston (253) surrendered more markers than Detroit.

A season-opening 6-2 loss at Boston on October 19 launched two club records for road futility. The Wings lost their first 14 games away from home and gained only one point from their first 19 road games.

There were a few reasons to smile. The moment he stepped on the ice, right-winger Gordie Howe, 38, set a record by playing in his 21st NHL season. "I'll play as long as these hold out," Howe said, tapping his knees.

Center Norm Ullman (26-44-70) and Howe (25-40-65) finished 3-4 in NHL scoring and along with captain Alex Delvecchio, represented Detroit in the NHL All-Star Game. Howe won the Lester Patrick Trophy, was an NHL Second Team All-Star selection and even tried to help fill Detroit's defensive void by playing a few games on the blueline.

Nothing they tried seemed to work, though. The Wings finished fifth at 27-39-4, out of the playoffs.

HOCKEYTOWN MOMENT
"Hum Line" shines for Detroit

A bright spot in a disappointing winter for Detroit was the forward unit of left-winger Paul Henderson, center Norm Ullman and right-winger Bruce MacGregor. All three players topped 20 goals.

Dubbed the "HUM Line," because left to right, those were the first initials of each player's surname, that's exactly what the trio did.

Henderson, a right-hand shot playing his wrong wing, possessed tremendous speed, scoring 21 times in just 46 games. "When he gets away, no one can catch him," New York Rangers coach Emile Francis said after Henderson tallied four goals against them in an October 26, 1966 game.

Ullman led the Wings with 26 goals and 70 points, was a crafty playmaker and like the other two, a tenacious forechecker. "We had two men on the puck all of the time," Ullman said.

MacGregor, who scored a team-leading 28 goals, was strong along the boards and in the corners. "For whatever reason, we happened to click," MacGregor said. "There was a diversity with each player and we helped each other."

Almost as quickly as they got in tune, the HUM was silenced. Late in the 1967-68 season, Henderson and Ullman were dealt to Toronto.

179

Wings of Legend
Bruce MacGregor

The Canadian Prairies pumped many a great player into Detroit. Gordie Howe, Sid Abel, (Black) Jack Stewart, Norm Ullman and Terry Sawchuk all traveled this pipeline to Hockeytown and so did Bruce MacGregor.

"Going back to the days when Detroit had a (WHL) farm club in Edmonton, when you came up from junior, you were basically a Red Wing," said MacGregor, who signed with Detroit in 1960, launching a 673-game stint with the team.

He was just 19 when making his debut with the club during the 1960-61 season. "I didn't see a lot of ice time," said MacGregor, who garnered one assist in 12 games. "It was a big step, one year out of junior."

A step he made permanently the following season, never again playing a game in the minor leagues, establishing a reputation as a player who was willing to do the dirty work along the boards and in the corners.

RED WINGS ARCHIVE

"My style was to play and play hard," MacGregor said. "I took checks and I gave checks. I didn't mind going into the corners. I wasn't going to try and beat people up, but I didn't shy away from the physical play."

His best season as a Red Wing came in 1966-67, when MacGregor led the club with 28 goals while playing right wing on the "HUM Line" with center Norm Ullman and left-winger Paul Henderson.

"That was the biggest of my NHL thrills, the opportunity to play on a line with Norm Ullman and Paul Henderson," MacGregor said. "We were friends and our wives were good friends. We got along and I think that's part of the reason why we worked so well together."

Three times, he produced 20-goal seasons working with that unit, reaching career highs with 28 goals and 47 points in 1966-67.

The unit was broken up the following spring when Ullman and Henderson were traded to Toronto and MacGregor never again scaled such offensive heights.

"When that happened, it was a tough blow," MacGregor said of the deal. "I just never got back on my feet in Detroit."

MacGregor was traded to the New York Rangers by new GM Ned Harkness in 1970. "We had such good leadership with Sid Abel," MacGregor said. "Sid treated everyone well and he really cared about the players. When he left, those things started to change."

MacGregor jumped to the Edmonton Oilers when they were a WHA team in 1973 and stayed with that organization after his playing days, working in the front office until his retirement following the 1999-2000 season.

- **BORN:**
  Edmonton, Alberta, April 26, 1941
- **ACQUIRED:**
  Signed to pro contract, September 1, 1960
- **BEST SEASON WITH RED WINGS:**
  1966-67 (28-19-47)

- **TOTALS WITH RED WINGS:**
  GP-673, G-151, A-184, PTS-335
- **HONORS:**
  Led team in goals, 1966-67

MOTOWN Classic

Henderson "masks" his illness

Who was that masked man? None other than Detroit winger Paul Henderson. Sent to Detroit's Henry Ford Hospital in December with throat discomfort, doctors determined Henderson was suffering from trachiatis, a viral infection which caused coughing spells whenever Henderson skated in the cold air of a hockey rink.

With the injury-riddled Wings trying to shake out of their doldrums, Henderson attempted to keep playing, donning a surgical mask for practice.

"Chances are he will have to play with a surgical mask on his face, if he plays at all," Detroit coach-GM Sid Abel said.

Henderson did play a few games wearing the mask, but still experienced uncontrollable coughing spells which induced nausea.

Eventually, he was sent on an Arizona vacation to help cure the ailment.

RED WINGS ARCHIVE

ASSEMBLY LINE

Trying to shore up his blueline, Wings coach-GM Sid Abel dealt Al Lebrun, Murray Hall and Rick Morris to Chicago December 20 for rambunctious rearguard Howie Young. Center Ray Cullen was grabbed from the New York Rangers in the NHL intra-league draft. Right-winger Doug Roberts was signed as a free agent from the Michigan State Spartans. Goalie George Gardner, defenseman Bob Falkenberg, center Pete Mahovlich and center Gerry Abel, the son of the coach, came up from the farm system.

RED WINGS ARCHIVE

Howie Young

Red Wings Facts

Longest Home Winning Streak

14 - January 21 to March 25, 1965
12 - Nov. 4 to Dec. 31, 1995
12 - Jan. 12 to Feb. 29, 1996
10 - Dec. 19, 2001 to Jan. 20, 2002
9 - Feb. 3 to March 23, 1952
8 - Dec. 29, 1955 to Jan. 26, 1956
8 - Feb. 6, 1987 to March 17, 1987
8 - Jan. 24, 2001 to March 13, 2001

Short Passes

The only NHLer to be born on blades, Detroit forward Paul Henderson came into the world January 28, 1943 on a horse-drawn sleigh, just 500 yards shy of the entrance to the hospital in Kincardine, Ont.

BACK in TIME

- **December 3, 1967**
Dr. Christian N. Barnard and team of four other surgeons preformed the first heart transplant on Louis Washkansky, who died 18 days later of lung complications.

- **January 31, 1968**
Communist guerrillas launched a broad Tet (New Year) attack against more than 100 Vietnamese cities and blasted the American Embassy in Saigon.

- **June 6, 1968**
Presidential hopeful Senator Robert F. Kennedy was shot in Los Angeles just minutes after claiming victory in the California primary and died 20 hours later.

quick cuts

Most Goals
Gordie Howe: 39

Most Assists
Alex Delvecchio: 48

Most Points
Gordie Howe: 82

Most Penalty Minutes
Kent Douglas: 126

Most Wins, Goaltender
Roy Edwards: 15

Lowest Goals-Against Average
Roger Crozier: 3.30

Most Shutouts
Roger Crozier: 1

NHL Award Winners
Gordie Howe - 1st Team All-Star

FINAL STANDINGS

East Division	W	L	T	PTS	GF	GA
Montreal	42	22	10	94	236	167
New York	39	23	12	90	226	183
Boston	37	27	10	84	259	216
Chicago	32	26	16	80	216	222
Toronto	33	31	10	76	209	176
DETROIT	27	35	12	66	245	257

West Division Winner - Philadelphia

Playoff Results
Did Not Qualify
Stanley Cup Champion
Montreal Canadiens

1967-68 Season in Review

Change was on the menu, around the NHL and in Detroit. Six expansion teams doubled the league's size, while 10 players who wore the Red Wings uniform during the 1967-68 season were wearing another team's jersey when the season ended.

There was one thing the Wings couldn't change - their playoff status. With 66 points, Detroit finished sixth and last in the new East Division, collecting fewer points than every NHL team except Oakland (47). It was the first time since 1929-30 and 1930-31 that the Wings were absent from the Stanley Cup tournament in successive seasons. Defense continued to be Detroit's Achilles' heel. The Wings allowed an NHL-high 257 goals, going through 11 rearguards in search of a capable corps.

The opposition onslaught took a toll on goalie Roger Crozier, who announced his retirement after the Wings blew a 4-1 third-period lead November 5 and lost 6-4 to Los Angeles. "Goalies are funny people in a funny business," said Crozier, who returned to the team later in the season. "If they tell you to sit on the bench, you wish you were playing and if they tell you to play, you wish you were sitting on the bench. There are times when you have to force yourself to go out there."

Right-winger Gordie Howe and center Norm Ullman represented the Wings in the NHL All-Star

RED WINGS ARCHIVE

Game. Howe set up Ullman for a goal and straightened out Toronto's Mike Walton in a third-period altercation. "It wasn't a fight," Howe said. "It was just a token swing, but I wasn't going to miss."

The Wings and Leafs both looked set to miss the playoffs and on March 3, these rivals made one of the most famous trades in hockey history. Detroit sent two-thirds of the "HUM Line" - Ullman and Paul Henderson, along with Floyd Smith, to Toronto for left-winger Frank Mahovlich, centers Pete Stemkowski and Garry Unger and the rights to former NHL All-Star defenseman Carl Brewer, out of the NHL since a 1965 contract dispute with Toronto.

The move didn't get either team into the playoffs, but Detroit would soon reap benefits from the deal.

HOCKEYTOWN MOMENT
NHL Expands, Wings join Eastern Division

Doubling its size, the NHL added six new teams - the Pittsburgh Penguins, St. Louis Blues, Philadelphia Flyers, Minnesota North Stars, Los Angeles Kings and California Seals, who were renamed the Oakland Seals a month into the season - grouping them all in the West Division. The existing teams - Detroit, Montreal, Toronto, New York, Boston and Chicago - formed the East Division and the phrase "Original Six" was coined to describe them.

During the expansion draft which stocked the new clubs, the Wings lost 20 players. Notables who depart-

ed were defenseman Leo Boivin and forwards Andy Bathgate, Ab McDonald and Val Fonteyne, all claimed by Pittsburgh. Oakland grabbed forward Billy Harris, while defenseman Bob Wall went to L.A. and Minnesota snared defenseman Bryan Watson and forwards Parker MacDonald and Ray Cullen.

Roger Crozier blanked St. Louis 1-0 October 22 in Detroit's first meeting with one of the new clubs. The Wings went 14-7-3 versus the expansion six, but it wasn't easy. "They check like demons on those new teams," Gordie Howe said.

Wings of Legend

Roy Edwards

When Roy Edwards turned professional, he was literally on top of the world.

In 1958, Edwards backstopped Canada to the World Championship at Oslo, Norway, posting a perfect 7-0 record with three shutouts and an 0.86 goals-against average.

Signing with Chicago, Edwards toured the minor leagues for the next nine seasons, making stops at seven cities in four leagues.

The Pittsburgh Penguins selected Edwards from Chicago in the 1967 NHL expansion draft, then dealt him to Detroit for Hank Bassen.

Edwards began the 1967-68 season with Fort Worth of the Central League, but after posting an 8-0-1 slate with four shutouts and a 1.33 GAA in his first nine games, he was elevated to Detroit.

Roger Crozier had shocked the Wings by announcing his retirement and in one day, Edwards, 30, went from career minor-leaguer to Detroit's No. 1 goalie, a position he refused to surrender. Edwards led the Wings in games and wins for the next four seasons.

His good luck appeared to run out December 6, 1970, during a 3-0 loss to St. Louis. While scoring for the Blues, Craig Cameron tumbled into Edwards, who fell back and hit his head on the goal post, suffering a hairline fracture of the skull.

Unable to shake headaches and dizzy spells, Edwards announced his retirement June 4, 1971. "The organization thought highly of Roy's goaltending abilities, but he owes his health and well-being to himself and his family," Detroit GM Ned Harkness said.

"Should he regain his health and consider returning to the game, the door to the Wings would always be open."

Edwards did reconsider, but made his comeback with the Penguins, who claimed him on waivers in the

RED WINGS ARCHIVE

spring of 1971. The Wings purchased his contract from Pittsburgh prior to the 1972-73 season and back with Detroit, Edwards enjoyed his finest season, winning 27 games and posting an NHL-leading six shutouts.

"It's confidence," Edwards said. "I don't worry about giving up bad goals the way I did. If you worry when you're playing, it hurts you." Perhaps his injury gave Edwards more perspective. Or maybe he simply appreciated the second chance. Whatever the reason for his change of attitude, he never revealed it.

"I'm not going to go into that," Edwards said. "I'm not going to talk about it. I just wish I had it 10 years ago."

As quickly as he returned, Edwards was gone again. After losing his first three decisions in 1973-74, he retired, making it stick this time.

"Detroit has been a fine organization and I enjoyed my finest years in professional hockey while in a Red Wing uniform," Edwards said.

- **BORN:**
Seneca Township, Ontario, March 12, 1937
- **ACQUIRED:**
September 7, 1967 trade with Pittsburgh
- **BEST SEASON WITH RED WINGS:**
1972-73 (27-17-7, 6 SO, 2.63 GAA)

- **TOTALS WITH RED WINGS:**
GP-222, W-90, L-80, T-34, SO-12, GAA-2.94
- **HONORS:**
Led NHL in shutouts, 1972-73; Led team in shutouts three times; Lead team in wins five times; Led team in GAA four times

184

MOTOWN Classic

Howe leads Wings in goal scoring for 15th time

Ageless and timeless, right-winger Gordie Howe continued to defy his biological clock, leading the Wings in scoring with 39-43-82 totals, good for third in the league and his 10th NHL First All-Star Team selection. Howe also produced club highs by netting 10 power-play goals and four game winners and although it looked as if it were effortless, he was the first to admit that Father Time was taking a toll on his 40-year-old body.

"I work harder now than I did 10 years ago," Howe said. "I also need a lot more rest before a game and now I generally stay in bed the day of a game. I really hate to be bothered then."

ASSEMBLY LINE

Blockbusters were in order this season, as the Wings pulled the trigger on three deals involving four or more players. The biggest saw Norm Ullman, Paul Henderson and Floyd Smith move to Toronto in exchange for left-winger Frank Mahovlich, centers Garry Unger and Pete Stemkowski and the rights to defenseman Carl Brewer. Left-winger John Brenneman was acquired from St. Louis for Craig Cameron, Larry Hornung and Don Giesebrecht. Brenneman, Bert Marshall and Ted Hampson went to the Oakland Seals for defenseman Kent Douglas. Bob McCord was dealt to Minnesota for defenseman Jean-Guy Talbot. Talbot was later lost on waivers to St. Louis. Left-wingers Nick Libett and Gary Marsh, defenseman Jim Watson and right-winger Ron Anderson were promoted from the farm system.

Garry Unger

Red Wings Facts

Highest Winning Percentage By A Coach

1. Tommy Ivan - .653 (262-118-90)
2. Scotty Bowman - .648 (410-203-88)
3. Jimmy Skinner - .591 (262-118-90)
4. Bryan Murray - .568 (124-91-29)
5. Jack Adams - .512 (413-390-161)
6. Jacques Demers - .502 (137-136-47)
7. Sid Abel - .501 (340-339-132)

Short Passes

Michigan Tech center Al Karlander, selected 15th overall by Detroit in 1967, was the first U.S. college player ever picked in the NHL amateur draft. Karlander played for the Wings from 1969-73.

- 1968  1969 -

BACK in TIME

• **October 20, 1968**

In a move that shocked the world, former first lady Jacqueline Kennedy married slipping magnate Aristotle Onassis on the Greek Island of Skorpios.

• **March 2, 1969**

Powered by four Rolls Royce Olympus engines, the French-British Concorde made its maiden flight when it jetted into the air in Toulouse, France and stayed airborne for 28 minutes.

• **July 20, 1969**

Apollo 11 American astronauts Neil A. Armstrong and Edwin E. Aldrin walked on the Moon's surface while Michael Collins orbited the Moon aboard the command ship.

quick cuts

Most Goals
Frank Mahovlich: 49

Most Assists
Gordie Howe: 59

Most Points
Gordie Howe: 103

Most Penalty Minutes
Bob Baun: 121

Most Wins, Goaltender
Roy Edwards: 18

Lowest Goals-Against Average
Roy Edwards: 2.54

Most Shutouts
Roy Edwards: 4

NHL Award Winners
Alex Delvecchio - Lady Byng Trophy
Gordie Howe - 1st Team All-Star
Frank Mahovlich - 2nd Team All-Star

FINAL STANDINGS

East Division	W	L	T	PTS	GF	GA
Montreal	46	19	11	103	271	202
Boston	42	18	16	100	303	221
New York	41	26	9	91	231	196
Toronto	35	26	15	85	234	217
DETROIT	33	31	12	78	239	221
Chicago	34	33	9	77	280	246

West Division Winner - St. Louis

Playoff Results
Did Not Qualify
Stanley Cup Champion
Montreal Canadiens

1968-69 Season in Review

Seeking to halt their woeful ways, the Wings reached back into their glorious past. Sid Abel stepped from behind the bench to focus solely on his GM's duties, handing the coaching reins to former Wings defenseman Bill Gadsby.

Gadsby wasted little time letting the team know who was boss. When Toronto edged Detroit 2-1 in the home opener at the Olympia, he criticized his players' lack of condition.

"We looked like we weren't in shape," Gadsby said. "Some of them could hardly stagger to the bench at the end of a shift."

The team was also seeking to get goalie Roger Crozier to shape up and just before the start of the season, moved to acquire veteran Terry Sawchuk from Los Angeles. Abel felt Sawchuk could serve as a mentor to the temperamental netminder, but Sawchuk showed them he still had some game left, posting back-to-back wins against Oakland and Toronto in late January, to extend Detroit's Olympia unbeaten streak to 12 games.

In his first full season as a Red Wing, left-winger Frank Mahovlich exploded for 49 goals, tying Howe's club record. Mahovlich collected four hat-tricks and along with linemates Gordie Howe and Alex Delvecchio, set an NHL record by combining for 118 goals. At 41, in his 23rd NHL season, Howe became the first Red Wing to crack the 100-point barrier, garnering 103 points.

Howe was selected to the NHL's First All-Star Team, while Mahovlich was a Second Team selection.

RED WINGS ARCHIVE

Both players also skated for Detroit in the NHL All-Star Game.

The Wings clung to the fourth and final playoff spot in the East for most of the season, thanks to two factors - a potent offense and their home-ice dominance. Detroit was 23-8-7 at the Olympia. As late as March 13, Detroit was still fourth, but successive losses to St. Louis and the New York Rangers dropped them to fifth. Owner Bruce Norris ordered Abel to go behind the bench down the stretch, but hobbled by a dismal 10-23-5 road mark, Detroit missed the playoffs. It marked the first time in history the franchise was absent from post-season play for three successive seasons.

HOCKEYTOWN MOMENT
Howe scores 700th goal

The Motor City was ready for the moment, but apparently the Steel City was unimpressed.

Detroit's Gordie Howe became the NHL's first 700-goal scorer December 4 at Pittsburgh's Civic Arena before a sparse gathering of 4,451, when he whipped a shot from the slot past Penguins goalie Les Binkley in a 7-2 victory.

Howe's only disappointment was that the moment didn't come at the Olympia. "They had 700 balloons ready for me in the rafters," he said.

The historic tally was part of a record season for Howe, who finished third in NHL scoring with 44-59-103 totals. His assists and points totals from 1968-69 still rank as club marks for a right-winger.

RED WINGS ARCHIVE

187

Wings of Legend

Frank Mahovlich

As a rookie, Frank Mahovlich beat out Bobby Hull for the Calder Trophy. In 1960-61, hockey fans anticipated Mahovlich would be a 50-goal scorer when he netted 35 times in Toronto's first 38 games and many expressed their disappointment when Mahovlich finished with 48 goals.

So went the on-again, off-again love affair between Maple Leafs fans and "The Big M."

By the time Mahovlich arrived in Detroit late in the 1967-68 season, his battles with the Toronto fans and coach Punch Imlach were well-documented.

Mahovlich feared he wouldn't be accepted as a Red Wing. "There was pressure at first," Mahovlich said. "Some of them heard the Frank Mahovlich stories and they were wondering if they were true. And I was never the kind of guy who tried to sell myself."

A sales pitch wouldn't be necessary, especially after Mahovlich lit the red lamp 49 times during the 1968-69 season.

Combined with Gordie Howe and Alex Delvecchio, this latest incarnation of the Production Line proved to be the most productive. Left-winger Mahovlich tallied 49 goals in 1968-69, tying the club mark for goals set by right-winger Howe in 1952-53. Howe produced 44-59-103 totals, finishing third in NHL scoring and becoming the first Red Wing to hit triple figures in points. Center Delvecchio added 25 goals and 83 points, earning his third Lady Byng Trophy.

Both Howe and Mahovlich were tabbed as NHL All-Stars. Mahovlich scored twice in the NHL All-Star Game and was named MVP.

"Frank skates for the holes," Howe said, describing Mahovlich's uncanny knack for finding open ice. "I've never seen a guy who could skate for those holes better than Frank."

The deal also united Frank with younger brother Pete, who became known as "The Little M."

"I would much sooner play with Frank than against him," said Pete, who was traded to Montreal in 1969.

Frank would soon follow. He scored 38 goals for the Wings in 1969-70, but had just 14 when he was

RED WINGS ARCHIVE

dealt to the Habs 38 games into the 1970-71 campaign.

"Leaving Detroit was tough," Frank Mahovlich said. "I had two really good years there and enjoyed playing with the Red Wings." The elder Mahovlich won six Stanley Cups in his career and joined the 500-goal club March 21, 1973. He was inducted into the Hockey Hall of Fame in 1981.

Today, Frank Mahovlich plays in the political arena. He's a member of the Canadian Senate.

- **BORN:**
  Timmins, Ontario, January 10, 1938
- **ACQUIRED:**
  March 3, 1968 trade with Toronto
- **BEST SEASON WITH RED WINGS:**
  1968-69 (49-29-78)
- **TOTALS WITH RED WINGS:**
  GP-198, G-108, A-88, PTS-196

- **HONORS:**
  Selected to NHL Second All-Star Team, 1968-69, 1969-70; Played in NHL All-Star Game, 1968-69, 1969-70; Elected to Hockey Hall of Fame, 1981

MOTOWN Classic

Delvecchio becomes third player to reach 1,000 points

The man in the middle of Detroit's explosive new forward unit made himself part of another unique trio on February 16, 1969.

In a 6-3 win over the Los Angeles Kings, Red Wings center Alex Delvecchio collected an assist on a goal by Gordie Howe for his 1,000th point in NHL regular-season play.

The Red Wings captain joined linemate Howe (1960) and Montreal's Jean Beliveau (1968) in this exclusive club, garnering the helper in his 1,143rd NHL game. By coincidence, Beliveau got his 1,000 point against the Red Wings, meaning Detroit was involved in all three milestone games.

Delvecchio capped his fine season by capturing his third Lady Byng Trophy as the NHL's best combination of talent and gentlemanly conduct.

RED WINGS ARCHIVE

ASSEMBLY LINE

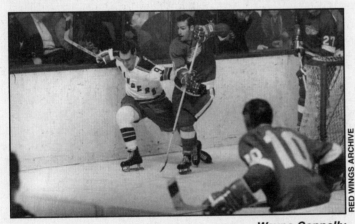

RED WINGS ARCHIVE

Wayne Connelly

The Wings dealt center Jim Peters Jr. to Los Angeles to give Terry Sawchuk his third chance to wear a Red Wings jersey. The first time Sawchuk pulled on a Detroit sweater, back in 1950, Jim Peters Sr. was his teammate. Danny Lawson was traded to Minnesota for Wayne Connelly. Howie Young, Doug Roberts, Chris Worthy and Gary Jarrett were shipped to Oakland for defensemen Bob Baun and Ron Harris, while Ron Anderson was traded to Los Angeles for defenseman Poul Popiel, a native of Sollested, Denmark. Right-winger Ed Hatoum, a native of Beirut, Lebanon, was called up from the minors, as were right-winger Rene Leclerc and left-winger Hank Monteith. Goaltender Jim Rutherford was Detroit's top pick in the amateur draft.

Red Wings Facts

Most Games Played As A Red Wing

Gordie Howe - 1,687
Alex Delvecchio -1,549
Steve Yzerman - 1,362
Marcel Pronovost - 983
Norm Ullman - 875
Ted Lindsay - 862
Nick Libett - 861
Red Kelly - 846
Syd Howe - 793
Nicklas Lidstrom - 853
Sergei Fedorov - 828
Terry Sawchuk - 734
Reed Larson - 708
Gary Bergman - 706

Short Passes

A 3-2 decision over the Toronto Maple Leafs on January 26, 1969 was the record 352nd and final victory for goaltender Terry Sawchuk in a Red Wings uniform.

- 1969 ☆ 1970 -

BACK in TIME

- **November 15, 1969**

Two hundred and fifty thousand Vietnam war protesters marched in Washington D.C., insisting that President Nixon's policy of gradual withdrawal was not good enough.

- **January 19, 1970**

Inflation reached 6.1 percent, the highest it had been since the Korean War.

- **April 10, 1970**

Due to personal, business and musical differences, Paul McCartney announced that he was leaving the Beatles, thereby disbanding one of the most successful pop groups in history.

quick cuts

Most Goals
Garry Unger: 42
Most Assists
Alex Delvecchio: 47
Most Points
Gordie Howe: 71
Most Penalty Minutes
Gary Bergman: 122
Most Wins, Goaltender
Roy Edwards: 24
Lowest Goals-Against Average
Roy Edwards: 2.59
Most Shutouts
Roy Edwards: 2
NHL Award Winners
Gordie Howe - 1st Team All-Star
Frank Mahovlich &
Carl Brewer - 2nd Team All-Star

FINAL STANDINGS

East Division	W	L	T	PTS	GF	GA
Chicago	45	22	9	99	250	170
Boston	40	17	19	99	303	221
DETROIT	40	21	15	95	246	199
New York	38	22	16	92	246	189
Montreal	38	22	16	92	244	201
Toronto	29	34	13	71	222	242

West Division Winner - St. Louis

Playoff Results
Lost to the Chicago Blackhawks in first round (4-0)
Leading Playoff Scorer
Wayne Connelly (4PTS)
Stanley Cup Champion
Boston Bruins

1969-70 Season in Review

A season which started and finished in bizarre fashion resulted in Detroit's first playoff appearance since the 1965-66 Stanley Cup final. For the first time since 1963-64, the Wings opened with consecutive victories and they celebrated by firing the coach.

Coach Bill Gadsby was let go and GM Sid Abel returned behind the bench. Abel guided the Wings to third place with a 40-21-15 slate, including a 20-10-8 road slate, Detroit's first winning season away from the Olympia since 1956-57.

Right-winger Gordie Howe led the team with 71 points - good for ninth in the league, the first season since 1948-49 that Howe wasn't among the NHL's top five scorers. His three-goal performance November 2 in a 4-3 win over Pittsburgh was Howe's record 18th and final hat trick as a Red Wing.

Center Garry Unger scored 42 goals and left-winger Frank Mahovlich netted 38 times for a team which featured seven 20-goal scorers. Howe was an NHL First Team All-Star choice, while Mahovlich and defenseman Carl Brewer, who ended a four-season retirement to join the Wings, both earned Second Team honors. All three skated in the NHL All-Star Game and Howe scored the game winner as the East downed the West 4-1.

RED WINGS ARCHIVE

The final game of the season at New York was irrelevant to the Wings, but was huge to the Rangers and Montreal, battling for the final playoff spot. Abel rested several regulars and the Rangers won 9-5. Coupled with Montreal's 10-2 loss to Chicago, it put New York in the playoffs and left several Canadiens fans furious with Detroit for not icing its best lineup.

"It's my prerogative to play who I want to play," Abel said. Chicago swept the Wings aside in the first round of the playoffs. Coupled with Detroit's losses in the final four games of the 1965-66 final against Montreal, the eight straight setbacks assembled a team-record Stanley Cup losing streak, as did the club's five consecutive home-ice playoff defeats.

HOCKEYTOWN MOMENT

Wings return to playoffs after three year absence

Just call it the spring of 4-2. Earning a place in the Stanley Cup playoffs for the first time since the 1967 NHL expansion, Detroit drew Chicago in the quarterfinals, the sixth post-season meeting between the two teams since the 1960-61 Stanley Cup final.

It wouldn't be as memorable as several of those series, but it certainly would prove symmetrical. Chicago swept the series, winning every game by a 4-2 count. It's the only time in NHL history that a four-game sweep was accomplished with the same final result in each contest.

"The scores show every game was up for grabs," Detroit coach-GM Sid Abel said.

Gordie Howe, playing despite a severe cold which left him unable to talk, scored twice in the series. Howe's tally in Game 3 would prove to be his final Stanley Cup goal in a Red Wings uniform.

Garry Unger

Garry Unger was the "Mr. Mod" of the Red Wings in the late 1960s. Unger was one of the first NHLers to add to his wardrobe the bright colors of the mod style of clothing which was popular in that era, also allowing his flowing blond locks to grow to shoulder length.

A western cowboy from the Alberta prairies, Unger owned 15 games of NHL experience when he arrived in Detroit as the sleeper in the March 3, 1968 trade with Toronto which also brought forwards Frank Mahovlich and Pete Stemkowski and defenseman Carl Brewer to Detroit.

"I hated to let Unger go untried" Toronto coach Punch Imlach said. Each member of this quartet of former Leafs played a key role in Detroit's return to the playoffs in 1969-70. Mahovlich and Brewer, paired with his old Toronto blue-line partner Bobby Baun, were NHL All-Stars, while Stemkowski and Unger blossomed on Detroit's second line with Wayne Connelly.

Stemkowski scored 25 times, Connelly netted 23 and Unger tallied a team-leading 42 times, with some of the credit being owed to a beauty queen.

Unger was stuck at seven goals around Christmas when Miss America, Pam Eldred, was invited to drop the puck in a ceremonial faceoff before a game at the Olympia. Unger promised in the faceoff circle that he'd score for her, but failed in his quest. After the game, he presented her with a stick, a puck and a guarantee to deliver on his goal, which he did, 35 times before season's end.

During the summer, Unger - whose hobbies included calf-roping, horseback riding, water-skiing and speedboat racing - was thrown from his mount while breaking a horse and cracked three small bones in his back. "I was in a wheelchair all through training camp

RED WINGS ARCHIVE

and the exhibition season, but I was in the lineup on opening night," recalled Unger, who would play an NHL-record 914 consecutive games.

If only he'd gotten a haircut, most of the those games might have been with the Red Wings.

Ned Harkness was Detroit's new coach in 1970-71 and he didn't care for Unger's look, ordering him to get a trim, going as far as to sketch potential hairstyle options for Unger on a napkin.

"What if the latest fashion became brush cuts again?" Unger asked.

"Would he have ordered me to grow my hair long?

"To me, the whole thing was irrelevant."

Harkness thought otherwise and traded Unger to St. Louis, where he was selected to play in seven straight NHL All-Star Games.

- **BORN:**
  Calgary, Alberta, December 7, 1947
- **ACQUIRED:**
  March 3, 1968 trade with Toronto
- **BEST SEASON WITH RED WINGS:**
  1969-70 (42-24-66)

- **TOTALS WITH RED WINGS:**
  GP-216, G-84, A-68, PTS-152
- **HONORS:**
  Led team in goals, 1969-70

Perfect Gadsby gets the axe

Detroit was tied for first place when coach Bill Gadsby arrived at the Olympia for an October 16 game with Minnesota. He left without a job. "I'm really shocked," said Gadsby, who was dismissed before the game with a 2-0 record. "There's no justice."

Wings owner Bruce Norris felt his team was underachieving, despite the unblemished record. "I thought we had a good team last year, yet we finished out of the playoffs," Norris said. "There were things in training camp and the exhibition season about which I wasn't happy. In my mind, the team was headed in the same direction as last year."

GM Sid Abel returned the coaching position to his portfolio, but he wasn't pleased with the additional duties. "I like coaching, but I don't like the idea of the two jobs," Abel said. "It's too much for one person."

Abel insisted he'd immediately hire a new coach, but instead stayed behind the bench the rest of the season.

RED WINGS ARCHIVE

ASSEMBLY LINE

The Wings acquired left-winger Garry Monahan from Montreal for Pete Mahovlich, then shipped Monahan and Brian Gibbons to Los Angeles for defensemen Dale Rolfe and Larry Johnston and left-winger Gary Croteau. Terry Sawchuk and Sandy Snow went to the New York Rangers for left-winger Larry Jeffrey, a former Wing. Defenseman Mike McMahon was claimed on waivers from Chicago and traded to Pittsburgh for right-winger Billy Dea, previously a Wing from 1956-58. Center Al Karlander and right-winger Doug Volmar were elevated from the farm system.

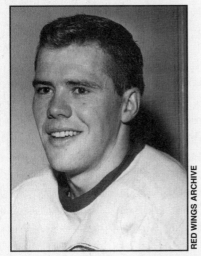

Bill Dea

RED WINGS ARCHIVE

Red Wings Facts

Best Winning Percentage Against An Opponent

Atlanta Thrashers	1.000
Tampa Bay Lightning	.804
Columbus Blue Jackets	.800
San Jose Sharks	.767
Nashville Predators	.738

Short Passes

The Wings traded center Pete Mahovlich to Montreal for left-winger Garry Monahan on June 6, 1969. Six years and one day earlier on June 5, 1963, Monahan and Mahovlich were selected 1-2 in the first NHL amateur draft.

- 1970 · 1971 -

BACK in TIME

• **December 31, 1970**
President Nixon signed the National Air Quality Control Act, designed to cut air pollution.

• **March 29, 1971**
Ford Motor Company recalled 220,000 Pintos because their engines were suspected of being prone to fire.

• **June 13, 1971**
Known as the Pentagon Papers, The New York Times began to publish this secret study of the Vietnam War conducted by the Department of Defense.

quick cuts

Most Goals
Tom Webster: 30
Most Assists
Tom Webster: 37
Most Points
Tom Webster: 67
Most Penalty Minutes
Gary Bergman: 149
Most Wins, Goaltender
Roy Edwards: 11
Lowest Goals-Against Average
Roy Edwards: 3.39
Most Shutouts
Jim Rutherford: 1
NHL Award Winners
None

FINAL STANDINGS

East Division	W	L	T	PTS	GF	GA
Boston	57	14	7	121	399	207
New York	49	18	11	109	259	177
Montreal	42	23	13	97	291	216
Toronto	37	33	8	82	248	211
Buffalo	24	39	15	63	217	291
Vancouver	24	46	8	56	229	296
DETROIT	22	45	11	55	209	308

West Division Winner - Chicago

Playoff Results
Did Not Qualify
Stanley Cup Champion
Montreal Canadiens

1970-71 Season in Review

Their third coach in as many seasons welcomed the Wings to training camp for a season which would contain more turmoil than any in Red Wings history. Ned Harkness owned a fine pedigree from U.S. college hockey, but had no pro coaching experience and that quickly led to problems.

"He thinks if you're not skating, you're not working," center Garry Unger said. "You can do that for 30 games in college hockey, but not for 80 in the NHL." Harkness and Unger continued to feud, with the coach ordering the player three times to the barber to get his long hair clipped. Perhaps there was some sort of Samson effect on the Wings, who started 2-6-1, launching a downward spiral in which they continued to sink.

"I never saw a situation crumble so quickly," left-winger Frank Mahovlich said. "Usually, when a team fails, it happens gradually, but this collapse happened so fast. There was a power struggle going on with management and we knew it had to affect us."

The low point came January 2, when the Wings were whipped 13-0 at Toronto, the most lopsided defeat in club history. A players-only meeting was held five days later in Buffalo and they took a petition to GM Sid Abel, requesting the removal of Harkness. The request was relayed to owner Bruce Norris, who instead removed Abel, promoted Harkness to GM and elevated Doug Barkley from Fort Worth of the Central League to take over as coach.

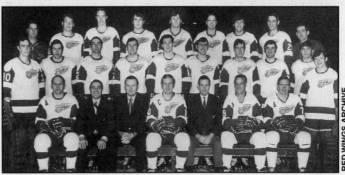

RED WINGS ARCHIVE

Harkness dramatically altered his lineup with a series of trades. Unger went to St. Louis, with ex-Michigan star Red Berenson coming to Detroit. Mahovlich was shipped to Montreal for a trio of young players, including right-winger Mickey Redmond. Right-winger Tom Webster, acquired from Buffalo for goalie Roger Crozier, posted 30-37-67 totals, becoming the only rookie in Wings history to led the club in all three offensive categories.

When Harkness was done, only seven regulars remained from the 1969-70 playoff team, but the changes had little effect. Detroit finished last in the seven-team East Division, behind the first-year expansion teams from Buffalo and Vancouver. The Wings' 55-point total from 78 games was their lowest since a 50-point effort during a 50-game campaign in 1946-47.

The era Wings fans would refer to as, "The Darkness With Harkness" was in full swing.

HOCKEYTOWN MOMENT

Ned Harkness named new coach of the Wings

Ned Harkness and Tommy Lynch

RED WINGS ARCHIVE

Rumors at the conclusion of the 1969-70 season suggested Ned Harkness would be named coach of the Red Wings and those rumors were confirmed April 10, 1970, when he was awarded the position.

The Ottawa-born Harkness became a naturalized U.S. citizen in 1949 and launched a successful coaching career in the NCAA, guiding RPI to a national championship in 1954 and taking Cornell to titles in 1967 and 1970. The Big Red posted a perfect 27-0-0 record in claiming the 1970 crown.

Harkness was the first NCAA coach to guide an NHL team, but he lasted just 38 games and was 12-22-4 when Sid Abel was fired as GM and Harkness was promoted to that position, with Doug Barkley taking over as coach.

Abel pulled no punches when asked his assessment of Harkness behind the bench. "I might as well be blunt," Abel said. "He can't coach."

Nick Libett

The Red Wings thought so highly of young Nick Libett, they sponsored the entire Stratford, Ontario minor-hockey system in 1960 to ensure they'd retain his NHL rights.

Libett was 15 at the time.

The investment paid off when Libett broke in with Detroit in 1967-68, launching a 14-season NHL career as an effective, two-way left-winger. Six times, Libett attained the 20-goal plateau, netting a career high of 31 goals in 1971-72. It was without the puck where Libett was most respected, however. His work as a checker rated him among the best in the NHL.

"We'd play against Montreal and we'd play against the (New York) Rangers," Libett said. "They had right wings like (Hall of Famers) Guy Lafleur and Rod Gilbert and I'd have to check them."

He checked them pretty well. Just ask Gilbert. "Every time I played against him, I cringed, because I knew I wouldn't have any room and I was going to have a tough time," Gilbert said.

"Checking was different then," Libett said. "Today, checkers can have only four goals. I wasn't a prolific scorer, but I knew I could score 20 or 25 (a season)."

A durable, hard-working sort, Libett missed only two games his first six NHL seasons and once played 389 consecutive games. "He had that determination and drive you'd like to see all the players on your team have," noted Dave Lewis, Libett's NHL opponent for seven seasons. "You'd slow him down and he'd keep coming. You'd hit him and he'd get back up. And he was relentless as a checker."

Libett performed these challenging and often dirty tasks for a team which made the playoffs just twice during his 12 seasons as a Red Wing. "Playing on a bad team, it's difficult, but the motivation comes from within," he explained. "I like to think I have a lot of pride."

Libett represented the Wings in the 1976-77 NHL All-Star Game and was picked to play for Canada at the 1979 World Championships. He was dealt by the Wings to Pittsburgh in 1979, where he concluded his playing days following the 1980-81 season.

After hockey, Libett won a 1988 battle with non-Hodgkin's lymphoma. "It gets your priorities straightened around," he said of his fight with cancer. Though he never played for a legitimate contender, Libett recalls his Red Wings career with fondness.

"I wouldn't say it was the wrong place, because I enjoyed my time," he said.

RED WINGS ARCHIVE

- **BORN:**
  Stratford, Ontario, December 9, 1945
- **ACQUIRED:**
  Signed to pro contract, March 22, 1966
- **BEST SEASON WITH RED WINGS:**
  1971-72 (31-22-53)

- **TOTALS WITH RED WINGS:**
  GP-861, G-217, A-250, PTS-467
- **HONORS:**
  Served as team captain, 1973-74, 1978-79; Played in NHL All-Star Game, 1976-77; Played for Canada, 1979 World Championships

MOTOWN Classic

Howe calls it quits

Falling out of the NHL's top-10 scorers for the first time since the 1940s and struggling with torn rib-cage muscles and arthritic wrists, Gordie Howe, 43, announced his retirement after 25 seasons as a Red Wing. "I could play one more year and I could play very badly," suggested Howe, who posted 23-29-52 totals in 1970-71 and was employed briefly as a defenseman by coach Ned Harkness in a failed experiment.

Howe finished his Red Wings days with 1,687 games played and 786-1,023-1,809 totals, all club records.

Rookie Tom Webster, Detroit's leading scorer in 1970-71, roomed on the road with Howe and admitted he had to get used to sleeping in the same room with a legend. "You'd be just nodding off, then you'd roll over, look at the other bed and think, 'That's Gordie Howe,' and you'd be wide awake again," Webster said.

RED WINGS ARCHIVE

ASSEMBLY LINE

A season which saw addresses change frequently began with an expansion draft that added Buffalo and Vancouver to the league. The Sabres claimed Jim Watson from the Wings, while the Canucks took Ed Hatoum and Poul Popiel. Shortly after the draft was completed, Detroit dealt Roger Crozier to Buffalo for right-winger Tom Webster. Pete Stemkowski went to the New York Rangers for center Don Luce. Defensemen Arnie Brown and Mike Robitaille and center Tom Miller were also acquired from the Rangers for Larry Brown and Bruce MacGregor, while a third deal with New York saw left-winger Jim Krulicki added for Dale Rolfe. Frank Mahovlich was shipped to Montreal for right-winger Mickey Redmond, right-winger Bill Collins and center Guy Charron. Center Red Berenson and right-winger Tim Ecclestone were picked up from St. Louis for Garry Unger and Wayne Connelly. Right wing Bob Cook was purchased from Vancouver. Defenseman Serge Lajeunesse was Detroit's top draft pick, while goalies Gerry Gray and Don McLeod, defensemen Gerry Hart and Jim Niekamp and left-winger Jim Shires moved up from the minors.

Mickey Redmond

RED WINGS ARCHIVE

Red Wings Facts

Longest Unbeaten Streaks

15 Games (8 wins, 7 ties)
Nov. 27 thru Dec. 28, 1952

13 Games
Dec. 25, 1932 thru Jan. 30, 1933

13 Games
Jan. 21, 1934 thru Feb. 20, 1934

13 Games
Mar. 3, 1996 thru Mar. 22, 1996

13 Games
Jan. 31, 2001 thru Mar. 2, 2001

Short Passes

Detroit defenseman Ron Harris practiced with five-pound lead weights in each shin guard, figuring the added weight developed increased strength. "If I find my legs feeling loggy during a game, then I put the weights on in practice for a while," Harris said.

BUDD LYNCH and BRUCE MARTYN

Gordie Howe, Ted Lindsay, Sid Abel, Red Kelly, Marcel Pronovost, Terry Sawchuk.

They were the heart and soul of the Detroit Red Wings' dynasty.

Budd Lynch and Bruce Martyn were the voices who described the greatness, serving as team broadcasters, on radio and television, sometimes doing both during the same game.

"We'd switch from the radio booth to the television booth between periods," Martyn recalled. "We both had black, horn-rimmed glasses and one night, we got them mixed up.

"Well, he's far-sighted and I'm near-sighted, so he couldn't read and I couldn't see for about a period until somebody ran down and changed our glasses."

Lynch was working for CKLW radio in Windsor, Ontario when World War II broke out. Lynch enlisted and was shipped overseas in 1942.

Serving with the Essex Scottish of the Canadian Armed Forces, he attained the rank of major and landed at Normandy, France during the D-Day invasion.

Lynch took a direct hit in the shoulder from a German 88-millimeter shell during the Allied assault on Caen, France in July of 1944. The seriousness of his wounds resulted in the amputation of Lynch's right arm.

After recuperating, he served in the radio branch of public relations at the Canadian Military Headquarters in London, England, rejoining the announcing staff of CKLW following the war.

WWJ asked Lynch to broadcast 12 Red Wings games in 1949-50 and was so impressive, the station hired him to call all 70 games the following season. Lynch added radio broadcasts to his duties in 1960 and was joined in the booth by Martyn in 1964.

"We had some great times together and we really hit it off," Lynch said.

"The phrase Bruce uses all the time is, 'He had no brother, I had no brother, but we are brothers.'"

Martyn, who first called hockey games in Sault Ste. Marie, also handled Detroit Lions and Michigan State football before earning his place as a voice of the Red Wings.

"I moved right into Budd's territory, but we were equal partners," Martyn said. "We developed a friendship that just continued and for thirty years, we never did have a disagreement."

Lynch retired from broadcasting in 1974-75 and moved in the Wings' public relations department. His dulcet tones can still be heard on the public-address system at every Detroit home game.

Martyn switched exclusively to radio in 1986 and retired following the 1995 Stanley Cup finals, but was invited back by new radio voice Ken Kal to call the second period of Game 4 of the 1997 finals with Philadelphia.

As it turned out, Martyn described Darren McCarty's goal which proved to be Detroit's first Cup-winning tally in 42 seasons.

Both men received the highest honor of their profession — the Foster Hewitt Memorial Award, induction into the broadcasting wing of the Hockey Hall of Fame. Lynch was enshrined in 1985; Martyn in 1991.

Two Hall of Fame voices who found a place in the heart of every Red Wings fan.

- 1971  1972 -

BACK in TIME

- **December 23, 1971**
President Nixon granted a personal pardon to Jimmy Hoffa, former president of Teamsters' Union, who had been imprisoned for jury tampering on a conspiracy charge.

- **March 22, 1972**
The Equal Rights Amendment was passed in the U.S. Senate by a vote of 84-8 and sent to the States for consideration.

- **July 26, 1972**
The Senate passed a 15 year ban on the killing of ocean mammals in U.S. waters.

quick cuts

Most Goals
Mickey Redmond: 42
Most Assists
Marcel Dionne: 49
Most Points
Marcel Dionne: 77
Most Penalty Minutes
Gary Bergman: 138
Most Wins, Goaltender
Al Smith: 18
Lowest Goals-Against Average
Joe Daley: 3.15
Most Shutouts
Al Smith: 4
NHL Award Winners
None

FINAL STANDINGS

East Division	W	L	T	PTS	GF	GA
Boston	54	13	11	119	330	204
New York	48	17	13	109	317	192
Montreal	46	16	16	108	307	205
Toronto	33	31	14	80	209	208
DETROIT	33	35	10	76	261	262
Buffalo	16	43	19	51	203	289
Vancouver	20	50	8	48	203	297

West Division Winner - Chicago

Playoff Results
Did Not Qualify
Stanley Cup Champion
Boston Bruins

200

1971-72 Season in Review

His revamped lineup starting to take shape, GM Ned Harkness felt better days were ahead for the Wings.

"We now have a solid, young base to build on, people like Mickey Redmond, Nick Libett and Tim Ecclestone and a leader in Red Berenson," Harkness said. First, they'd have to lay a foundation, but all the Wings accomplished in October was to lay an egg, losing their first three games and sitting at 2-8 after 10 contests.

That was enough for coach Doug Barkley, who handed in his resignation on Halloween. "It's obvious they weren't responding to me, but I think they have the talent to make the playoffs," Barkley said. "I wanted to give a new man a chance, before they get too far behind."

That new man was an old Wing, Johnny Wilson, who was promoted from his position as coach with Detroit's Tidewater AHL farm club. But the team didn't respond any better to Wilson, going 1-5-4 in his first 10 games behind the bench.

At that point, somebody threw the switch and Detroit turned it on, winning 23 and tying five of its next 40 games, moving into a race with Toronto for the East Division's fourth and final playoff spot. But the Wings lost 10 of their last 18 games and even though they won 33 times, the same number as the Leafs, Toronto posted four more draws than Detroit and that created a four-point difference in the standings, putting the Leafs in the playoffs.

The Wings did find plenty of cause for optimism during the season. Right-winger Redmond blasted 42 goals and rookie center Marcel Dionne led the team with 49 assists and 71 points. Left-winger Nick Libett potted a career-high 31 goals, while Berenson (28), Bill Collins (25) and captain Alex Delvecchio (20) all ascended to the 20-goal plateau.

Berenson played in the NHL All-Star Game and expressed a belief that Detroit's troubles were all in the past.

"There was something different about the team in 1971-72," he said. "It was our attitude. The problem a year ago was that we weren't happy because there was trouble in the front office. It was better this season and should be even better next year."

HOCKEYTOWN MOMENT

Wings select Dionne second overall in draft

The one advantage to Detroit's dismal 1970-71 campaign was that it afforded the team second pick in the NHL amateur draft, a choice they used to select center Marcel Dionne from the St. Catharines Black Hawks of the Ontario Hockey Association's Junior A series.

The OHA's leading scorer in each of his last two seasons of junior hockey, Dionne showed he could put up numbers as a Red Wing from Day 1. His 28-49-77 totals in 1971-72 were club rookie marks at the time and his 49 assists remain on the books as the standard for Detroit freshmen.

At 5-foot-9 and 190 pounds, hockey people questioned whether Dionne could withstand NHL punishment, but he wasn't among them. "They say I'm too small, but what about little centers like (Toronto's Dave) Keon and (Montreal's Henri) Richard?" Dionne asked. "Besides, I'm just short. I'm heavy and strong."

Red Berenson

Looking for a new hero after Gordie Howe hung up his skates, Red Wings fans turned their lonely eyes to another Gord - Gordon (Red) Berenson. "Nobody replaces Howe," Berenson said. "But if I can set an example by playing solid positional hockey and covering my man at all times, them I'm ready for that responsibility."

"The Red Baron," as he was affectionately known, was not unfamiliar to area hockey fans. Berenson was a two-time All-American at the University of Michigan, where he led the nation with 43 goals in 1961-62 and also graduated with Bachelor's and Masters' degrees in business administration.

Berenson assembled quite a hockey resume before ever lacing up his skates in NHL competition, winning a World Championship with Canada in 1959 and playing in the NCAA Tournament for Michigan. He jumped from the Wolverines directly into the lineup of the Montreal Canadiens late in the 1961-62 season, but didn't hit it off with Habs coach Toe Blake.

"He knew I was a college man and I don't think he believed I could make it," said Berenson, who also had a stint with the New York Rangers before finding a home in St. Louis.

Playing for the Blues on November 7, 1968, Berenson scored six times in an 8-0 shutout of Philadelphia, becoming the first NHLer to register that many goals in a game since 1944, when Detroit's Syd Howe had a six-goal game against the Rangers at the Olympia.

Soon, Berenson would call the same rink home.

Detroit was struggling during the 1970-71 season and St. Louis was entering a rebuilding phase, so the two teams made a four-forward swap, with the Wings getting Berenson and Tim Ecclestone for Garry Unger and Wayne Connelly. "Berenson is a real superstar and has the leadership qualities we want," Wings GM Ned Harkness said.

RED WINGS ARCHIVE

Berenson produced a pair of 20-goal, 60-point seasons for the Wings, but couldn't guide the team into post-season play and early in the 1974-75 season, was traded back to the Blues, where he concluded his NHL career in 1977-78. "When I look back, I didn't make the best of those years in Detroit," Berenson said. "The team was playing poorly and I was playing poorly."

After retiring as a player, Berenson coached the Blues, winning the Jack Adams Trophy as the NHL's top bench boss in 1980-81. Today, he's a frequent visitor to Joe Louis Arena in his position as coach of the Wolverines, a team he has guided to a pair of NCAA titles.

- **BORN:**
  Regina, Saskatchewan, December 8, 1939
- **ACQUIRED:**
  February 6, 1971 trade with St. Louis
- **BEST SEASON WITH RED WINGS:**
  1971-72 (28-41-69)

- **TOTALS WITH RED WINGS:**
  GP-283, G-73, A-128, PTS-201
- **HONORS:**
  Played in NHL All-Star Game, 1970-71, 1971-72, 1973-74

MOTOWN Classic

Brown is NHL's last maskless netminder

Whether he was at work or having fun, Andy Brown was a guy who enjoyed living on the edge. In the summer, Brown drove stock cars as a hobby. He earned his living stopping pucks as an NHL goalie, but wasn't content with the mere thrill of someone whistling 14 ounces of vulcanized rubber at him at speeds of more than 100 m.p.h. Brown was the last netminder in NHL history who tended goal without the added protection of a face mask.

The son of former Red Wings forward Adam Brown, Andy made his Detroit debut February 20, 1972 in a 4-3 loss to the New York Rangers at Madison Square Garden.

He played 17 games with the Wings before a 1973 trade sent him to Pittsburgh, where Brown set an NHL record for netminders by garnering 60 penalty minutes. "I only played 36 games, too," he boasted.

Brown's final NHL appearance came April 7, 1974 in Pittsburgh's 6-3 loss to Atlanta. NHL goalies have been covering up their faces ever since.

RED WINGS ARCHIVE

ASSEMBLY LINE

Deals were nearly as plentiful as in 1970-71. GM Ned Harkness sent his leading scorer, Tom Webster, to California for defenseman Ron Stackhouse. Center Danny Johnson was claimed on waivers from Vancouver and center Bill Sutherland was purchased from St. Louis. Left-winger Ab McDonald, defenseman Bob Wall and minor-leaguer Mike Lowe came from St. Louis as future considerations for a February, 1971 deal which sent Carl Brewer to St. Louis. Jim Niekamp was shipped to Vancouver for center Ralph Stewart. Kerry Ketter was sent to Montreal for right-winger Leon Rochefort and left-winger Brian Conacher, a former NHLer, was signed from the Canadian national team. Completely revamping his goaltending, Harkness dealt Don Luce and Mike Robitaille to Buffalo for Joe Daley, claimed Al Smith from Pittsburgh in the NHL intra-league draft and selected Andy Brown from Baltimore (AHL) in the inter-league draft, while losing Jim Rutherford to Pittsburgh in the intra-league draft. The NHL amateur draft produced centers Marcel Dionne and Henry Boucha.

Henry Boucha

RED WINGS ARCHIVE

Red Wings Facts

Vezina Trophy Winners
(Award Established in 1926)

Normie Smith 1936-37

Johnny Mowers 1942-43

Terry Sawchuk 1951-52

Terry Sawchuk 1952-53

Terry Sawchuk 1954-55

Short Passes

The United States won the silver medal at the 1972 Olympic hockey tournament in Sapporo, Japan and five members of that team - Mark Howe, Robbie Ftorek, Tom Mellor, Tim Sheehy and Henry Boucha - later played for the Red Wings.

- 1972  1973 -

BACK in TIME

1926 1928 1943

- **September 15, 1972**

Two former White House aides, E. Howard Hunt and G. Gordon Liddy, were among seven men indicted on charges of conspiracy to break into the Democratic national headquarters at Washington's Watergate complex.

- **January 20, 1973**

In Roe vs. Wade, the Supreme Court held that women's interest in privacy meant states could not prohibit abortion in the first trimester of pregnancy.

- **May 25, 1973**

The first Skylab mission was launched followed by 28 days of experimentation by three man crew, while the space station orbited Earth.

quick cuts

Most Goals
Mickey Redmond: 52
Most Assists
Alex Delvecchio: 53
Most Points
Mickey Redmond: 93
Most Penalty Minutes
Larry Johnston: 169
Most Wins, Goaltender
Roy Edwards: 27
Lowest Goals-Against Average
Roy Edwards: 2.63
Most Shutouts
Roy Edwards: 6
NHL Award Winners
Mickey Redmond - 1st Team All-Star

FINAL STANDINGS

East Division	W	L	T	PTS	GF	GA
Montreal	52	10	16	120	329	184
Boston	51	22	5	107	220	235
New York	47	23	8	102	297	208
Buffalo	37	27	14	88	257	219
DETROIT	37	29	12	86	265	243
Toronto	27	41	10	64	247	279
Vancouver	22	47	9	53	233	339
NY Islanders	12	60	6	30	170	347

West Division Winner - Chicago

Playoff Results
Did Not Qualify
Stanley Cup Champion
Mortreal Canadiens

1972-73 Season in Review

The Red Wings got off to a never before seen beginning, but the end result was all too familiar.

Breaking from the starting gate with a club-record six-game winning streak, Detroit found itself atop the NHL's East Division. By mid-December, though, the landscape took on a more common look. The Wings had slumped to 11-14-3 and were settling into a dogfight for the last playoff spot.

This year, the battle would be against Buffalo for fourth place and a 2-4-1 mark in their last six games doomed the Wings to their second straight fifth-place finish, coming home two points back of the Sabres.

A 4-2 afternoon victory January 28 on national television over the Montreal Canadiens saw Detroit center Henry Boucha tally just six seconds after the opening faceoff to set an NHL record. Goalie Roy Edwards led the NHL with six shutouts.

Defenseman Gary Bergman was Detroit's lone representative in the NHL All-Star Game and Bergman, centers Marcel Dionne and Red Berenson, and right-winger Mickey Redmond were all part of the Team Canada squad which edged the Soviet Union 4-3-1 in an eight-game Summit Series played in September across Canada and in Moscow.

"In all my years in hockey, that was one of the greatest experiences I ever had," Redmond said of defeating the Soviets.

RED WINGS ARCHIVE

Redmond was the story of the season, becoming the first Red Wing to record a 50-goal campaign, finishing the year with 52 markers, the second-highest total in the NHL. Redmond finished seventh in the NHL scoring race with 93 points and was selected to the NHL's First All-Star Team.

Dionne collected 40 goals and 90 points. In his 23rd campaign as a Red Wing, captain Alex Delvecchio recorded 53 assists and 71 points.

Late in the season, coach Johnny Wilson sought permission from GM Ned Harkness to ask Gordie Howe to make a comeback and assist in Detroit's playoff bid. "I knew doggone well that if we'd have had Gordie, he would've been the best player on the team," Wilson said.

Harkness rejected the idea and that summer, Howe signed with the WHA's Houston Aeros.

HOCKEYTOWN MOMENT

Wings miss playoffs, despite winning record

Detroit and Buffalo both finished the 1972-73 season with 37 wins, but Buffalo garnered two more ties than Detroit, creating the two-point difference which gave the Sabres their first playoff spot in franchise history.

If the Wings had played as well against poor teams as they did against the Sabres, all would have turned out fine. Detroit took four of five meetings with Buffalo, but inexplicably lost nine times to teams which wouldn't make the playoffs, including a 4-2 loss to the New York Islanders on February 24, a team which lost 60 times in 78 games.

Detroit's 37-29-12 record was the club's best output since 1969-70 and would prove to be their last winning season until 1987-88. But missing the play-

RED WINGS ARCHIVE

offs cost coach Johnny Wilson his job. He was fired at the end of the season, despite an overall mark of 67-56-22 at Detroit's helm.

Wings of Legend
Mickey Redmond

The howitzer-like slapshot which carried Mickey Redmond to consecutive 50-goal seasons was fashioned in the bowels of the Peterborough Memorial Centre.

It was there that the young Redmond would spend hours blasting a puck-shaped metal orb at a wall to add velocity to his shot. "Before every junior game in Peterborough, I would go down under the stands and shoot a three-pound steel puck," Redmond said. "The result was that when the game would start, the puck would feel like a quarter."

Not to mention that Redmond developed a powerful shot which was the scourge of NHL netminders.

"I'd say that Mickey had the hardest shot in the league," Wings goalie Roy Edwards said when Redmond blasted a club-record 52 goals in 1972-73. "I was very proud to have accomplished that, though at the same time, very disappointed those goals weren't used better, because we missed the playoffs," Redmond said of his first 50-goal season.

It earned him NHL First All-Star Team selection and his encore performance saw Redmond count 51 goals in 1973-74, including an NHL-best 21 power-play goals, which still stands as a club record.

"I had good centers feeding me the puck - Alex Delvecchio, Guy Charron and Bill Hogaboam," Redmond said of his two 50-goal campaigns. "When you're getting six or seven shots a game, you're going to score."

Redmond wasn't the happiest camper when he was dealt to Detroit during the 1970-71 season, coming over from Montreal with Charron and Bill Collins in exchange for Frank Mahovlich. "They had a super organization," said Redmond, who won two Stanley Cups with the Canadiens. "I was originally disappointed, but I wasn't playing regularly in Montreal and that's what every player wants." Redmond's brother Dick also played in the NHL and their father Eddie was a minor-pro player. "We had the best hockey coach we ever had, right under our own roof," Redmond said.

After his two 50-goal seasons, Redmond's back went south and took his career with it. He appeared in

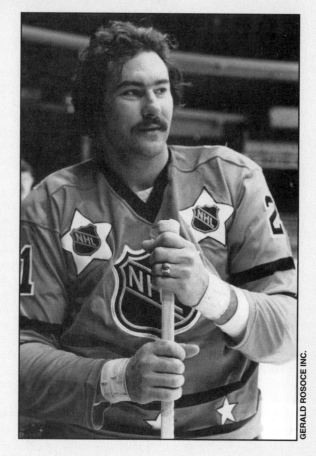

GERALD ROSOCE INC.

only 66 more games, producing 26 goals. "I had a ruptured disc," said Redmond, who was forced to retire in the fall of 1976. "I probably waited too long to have surgery on it and did some permanent nerve damage to my right leg."

Redmond staged a failed comeback bid with the Wings in 1979, then moved into the television booth. He's worked as an analyst on Red Wings telecasts since 1985, sharing the booth with three play-by-play men – Dave Strader, Mike Goldberg and Ken Daniels.

- **BORN:**
  Kirkland Lake, Ontario, December 27, 1947
- **ACQUIRED:**
  January 13, 1971 trade with Montreal
- **BEST SEASON WITH RED WINGS:**
  1972-73 (52-41-93)
- **TOTALS WITH RED WINGS:**
  GP-317, G-177, A-132, PTS-309

- **HONORS:**
  Selected to NHL First All-Star Team, 1972-73; Selected to NHL Second All-Star Team, 1973-74; Played in NHL All-Star Game, 1973-74; Played for Team Canada in 1972 Summit Series; First Red Wing to score 50 goals in a season; Set club record with 21 power-play goals, 1973-74

MOTOWN *Classic*

Redmond breaks 50-goal plateau

It may have been the only sucker bet in sports history to pay off.

Jean Murney, a neighbor of Red Wings right-winger Mickey Redmond's parents in their hometown of Peterborough, Ont., sent Redmond and his teammates a supply of homemade taffy suckers prior to Detroit's March 27 game at Toronto's Maple Leaf Gardens.

Redmond entered the contest one goal away from becoming the first Detroit player to post a 50-goal campaign and Murney felt the candy treats would bring good fortune.

"Sure, I ate mine," Redmond said. "She made some for her son's bantam team after they had some trouble and after they ate up the suckers, they went on to win their tournament and her son, the goaltender, was the most valuable player."

It proved to be a recipe for success for Redmond, who beat Toronto goalie Ron Low twice in an 18-second span during an 8-1 Detroit victory to become the seventh 50-goal scorer in NHL history.

ASSEMBLY LINE

In the spring, the NHL's latest expansion teams, the New York Islanders (Gerry Hart) and Atlanta Flames (Ron Harris, Randy Manery), combined to select three Detroit players. On the trade front, defensemen Gary Doak and Rick Newell were acquired from the New York Rangers for Joe Zanussi and a 1973 first round draft pick (Al Blanchard). Doak was then dealt to Boston for defenseman Murray Wing and left-winger Garnet (Ace) Bailey. Ralph Stewart and Bob Cook were shipped to the Islanders for defenseman Ken Murray and left-winger Brian Lavender. Arnie Brown and Gerry Gray also went to the Isles for goalie Denis DeJordy and minor-leaguer Don McLaughlin. Leon Rochefort was traded to Atlanta for center Bill Hogaboam. Goalie Roy Edwards was purchased from Pittsburgh. Swedish defenseman Thommie Bergman, Detroit's first European-trained player, was signed as a free agent and right-winger Len Fontaine was promoted from the farm system.

Arnie Brown

Red Wings Facts

Selke Trophy Winners
(Award Established in 1977)

Sergei Fedorov 1993-94

Sergei Fedorov 1995-96

Steve Yzerman 1999-00

Short Passes

Center Alex Delvecchio picked up 383 penalty minutes in 24 seasons and 1,549 games as a Red Wing – 15 minutes less than the single-season club-record 398 minutes Bob Probert was assessed during the 1987-88 campaign.

- 1973 1974 -

BACK in TIME

• **November 21, 1973**

The White House revealed there was a mysterious 18.5 minute gap in a key Watergate tape.

• **March 15, 1974**

A federal Grand Jury convicted President Nixon as a co-conspirator in the Watergate affair, bringing about his resignation on August 8, 1974.

• **April 15, 1974**

Newspaper heiress Patricia Hearst assisted the Symbionese Liberation Army in its holdup of a San Francisco bank and pointed a rifle at a bank teller.

quick cuts

Most Goals
Mickey Redmond: 51

Most Assists
Marcel Dionne: 54

Most Points
Marcel Dionne: 78

Most Penalty Minutes
Larry Johnston: 139

Most Wins, Goaltender
Doug Grant: 15

Lowest Goals-Against Average
Bill McKenzie: 3.58

Most Shutouts
Doug Grant - Terry Richardson: 1

NHL Award Winners
Alex Delvecchio - Lester Patrick Trophy
Mickey Redmond - 2nd Team All-Star

FINAL STANDINGS

East Division	W	L	T	PTS	GF	GA
Boston	52	17	9	113	349	221
Montreal	45	24	9	99	293	240
New York	40	24	14	94	300	251
Toronto	35	27	16	86	274	230
Buffalo	32	34	12	76	242	250
DETROIT	29	39	10	68	255	319
Vancouver	24	43	11	59	224	296
NY Islanders	19	41	18	56	182	247

West Division Winner - Montreal Canadiens

Playoff Results
Did Not Qualify
Stanley Cup Champion
Philadelphia Flyers

1973-74 Season in Review

For the sixth time since the start of the 1969-70 season, the Wings welcomed a new coach. And for the fourth time in five seasons, they bid him adieu in the midst of the season.

Ted Garvin, a successful minor-league mentor with Toledo of the IHL, was hired by GM Ned Harkness, but Garvin was gone after 12 games, in which he posted a 2-9-1 slate. He left the bench with 2:55 to play in his farewell game, a 4-1 loss to Philadelphia, having been informed before the game it would be his last as coach.

"I tried, I really tried," was Garvin's departing statement.

Alex Delvecchio, Wings captain since the 1962-63 season, announced his retirement November 7 to accept the coaching position. Detroit won its first three games under Delvecchio's leadership, but were already behind the eight-ball, due to the poor start.

"We're so far out of it now, all we can hope is we get together and play well," center Guy Charron said.

The Wings captaincy, Delvecchio's domain since 1962-63, took on a committee approach. Nick Libett, Red Berenson, Mickey Redmond, Gary Bergman, Ted Harris and Larry Johnston all took turns wearing the "C."

Posting a more respectable 28-31-9 with Delvecchio as coach, the Wings finished sixth in the East Division, out of the playoffs for the the fourth straight season. That development led to the departure

of Harkness, who resigned February 6. Former Wings coach Jimmy Skinner took over as interim GM.

Redmond fired 51 goals to become the first Red Wing to post successive 50-goal campaigns. He potted the game winner in nine of Detroit's 29 victories and tied a club record with four points in one period of an 11-2 win over the California Golden Seals on October 21.

Center Marcel Dionne led the club in scoring with 78 points. Berenson and Redmond appeared for the Wings in the NHL All-Star Game, with Berenson setting up Redmond for a goal. Delvecchio was presented with the Lester Patrick Trophy for service to hockey in the United States. The Jack Adams Award, which would go annually to the NHL's best coach, was introduced to honor the legendary Detroit boss.

HOCKEYTOWN MOMENT

Delvecchio retires to take Wings coaching duties

Midway through the 1972-73 season, captain Alex Delvecchio hinted that his retirement was imminent, suggesting he'd like to remain with the Red Wings organization.

"I wouldn't want to coach, though," Delvecchio insisted. "What with the travel and all, it would be the same as playing."

Yet there he was, making his debut behind the bench less than a year later, asked to retire as a player and replace the fired Ted Garvin.

"I wanted to stay with the club in some capacity," Delvecchio said. "I was thinking about an assistant manager's job, or something like that. But when they asked me to coach, I said, 'Yes.'

"I didn't think I was having a great year (1-4-5 in 11 games), so this kind of lets me off the hook."

Wings of Legend

Marcel Dionne

In 18 NHL seasons, Marcel Dionne scored 731 goals, but never played in a Stanley Cup final.

Not winning a championship is Dionne's greatest regret from his playing days. Leaving Detroit is a close second.

"My biggest disappointment is that my career with the Red Wings didn't work out," Dionne said. "My decision to leave was strictly business, but in retrospect, I'm convinced that I should have remained in Detroit and finished my career there.

"I realize now it's a great hockey town and a wonderful place to play." Certainly, the start to Dionne's Red Wings days were wonderful. Selected second overall in the 1971 NHL amateur draft, he led the club in scoring with 77 points in 1971-72, registering a club rookie-record 49 assists. The next year, he improved to 90 points and his combined totals of 167 points were the best first two seasons ever recorded by an NHL player.

The problems began during the 1972-73 season, when Dionne skipped a December game against Vancouver. He was suspended for a game the following season by coach Ted Garvin and submitted a trade request, but relented after Alex Delvecchio replaced Garvin as coach.

Named captain of the Wings at age 23 to commence the 1974-75 season, Dionne switched from No. 5 to the No. 12 Sid Abel wore on his back as Wings captain. "I gave this a great deal of thought and I'm convinced Marcel Dionne has both the talent to inspire and the ability to lead our club the way Sid did," Delvecchio said.

He looked a prophet when Dionne set a club single-season record by registering 121 points and won the Lady Byng Trophy, but Dionne played out his option and signed a five-year, $1 million deal with the Los Angeles Kings, rejecting a four-year, $1 million offer from the Wings, who received winger Dan Maloney and defenseman Terry Harper as compensation from L.A., since Dionne was a restricted free agent.

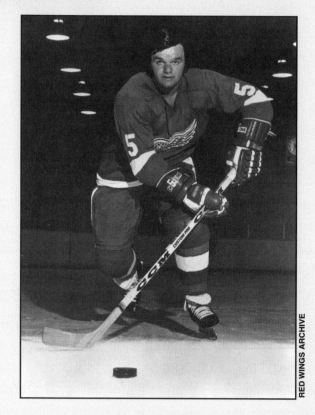

RED WINGS ARCHIVE

"It was not an easy decision to leave Detroit," Dionne said. "We loved the city because it was very sports-oriented and we loved the people."

Dionne won an NHL scoring title in L.A. and was elected to the Hockey Hall of Fame in 1992, five years before Detroit ended its 42-season Stanley Cup drought.

"The reason Detroit was able to win two Stanley Cups (in the 1990s) is because (owner) Mike Ilitch was willing to build from the bottom," Dionne said. Dionne only wishes Ilitch had arrived before he left.

- **BORN:**
  Drummondville, Quebec, August 3, 1951
- **ACQUIRED:**
  Selected second overall in the June 10, 1971 NHL amateur draft
- **BEST SEASON WITH RED WINGS:**
  1974-75 (47-74-121)
- **TOTALS WITH RED WINGS:**
  GP-309, G-139, A-227, PTS-366

- **HONORS:**
  Won Lady Byng Trophy, 1974-75; Played in NHL All-Star Game, 1974-75; Led team in scoring, 1971-72; 1973-74; 1974-75; Set team record for assists by rookies (49), 1971-72; Selected to Team Canada for 1972 Summit Series

MOTOWN Classic

Redmond scores 50 . . . again

Beating Ed Giacomin in Detroit's 5-3 victory over the New York Rangers on March 23, Detroit right-winger Mickey Redmond ascended to the 50-goal plateau for the second straight season.

The performance earned Redmond a spot on the NHL's Second All-Star Team. He was the third NHLer, following Bobby Hull and Phil Esposito, to post multiple 50-goal seasons. Redmond also led the NHL with 21 power-play goals, a Red Wings record.

"I had a good shot, so every practice, I practiced shooting the puck," Redmond said. "I'd shoot a lot of times from bad angles. I used to try to bank them in off goaltenders, or shoot them at their heads to get them up on their toes. Whatever it took."

RED WINGS ARCHIVE

ASSEMBLY LINE

Jim Rutherford

There were trades aplenty, as the Wings continued their search for a successful squad. Gary Bergman was dealt to Minnesota for defenseman Ted Harris. Harris, Garnet (Ace) Bailey and Bill Collins were moved to St. Louis later in the season for defensemen Chris Evans, Jean Hamel and Bryan (Bugsy) Watson. Defenseman Brent Hughes was purchased from Philadelphia, Tim Ecclestone was traded to Toronto for left-winger Pierre Jarry and defenseman Jack Lynch and goalie Jim Rutherford were acquired from Pittsburgh for Ron Stackhouse. Defenseman/right-winger Doug Roberts was purchased from Boston. Serge Lajeunesse was traded to Philadelphia for defenseman Rick Foley. Free-agent signees included left-winger Nelson Debenedet, Swedish left-winger Tord Lundstrom, defenseman Al McLeod, center Robbie Ftorek and goalies Doug Grant and Bill McKenzie. The NHL amateur draft supplied left-winger Danny Gruen, goalie Terry Richardson, defenseman Tom Mellor and center Blair Stewart.

RED WINGS ARCHIVE

Red Wings Facts

Adams Trophy Winners
(Award Established in 1974)

Bobby Kromm 1977-78

Jacques Demers 1986-87

Jacques Demers 1987-88

Scotty Bowman 1995-96

Short Passes

Detroit operated a farm club in London, England during the 1973-74 season. The London Lions played an exhibition slate against European teams and included such future Wings as Dennis Polonich, Mike Korney, Nelson Pyatt and Bill McKenzie.

- 1974  1975 -

BACK in TIME

- **November 21, 1974**

Overriding President Ford's veto, Congress passed the Freedom of Information Act, increasing public access to government files.

- **February 11, 1975**

Magaret Thatcher became England's first woman prime minister by defeating incumbent Edward Heath.

- **July 19, 1975**

In separate launchings, American and Soviet astronauts began a joint mission to dock their Apollo and Soyuz space-crafts in space.

quick cuts

Most Goals
Danny Grant: 50
Most Assists
Marcel Dionne: 74
Most Points
Marcel Dionne: 121
Most Penalty Minutes
Bryan Watson: 238
Most Wins, Goaltender
Jim Rutherford: 20
Lowest Goals-Against Average
Jim Rutherford: 3.74
Most Shutouts
Jim Rutherford: 2
NHL Award Winners
Marcel Dionne - Lady Byng Trophy
Bruce A. Norris - Lester Patrick Trophy

FINAL STANDINGS

Norris Division	W	L	T	PTS	GF	GA
Montreal	47	14	19	113	374	225
Los Angeles	42	17	21	105	269	185
Pittsburgh	37	28	15	89	326	289
DETROIT	23	45	12	58	259	335
Washington	8	67	5	21	181	446

OTHER DIVISION WINNERS
Adams Division: Buffalo Sabres
Patrick Division: Philadelphia Flyers
Smythe Division: Vancouver Canucks

Playoff Results
Did Not Qualify
Stanley Cup Champion
Philadelphia Flyers

1974-75 Season in Review

RED WINGS ARCHIVE

"It would be foolish to promise miracles," Wings coach Alex Delvecchio said when the Wings commenced the season looking for their first playoff position since 1969-70. "I can only promise effort, because there's a very big job ahead."

He wasn't kidding.

The addition of new franchises in Kansas City and Washington, D.C. turned the NHL into a four-division, 18-team league. All four divisions were named for NHL pioneers and Detroit was fittingly grouped in the Norris Division, named for former club owner James Norris Sr., along with Montreal, Los Angeles, Pittsburgh and the newly-formed Washington Capitals.

Bruce Norris, current owner of the team, won the Lester Patrick Trophy for service to hockey in the U.S.A.

The home opener provided hope when Guy Charron's goal with 37 seconds to play earned the Wings a 2-1 victory over Chicago. Detroit was 5-1 through six games.

"We'll make the playoffs, I'm sure of it," Delvecchio boldly predicted. "I won't even concede first place to Montreal." That bravado looked misplaced when the Wings were drilled 10-1 in Atlanta, launching an eight-game winless skid.

Detroit won just six of its next 38 games and ended up fourth in the division at 23-45-6, 31 points out of a playoff spot.

"Obviously, the area we have to work on is defensive play," Delvecchio said. The Wings finished 17th in the NHL in goals against, allowing 335 goals in 80 games.

Offensively, there was no concern. Newly-acquired left-winger Danny Grant scored 50 goals and was a helpful addition, considering a back injury limited two-time 50-goal sniper Mickey Redmond to 15 goals in 29 games.

But the story of the year was Marcel Dionne. Named captain of the team, he donned Sid Abel's old No. 12 and dominated, producing a club-record 121 points, beating Gordie Howe's old mark by 18 points.

Dionne played in the NHL All-Star Game, set a league record with 10 shorthanded goals, won the Lady Byng Trophy and accolades from everywhere. "Dionne can do it all," Delvecchio said. "He's got all the moves. He's probably the most colorful player in the NHL today."

HOCKEYTOWN MOMENT
Delvecchio takes on dual role

RED WINGS ARCHIVE

From player and captain to coach and general manager, all in the space of seven months. That was the course traversed by Alex Delvecchio, who added the GM's portfolio to his coaching position on May 21, 1974.

Jimmy Skinner, who had filled the GM's chair on an interim basis after Ned Harkness departed, was retained as assistant GM and former Wings forward Billy Dea was hired as an assistant coach.

"The three of us will talk over whatever situations arise and make a decision," Delvecchio said. "Then it will be presented to (Wings owner Bruce) Norris for approval."

Norris admitted he'd been turned down by Ted Lindsay before offering the position to Delvecchio.

"Alex did a wonderful job as coach," Norris said in announcing Delvecchio's appointment as GM. "I feel in order to win, we have to put our losing attitude behind us and I'm certain Alex is the man to do it.

"We've had a lot of problems lately, but I guess you can say Alex is the 'heavy' in the Red Wings situation now."

Gary Bergman

RED WINGS ARCHIVE

Maybe he wasn't the best defenseman in the game, but what every man who coached Gary Bergman knew was they'd get his best every game.

"Sid Abel always said to me, 'I always know that even if you come to the rink with only eight gallons in the tank, I'm going to get eight gallons out of you that night,'" Bergman recalled.

Originally property of the Montreal Canadiens, Bergman was stuck behind many great defenseman with the talent-rich Habs, but jumped right into Detroit's lineup when the Wings claimed him during the 1964 NHL intra-league draft.

He helped the team to a first-place finish as a rookie and was the man tangled up with Montreal's Henri Richard when Richard scored the Stanley Cup-winning goal against Detroit in overtime during Game 6 of the 1965-66 final series.

Bergman, like all Wings from that season, was convinced Richard pushed the puck in with his glove and the goal should not have counted.

"I took him down and held his stick in my hand," Bergman said. "There was no way he could score."

That Stanley Cup final would be the last team glory Bergman experienced in Detroit. He'd play in just one more playoff series, never winning another Stanley Cup game, but his numbers remained impressive for someone performing on a poor club. He posted career highs with 13 goals and 41 points in 1967-68. Detroit missed the playoffs in 1968-69, but Bergman logged an astonishing plus-45 rating.

"He was a mobile defenseman who could skate well, carry the puck and contribute to the attack," said Jackie Gordon, who coached Bergman in Minnesota, which acquired him from the Wings in 1973, then traded him back to Detroit a year later.

It was that sort of style Harry Sinden was seeking from his Team Canada defense for the 1972 Summit Series with the Soviet Union and Bergman was a surprise pick.

"He was one of the great unsung heroes of that series," former Wing Paul Henderson said. "He played incredible hockey."

Bergman played every game, collecting three assists and his plus-five rating was second-best on the squad.

"The steadiness of his play is what I remember most," fellow Team Canada defenseman Bill White said. "He was an above-average player in the NHL at that time and he proved it during that series."

Canada rallied to win the last three games and take the set 4-3-1. "We were on the edge of the envelope," Bergman said. "That's the way everyone was the last three games. By then, we were letting it all hang out.

"Every shift, you played like your life depended on it. And it did." Bergman's second stint with Detroit lasted one season. He was traded to the Kansas City Scouts, where he wrapped up his NHL career in 1975-76.

- **BORN:**
  Kenora, Ontario, October 7, 1938
- **ACQUIRED:**
  Selected from Montreal in NHL intra-league draft, June 10, 1964
- **BEST SEASON WITH RED WINGS:**
  1967-68 (13-28-41)

- **TOTALS WITH RED WINGS:**
  GP-706, G-60, A-243, PTS-303
- **HONORS:**
  Played in NHL All-Star Game, 1972-73; Selected to Team Canada for 1972 Summit Series

MOTOWN *Classic*

Newcomer Grant adds offensive spark

RED WINGS ARCHIVE

As teammates with the junior Peterborough Petes, Danny Grant and Mickey Redmond were both 40-goal scorers. As teammates with the Red Wings, they were both 50-goal scorers. Detroit coach-GM Alex Delvecchio dealt speedy center Henry Boucha to the Minnesota North Stars for left-winger Grant on August 27, 1974.

Grant arrived with a pedigree as a scorer, producing three 30-goal seasons in Minnesota, including a 34-goal campaign in 1968-69 which earned him the Calder Trophy as NHL rookie of the year. But he saved his best season for Detroit.

Grant beat Washington goalie John Adams for his 50th goal of the season April 2 in an 8-3 Red Wings victory, joining Redmond, who achieved the milestone in 1971-72 and 1972-73, as Detroit's only 50-goal scorers.

"It helps to have a center like Marcel Dionne making plays for you," Grant said.

Dionne moved to L.A. next season and Grant's potency also disappeared. He scored just 14 more goals for Detroit over the next three seasons and was himself dealt to Los Angeles in 1978.

ASSEMBLY LINE

RED WINGS ARCHIVE

Walt McKechnie

The roster shuffling of recent seasons continued. Ken Murray, Chris Evans and Brent Hughes (Kansas City) were expansion draft losses. Henry Boucha was shipped to Minnesota for left-winger Danny Grant, while Guy Charron and Claude Houde were sent to Kansas City for defensemen Bart Crashley and Larry Giroux and right-winger Ted Snell. Red Berenson went to St. Louis for right-winger Phil Roberto and a 1975 third-round draft pick (Blair Davidson). Blair Stewart was traded to Washington for left-winger Mike Bloom and defenseman Gary Bergman returned to the Wings from Minnesota for a 1975 third-round draft choice (Alex Pirus). Jack Lynch was sent to Washington for left-winger Dave Kryskow. Pittsburgh acquired Nelson Debenedet for left-winger Hank Nowak and a 1974 third round draft pick (Dan Mandryck), then Nowak and Earl Anderson went to Boston for center Walt McKechnie and a 1975 third-round draft pick (Clarke Hamilton). Defenseman Frank Bathe and left-winger Brian McCutcheon were free-agent additions. Defenseman Barry Salovaara earned promotion from the minors and the NHL amateur draft supplied right-wingers Mike Korney and Michel Bergeron and left-winger Bill Lochead.

Red Wings Facts

Hart Trophy Winners

(Award Established in 1923)

Ebbie Goodfellow - 1939-40
Sid Abel - 1948-49
Gordie Howe - 1951-52
Gordie Howe - 1952-53
Gordie Howe - 1956-57
Gordie Howe - 1957-58
Gordie Howe - 1959-60
Gordie Howe - 1962-63
Sergei Fedorov - 1993-94

Short Passes

Michigan Wolverines left-winger Don Dufek was selected 99th overall by the Wings in the 1974 NHL amateur draft. Also a member of the U of M football team, Dufek opted to take that route, playing safety for the NFL's Seattle Seahawks from 1976-84.

Red Wing
HOCKEY MAGAZINE

PRINCE OF WALES
'56-'57

PRINCE OF WALES
STANLEY CUP
'54-'55

PRINCE OF WALES
STANLEY CUP
'53-'54

PRINCE OF WALES
'52-'53

PRINCE OF WALES
STANLEY CUP
'51-'52

PRINCE OF WALES
'50-'51

PRINCE OF WALES
STANLEY CUP
'49-'50

PRINCE OF WALES
'48-'49

PRINCE OF WALES
STANLEY CUP
'42-'43

PRINCE OF WALES
STANLEY CUP
'36-'37

PRINCE OF WALES
STANLEY CUP
'35-'36

PRINCE OF WALES
'33-'34

25¢

OLYMPIA STADIUM
DETROIT

THE ALL-TIME RED WINGS TEAM:
SECOND ERA (1950–75)

CENTER — ALEX DELVECCHIO

Only Gordie Howe played more seasons and games as a Red Wing than "Fats," who skated in 1,549 games over 24 seasons, both NHL marks for a player who spent his entire career with one team. Three times, Delvecchio was awarded the Lady Byng Trophy as the NHL's most sportsmanlike player and he also won the Lester Patrick Trophy for service to hockey in the U.S. A two-time NHL Second All-Star Team selection, Delvecchio played in 13 NHL All-Star Games and served a captain, coach and GM of the Wings. He was elected to the Hockey Hall of Fame in 1977.

LEFT WING — TED LINDSAY

Perhaps the most determined competitor ever to lace up a pair of skates, opponents knew Lindsay as "Terrible Ted" or "Scarface." His mixture of talent and toughness allowed Lindsay to lead the NHL in scoring in 1949-50 and to top the league in penalty minutes in 1958-59. When Lindsay retired in 1965, he stood as the NHL's career penalty-minute leader, a mark he held for more than a decade. Eight times placed on the NHL's First All-Star Team, Lindsay also made one appearance on the Second Team and skated in 10 NHL All-Star Games as a Wing. He ended a four-season retirement to make a stirring comeback at age 39 with Detroit in 1964-65, scoring 19 goals and leading the team with 173 penalty minutes. Lindsay was enshrined in the Hockey Hall of Fame in 1967.

RIGHT WING — GORDIE HOWE

Teammate Bill Gadsby summed up Howe's uniqueness when he stated, "He's not merely the greatest hockey player I've ever seen, but also the greatest athlete." A Detroit career which spanned 25 seasons saw Howe finish as the club's all-time scoring leader with 786-1,023-1,809 totals, Howe captured six Art Ross Trophies as NHL scoring champion and six Hart Trophies as MVP of the league. He earned a dozen selections to the NHL's First All-Star Team and made an additional nine appearances on the Second Team. Howe played in 22 NHL All-Star Games as a Red Wing. In 1967, he won the Lester Patrick Trophy for meritorious service to hockey in the United States and Howe was inducted into the Hockey Hall of Fame in 1972.

DEFENSEMAN — RED KELLY

A rare breed of blueliner who combined outstanding defensive ability with gentlemanly play, Kelly was awarded the Lady Byng Trophy as the NHL's best combination of sportsmanship and talent on three occasions, a league record for defensemen. In 1953-54, he was also the first winner of the Norris Trophy as the NHL's most outstanding rearguard. A winner of four Stanley Cups as a Wing, six times, Kelly was an NHL First All-Star Team choice and twice he achieved Second Team honors. Leaving Detroit in a 1960 trade with Toronto, Kelly won four more Cups as a Leaf and another Lady Byng after switching to center. He was enshrined in the Hockey Hall of Fame in 1969.

DEFENSEMAN — MARCEL PRONOVOST

One of the most underrated rearguards in NHL history, Pronovost made his Red Wings debut in the 1949-50 Stanley Cup playoffs and was a fixture on the Detroit blueline for 16 seasons, winning four Stanley Cups. Twice Pronovost was tabbed for selection to the NHL's First All-Star Team and he also earned Second Team status on a pair of occasions. He finished as runner-up in the Norris Trophy voting in 1960-61. A skilled puckhandler, Pronovost twice topped the 30-point plateau and netted 11 goals in 1958-59. Appearing in nine NHL All-Star Games as a Red Wing, Pronovost was inducted into the Hockey Hall of Fame in 1978.

GOALTENDER — TERRY SAWCHUCK

The NHL's all-time leader in shutouts (103) and games played (971) by a goalie, the man the Wings called "Ukey" set the standard for modern-day netminders. He backstopped Detroit to three Stanley Cups during his tenure, winning the Calder Trophy as the NHL's top rookie in 1950-51 and capturing three Vezina Trophies. He set a club record with 12 shutouts in 1951-52 and tied the mark in 1954-55. Three times, Sawchuk was selected to the NHL's First All-Star Team and he was a Second Team choice on four occasions, earning election to the Hockey Hall of Fame in 1971.

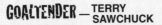

217

- 1975 1976 -

BACK in TIME

- **October 20, 1975**

The Supreme Court held that school administrators may hit students to punish them even if parents objected.

- **February 2, 1976**

The Government authorized limited U.S. landings by the supersonic Anglo-French Concorde aircraft; the first transatlantic flights began.

- **April 21, 1976**

The last Cadillac Eldorado rolled off the assembly lines and the U.S. auto industry ceased the production of convertibles due to declining sales.

quick cuts

Most Goals
Michel Bergeron: 32
Most Assists
Walt McKechnie: 56
Most Points
Walt McKechnie: 82
Most Penalty Minutes
Bryan Watson: 322
Most Wins, Goaltender
Jim Rutherford: 13
Lowest Goals-Against Average
Ed Giacomin: 3.45
Most Shutouts
Jim Rutherford: 4
NHL Award Winners
None

FINAL STANDINGS

Norris Division	W	L	T	PTS	GF	GA
Montreal	58	11	11	127	337	174
Los Angeles	38	33	9	85	263	265
Pittsburgh	35	33	12	82	339	303
DETROIT	26	44	10	62	226	300
Washington	11	59	10	32	224	394

OTHER DIVISION WINNERS
Adams Division: Boston Bruins
Patrick Division: Philadelphia Flyers
Smythe Division: Chicago Blackhawks

Playoff Results
Did Not Qualify
Stanley Cup Champion
Montreal Canadiens

1975-76 Season in Review

General manager of a team which hadn't qualified for post-season play since 1969-70, Alex Delvecchio was surprisingly upbeat when the season commenced, even though top scorer Marcel Dionne was gone in a sign-and-trade deal with Los Angeles.

"That's got to hurt, he's one of the best players in the league," Delvecchio acknowledged, "but I don't see that the situation is hopeless. Our record was bad and we were 31 points out of a playoff spot, but look at the things that happened to us."

Delvecchio pointed to injuries to forwards Bill Hogaboam, Bill Lochead and Mickey Redmond and defenseman Bryan Watson as causing Detroit's slide. "We just didn't have the depth to overcome injuries like that," he said.

The Wings did have a new coach when Doug Barkley was rehired. He'd previously been bench boss for 51 games during the 1970-71 and 1971-72 seasons.

The former Detroit defenseman wasn't coach for long. The Wings got off to the worst start in franchise history, going winless (0-7-3) in their first 10 games, including the worst home-ice start (0-2-3) in club history.

By early December, Barkley was done, leaving after 26 games with a 7-15-4 record.

Delvecchio assumed coaching duties, but moved assistant Billy Dea behind the bench commencing December 31, although Delvecchio retained the title as head coach.

Jim Rutherford blanked the Washington Capitals 4-0 that night, the first of three consecutive shutouts he'd post, tying a club record shared by Terry Sawchuk and Glenn Hall.

Forward Danny Grant and defenseman Terry Harper shared duties as captain. Left-winger Dan Maloney represented Detroit in the NHL All-Star Game, picking up a goal and an assist for the Wales Conference in a 7-5 win over the Campbell Conference.

Center Walt McKechnie led the club with 56 assists and 82 points, while right-winger Michel Bergeron netted a team-high 32 goals, including a four-goal performance March 18 in a 6-3 win over St. Louis.

On the rugged side of the ledger, forward Dennis Polonich collected a club-record eight penalties March 24 in a 7-3 win over Washington and Watson surpassed former Wing Ted Lindsay (1,808) as the NHL's career penalty-minute leader, finishing the season with 1,879 minutes in 13 seasons after a club-record 322 PIM in 1975-76.

There would be no playoffs again for the Wings, who finished fourth in the Norris Division at 26-44-10.

HOCKEYTOWN MOMENT
Dionne dealt to the L.A. Kings

Becoming the first NHL team ever to be involved in compensation for the loss of a restricted free agent wasn't the way the Wings sought to make history. Especially since the restricted free agent in question was Marcel Dionne, their best player.

Dionne played out his option and when he rejected a four-season, $1 million offer from the Wings, they told him to seek his own deal with another team. It was the Los Angeles Kings he chose, even though the money - $1 million over five years - was less than the Detroit offer.

"I had all summer to think things over," Dionne said. "It's not much fun to play on a loser for four seasons."

The teams worked out a deal with left-winger Dan Maloney and defenseman Terry Harper, two of the NHL's toughest players, coming to Detroit for Dionne and defenseman Bart Crashley.

Jim Rutherford

Jim Rutherford was the little goalie who could, but was unfortunately saddled with the difficult task of playing behind several teams which couldn't.

In 13 NHL seasons, he participated in the playoffs just three times.

The Wings claimed Rutherford from the OHA Junior A Hamilton Red Wings with the 10th pick in the 1969 NHL amateur draft, the earliest the team has ever selected a goaltender on draft day.

After one campaign of minor-league seasoning, Rutherford was called up just in time for the disappointing 1970-71 season.

The Wings elected not to protect Rutherford that spring and Pittsburgh claimed him in the NHL intra-league draft. Detroit reacquired him from Pittsburgh January 18, 1974 for defenseman Ron Stackhouse, a deal which would unwittingly turn Rutherford into the Picasso of puckstoppers.

While with Pittsburgh, Rutherford painted his goalie mask blue to match the Penguins colors.

Luckily for him, one of Detroit's first games after the trade was in Toronto, home of goalie-mask designer Greg Harrison.

"I dropped the mask off to Greg and he said he'd have it ready by game time," Rutherford said. "I told him to paint it white," but Harrison had other ideas. "When he showed up with it, the mask was white and had red wings painted over each eye," Rutherford said. Using the eye holes in Rutherford's mask as the wheels, Harrison depicted two Red Wings logos on the front, but his client was unimpressed by the artwork.

"I said, 'I don't want that,'" Rutherford remembered. "I was upset by the trade and I didn't want to draw any more attention to myself."

"There wasn't enough time to do anything about it, so I wore it and everybody loved it," said Rutherford, who starred in a 2-2 tie with the Leafs. Athletes being the superstitious sort, Rutherford wasn't about to alter a successful formula and the goalie mask as art was here to stay.

"After that, all goalies started having things painted on their mask," he said. Rutherford etched another

RED WINGS ARCHIVE

mark in Detroit history in 1975-76. He blanked Washington 4-0 on Dec. 31 and followed up with a 1-0 whitewash of Toronto January 3 and a 5-0 shutout of Minnesota January 8, joining Terry Sawchuk, Clarence (Dolly) Dolson and Glenn Hall as the only Detroit goalies to post shutouts in three consecutive starts.

"Hall was always my favorite goaltender," Rutherford said.

A 1980 trade to Toronto allowed Rutherford to share another unique trio with Sawchuk. The Wings signed him as a free agent in 1982, making Rutherford and Sawchuk the only three-time Red Wings.

Some suggested Rutherford, at 5-foot-8 and 168 pounds, was too small to be an NHL goalie, but Alex Delvecchio, his teammate and later Rutherford's coach and GM, disagreed.

"Size doesn't make any difference," Delvecchio said. "As long as you keep the puck out, which Jimmy did, it doesn't matter how you're built."

- **BORN:**
  Beeton, Ontario, February 17, 1949
- **ACQUIRED:**
  Selected 10th overall in the June 12, 1969 NHL amateur draft
- **BEST SEASON WITH RED WINGS:**
  1977-78 (20-17-4, 1 SO, 3.26 GAA)

- **TOTALS WITH RED WINGS:**
  GP-314, W-96, L-164, T-43, SO-10, GAA-3.69
- **HONORS:**
  Led team in wins four times; Led team in shutouts five times; Led team in GAA four times; Played for Canada, 1977 and 1979 World Championships

MOTOWN Classic

Eddie Giacomin

A rare big night for the Red Wings proved to be one of the most emotional evenings in New York Rangers history. The Wings claimed goalie Eddie Giacomin on waivers from the Rangers October 31, 1975 and Rangers fans were insulted that their Vezina Trophy-winning netminder would be discarded like a piece of old furniture.

It was also bad timing on the Rangers' part, because the Wings were due to play at Madison Square Garden two nights later. Giacomin got the start and chants of "Eddie, Eddie" from the Garden faithful drowned out the National Anthem. "I was shaking before the game, I was so nervous," said Giacomin, who couldn't hold back the tears. "When I think of what the fans did for me, it was an honor."

With Giacomin playing brilliantly and his old Rangers teammates apologizing for scoring on him, the Wings posted a 6-4 victory.

"It must have been awfully hard for the Ranger players," Giacomin said. "You could see it in their eyes."

RED WINGS ARCHIVE

ASSEMBLY LINE

Making a little unwanted history, the Wings were part of the NHL's first free-agent compensation case, arranging to deal Marcel Dionne and Bart Crashley to Los Angeles for left-winger Dan Maloney and defenseman Terry Harper after Dionne signed as a free-agent with L.A. Left-winger Dennis Hextall was acquired from Minnesota for Bill Hogaboam and his brother, center Bryan Hextall, was picked up from Atlanta for Dave Kryskow, then dealt to Minnesota for right-winger Rick Chinnick. Goalie Eddie Giacomin was claimed on waivers from the Rangers and Phil Roberto went to Atlanta for right-winger Buster Harvey. Pierre Jarry was shipped to Minnesota for right-winger Don Martineau. Center J.P. LeBlanc was added from Chicago for Jean Savard. Defensemen Rick Lapointe and Al Cameron and center Mike Wong were added through the NHL amateur draft.

Terry Harper

RED WINGS ARCHIVE

Red Wings Facts

Most Points In One Season

131 - (1995-96)
116 - (2001-02)
111 - (2000-01)
108 - (1999-00)
103 - (1997-98)
103 - (1992-93)
101 - (1950-51)
100 - (1951-52)
100 - (1993-94)

Short Passes

Brothers Bryan and Dennis Hextall, linemates with the Wings for part of the 1975-76 season, were part of a three-generation NHL family. Their father was Hall of Fame right-winger Bryan Hextall Sr. of the New York Rangers and Ron Hextall, the son of Bryan Jr., won the 1986-87 Conn Smythe Trophy as goalie for the Philadelphia Flyers.

- 1976   1977 -

BACK in TIME

- **August 28, 1976**
A breakthrough in genetic engineering took place when a bacterial gene was constructed in the lab and implanted in a lung cell, and it functioned normally.

- **January 21, 1977**
President Carter signed an unconditional pardon for nearly all Vietnam era draft evaders.

- **October 26, 1977**
The world's last known case of smallpox developed in Somalia; two years later the disease was considered eradicated.

quick cuts

Most Goals
Walt McKechnie: 25

Most Assists
Walt McKechnie: 34

Most Points
Walt McKechnie: 59

Most Penalty Minutes
Dennis Polonich: 274

Most Wins, Goaltender
Ed Giacomin: 8

Lowest Goals-Against Average
Ed Giacomin: 3.58

Most Shutouts
Ed Giacomin: 3

NHL Award Winners
None

FINAL STANDINGS

Norris Division	W	L	T	PTS	GF	GA
Montreal	60	8	12	132	387	171
Los Angeles	34	31	15	83	271	241
Pittsburgh	34	33	13	81	240	252
Washington	24	42	14	62	221	307
DETROIT	**16**	**55**	**9**	**41**	**183**	**309**

OTHER DIVISION WINNERS:
Adams Division - Boston Bruins
Patrick Division - Philadelphia Flyers
Smythe Division - St. Louis Blues

Playoff Results
Did Not Qualify
Stanley Cup Champion
Montreal Canadiens

1976-77 Season in Review

There were plenty of records established in Hockeytown this season, but they were of the sort teams don't seek to achieve.

The Wings finished as the NHL's worst team for just the third time in club history.

Posting a 16-55-9 slate, Detroit won the fewest games in the league and lost the most, finishing 13 points behind the Colorado Rockies, who were the NHL's second-worst team. With 183 goals, Detroit owned the NHL's most anemic offense and were blanked 11 times. Only the New York Rangers (310) allowed more goals than the 309 surrendered by the Wings.

Another coaching change saw GM Alex Delvecchio hand bench duties to former Wing Larry Wilson for the final 36 games. Wilson's brother Johnny coached the Wings from 1971-73.

Amazingly, this sad state of affairs had a happy beginning. The Wings fashioned a 3-3 tie with Washington in the season opener, then Ed Giacomin blanked Buffalo 4-0. Giacomin posted three shutouts, one coming November 7 in a 0-0 draw with Atlanta, Detroit's first scoreless tie since October 13, 1962.

The Wings owned 13 wins after a 4-2 decision December 31 over the Cleveland Barons, but little would be resolved in Detroit's favor during the New Year. Detroit was 1-9-2 in January, 2-9-2 in February and a combined 0-17-1 in March and April, ending the season on a team-record 19-game winless skid. The Wings suffered a record 33 road defeats, going 0-23-3 away from home from December 15 through the end of the season.

Things weren't much better at the Olympia, where the Wings won just five times in their last 23 home dates, closing the season 0-8-1. At least the fans felt rewarded March 31, which the Wings billed as "Guaranteed Win Night" at the Olympia. When Minnesota handed Detroit a 3-1 setback, all 8,427 in attendance received a free ticket to the Wings' final home game against Pittsburgh.

Left-winger Nick Libett was Detroit's representative in the NHL All-Star Game and goalie Jim Rutherford and center Walt McKechnie played for Canada at the World Championships.

A club-record seven straight seasons out of the playoffs left some people referring to the team as, "The Dead Wings," but they were about to rise again.

HOCKEYTOWN MOMENT
Lindsay returns to the Wings

Three years earlier, Ted Lindsay rejected an offer to be GM of the team for which he was a star. This time, he jumped at the chance.

Lindsay was signed to a five-year contract as GM of the club on March 15, 1977, replacing former teammate Alex Delvecchio.

"Don't give up on us," Lindsay begged Detroit fans. "I promise you, we'll have men on the ice at all times. If the players don't work and produce, the fans won't have to look at them for long."

One-third of Detroit's famed Production Line along with Sid Abel and Gordie Howe, Lindsay was running an auto parts business with former teammate Marty Pavelich and coaching the hockey team at Hillsdale College when the Wings came calling.

Wings of Legend

Dennis Polonich

As diamonds in the rough go, Dennis Polonich was pretty rough. An undersized terror who feared no one, Polonich was one of the few gems to be unearthed during Detroit's frustrating 1976-77 campaign.

In his second full season as a Red Wing, Polonich served as captain and finished second on the club with 18-28-46 totals, while slugging his way to a team-leading 274 penalty minutes, even though he checked in at just 5-foot-6 and 168 pounds.

Well, that's what it said in the yearbook.

"When I was a kid, about 16 or 17, I tried to get a job in the zinc mines up in Flin Flon (Manitoba)," Polonich said. "We had to take a physical."

Polonich's height measured barely over 5-foot-4, too small to work underground. But not too small to play eight seasons for the Wings.

"In my hometown (of Foam Lake, Saskatchewan), there were better players in minor hockey than I was," Polonich said. "I just pursued it, I kept working." The man with the bowling-ball build was a thorn in the side of the opposition. And he never shied away from dropping the mitts.

On March 24, 1976 in a 7-3 win over Washington, Polonich established a club record by sitting out eight penalties - five minors, a major and a misconduct. Looking back, Polonich wishes he'd spent less time in the sin bin and more on the ice. "If I had stayed out of the box a little more, I might have scored 20 or 25 goals," he said. "You have to have a mighty long stick to score from the penalty box."

Polonich also wishes the Wings had enjoyed more stability during his tenure in Detroit, which saw the club make a lone playoff appearance.

"There were just too many general managers and I had 11 coaches in eight years," he said. "There were some good coaches, but they weren't allowed to stay behind the bench long enough to really do anything with the team."

Polonich is perhaps best remembered for winning an $850,000 legal settlement from Colorado's Wilf

RED WINGS ARCHIVE

Paiement, who clubbed Polonich in the face with a baseball-swing slash in an October 25, 1978 game, leaving the Detroit player with a broken nose requiring reconstructive surgery, a concussion and several facial lacerations. Polonich endured breathing problems the remainder of his career and within two seasons of the slash, was sent to the minor leagues.

"It wasn't just a broken nose as some people said," Polonich noted. "If they had to go through the pain I went through – the marking, disfigurement and the psychological problems – they'd say it wasn't worth $850,000."

- **BORN:**
  Foam Lake, Saskatchewan, December 4, 1953
- **ACQUIRED:**
  Selected 123rd overall in the May 15, 1973 NHL amateur draft
- **BEST SEASON WITH RED WINGS:**
  1976-77 (18-28-46)

- **TOTALS WITH RED WINGS:**
  GP-390, G-59, A-82, PTS-141
- **HONORS:**
  Served as team captain, 1976-77; Led team in penalty minutes, 1976-77, 1977-78

MOTOWN Classic

McKechnie is Wings' top scorer

Offensively, Walt McKechnie was the best of the bunch for the Wings in 1976-77, but like most everything else to do with that club, it was nothing to brag about. McKechnie's 25 goals were the lowest output to lead the team since Adam Brown topped the club with 20 in 1945-46. And McKechnie's 59 points were the tiniest team-leading total since Ted Lindsay and Sid Abel shared club honors with 54 points in 1948-49.

Acquired from Boston in 1974-75, McKechnie tried to pick up the void left at center by the departed Marcel Dionne in 1975-76, scoring a club-high 82 points for the Wings.

"We think we've got ourselves one of the best young centers around," Detroit GM Alex Delvecchio said. But McKechnie wasn't around long, going to Washington in 1977 as compensation for Detroit's signing of free-agent goalie Ron Low.

Moving was nothing new to the man they called "McKetch." McKechnie changed teams 12 times during his career, returning to the Wings as a free agent in 1981.

ASSEMBLY LINE

Rick Lapointe, Detroit's top draft pick in 1975, was dealt to Philadelphia for left-winger Bob Ritchie, right-wingers Steve Coates and Dave Kelly and defenseman Terry Murray. Doug Grant was traded to St. Louis for defenseman Rick Wilson. Bryan Watson went to Washington for defenseman Greg Joly. Center Bobby Sheehan was signed as a free agent and defensemen Jim Nahrgang and Reed Larson and center Fred Williams were supplied by the NHL amateur draft.

Rick Lapointe

Red Wings Facts

Most Playoff Shut-outs In one Season

6 - 2002

4 - 1952

3 - 1937

3 - 1950

2 - Several Occasions

Short Passes

The first time brothers ever coached against each other in a Red Wings game saw Johnny Wilson's Colorado Rockies down Larry Wilson's Red Wings 3-1 at the Olympia on January 20, 1977.

225

BACK in TIME

- **December 7, 1977**
While a member of the World Hockey Association's New England Whalers team, Gordie Howe scored his 1,000th career goal.

- **April 18, 1978**
The Senate ratified a second Panama Canal treaty which would turn the waterway over to Panama in 1999.

- **July 25, 1978**
The first test tube baby conceived outside the human body was born to a British couple and weighed 5 lbs, 2 oz.

quick cuts

Most Goals
Dale McCourt: 33

Most Assists
Reed Larson: 41

Most Points
Dale McCourt: 72

Most Penalty Minutes
Dennis Polonich: 254

Most Wins, Goaltender
Jim Rutherford: 20

Lowest Goals-Against Average
Jim Rutherford: 3.26

Most Shutouts
Jim Rutherford & Ron Low: 1

NHL Award Winners
Bobby Kromm - Jack Adams Award

FINAL STANDINGS

Norris Division	W	L	T	PTS	GF	GA
Montreal	59	10	11	129	359	183
DETROIT	32	34	14	78	252	266
Los Angeles	31	34	15	77	243	245
Pittsburgh	25	37	18	68	254	321
Washington	17	49	14	48	195	321

OTHER DIVISION WINNERS:
Adams Division - Boston Bruins
Patrick Division - NY Islanders
Smythe Division - Chicago Blackhawks

Playoff Results
Defeated the Atlanta Flames in Series "D" (2-0)
Lost to the Montreal Canadiens in Series "E" (4-1)
Leading Playoff Scorers
Vaclav Nedomansky (8PTS) - Dale McCourt (6PTS)
Stanley Cup Champion
Montreal Canadiens

1977-78 Season in Review

A new team was in charge of the NHL's worst team at the start of the season. Ted Lindsay was hired as Detroit GM late in the 1976-77 season, while Bobby Kromm took over as coach.

"Ted and I realize we're not going to turn the corner in a year or two," Kromm said. "But the main thing is to make progress every year."

After one year, both men were delighted by the progress made. The Wings rebounded strongly - a 37-point improvement from their dismal 41-point performance of 1976-77 - while discovering a couple of young cornerstones to build the team around.

Center Dale McCourt, the first overall choice in the 1977 NHL amateur draft, provided immediate impact, leading the team with 33-39-72 totals, firing a club rookie-record three hat tricks.

Back on defense, Reed Larson, a late-season addition in 1976-77, blossomed, leading all Wings blueliners with 19 goals and 60 points. The latter total was an NHL record for rookie defenders and the most points ever recorded by a Detroit rearguard in a single season.

Another surprise newcomer was speedy left-winger Paul Woods. Claimed from Montreal in the NHL waiver draft, Woods set a rookie playoff mark with five assists.

Center Andre St. Laurent, acquired from the New York Islanders, collected 31 goals and 70 points, while forwards Bill Lochead, Errol Thompson and Nick Libett, the lone holdover from Detroit's last playoff

RED WINGS ARCHIVE

team in 1969-70, all reached the 20-goal plateau. A 4-0 win April 9 over Montreal clinched second place for the Wings. "It was really enjoyable playing for the Red Wings that year, even more so than the years I played in Montreal," recalled defenseman Terry Harper, who won five Stanley Cups with the Canadiens.

The Wings also made news in the boardroom, where Detroit vice-president John Ziegler was named president of the NHL.

In their first playoff game since 1970, the Wings scored a team-record three power-play goals in the first period en route to a 5-3 verdict over Atlanta. Detroit swept the Flames, then dropped a best-of-seven series to Montreal in five games.

"Aggressive hockey is back in town," Lindsay liked to say. More significantly, so was playoff hockey.

HOCKEYTOWN MOMENT
Red Wings return to playoff action

The seven-year itch for playoff hockey ended April 11, when the Wings defeated the Atlanta Flames 5-3 at the Omni, coming home to sweep the best-of-three set two nights later, winning 3-2 on two third-period goals by Bill Lochead. The largest crowd in Olympia history, 16,671, watched Detroit win its first playoff series in 11 seasons. "If we never win another game, it's been a fabulous season," Wings coach Bobby Kromm said.

They did win again, taking Game 2 of their quarter-final series with the defending Stanley Cup champion

Montreal Canadiens, roaring back from a 2-0 deficit to win 4-2 at the Forum.

Back home, the Wings squandered a 2-0 third-period lead in Game 3, losing 4-2. Octopi rained down and late in the game, Montreal coach Scotty Bowman donned a helmet. "A kid right near our bench got hurt by somebody tossing a golf ball," Bowman explained. Montreal routed Detroit 8-0 in Game 4, clinching the set with a 4-1 triumph in Game 5.

Dale McCourt

Dale McCourt liked Detroit so much, he went to court to ensure he'd remain in the Motor City.

The Wings signed free-agent goalie Rogie Vachon of the Los Angeles Kings in the summer of 1978 and McCourt, Detroit's leading scorer, was awarded to L.A. as compensation for the loss of the two-time NHL All-Star netminder.

McCourt refused to report to the Kings, taking his battle to remain a Red Wing to the U.S. Federal District Court, where Judge Robert DeMascio granted a temporary injunction, allowing McCourt to play for Detroit during the 1978-79 season.

An appeal after the season once again awarded McCourt to the Kings, but he spurned a six-year, $3 million contract offer from the team. "What I offered Dale McCourt would have made him the highest-paid player in the history of hockey," L.A. owner Jerry Buss said. "I was very surprised when he turned it down, but I had to convince myself that he did not want to play in L.A. That convinced me."

The teams worked out a deal where McCourt's rights were dealt back to Detroit for center Andre St. Laurent and a pair of first-round draft picks.

McCourt was delighted and so were the Wings. They'd selected the center first overall in the 1977 NHL amateur draft after he'd captained the Hamilton Fincups to the 1975-76 Memorial Cup championship.

"People build successful franchises from within," Detroit GM Ted Lindsay said. "Dale is the best junior in Canada."

McCourt lit it up as a rookie, leading the club with 33-39-72 totals. A nephew of former Toronto Maple Leafs captain George Armstrong, McCourt led the club in scoring two more times – in 1979-80 and 1980-81 – and similarities were noted between McCourt and another famous NHLer.

"The best way I can describe him is to compare him to Stan Mikita," Lindsay said of the Hall of Fame Chicago center. "Dale does a lot of things like Stan. He's unselfish. If you look at the stats, his wingers always seem to have good years."

McCourt never fell below 28 goals or 71 points during his first four seasons with the Wings, but the team continued to sink further from playoff contention and the club took a drastic step, dealing three former first-round draft picks - McCourt, right-winger Mike Foligno and center/right-winger Brent Peterson - to the Buffalo Sabres for forwards Danny Gare and Derek Smith and defenseman Jim Schoenfeld on December 2, 1981.

"That's the business, I guess," McCourt said after the deal. Unlike the Los Angeles situation, this time time, McCourt willingly departed Detroit. "That was a different thing," he said of being awarded to the Kings. "If it had been a trade, I would have gone."

McCourt played just two more NHL campaigns, splitting the 1983-84 season between Buffalo and Toronto, then spent seven campaigns with Ambri-Piotta of the Swiss League.

- **BORN:**
  Falconbridge, Ontario, January 26, 1957
- **ACQUIRED:**
  Selected first overall in the June 14, 1977 NHL amateur draft
- **BEST SEASON WITH RED WINGS:**
  1980-81 (30-56-86)

- **TOTALS WITH RED WINGS:**
  GP-341, G-134, A-203, PTS-337
- **HONORS:**
  Led team in scoring, 1977-78, 1979-80, 1980-81; Played for Canada, 1979 and 1981 World Championships

MOTOWN Classic

Kromm wins Jack Adams Award

Bobby Kromm arrived in Detroit with a suitcase full of accomplishments. He coached Canada to a world title in 1961 and led the WHA's Winnipeg Jets to the 1975-76 Avco Cup as champions of that league. He'd also guided the Trail, B.C. Smoke Eaters to an Allan Cup as Canadian senior champs and won a CHL title in Dallas.

What he did in his first season as coach of Detroit, though, might just have been his most impressive performance. He took a team that was the NHL's worst at 16-55-9 the season before and led them into the playoffs for the first time since 1969-70, earning second place in the NHL's Norris Division. The Wings also won their first playoff series since 1965-66 under Kromm's guidance. "He was the boss," GM Ted Lindsay said. "He's a hell of a coach."

RED WINGS ARCHIVE

These achievements did not go unrecognized and Kromm was the 1977-78 recipient of the Jack Adams Trophy, which goes to the NHL's coach of the year, becoming the first Red Wing coach to win the award named for the Hall of Fame Detroit bench boss.

ASSEMBLY LINE

Shaking up what had been the NHL's worst team, GM Ted Lindsay moved Michel Bergeron to the New York Islanders for center Andre St. Laurent. Defenseman Perry Miller and former Wing Thommie Bergman jumped with coach Bobby Kromm from Winnipeg of the WHA and right-winger Al McDonough, acquired in a 1974 deal with Atlanta, also jumped to Detroit from the WHA. Left-winger Paul Woods was claimed from Montreal in the NHL waiver draft. Free-agent goalie Ron Low was signed from Washington, costing Walt McKechnie as compensation. Right-winger Rick Bowness was purchased from Atlanta and left-winger Dennis Hull was acquired from Chicago for a 1977 fourth-round draft pick (Carey Wilson). Dan Maloney went to Toronto for left-winger Errol Thompson. Right-winger Vaclav Nedomansky and center Larry Wright were signed as free agents and the NHL amateur draft provided center Dale McCourt and left-winger Rob Plumb.

Ron Low

RED WINGS ARCHIVE

Red Wings Facts

Most Goals Scored By A Defenseman in one Season

27	Reed Larson	1980 - 81
23	Reed Larson	1983 - 84
22	Reed Larson	1979 - 80
22	Reed Larson	1982 - 83
21	Reed Larson	1981 - 82
20	Flash Hollett	1944 - 45
20	Nicklas Lidstrom	1999 - 00
19	Red Kelly	1952 - 53
19	Reed Larson	1977 - 78
19	Reed Larson	1985 - 86

Short Passes

Wings defenseman Dave Hanson portrayed Jack Hanson, one of the infamous Hanson Brothers in the 1977 hockey film Slap Shot and he's also given credit for coining the phrase, "Aggressive Hockey Is Back In Town," which became Detroit's marketing slogan in 1977-78.

- 1978  1979 -

BACK in TIME

- **December 5, 1978**

Pete Rose, a free agent in professional baseball, signed a $3.2 million contract with the Philadelphia Phillies, making him baseball's highest paid player.

- **March 5, 1979**

In a 6-3 vote, the Supreme Court ruled that it is unconstitutional sex discrimination for state laws to require husbands to pay alimony.

- **March 26, 1979**

Egyptian president Anwar Sadat and Isreal's Prime Minister Menachem Begin signed a peace treaty at the White House, ending 31 years of warfare.

quick cuts

Most Goals
Vaclav Nedomansky: 38

Most Assists
Reed Larson: 49

Most Points
Vaclav Nedomansky: 73

Most Penalty Minutes
Dennis Polonich: 208

Most Wins, Goaltender
Jim Rutherford: 13

Lowest Goals-Against Average
Jim Rutherford: 3.27

Most Shutouts
Jim Rutherford: 1

NHL Award Winners
None

FINAL STANDINGS

Norris Division	W	L	T	PTS	GF	GA
Montreal	52	17	11	115	337	204
Pittsburgh	36	31	13	85	281	279
Los Angeles	34	34	12	80	292	286
Washington	24	41	15	63	273	338
DETROIT	23	41	16	62	252	295

OTHER DIVISION WINNERS:
Adams Division - Boston Bruins
Patrick Division - NY Islanders
Smythe Division - Chicago Blackhawks

Playoff Results
Did Not Qualify
Stanley Cup Champion
Montreal Canadiens

1978-79 Season in Review

"We'll be better this year," GM Ted Lindsay boasted at the start of the 1978-79 season. "We won't be 37 points better, like last season, but we will be improved."

His reason for optimism was between the pipes, where Lindsay had boldly signed restricted free agent Rogie Vachon, a former Vezina Trophy winner and a three-time Stanley Cup champion, away from the Los Angeles Kings.

The Kings were awarded Dale McCourt, Detroit's leading scorer, as compensation for the loss of Vachon, but the Wings looked to be a on a roll when McCourt gained a court injunction which would keep him in Detroit.

RED WINGS ARCHIVE

Appearances can be deceiving, however.

When the season began, things started to go horribly wrong, beginning with Vachon, who struggled to find his confidence all season, managing just 10 wins in 50 games. Rookie forward Brent Peterson broke his leg. Defenseman Greg Joly fractured his wrist. Feisty center Dennis Polonich had his nose splintered by the stick of Colorado's Wilf Paiement.

Sitting a respectable 4-2-3 nine games into the season, the Wings hit the skids, winning only five of their next 41 games, missing the playoffs with a 23-41-16 record, leaving them last in the Norris Division.

One highlight was a 1-0 win over reigning Stanley Cup champion Montreal in the season finale. Jim Rutherford posted the shutout, McCourt got the goal and the reverse cost the Habs first overall in the NHL standings.

"What were we, 55 points ahead of them?" Montreal coach Scotty Bowman asked incredulously. "It's hard to believe. Where have they been all year?"

Center Vaclav Nedomansky led the Wings with 38 goals and 73 points, while Polonich, with 208, was the club penalty-minute leader for the third straight season. McCourt, Rutherford and left-wingers Paul Woods and Nick Libett played for Canada at the World Championships, while left-winger Dan Labraaten suited up for Sweden and left-winger Danny Bolduc played for the U.S.

HOCKEYTOWN MOMENT

Wings sign free agent Vachon

RED WINGS ARCHIVE

Were the playoff chances of the Red Wings scuttled on the beaches of Honolulu during the summer of 1978? Hawaiian legend says so.

With the ink still drying on a new $1.9 million contract from the Wings, goalie Rogie Vachon and wife Nicole headed to the Pacific on vacation. While there, Nicole picked up a souvenir statue of the Hawaiian Goddess of Fire.

Legend has it that anyone who removes the Goddess of Fire from the Islands will be cursed, which might explain Vachon's injury later that summer during the Superstars competition, or the concussion he suffered which affected his co-ordination and concentration. It could also have been responsible for Vachon's 3.90 goals-against average, nearly a goal higher than his career GAA of 2.99.

Nicole shipped the statue back to Hawaii later in the season, but the damage was done. When the Wings placed the two-time NHL All-Star on waivers in March, not one team was willing to cough up $2,500 to claim Vachon.

Wings of Legend

Vaclav Nedomansky

Long before Igor Larionov and Viacheslav Fetisov brought down the Iron Curtain, Vaclav Nedomansky boldly leaped over it to freedom.

The star of Czechoslovakia's national team and considered by some to be the best player skating outside of the NHL, Nedomansky and teammate Richard Farda, escaped to the West in the summer of 1974 to sign with the WHA's Toronto Toros. "I couldn't get out legally, so I had to do it this way," said Nedomansky, who defected with his wife Vera and son Vaclav Jr. while vacationing in Switzerland.

Nedomansky was a star in Europe, with both Slovan Bratislava of the Czech League, for whom he scored 369 goals in 419 games and the Czech national team, registering 78 goals in 93 games for his country.

He played in two Olympics, winning silver and bronze medals and led Czechoslovakia to the 1972 World Championship.

The political battles between Czechoslovakia and the Soviet Union, stemming from the latter's 1968 invasion of the former, often carried over into athletic competition, as former Wing Mark Howe discovered while watching the Soviet-Czech game at the 1972 Olympics.

"To this day, I've never seen a game more brutal than that one," Howe remembered. "The Czech goalie must have broken five sticks over Russian players.

"The Russians were ahead in the third period and the Czechs were on the power play, with a faceoff in the Russian end. They won the draw and the puck went to Nedomansky, but he just turned and wired a shot into the Russian bench."

That level of intensity made Nedomansky a success in North America, where he wasn't afraid to mix it up. "Defensemen around the league have just been given a king-sized headache," New York Rangers GM John Ferguson said when Nedomansky signed as a free agent with the Wings in 1977.

"Big Ned is an outstanding acquisition," noted Wings legend Gordie Howe, who played against

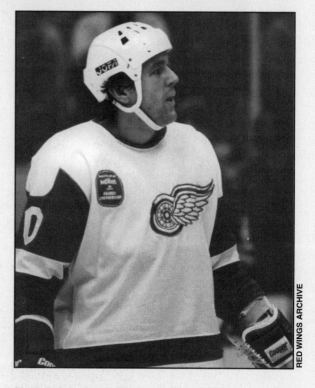

RED WINGS ARCHIVE

Nedomansky in the WHA. "He does what Phil Esposito does in the slot – takes up space, gets the puck and snaps shots on goal.

"He should score 30 goals for Detroit."

Howe was right. In 1978-79, his first full season as a Wing, the 6-foot-2, 205-pound center scored 38 times, becoming the first player in franchise history to register hat tricks in consecutive games. Nedomansky produced 35 more goals in 1979-80.

His production fell off to 12 goals in each of the next two seasons and Nedomansky, 38 at the time, was let go, joining the Rangers in 1982-83, his last NHL season.

After retiring, Nedomansky coached in Austria and Germany and worked as an NHL scout.

- **BORN:**
  Hodonin, Czechoslovakia, March 14, 1944
- **ACQUIRED:**
  Signed as a free agent, November 15, 1977
- **BEST SEASON WITH RED WINGS:**
  1979-80 (35-39-74)
- **TOTALS WITH RED WINGS:**
  GP-344, G-108, A-139, PTS-247
- **HONORS:**
  Led team in goals and points, 1978-79; First Wing to score back-to-back hat tricks, February 25 and 28, 1979

232

MOTOWN Classic

Larson sets defenseman scoring record

A true All-American performer, Minnesota-born Reed Larson wasted little time establishing his credentials as a point-producing blueliner.

"Reed is going to be one of the better defensemen in the league," predicted Detroit teammate Dennis Hextall. "The kid just skates and shoots so well." Known as the "Riverboat Gambler" because he so often jumped up to join the rush, Larson tallied 60 points in 1977-78, his first full NHL season, setting a club record for defensemen, earning a spot in the NHL All-Star Game as a rookie.

He then trumped that card in 1978-79. Larson collected 49 assists and 67 points, both new Wings marks for rearguards. His 49 assists led the team, just as his 41 helpers had in 1977-78.

"He could shoot the puck harder than anybody," said former Wing Mark Howe. That booming shot helped Larson count 37 goals in his first 168 NHL games.

RED WINGS ARCHIVE

ASSEMBLY LINE

Signing restricted free-agent goalie Rogie Vachon from Los Angeles nearly cost the Wings Dale McCourt, but after a two-year court battle, the Kings accepted Andre St. Laurent and two first-round draft picks as compensation. Other free-agent pick-ups included former Wings center Bill Hogaboam and left-wingers Danny Bolduc and Dan Labraaten. Center Greg Carroll was claimed on waivers from Washington. Defensemen Willie Huber, Larry Gloeckner, John Hilworth and John Taft, centers Fern LeBlanc and Roland Cloutier and center/right-winger Brent Peterson were added through the NHL amateur draft. Center Bjorne Skaare, another draftee, skated in one game to become the first Norwegian-born NHLer.

RED WINGS ARCHIVE

Bill Hogaboam

Red Wings Facts

Most Career Victories By A Goaltender

Terry Sawchuk - 352
Chris Osgood - 221
Harry Lumley - 163
Roger Crozier - 131
Tim Cheveldae - 128
Greg Stefan - 115
Jimmy Rutherford - 97
Roy Edwards - 95
Norm Smith - 76
Glenn Hall - 74
Johnny Mowers - 65
Glen Hanlon - 65

Short Passes

Dan Labraaten recorded a goal and two assists as the Red Wings defeated the Wings of the Soviet 6-5 in an exhibition game against the touring Russian team played January 4, 1979 at the Olympia.

JOE LOUIS ARENA

When you get right down to it, the place is only a building. Four walls and a roof.

It's the memories which make Joe Louis Arena special. And, oh, what memories have been made there.

Named for the Detroit-born boxer who reigned as heavyweight champion of the world from 1937-48, Joe Louis Arena, like its predecessor, the Olympia, wasn't christened with a hockey game.

The inaugural event, a college basketball game between Michigan and Detroit, was witnessed by 12,000 fans on December 12, 1979. Unlike the Olympia, the JLA was ahead of schedule by 19 days. Olympia's birth in 1927 was nine months late in arrival.

Hockey took over on December 27, with the Wings moving in as main tenants, losing a 3-2 decision to the St. Louis Blues before 19,742, a Detroit-record crowd which would last less than a month.

There were 19,905 packed into the rink January 12 to watch Wings legend Gordie Howe make his NHL return to Detroit with the Hartford Whalers. A month later, 21,002 took in the NHL All-Star Game, in Detroit for the first time since 1955.

"It's a beautiful arena, but it's the people who make it," Howe said.

The affair between Red Wings fans and their new home wasn't a case of love at first sight. Those early years were a struggle for the Wings, both on and off the ice. The turnaround began when Mike Ilitch bought the team in 1982 and when Steve Yzerman was drafted a year later. "I want to make this the best arena in the country," Ilitch said and progress was being made in that direction. A gathering of 21,019 — at the time an NHL-record crowd for a regular-season game — watched the Wings defeat Pittsburgh 5-2 on November 25, 1983. By 1987-88, after successive appearances in the Stanley Cup final four, tickets to Wings games were as scarce and as valuable as precious metals.

"St. Louis was a pretty good hockey town, but even it doesn't compare to here," Detroit left-winger Brendan Shanahan said. "You quickly get a sense of the passion here, of how much the people in the city care about their hockey team."

That passion is evident in the mass of Red Wings jerseys which fill the JLA seats as the Wings take the ice each night. This is the rink where Howe made his final Detroit NHL appearance, where Yzerman scored his 500th and 600th goals and where visiting teams rarely depart with a smile on their face.

So many memories have unfolded on the ice below, none more significant than the night of June 7, 1997, when the Wings won their first Stanley Cup in 42 years.

"You got a sense that the whole city of Detroit was behind this team," remembered goalie Mike Vernon.

The Wings entered the 2001-02 season with a 463-293-105-2 record at Joe Louis Arena. More impressively, displaying that passion for the game which Shanahan expressed, Wings fans have packed the place for 223 consecutive sellouts.

Just a building? Sure. And the Mona Lisa is just a painting.

- 1979 1980 -

BACK in TIME

• December 10, 1979
Mother Theresa, known for her empire of 700 shelters and clinics and her direct work with India's poor, was awarded the Nobel Prize.

• February 7, 1980
The FDA upheld the 1969 federal ban on the sale of the sugar substitute Cyclamate, as a cancer danger.

• July 19, 1980
The Summer Olympics opened in Moscow without the United States, West Germany and Japan, who refused to attend in protest against the Soviet intervention in Afganastan.

quick cuts

Most Goals
Mike Foligno: 36
Most Assists
Dale McCourt: 51
Most Points
Dale McCourt: 81
Most Penalty Minutes
Willie Huber: 164
Most Wins, Goaltender
Rogie Vachon: 20
Lowest Goals-Against Average
Rogie Vachon: 3.61
Most Shutouts
Rogie Vachon: 4
NHL Award Winners
None

FINAL STANDINGS

Norris Division	W	L	T	PTS	GF	GA
Montreal	47	20	13	107	328	240
Los Angeles	30	36	14	74	290	313
Pittsburgh	30	37	13	73	251	303
Hartford	27	34	19	73	303	312
DETROIT	26	43	11	63	268	306

OTHER DIVISION WINNERS:
Adams Division - Buffalo Sabres
Patrick Division - Philadelphia Flyers
Smythe Division - Chicago Blackhawks

Playoff Results
Did Not Qualify
Stanley Cup Champion
New York Islanders

236

1979-80 Season in Review

Despite sliding out of the playoff picture for the eighth time in nine years, Wings GM Ted Lindsay saw positive signs entering a new season. "We were out of only seven games all last year," Lindsay said. "The rest could have gone either way."

Coach Bobby Kromm echoed Lindsay's hopeful tone. "I think we actually played better last year (than in 1977-78), except for the last three minutes of a bunch of games," Kromm said.

On the one hand, their hope was rewarded. The Wings won 26 games, three more than in 1978-79 and netted a club-record 268 goals, suiting up five 30-goal scorers. Vaclav Nedomansky scored 35 goals, Errol Thompson had 34 and Dale McCourt and Dan Labraaten 30 apiece. Pacing the attack was left-winger Mike Foligno, Detroit's first draft pick, who scored 36 times to set a team mark for rookies. Foligno garnered his first NHL hat trick January 27 in a 7-6 win over Quebec, then collected another four days later in a 4-3 decision against Pittsburgh.

Quebec, which joined the NHL along with Winnipeg, Hartford and Edmonton in the NHL-WHA merger, also supplied the opposition December 15 in the closing game at the Olympia, which resulted in a 4-4 tie. Detroit opened the new Joe Louis Arena on December 27, losing 3-2 to St. Louis. Foligno had two assists and was selected first star.

RED WINGS ARCHIVE

Fifty-two years earlier on November 22, 1927, Detroit was also a one-goal loser, that time to Ottawa, in the very first contest at the Olympia.

Defenseman Reed Larson scored 22 times, a new mark for Detroit blueliners and played in the NHL All-Star Game, held February 5 at the JLA.

The new-found offense couldn't offset Detroit's defensive woes, which increased the club's total in the loss column from 41 to 43 and cost Kromm his job.

Former Wings defenseman Marcel Pronovost coached the last nine games of the season, as Detroit missed the playoffs for the ninth time in 10 seasons.

HOCKEYTOWN MOMENT
Goodbye Olympia...Hello Joe Louis Arena

They bid farewell to the Olympia on December 15, 1979, as 15,609 watched Detroit rally from a 4-0 deficit to gain a 4-4 tie with the Quebec Nordiques. Wings defenseman Greg Joly earned the honor of scoring the final goal in the rink, but doesn't recollect the moment. "I didn't score too many goals in my career, so you would think the ones that did go into the net would be engraved in my mind," Joly said. "That just shows you what kind of memory I have."

Twelve days later, 19,472 crammed into the new Joe Louis Arena to see the Wings and St. Louis Blues do battle. Brian Sutter gave the Blues the lead, but Dennis Sobchuk and Danny Bolduc made it 2-1 Detroit entering the final period. Bernie Federko tied it, then Blair Chapman tallied the game-winner with Detroit's Barry Long in the penalty box and the Wings lost for the sixth time in nine games.

RED WINGS ARCHIVE

"The only difference between this place and Olympia is 5,000 seats," groused Wings GM Ted Lindsay, more concerned with his team's struggles than their cozy, new home.

Reed Larson

When Reed Larson wound up at the point, players scattered and goalies prayed he'd shoot wide.

"I faced a lot of shots, but no shooter fired the puck harder than Reed Larson," said goalie Ron Low, who dealt with Larson as an opponent and in practice as a Detroit teammate. "No matter what anyone says, Bobby Hull never shot the puck as hard as Reed did."

Those powerful blasts allowed Larson to rewrite the record book for Red Wings defensemen and for American-born NHL players. A native of Minneapolis, Larson won an NCAA title with the University of Minnesota in 1976, the year the Wings drafted him. "Reed has unlimited potential," Detroit GM Ted Lindsay said. "The potential to be an all-star."

He made his NHL debut late in the 1976-77 campaign, then rocketed to stardom the following season.

His 41 assists and 60 points were new records for Detroit defensemen, let alone for Wings rookie rearguards. But, like Babe Ruth's home-run numbers, Larson just kept breaking his own marks.

"He moves so effortlessly and he's got a lot of talent," assessed fellow Wings defenseman Terry Harper.

Larson collected 67 points in 1978-79 and tallied 22 goals in 1979-80, breaking the club mark for goals by a defenseman of 20, set by Flash Hollett in 1944-45. Not satisfied to stop there, Larson bagged 27 goals in 1980-81, one of six 20-goal seasons during his career. He garnered 52 asissts and 74 points in 1982-83, once again bettering his own records.

Larson is one of only three defensemen in NHL history to record at least nine straight seasons with 50 or more points. His nine successive 50-point campaigns came from 1977-78 through 1985-86, joining Paul Coffey (15) and Phil Housley (11) in this select group.

Larson posted five consecutive 20-goal seasons from 1979-80 through 1983-84. Among NHL defensemen, only Bobby Orr (seven) ever put together a longer stretch of 20-goal performances.

Serving as Detroit captain in 1980-81 and 1981-82, Larson played for the United States in the 1981 World Championships and Canada Cup. He collected his

RED WINGS ARCHIVE

451st point as a Wing on October 1, 1984 to surpass Red Kelly as the all-time leading scorer among Detroit defenders. Larson was the first U.S.-born NHLer to collect 500 points and the fifth Red Wing to reach this plateau.

"He was a good skater, moved the puck well and had quite a shot," was current Wings coach Scotty Bowman's scouting report on Larson.

Detroit endured a dismal 1985-86 campaign and entered a rebuilding mode. Larson was dealt to the Boston Bruins for defenseman Mike O'Connell, currently the Bruins GM. Larson spent four more seasons in the NHL, playing for Boston in the 1988 Stanley Cup final. He skated for three years in the Italian League and made a brief comeback with the IHL's Minnesota Moose in 1994-95.

He was inducted into the U.S. Hockey Hall of Fame in 1996.

- **BORN:**
  Minneapolis, Minnesota, July 30, 1956
- **ACQUIRED:**
  Selected 22nd overall in the June 1, 1976 NHL amateur draft
- **BEST SEASON WITH RED WINGS:**
  1982-83 (22-52-74)
- **TOTALS WITH RED WINGS:**
  GP-708, G-188, A-382, PTS-570

- **HONORS:**
  Played in NHL All-Star Game, 1977-78, 1980-81, 1981-82; Played for the United States, 1981 World Championship, 1981 Canada Cup; Led team in assists, 1977-78, 1978-79, 1979-80; Led team in penalty minutes, 1981-82; Elected to U.S. Hockey Hall of Fame, 1996

MOTOWN Classic

All-Star Game marks Howe's return to Detroit

Joe Louis Arena played host to the NHL All-Star Game February 5, 1980 and an unofficial love-in for Wings legend Gordie Howe.

Added to the Wales Conference team by coach Scotty Bowman, Howe – who had returned to the NHL with the Hartford Whalers – received a two-minute standing ovation from the crowd of 21,002. "It meant everything to be back in the home town again," said Howe, who registered an assist as the Wales beat the Campbells 6-3. Howe, 51, made three appearances at the JLA in what would be his final NHL season. He was named the first star of Hartford's 6-4 victory on January 12 and in a 4-4 tie on March 13, took the opening faceoff at center, flanked by sons Mark and Marty on the wings.

"Why not?" said Hartford coach Don Blackburn, who sent out the all-Howe line "Gordie's deserving of every accolade and it gave the kids a chance to enjoy something very meaningful."

PHOTO COURTESY OF WINDSOR STAR

ASSEMBLY LINE

"You don't end up in last place and stand pat," said Wings GM Ted Lindsay, who traded a 1981 fifth-round draft pick (Dave Michayluk) to Philadelphia for center Dennis Sobchuk and dealt veteran Nick Libett to Pittsburgh for center Pete Mahovlich, a former Wing. Right-winger Tom Webster, Detroit's leading scorer in 1970-71, was signed as a free agent and right-winger Alex Pirus was purchased from Minnesota. Left-wingers George Lyle (Hartford) and Glenn Hicks and defenseman Barry Long (Winnipeg) were reclaimed prior to the expansion draft which stocked the four former WHA teams involved in the merger with the NHL. Expansion draft losses included Ron Low and Roland Cloutier (Quebec) and Clarke Hamilton and Al Cameron (Winnipeg). The newly-named NHL entry draft supplied right-winger Mike Foligno, left-winger John Ogrodnick and defensemen Rick Vasko and Jim Korn.

RED WINGS ARCHIVE

Dennis Sobchuk

Red Wings Facts

Most Losses In one Season

57 (1985-86)
55 (1976-77)
47 (1981-82)
45 (1970-71)
45 (1974-75)
44 (1975-76)
44 (1982-83)
43 (1979-80)
43 (1980-81)
42 (1983-84)

Short Passes

Dennis Sobchuk, who scored the first Detroit goal at Joe Louis Arena, could boast that he played major pro hockey in three Detroit rinks – at the Olympia and the JLA with the Wings and at Cobo Arena with the WHA's Phoenix Roadrunners against the Michigan Stags in 1974-75.

- 1980 [ ] 1981 -

BACK in TIME

- **November 21, 1980**
An estimated 83 million Americans tuned into the CBS prime time soap opera Dallas to find out "who shot JR."

- **March 30, 1981**
Newly elected President Ronald Reagan was shot in the chest by John W. Hinckley, Jr. after delivering a speech at the Washington Hilton Hotel.

- **July 17, 1981**
Eleven people were killed and nearly 200 injured when two aerial walkways in the Hyatt Regency Hotel in Kansas City, Missouri collapsed.

quick cuts

Most Goals
John Ogrodnick: 35
Most Assists
Dale McCourt: 56
Most Points
Dale McCourt: 86
Most Penalty Minutes
Jim Korn: 246
Most Wins, Goaltender
Gilles Gilbert: 11
Lowest Goals-Against Average
Gilles Gilbert: 4.01
Most Shutouts
None
NHL Award Winners
None

FINAL STANDINGS

Norris Division	W	L	T	PTS	GF	GA
Montreal	45	22	13	103	332	232
Los Angeles	43	24	13	99	337	290
Pittsburgh	30	37	13	73	302	345
Hartford	21	41	18	60	292	372
DETROIT	19	43	18	56	252	339

OTHER DIVISION WINNER:
Adams Division - Buffalo Sabres
Patrick Division - NY Islanders
Smythe Division - St. Louis Blues

Playoff Results
Did Not Qualify
Stanley Cup Champion
New York Islanders

1980-81 Season in Review

It wasn't the worst season in Red Wings history, but it was close. And it was the worst start to a season the franchise had ever experienced. A three-game losing streak during a season-opening road trip launched an 0-5 beginning for the Wings, which was halted with a 5-1 home-ice victory October 23 over the Colorado Rockies.

The Wings defeated the New York Rangers 4-2 in their next game, then proceeded to win just once in their next 17 games, costing Ted Lindsay, who had dropped down from GM to assume the coaching duties, his job. Wayne Maxner took over behind the bench and a 7-2-4 stretch in December got people excited. But the excitement was short-lived.

The Wings skidded back into oblivion, winning two of 14 January contests, suffering a pair of double-digit setbacks in a five-day span - 10-0 January 15 at Calgary and 11-4 January 20 at Los Angeles. Not surprisingly, these defeats came on the road, where Detroit was a dismal 3-28-9, the fewest away wins recorded by the team since posting a 3-17-4 slate in 1931-32.

The Wings were fit to be tied, posting 18 draws, equaling a club record set in 1952-53. They recorded four consecutive ties between March 1-10, but never posted a shutout, the first season in club history in which the Wings failed to register a clean sheet. They

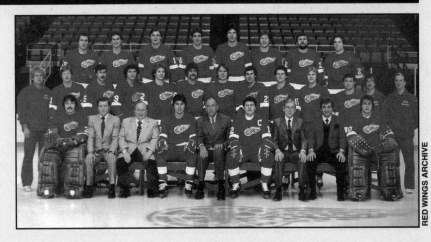

RED WINGS ARCHIVE

held the opposition to a solitary goal in only five of 80 games.

Down the stretch, Detroit closed 1-14-6 in its last 21 games, finishing last in the Norris Division for the third consecutive season, winning just 19 times.

Second-year left-winger John Ogrodnick fired a team-high 35 goals, while linemate Dale McCourt was out front with 56 assists and 86 points. But the story of the season for the Wings was defenseman Reed Larson, whose 27 goals bettered his own club mark by five. Scoring three goals in a 6-4 loss to Pittsburgh January 3, Larson joined Red Kelly and Flash Hollett as the only Detroit defenders to register hat tricks.

Larson and defenseman Jim Korn played for the U.S. in the World Championships, while McCourt, Ogrodnick, right-winger Mike Foligno and defenseman Willie Huber were part of the Canadian team.

HOCKEYTOWN MOMENT
Skinner New Red Wings G.M.

The old GM was now the coach and the old coach was now the GM. Ted Lindsay, hired as GM of the Wings late in the 1976-77, assumed the coaching chores of the team, while Jimmy Skinner, coach when Detroit won its last Stanley Cup in 1954-55, took over in the role of GM.

"I thought Ted would infuse some of his drive into the team," Skinner said.

It was an arrangement which didn't last long. With a 3-14-3 slate, Lindsay was out of work 20 games into the season and Wayne Maxner, who coached the Windsor Spitfires juniors across the Detroit River in Windsor, Ontario, was named to replace Lindsay behind the bench. Lindsay was philosophical upon his departure. "Our record is not that impressive," he said. "As a player or a coach, if you want accolades, you have to earn them."

RED WINGS ARCHIVE

Jimmy Skinner

Wings of Legend

Mike Foligno

If vertical leap were a statistic tabulated by the NHL, Mike Foligno would have been a perennial leader.

The Detroit right-winger quickly became a fan favorite during the 1979-80 campaign, his inaugural NHL season – because he set a club mark for rookies with 36 goals and because of the way he celebrated each of them.

Every time he tallied, Foligno's unique method of celebration was to leap into the air as high as he could while tucking his knees into his chest.

He's the only NHL player remembered for his hang time.

"Everywhere I would go, kids would yell to me, 'Hey Foligno, do the jump,'" Foligno recalled.

He isn't sure when he originated the Foligno Flip – he thinks it was in junior with the Sudbury Wolves – but Foligno vividly recollects the reaction on the two occasions he elected not to jump – while playing for Buffalo after scoring the final goal in a 8-1 rout of the New Jersey Devils and his first goal with Toronto after recuperating from a broken leg.

"I received a lot of fan mail from people telling me I had to jump," Foligno said. "I decided that I had better be sure to do it after all my goals."

The Wings certainly jumped for joy after Foligno's rookie season, which saw his 36 goals lead the team. He finished second to Boston Bruins defenseman Ray Bourque in the Calder Trophy balloting for NHL rookie of the year.

"He's a complete hockey player, a guy with a great deal of talent who comes to play every night," Detroit GM Ted Lindsay said after drafting Foligno.

Born in Sudbury, Foligno's family moved to Italy when he was a toddler, but returned to Canada when Mike was seven, about the time he became a Wings fan.

"It was because of Alex Delvecchio," Foligno said. "The family always talked about Alex, because he was Italian. They never mentioned Gordie Howe, though."

RED WINGS ARCHIVE

Foligno slipped to 28 goals in 1980-81 and had 13 goals in 26 games the following season when the Wings unleashed a blockbuster deal, sending Foligno, Dale McCourt and Brent Peterson to Buffalo for forwards Danny Gare and Derek Smith and defenseman Jim Schoenfeld.

"I hope I've given the fans some entertainment in the time I've been here," Foligno said. "If they ever want me back, I'll come."

Foligno did come back, but only to haunt Wings fans in enemy uniforms. Playing for the Leafs in a 1993 playoff series against Detroit, he scored an overtime winner in Game 5 of the series at Joe Louis Arena, helping Toronto take a seven-game decision.

Foligno finished his playing days with the Florida Panthers in 1993-94 and today is head coach of the AHL's Hershey Bears.

- **BORN:**
  Sudbury, Ontario, January 29, 1959
- **ACQUIRED:**
  Selected third overall in the August 9, 1979 NHL entry draft
- **BEST SEASON WITH RED WINGS:**
  1979-80 (36-35-71)
- **TOTALS WITH RED WINGS:**
  GP-186, G-77, A-83, PTS-160

- **HONORS:**
  Runner up in Calder Trophy voting, 1979-80; Set club rookie record with 36 goals, 1979-80; Led team in goals, 1979-80; Played for Canada, 1981 World Championships

MOTOWN Classic

Super sophomore effort by Ogrodnick

The 1979 NHL entry draft was the first season that the draft age was lowered to 18, meaning several 19-year-old players were overlooked in the early rounds. One of those overlooked was John Ogrodnick.

The left-winger from the Western Hockey League's New Westminster Bruins was still available in the fourth round when Detroit pegged him with the 66th pick, even though he'd tallied 107 goals in his last two seasons of junior hockey.

Scoring only eight times in 41 games as a rookie, it was easy to overlook Ogrodnick during his first season with the Wings, but in 1980-81, he opened some eyes, leading the team with 35 goals. His efforts were recognized when he was selected to play in the NHL All-Star Game and invited to suit up for Canada at the World Championships.

It was the beginning of a trend for Ogrodnick, who would lead the club in goals for each of the next six seasons.

ASSEMBLY LINE

Goaltenders were on the move, as Jim Rutherford went to Toronto for center Mark Kirton and Rogie Vachon was dealt to Boston for Gilles Gilbert in an exchange of netminders. Errol Thompson was shipped to Pittsburgh for left-winger Gary McAdam, while Rick Vasko went to Calgary for rugged right-winger Brad Smith, dubbed "Motor City Smitty" by Detroit fans. Dan Labraaten also was sent to Calgary in a deal for center Earl Ingarfield Jr. Defenseman Rick Smith was claimed in the NHL waiver draft from Boston, but later lost on waivers to Washington. Defenseman Tom Bladon and left-winger Mal Davis were signed as free agents, while goalies Al Jensen, Claude Legris and Larry Lozinski, defenseman John Barrett, right-wingers Mike Blaisdell and Jody Gage and left-winger Joe Paterson were NHL entry-draft selections.

Gilles Gilbert

Red Wings Facts

Most Goals Scored In One Game

15
vs N.Y. Rangers January 23, 1944
12
vs N.Y. Rangers November 5, 1942
12
vs N.Y. Rangers February 3, 1944
12
vs Calgary October 29, 1981
12
vs Chicago December 4, 1987
11
on eight occasions

Short Passes

The Wings failed to post a shutout in 1980-81, the first time in franchise history they'd been blanked in this department. Detroit also played the entire 1981-82 and 1984-85 seasons without registering a shutout.

 **Little Caesars**®

Salutes

The Detroit

Red Wings®

on **75** *Years*

of Great Hockey!

THE ILITCH ERA

She took them to Joe Louis Arena box office and pointed towards the telephones. "Get on those telephones and talk people into buying season tickets," were her instructions.

The Ilitches lost money the first five seasons they owned the Wings and at one point were forced to give away cars during games just to get people into the rink.

"Those years could have been very frustrating," Mike Ilitch said of his early tenure as Wings owner. "I was confused for a while, but I learned to look at hockey as a business."

Today, the franchise is estimated to be worth more than $120 million and Wings games are the hottest ticket in town.

The Ilitches added to their empire in 1992, purchasing the Detroit Tigers for a reported $85 million. The following year, they opened the Detroit Second City Comedy Theatre. Already in place was the 5,000-seat Fox Theatre in downtown Detroit, restored at a cost of $65 million.

A hands-on owner, Mike Ilitch has never been afraid to make a daring move or a difficult decision, if he thought it would help his team win.

"If the difference is money, I'll spend money," he said. "But it's not always a matter of spending money. You've got to have good management and all the rest."

Good management hasn't been a concern since the Ilitches took over in Hockeytown.

One great ownership group passed the torch to another when the Norris family sold the Red Wings to the Ilitch family in 1982.

The parallels between the two hockey families are many. James Norris Sr. made his fortune in the grain business and Mike Ilitch employed some of that grain while building his wealth through his Little Caesars Pizza chain.

When Norris took over the club in 1932, it was in financial ruin. When Ilitch purchased the club from Norris' son Bruce, the Wings were also a franchise in dire straits.

"We worked our way out of the quicksand and back on the road," Ilitch said of those early days running the Wings. "Then we saw how good it felt to put the top down and cruise along."

The elder Norris turned the Red Wings into an NHL powerhouse, just as Ilitch has done. And like Norris, the rest of the Ilitch family is also involved in the operation of the team.

Marian Ilitch is co-owner of the team with her husband and secretary-treasurer of the Wings. Sons Christopher and Atanas and daughter Denise have served as vice-presidents and alternate governors on the NHL board.

Marian Ilitch remembered how excited their seven children were when told the family had bought the team for $8 million. "They said, 'Is this ever glamorous,' And I said, 'I'll show you how glamorous it is.'"

"It's most gratifying to have had a little part in taking a franchise that was one of the worst in the NHL, setting out without a real game plan or anything to develop one from and turning it into a successful franchise," Mike Ilitch said.

- 1981 1982 -

BACK in TIME

• **August 12, 1981**
IBM introduced its first personal computer with an operating system produced by Microsoft.

• **April 2, 1982**
In the Falkland Islands, Argentinian forces overran the island and captured the British troops stationed there.

• **April 25, 1982**
In compliance with the 1978 Camp David Accords and the 1979 Egyptian-Israeli peace treaty, Israel completed withdrawal of its troops from the Sinai.

quick cuts

Most Goals
John Ogrodnick: 28
Most Assists
Mark Osborne: 41
Most Points
Mark Osborne: 67
Most Penalty Minutes
Reed Larson: 112
Most Wins, Goaltender
Bob Sauve: 11
Lowest Goals-Against Average
Bob Sauve: 4.19
Most Shutouts
None
NHL Award Winners
None

FINAL STANDINGS

Norris Division	W	L	T	PTS	GF	GA
Minnesota	37	23	20	94	346	288
Winnipeg	33	33	14	80	319	332
St. Louis	32	40	8	72	315	349
Chicago	30	38	12	72	332	363
Toronto	20	44	16	56	298	380
DETROIT	21	47	12	54	270	351

OTHER DIVISION WINNERS:
Smythe Division - Edmonton Oilers
Adams Division - Montreal Canadiens
Patrick Division - NY Islanders

Playoff Results
Did Not Qualify
Stanley Cup Champion
New York Islanders

1981-82 Season in Review

Realignment in the NHL kept the Wings in the Norris Division, where they were joined by Toronto, St. Louis, Minnesota, Winnipeg and Chicago. Opening the season with a 5-2 victory at Madison Square Garden over the New York Rangers, the Wings lost only two of their first seven games. "We can play better, there's no question in my mind," coach Wayne Maxner said.

A 12-4 win over Calgary October 29, followed by a 10-2 rout of Los Angeles two games later had people believing him, but that belief was quickly squelched.

A 1-9-3 mark after the decisive win over L.A. led to dramatic changes. The Wings moved Dale McCourt, Mike Foligno and Brent Peterson to Buffalo, getting three players back, including right-winger Danny Gare, a two-time 50-goal scorer and defenseman Jim Schoenfeld, an NHL All-Star selection in 1979-80. Also coming from Buffalo in a separate deal was Vezina Trophy-winning goalie Bob Sauve.

Maxner's spirits were buoyed by the moves.

"We're better than St. Louis, we're better than Winnipeg and Toronto and maybe Chicago, too," Maxner said. "If we don't make the playoffs, I'll be the most disappointed guy in town."

But the Wings kept stumbling. Facing Edmonton before a Joe Louis Arena regular-season record crowd of 20,682, a 4-1 advantage was frittered away in a 4-4 saw off with the Oilers. Another 4-1 third-period lead disappeared in a 4-4 tie with Vancouver, the Canucks getting two goals on penalty shots.

"Just another chapter in the story of the Detroit Red Wings," Gare said.

Bruce Norris and Mike Ilitch

The last chapter saw the Wings lose a team-record 14 straight games from February 24-March 25, including a club-record seven successive home defeats. Maxner was fired, replaced by Billy Dea and the club missed the playoffs for the 10th time in 11 seasons.

Wings owner Bruce Norris dropped hints that the team might be on the market and by the end of the season, he was no longer hinting. "It was a difficult decision to make, giving up a tradition that has been part of your family for 50 years," Norris said.

The Chicago brokerage firm of Thomson-McKinnon Securities, Inc. was hired to oversee the transfer.

The Wings were for sale.

HOCKEYTOWN MOMENT
Wings and Sabres make blockbuster deal

Seeking to shake his team up, Wings GM Jimmy Skinner traded the future for the present. With Detroit mired in an eight-game winless skid, on December 2, three players the Wings picked in the first round of the NHL draft – forwards Mike Foligno, Dale McCourt and Brent Peterson – were dealt to Buffalo for veteran forwards Danny Gare and Derek Smith and defenseman Jim Schoenfeld.

"There will be some controversy, but that's part of my job," Skinner said. "It's tough trading the kids, but we weren't winning games."

Gare, a 56-goal scorer for the Sabres in 1979-80, brought offense to Detroit, while Schoenfeld would help solidify the blueline crew. Of the three who departed, Foligno was the most devastated. "I'm sorry to be leaving Detroit," Foligno said. "The people have been so good to me."

Danny Gare

Willie Huber

Some called him a Gulliver among the Lilliputians when he skated down the ice. Others saw him as a dinosaur, towering over the cavemen. Willie Huber was a giant among men, but he wasn't a bully and therein lay the problem.

Performing effectively on defense wasn't Huber's problem in Detroit. It was playing the way the fans wanted him to play which created the dilemma.

Detroit's top pick in the 1978 NHL amateur draft, Huber arrived in a 6-foot-5, 228-pound package.

People expected him to topple forwards like bowling pins, but that wasn't Huber's style. He wasn't afraid of physical play, it simply wasn't the No. 1 facet of his game.

"I don't go out looking for trouble," Huber explained. "But if someone starts getting rough with me, you can bet that I just won't shy away." The numbers were there to back up his statement. Huber led the Wings with 164 penalty minutes in 1979-80, his second NHL campaign. But his game was skill.

Huber was an amazingly agile skater for his size, an excellent puck-control defenseman with a booming shot, which he employed effectively from the point. In 1981-82, Huber and winger Mark Osborne shared the team lead in power-play goals with five apiece.

"He was our most consistent defenseman, throughout the season," Wings coach Wayne Maxner said during the 1981-82 campaign, a season in which Huber and Greg Smith formed Detroit's No. 1 defense pairing.

The Wings tried to groom Huber slowly, sending him for a 10-game stint with Kansas City of the CHL during his first NHL season in 1978-79. Huber still managed to garner seven goals and 31 points in 68 games and was named Detroit's rookie of the year.

"If we can develop two or three young men like Huber, I think our future will be bright," said Bobby Kromm, the Wings coach at the time.

The German-born Huber moved with his family to Canada as an infant. Huber was a junior teammate of fellow Red Wing Dale McCourt in Hamilton, where they won a Memorial Cup together in 1975-76. The

RED WINGS ARCHIVE

following season, Huber played for Canada in the World Junior Championship.

Huber played for his country again at the 1981 World Championship, but a broken cheekbone kept him out of the 1982 tournament.

A consistent goal-scoring machine from his defense position, Huber tallied 17 times in 1979-80 and scored 15 goals each in the 1980-81 and 1981-82 campaigns. He was selected to play in the 1983 NHL All-Star Game and put together a string of four 40-point seasons between 1979-80 and 1983-84.

The last one came with the New York Rangers, after a June 13, 1983 trade which sent Huber, Osborne and Mike Blaisdell to Broadway for Eddie Mio, Ron Duguay and Eddie Johnstone.

Huber spent the next four seasons in New York and split the 1987-88 season, his final one in the NHL, between the Rangers, Vancouver and Philadelphia.

- **BORN:**
  Strasskirchen, Germany, January 16, 1958
- **ACQUIRED:**
  Selected ninth overall in the June 19, 1978 NHL amateur draft
- **BEST SEASON WITH RED WINGS:**
  1980-81 (15-34-49)

- **TOTALS WITH RED WINGS:**
  GP-371, G-68, A-140, PTS-208
- **HONORS:**
  Played in NHL All-Star Game, 1982-83, Led team in penalty minutes, 1979-80; Played for Canada, 1981 World Championship

MOTOWN *Classic*

Rookie Osborne leads Wings in points

Following the path already created in recent seasons by Reed Larson, Dale McCourt and Mike Foligno, Mark Osborne was Detroit's rookie sensation of 1981-82.

The left-winger tallied 26 goals and 41 assists in his rookie season, to lead the team in scoring with 67 points. His impressive first season included a hat trick December 1 against St. Louis and a five-assist contest February 7, with the Blues again being victimized.

The first Detroit player to go by the nickname "Ozzie" – goalie Chris Osgood would carry the same handle in the 1990s - Osborne joined a select group by leading the Wings in points during his first NHL season.

Osborne, Tom Webster (1970-71), Marcel Dionne (1974-75), McCourt (1977-78) and Steve Yzerman (1983-84) are the only rookies to lead the Wings in scoring.

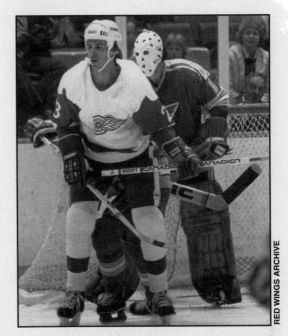

RED WINGS ARCHIVE

ASSEMBLY LINE

A six-player deal moved Mike Foligno, Dale McCourt and Brent Peterson to Buffalo for defenseman Jim Schoenfeld, right-winger Danny Gare and center Derek Smith. Goaltender Bob Sauve was acquired from Buffalo for future considerations, but was returned to the Sabres before the 1982-83 season. A 1982 first-round draft pick, which turned out to be Brian Bellows, was shipped to Minnesota for defenseman Greg Smith and right-winger Don Murdoch and a 1982 first-round draft pick (Murray Craven). Gary McAdam and a 1983 fourth-round draft pick (John Bekkers) were traded to Calgary for left-winger Eric Vail. Center Walt McKechnie was signed as a free agent. Al Jensen was dealt to Washington for center/right-winger Mark Lofthouse. Centers Ted Nolan and Claude Loiselle, goalie Corrado Micalef and left-winger Mark Osborne were NHL entry draft selections.

Eric Vail

RED WINGS ARCHIVE

Red Wings Facts

Individual Goal-Scoring Streak for Playoffs

5 Gordie Howe (1949 & 1964)

5 Ted Lindsay (1952)

Short Passes

The Wings celebrated 50 years of ownership by the Norris Family with a pre-game ceremony at Joe Louis Arena February 4, 1982, then beat the Chicago Blackhawks 6-4 on third-period goals by Mark Osborne and Danny Gare.

BACK in TIME

• **November 13, 1982**

The Vietnam Veterans' Memorial in Washington D.C. was dedicated with 150,000 observers as witnesses.

• **April 20, 1983**

President Reagan signed legislation designed to keep the Social Security system out of debt for the next 75 years.

• **June 24, 1983**

After a six day mission, Sally K. Ride, the first U.S. woman in space, landed safely aboard the space shuttle Challenger at Edwards Air Force base in California.

quick cuts

Most Goals
John Ogrodnick: 41

Most Assists
Reed Larson: 52

Most Points
John Ogrodnick: 85

Most Penalty Minutes
Danny Gare: 107

Most Wins, Goaltender
Corrado Micalef: 11

Lowest Goals-Against Average
Corrado Micalef: 3.62

Most Shutouts
Corrado Micalef: 2

NHL Award Winners
None

FINAL STANDINGS

Norris Division	W	L	T	PTS	GF	GA
Chicago	47	23	10	104	338	268
Minnesota	40	24	16	96	321	290
Toronto	28	40	12	68	293	330
St. Louis	25	40	15	65	285	316
DETROIT	21	44	15	57	263	344

OTHER DIVISION WINNERS:
Smythe Division - Edmonton Oilers
Adams Division - Boston Bruins
Patrick Division - Philadelphia Flyers

Playoff Results
Did Not Qualify
Stanley Cup Champion
New York Islanders

1982-83 Season in Review

James Norris Sr. bought the Detroit Red Wings in 1932 and turned them into a NHL dynasty, but the team his son Bruce Norris sold to Mike and Marian Ilitch was a shadow of that once-great powerhouse.

That was beside the point, noted Mike Ilitch, who gave his team one directive – look ahead.

"It's been played and replayed and I don't see any benefit talking about the past," Ilitch said. Along those lines, a complete house-cleaning took place in the club's offices. Everyone from the training staff through to GM Jimmy Skinner was replaced.

Jimmy Devellano, assistant GM of the four-time Stanley Cup champion New York Islanders, was the new GM and he vowed to build through the draft, increasing the scouting staff from three to six.

Nick Polano, an assistant coach with Buffalo, was the new coach, setting as his first objective to change the NHL's perception of the Wings. "I don't think that teams had respect for the Red Wings," Polano said. "They thought the Wings were easy."

"We'll play better hockey," Devellano said. "It's conceivable for us to make the playoffs. But there will be some pain along the way."

Such as an 0-4 start on home ice, not exactly the beginning the new regime sought.

Left-winger John Ogrodnick scored 41 goals and 85 points, but only two other players reached 20 goals

Mike Ilitch, Jimmy Devellano and Nick Polano

and Reggie Leach, a former 60-goal scorer signed as a free agent, was held to 15 goals. Defenseman Willie Huber scored 14 goals and played in the NHL All-Star Game.

Detroit finished 18th in the NHL in goals with 263 and 18th in goals against, allowing 344 tallies. The Wings improved by three points to 57 from 54 and moved up to fifth from sixth in the Norris Division, but finished eight points out of a playoff spot.

"We had more problems than I originally thought," Devellano admitted. "We're like an old house. First the plumbing went, then the roof, then the furnace."

Things were starting to shape up in Hockeytown, but they were still a long way from being ship-shape.

HOCKEYTOWN MOMENT

Wings sold to Mike and Marian Ilitch

The Norris era officially ended June 7, 1982, when Mike and Marian Ilitch were announced as the new owners of the Red Wings.

Founders of the Little Caesars pizza chain, which grew from a local restaurant to an international corporation, the Ilitches were raised in Detroit and had sponsored amateur hockey leagues in the area since 1964. Mike Ilitch was a professional baseball player who played shortstop in the Detroit Tigers chain.

"I think this is the best franchise in the world," Mike Ilitch said.

"It's a sleeping giant waiting for someone to do something with it." Previous owner Bruce Norris rejected a bid for the team by the Ilitch family in 1981 and the Ilitches had pulled out of negotiations, but reentered the picture after other bidders fell by the wayside.

Marian & Mike Ilitch and John Ziegler

251

Paul Woods

He arrived as part of an experiment and he still hasn't left.

The NHL waiver draft was inaugurated in the fall of 1977 and most NHL people chuckled when the Red Wings plopped down $50,000 to claim Paul Woods, a minor-league left-winger from the Montreal Canadiens' farm system.

By the end of the 1977-78 season, many of the same people were calling it Detroit's best deal in years. Woods, who won two AHL Calder Cup titles with the Nova Scotia Voyageurs in 1975-76 and 1976-77, was a speedster on skates who was most effective in a checking role.

"He does so many things well, he sparks the club with his great attitude, intensity and will to win," Detroit coach Bobby Kromm said of his speedy rookie, who, skating on a line with Dale McCourt and Bill Lochead, produced 19-23-42 totals in 1977-78 and was voted Detroit's most exciting player.

"He skates so smooth and easy, just like a Montreal Canadien," said Wings GM Ted Lindsay, who forked out the $50,000 for Woods, calling it, "The best investment the team has made."

When Detroit ventured into the 1977-78 playoffs, Woods again shone, collecting a club rookie-record five assists and turning the head of a pretty knowledgeable hockey man. "My God, that Woods can skate," said Hall of Fame coach Toe Blake after watching his work as a checker against Canadiens star Guy Lafleur in the Stanley Cup playoffs.

His rookie numbers would stand as career highs for Woods, whose role evolved into a defensive specialist as his career continued.

"Woodsie was amazing," teammate Dennis Hextall said. "His worth wasn't in scoring 25-30 goals a season, it was his hustle. For all the assignments he got killing penalties as a first-year man, it really showed his value."

It was a role Woods cherished. "I enjoyed playing defense and killing penalties," he said. "It was exciting to go out in a tight situation and check. In junior, I was known strictly as an offensive player. Shows how you can change."

JOHN HARTMAN

It was a switch Woods knew he'd have to make to be an NHLer. "My lifelong dream was to play in the NHL," he said. "And it was the only way I could play in the NHL. I didn't have an extraordinary shot or extraordinary skills like some other players. I just had to play hard all of the time."

Which he did for seven seasons in Detroit, becoming a fan favorite. Woods finished his pro career with Adirondack of the AHL in 1984-85, but soon returned to Joe Louis Arena.

He's been ensconced as the radio analyst on Red Wings broadcasts for several years, currently working alongside play-by-play voice Ken Kal, who Woods constantly taunts with his vast knowledge of hockey trivia.

- **BORN:**
  Hespeler, Ontario, April 12, 1965
- **ACQUIRED:**
  Claimed from Montreal in October 10, 1977 NHL waiver draft
- **BEST SEASON WITH RED WINGS:**
  1977-78 (19-23-42)

- **TOTALS WITH RED WINGS:**
  GP-501, G-72, A-124, PTS-196
- **HONORS:**
  Served as team captain, 1978-79; Played for Canada, 1979 World Championship

MOTOWN Classic

Larson sets new assists record

Seeing that the new ownership sought a fresh start, defenseman Reed Larson handed in his resignation as captain after two seasons and the "C" was given to right-winger Danny Gare.

Fortunately for the Wings, Larson didn't seek a fresh start on the ice. He merely picked up where he'd left off.

His best season as an NHLer saw Larson register 52 assists and 74 points, both new club records for a defenseman. He owned both of the previous standards with 49 assists in 1977-78 and 67 points in 1978-79. Larson lit up the Pittsburgh Penguins for three goals February 15 in a 7-3 Wings victory. It was Larson's second career hat trick and with it, he became the first Detroit rearguard to register multiple hat tricks.

ASSEMBLY LINE

Dwight Foster

Center Ivan Boldirev was acquired from Vancouver for Mark Kirton. Right-winger Dwight Foster's contract was purchased for one dollar from New Jersey and right-wingers Tom Rowe and Reggie Leach, center Kelly Kisio and defensemen Colin Campbell and Randy Ladouceur were signed as free agents. Center Stan Weir was purchased from Edmonton. Left-winger Ken Solheim was acquired from Minnesota for future considerations. Yves Courteau was dealt to Calgary for center Bobby Francis. The NHL entry draft provided left-winger Murray Craven, goalie Greg Stefan and defenseman Larry Trader.

Red Wings Facts

Most Road Victories in one Season

1995-96:	**26**
1993-94:	**23**
2001-02:	**23**
2000-01:	**22**
1992-93:	**22**
1951-52:	**20**
1969-70:	**20**
1950-51:	**19**
1952-53:	**19**
1991-92:	**19**
1997-98:	**19**
1996-97:	**18**
1954-55:	**17**
1987-88:	**17**

Short Passes

Posting a 2-0 victory over the Stanley Cup champion New York Islanders on December 8, 1982, Detroit goalie Corrado Micalef ended the club's 218-game streak without a shutout, which dated back to Rogie Vachon's 3-0 decision against St. Louis on February 3, 1980.

- 1983   1984 -

BACK in TIME

- **October 25, 1983**
In an effort to protect American citizens against the policies of the new Marxist government, 3,000 U.S. Marines invaded Grenada.

- **February 3, 1984**
The first baby from a donated embryo is born to an infertile woman.

- **July 23, 1984**
Vanessa Williams became the first Miss America to resign when Penthouse magazine announced it would publish nude pictures of her.

quick cuts

Most Goals
John Ogrodnick: 42
Most Assists
Brad Park: 53
Most Points
Steve Yzerman: 87
Most Penalty Minutes
Joe Paterson: 148
Most Wins, Goaltender
Greg Stefan: 19
Lowest Goals-Against Average
Greg Stefan: 3.51
Most Shutouts
Greg Stefan: 2
NHL Award Winners
Brad Park - Bill Masterton Trophy

FINAL STANDINGS

Norris Division	W	L	T	PTS	GF	GA
Minnesota	39	31	10	88	345	344
St. Louis	32	41	7	71	293	316
DETROIT	31	42	7	69	298	323
Chicago	30	42	8	68	277	311
Toronto	26	45	9	61	303	387

OTHER DIVISION WINNERS
Smythe Division - Edmonton Oilers
Adams Division - Boston Bruins
Patrick Division - NY Islanders

Playoff Results
Lost to the St. Louis Blues in Series "F" (3-1)
Leading Playoff Scorers
Steve Yzerman (6PTS), Ron Duguay & Ivan Boldirev (5PTS each)
Stanley Cup Champion
Edmonton Oilers

1983-84 Season in Review

Detroit coach Nick Polano noticed the improvement the first day of training camp.

"Last year, I could tell very little difference between the two groups in camp (pros and rookies)," Polano said. "Now, there's a difference."

Knowing the club needed an offensive boost, GM Jimmy Devellano dealt with the New York Rangers for former 40-goal scorer Ron Duguay and with Philadelphia for former 50-goal sniper Rick MacLeish.

"I don't know if I got the best goal-scorer in the league, but I sure got the prettiest," Wings owner Mike Ilitch said of Duguay, who had a playboy reputation in New York.

Goals were no longer an issue. Duguay fired 33, Ivan Boldirev had 35 and John Ogrodnick a team-leading 42. Rookies also contributed. First-round draft pick Steve Yzerman established himself as an all-star his first season, leading the club with 39-48-87 totals. Right-winger Lane Lambert was one of three players with 20 goals, as the Wings produced a club-record 298 goals.

Three-time Norris Trophy runner-up Brad Park was signed as a free agent from Boston and he won the Masterton Trophy for perseverance and dedication to hockey. Ogrodnick and Yzerman skated in the NHL All-Star Game.

The Wings went winless in their first five games, then ran off a six-game winning streak. There were other struggles, including eight and nine-game losing skids, but instead of coming apart, this team came

together, nipping Chicago by a point for third spot in the Norris Division and Detroit's first playoff berth since 1977-78.

Only defenseman Reed Larson and left-winger Paul Woods remained from that 1977-78 playoff squad when the Wings opened the post-season against the St. Louis Blues in a best-of-five series.

They split the first two games in St. Louis, the Wings winning Game 2 by a 5-3 count, thanks to two Danny Gare goals, but the Blues took a pair of overtime decisions in the first Stanley Cup games ever played at Joe Louis Arena and Detroit's season was over.

"It's a different feeling making the playoffs," Polano said. "Everyone's happy, everyone's able to enjoy the summer."

HOCKEYTOWN MOMENT
Wings select Yzerman in '83 draft

The moment he became a Red Wing, it was evident center Steve Yzerman would be a franchise player.

Selected with the third pick of the 1983 NHL entry draft from the OHL's Peterborough Petes, "Stevie Y" had all the answers in his rookie season, leading the team in scoring with rookie records of 39 goals and 87 points. His 13 power-play markers were also a team mark for first-year players and Yzerman finished as runner-up to Buffalo goalie Tom Barrasso in the NHL rookie-of-the-year balloting.

The Sporting News selected Yzerman as the NHL's top rookie and the rest of the league was so impressed, Yzerman was picked to play in the NHL All-Star Game. At 18 years, eight months and 22 days, he was the youngest player ever selected to participate in the mid-season classic.

"He's done some tricks with the puck that only the very good ones can do," Wings coach Nick Polano said, marveling at the skill of his new phenom.

Steve Yzerman and Mike Ilitch

Wings of Legend

Danny Gare

A veteran right-winger who had captained the Buffalo Sabres for five seasons, Danny Gare was the first on-ice leader for the Red Wings in the Mike Ilitch era and so far, the only man besides Steve Yzerman to wear the "C" during the Ilitch regime.

Gare certainly brought plenty of experience to the role. He was a two-time 50-goal scorer for the Sabres – in 1975-76 and 1979-80, netting his 50th goal in the latter campaign during a 10-1 win over Detroit on March 27, 1980.

He accumulated less than 20 goals in a season just once in his first nine NHL campaigns. He played in the 1974-75 Stanley Cup final with the Sabres and appeared for Canada in both the 1976 and 1981 Canada Cups.

Acquired in a six-player deal with the Sabres in 1981, Gare didn't flinch at the thought of joining the Wings, who were one of the NHL's weaker sisters at the time.

"I think I can help turn the team around," he said.

He was right, although Gare's helping hand would be delivered in a completely different role than the one he'd filled in Buffalo.

About a month into the 1983-84 season, Detroit coach Nick Polano combined the former NHL All-Star selection with center Dwight Foster and left-winger Bob Manno to form a checking line.

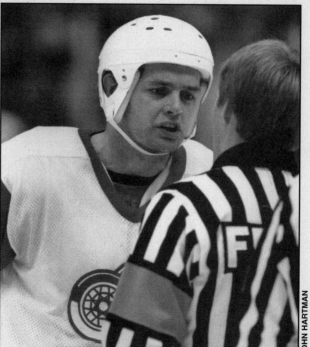

JOHN HARTMAN

They were an eclectic group. Gare, the former sniper; Foster, whose contract was purchased for one dollar from New Jersey; and Manno, a converted defenseman who was signed as a free agent from HC Merano of the Italian League.

Detroit fans quickly dubbed the trio the "Troll Line."

"The Washington Redskins have "The Hogs" and we have "The Trolls," Detroit defenseman Brad Park said.

"That line was incredible," Polano said. "Not only did they shut down the opposition, but they scored some big goals themselves."

Gare fired two hat tricks as a Red Wing and scored the game-winner in a 6-4 decision over the Calgary Flames on March 22, 1984, a victory which clinched Detroit's first trip to the playoffs since 1977-78.

He scored twice in a 5-3 triumph over St. Louis in Game 2 of their first-round playoff series that spring, the first post-season win by the Wings in six years.

"As captain, I felt an obligation to contribute," Gare said.

Gare produced 27-29-56 totals with the Wings in 1984-85, but slumped to seven goals the next year and was released following the 1985-86 season.

Gare closed out his playing days with the Edmonton Oilers the following season.

One of the most popular players to wear the Sabres uniform, today, Gare works on the team's broadcasts.

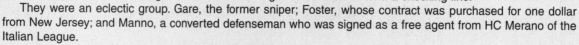

- **BORN:**
  Nelson, British Columbia, May 15, 1954
- **ACQUIRED:**
  December 2, 1981 trade with Buffalo
- **BEST SEASON WITH RED WINGS:**
  1982-83 (26-35-61)

- **TOTALS WITH RED WINGS:**
  GP-306, G-86, A-95, PTS-181
- **HONORS:**
  Served as team captain, 1982-83 to 1985-86; Led team in penalty minutes, 1982-83, 1984-85

MOTOWN Classic

Park signs on as a free agent

Brad Park, 35, a five-time NHL First All-Star Team selection and a three-time runner-up to Bobby Orr in the Norris Trophy voting, signed a two-year contract with the Wings, which didn't sit well with Boston GM Harry Sinden, who claimed a personal services contract Park had signed with the Bruins made him Boston property, meaning Boston should receive compensation.

Detroit GM Jimmy Devellano insisted Sinden was mistaken. "His name does not appear on the NHL reserve list as a member of the Boston Bruins," Devellano said.

Club lawyers agreed with him and so did the NHL. The Bruins received no compensation, but the Wings certainly got a boost from Park.

"I've never missed a playoff in my entire career and I don't intend on missing them now," said Park, who helped the Wings reach the post-season in each of his two Detroit campaigns.

ASSEMBLY LINE

Ron Duguay

Seeking to boost their goal scoring, the Wings dealt Mike Blasidell, Mark Osborne and Willie Huber to the New York Rangers for center/right-winger Ron Duguay, goalie Eddie Mio and left-winger Eddie Johnstone. Seven-time NHL All-Star defenseman Brad Park was signed as a free agent. Center Rick MacLeish, a former 50-goal scorer, was acquired from Philadelphia for future considerations. Center Blake Dunlop and defensemen Bob Manno and Barry Melrose were signed as free agents, as were goaltender Ken Holland, who would become the Wings GM in 1997 and right-winger Brian Johnson, who became the first African-American to play for the Wings. Left-winger Pierre Aubry was purchased from Quebec, while the NHL entry draft supplied center Steve Yzerman and right-winger Lane Lambert.

Red Wings Facts

Best Power-Play Percentage Since 1967

24.9%
1992 - 93
(113 P.P. Goals on 454 Advantages)

24.2%
1994 - 95
(52 P.P. Goals on 215 Advantages)

22.1%
2000 - 01
(85 P.P. goals on 389 Advantages)

Short Passes

A 6-6 tie with the Jets at Winnipeg in the October 5 season opener led to the first regular-season overtime period in a Detroit game since a 3-3 tie with Chicago on November 8, 1942. The rule, taken off the NHL books during World War II, was reintroduced in 1983-84.

- 1984   1985 -

BACK in TIME

• **September 25, 1984**
Texas billionaire Ross Perot purchased one of only 17 copies of the Magna Carta for $1.5 million and donated it to the National Archives.

• **April 23, 1985**
Coca Cola announced it was replacing its 99 year old formula with a sweeter tasting formula.

• **May 1, 1985**
President Reagan ordered a trade embargo on Nicaragua, denouncing the Sandinista regime as a threat to U.S. national security.

quick cuts

Most Goals
John Ogrodnick: 55
Most Assists
Steve Yzerman: 59
Most Points
John Ogrodnick: 105
Most Penalty Minutes
Danny Gare: 163
Most Wins, Goaltender
Greg Stefan: 21
Lowest Goals-Against Average
Greg Stefan: 4.33
Most Shutouts
None
NHL Award Winners
John Ogrodnick - 1st Team All-Star

FINAL STANDINGS

Norris Division	W	L	T	PTS	GF	GA
St. Louis	37	31	12	86	299	288
Chicago	38	35	7	83	309	299
DETROIT	27	41	12	66	313	357
Minnesota	25	43	12	62	268	321
Toronto	20	52	8	48	253	358

OTHER DIVISION WINNERS:
Smythe Division - Edmonton Oilers
Adams Division - Montreal Canadiens
Patrick Division - Philadelphia Flyers

Playoff Results
Lost to the Chicago Blackhawks in Series "F" (3-0)
Leading Playoff Scorers
Steve Yzerman & Ivan Boldirev (3PTS each)
Stanley Cup Champion
Edmonton Oilers

1984-85 Season in Review

Wings GM Jimmy Devellano hoped for a 10 per cent improvement over last season as his club broke training camp. "That would mean 76 points, which would almost be .500 hockey," he said.

"This team hasn't made the playoffs back-to-back in 20 years. It would be a nice thing."

Devellano didn't get his first wish. The Wings slipped back from 69 to 66 points, but that was still enough to maintain third spot in the weak Norris Division and enter post-season play for the second consecutive season.

Steady John Ogrodnick had a career year, leading the team with 105 points and a club-record 55 goals. He also tied a club mark with four points in the third period of a 7-6 win over Toronto, helping the Wings rally from a 6-2 deficit.

Steve Yzerman counted 30 goals and 89 points, setting a team record by sniping three goals March 30 in the third frame of a 9-3 decision, also against the Leafs.

"He does stuff, like that spin and turn, that only Dorothy Hamill can do," Wings forward Dave (Tiger) Williams said, comparing Stevie Y to the 1976 Olympic figure skating gold medalist.

Ron Duguay also reached the 30-goal plateau, registering three hat tricks among his 38 goals.

Ogrodnick was selected to the NHL's First All-Star Team and was voted a starter to the NHL All-Star

Game. In the fall, Yzerman helped Canada to victory in the Canada Cup and after the playoffs, jetted to Prague, Czechoslovakia, scoring three goals in 10 games as Canada won a silver medal at the World Championship.

The post-season was quick for Detroit. The Wings were swept by Chicago in a best-of-five series, losing the three games by a combined score of 23-8. The Blackhawks raced to a 4-0 lead in every game of the set before Detroit got on the board.

"It was all Chicago," Polano said. "I was very disappointed. I thought we were ready."

HOCKEYTOWN MOMENT
Wings acquire two ex-Leafs

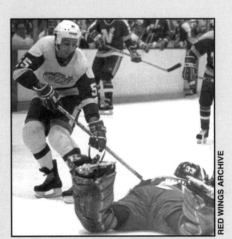

Tiger Williams

Feeling that the team was being pushed around too much, the Wings brought in left-winger Dave (Tiger) Williams, a three-time NHL penalty-minute champion.

Williams was a former Toronto Maple Leaf and so was center Darryl Sittler, a two-time 100-point scorer who was picked up from Philadelphia in exchange for young forwards Murray Craven and Joe Paterson. It was felt Sittler would provide experience down the middle to go with second-year star Steve Yzerman, but neither move panned out. Williams was dealt to Los Angeles in March, while Sittler registered 11-16-27 totals in 61 games and retired at the end of the season. Wings GM Jimmy Devellano lists the Sittler trade as one of his biggest regrets.

"Craven became a solid NHL player," Devellano said of Detroit's 1982 first-round draft choice, who played 18 NHL seasons, scored 20 goals in six of those seasons and appeared in three Stanley Cup finals.

Wings of Legend

John Ogrodnick

Like any deadly sniper, John Ogrodnick snuck into town quietly, took care of his business, then went on his way.

"Johnny O" was not one to brag, even though he had plenty to brag about.

"He was a great scorer," former Wings coach Jacques Demers said of Ogrodnick. "He could score from any angle 10 feet inside the blueline." Ogrodnick's key to success was a powerful slapshot.

At 16, he scored 54 goals in 67 games for the Maple Ridge Bruins of the B.C. Junior League. The following season, Ogrodnick tallied 59 times for the WHL's New Westminster Bruins. He added another 48 goals in 1978-79 and was touted as a sure first-rounder in the 1979 NHL entry draft.

The big left-winger slid all the way to the fourth round, though, where the Wings got him with the 66th choice.

"I was disappointed," Ogrodnick remembered of draft day. "They said I might be a first-round pick. My agent (Art Kaminsky) told me there was no way I'd be worse than a second-rounder.

The setback was temporary and Ogrodnick employed it as motivation, an opportunity to prove the experts wrong.

He tallied 35 goals in 1980-81, launching six straight seasons as Detroit's leading goal scorer, earning the first of five selections to play in the NHL All-Star Game. He scored 41 goals in 1981-82 and 42 the following season, then hit the mother lode in 1984-85.

Ogrodnick piled up a club-record 55 goals, joining Mickey Redmond and Danny Grant in Detroit's exclusive 50-goal club. His 105 points also put Ogrodnick in heady company. Gordie Howe and Marcel Dionne were the only Red Wings who'd previously recorded 100-point campaigns.

"If you look back at my record, you can't say I had one fluke year and scored 40 goals," Ogrodnick said. "I averaged 40 goals for six seasons."

Ogrodnick was selected to the NHL's First All-Star Team and was voted as the starting left-winger for the

RED WINGS ARCHIVE

NHL All-Star Game alongside Edmonton stars Wayne Gretzky and Jari Kurri.

"He deserves it," Gretzky said. "John's a great player."

Slipping to 38 goals in 1985-86 Ogrodnick was dealt to Quebec in a six-player deal on January 12, 1987.

"It's part of the business," he said of being traded. "When a team has been in a losing situation, somebody comes in and cleans house." Ogrodnick later played for the New York Rangers and made a 19-game comeback with the Wings in 1992-93, his final NHL season.

"I look back and believe it or not, I wish I could have done more," said Ogrodnick, who still resides in suburban Detroit and works as an investment counselor with a local brokerage firm.

- **BORN:**
  Ottawa, Ontario, June 20, 1959
- **ACQIURED:**
  Selected 66th overall in the August 9, 1979 NHL entry draft
- **BEST SEASON WITH RED WINGS:**
  1984-85 (55-50-105)
- **TOTALS WITH RED WINGS:**
  GP-558, G-265, A-281, PTS-546

- **HONORS:**
  Selected to NHL First All-Star Team, 1984-85; Played in five NHL All-Star Games; Led club in goals for six seasons; Led club in points, 1982-83, 1984-85; Played for Canada, 1981 World Championship

MOTOWN Classic

Ogrodnick nets 55 goals

Beating Edmonton's Grant Fuhr in a 7-6 loss to the Oilers on March 13, left-winger John Ogrodnick became the third Red Wing to register 50 goals, but he didn't stop there. By the end of the season, Ogrodnick had tallied 55 times, wiping out Mickey Redmond's 1972-73 club record of 52 goals.

"It was nice to be able to do something like that with the Red Wings," Ogrodnick said.

His 55 goals and 105 points led the team and remain team marks for a left-winger.

"He's one of the elite players in the NHL," said St. Louis coach Jacques Demers, who would coach Ogrodnick with Detroit two years later. "If we had Johnny Ogrodnick, we'd be so far ahead in our division, nobody would see us again."

RED WINGS ARCHIVE

ASSEMBLY LINE

Two members of the the 1980 gold-medal winning U.S. Olympic squad were acquired. Right-winger Dave Silk was claimed on waivers from Boston, while center Rob McClanahan was picked up from the New York Rangers and later traded to Vancouver for left-winger Dave (Tiger) Williams. Murray Craven and Joe Paterson went to Philadelphia for center Darryl Sittler. Two players were added from Czechoslovakia. Left-winger/right-winger Frank Cernik was signed as a free agent and defenseman Milan Chalupa was selected in the NHL entry draft. Right-winger Joe Kocur, left-winger Gerard Gallant and defenseman Rick Zombo were other entry draft additions.

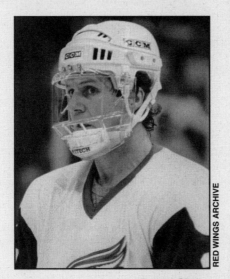

RED WINGS ARCHIVE

Darryl Sittler

Red Wings Facts

Scoreless Ties Since 1960

October 13, 1962
vs Chicago
Terry Sawchuk & Glenn Hall

November 7, 1976
vs Atlanta
Ed Giacomin & Phil Myre

December 10, 1996
vs Edmonton
Chris Osgood & Curtis Joseph

April 1, 2000
vs St. Louis
Chris Osgood & Roman Turek

Short Passes

Wings goalie Greg Stefan was a boyhood friend and teammate of Wayne Gretzky in Brantford, Ontario. Wings goalie Eddie Mio served as best man at Gretzky's 1988 wedding to actress Janet Jones.

BACK in TIME

• **November 14, 1985**

The Center of Science in the Public Interest indicted fast-food chains for deep frying with beef fat rather than with oils lower in saturated fats.

• **January 28, 1986**

In the worst disaster of the U.S. space program, seven astronauts lost their lives when the Challenger exploded while spectators in Florida and millions of television viewers watched in horror.

• **April 14-15, 1986**

American pilots bombed Libya following Libya's missile attack on U.S. ships on maneuvers in the Golf of Sidra.

quick cuts

Most Goals
John Ogrodnick: 38

Most Assists
Kelly Kisio: 48

Most Points
Doug Shedden: 71

Most Penalty Minutes
Joe Kocur: 377

Most Wins, Goaltender
Greg Stefan: 10

Lowest Goals-Against Average
Greg Stefan: 4.50

Most Shutouts
Greg Stefan & Mark Laforest (1 each)

NHL Award Winners
none

FINAL STANDINGS

Norris Division	W	L	T	PTS	GF	GA
Chicago	39	33	8	86	351	349
Minnesota	38	33	9	85	327	305
St. Louis	37	34	9	83	302	291
Toronto	25	48	7	57	311	386
DETROIT	17	57	6	40	266	415

OTHER DIVISION WINNERS
Smythe Division - Edmonton Oilers
Adams Division - Quebec Nordiques
Patrick Division - Philadelphia Flyers

Playoff Results
Did Not Qualify
Stanley Cup Champion
Montreal Canadiens

1985-86 Season in Review

In Hockeytown, 1985-86 will be remembered as the season of living dangerously.

Despite successive playoff appearances, Nick Polano was out as coach, promoted to assistant GM, with veteran Harry Neale taking over behind the bench.

The club signed a half-dozen college free agents and Czech defector Petr Klima. Several veteran free agents were also inked, including left-winger Warren Young, a 40-goal scorer on Mario Lemieux's left wing with Pittsburgh in 1984-85.

"I'm curious and excited," Wings GM Jimmy Devellano said after the sweeping changes. "There's that unknown factor."

The Wings would soon find out that what you don't know can hurt you. Of the newcomers, only left-winger Klima and center Adam Oates became solid NHLers and Oates did so after being traded away by the Wings in 1989.

It was that bad. And then it got worse.

With No. 1 goalie Greg Stefan sitting out an eight-game suspension stemming from an incident in the 1984-85 playoffs, the Wings broke from the gate 0-8-1. Center Steve Yzerman missed 39 games with a broken collarbone.

The club was mired in last place in the Norris Division with eight wins when Neale was replaced by Brad Park on December 30. "Most nights, there was nothing wrong with the effort," Neale said. "We were just outmanned."

The Wings allowed seven or more goals in 19 of 80 games, surrendering a club-record 415 goals.

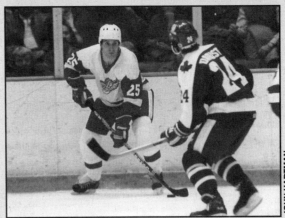

JOHN HARTMAN

Detroit finished as the NHL's worst team, with 40 points from a 17-57-6 record. The 57 losses were a club high and 40 points the lowest total by the Wings since a 35-point output during the 48-game 1937-38 campaign. Detroit's 26 home losses were a team mark. There was a record 10-game (0-9-1) winless skid at Joe Louis Arena from December 11 to January 18. The team surrendered 111 power-play goals while accumulating a record 2,393 penalty minutes, led by right-winger Joe Kocur, who topped the NHL with 377 minutes. Kocur set club marks for penalty minutes in a period (37) and game (42) on November 2 against St. Louis.

On the positive side, defenseman Reed Larson scored 11 power-play goals and left-winger John Ogrodnick skated in the NHL All-Star Game.

HOCKEYTOWN MOMENT
Neale named Red Wings Head Coach

Adjustment in Detroit's managerial team saw coach Nick Polano promoted to assistant GM and former Vancouver coach-GM Harry Neale brought in to coach the club.

"All I'm leaving the new man is my aspirin and Maalox," Polano said. Neale would need it.

"I'm delighted to be back in the NHL," said Neale, who wasn't back for long. He was fired after the Wings went 8-23-4 in their first 35 games. "They could bring in God and I don't think He could keep them from making the same individual errors," Neale said.

It was former Wings defenseman Brad Park who got the call. Park was named coach and director of player personnel. "Brad is in total control of our hockey team, on and off the ice," Wings GM Jimmy Devellano said. It turned out he was just the new skipper of an already sinking ship. The Wings went 9-34-2 under Park and he was fired at the end of the season.

RED WINGS ARCHIVE

Greg Stefan

The ice surface of Greg Stefan's goal crease was his turf and anyone foolish enough to venture inside the lines paid a severe price. "I controlled the area around my net really well," Stefan said. "I knew where everybody was."

If they were where they shouldn't be, Stefan would remind them that it was time to move elsewhere. Sometimes, those reminders weren't very subtle and the NHL took notice.

An altercation with Chicago's Al Secord during the 1984-85 playoffs cost Stefan an eight-game suspension to commence the 1985-86 season. When he clipped the head of Pittsburgh forward Dan Frawley with the paddle of his goal stick in a 5-2 loss on December 4, 1985, the league set Stefan down for another six games. He also missed a month of the 1985-86 campaign due to a back injury and his absence was noticeable. Without Stefan to begin the season, the Wings got off to an 0-8-1 start.

"When that happened, we started doubting some of the things we were doing," Stefan said. "We started to second-guess ourselves and it only got worse."

Stefan was in net for 10 of Detroit's 17 victories, despite playing only 37 games. Detroit's other four goaltenders were a combined 7-37-1 in 1985-86.

"I began to get the feeling I had to play if we were going to stand a chance of winning," he said. "When my suspension ended, I played about 22 straight and that ended up hurting both me and the team." Realizing his importance to the team, a new Stefan appeared the following season - one more focused on stopping shots, rather than delivering them.

"He stands there and challenges the shooters," assistant GM Nick Polano said, noting Stefan's refinement from the guy who garnered 23 penalty minutes the season before. "He doesn't go into the corners trying to bodycheck people anymore."

"I think I learned the hard way," Stefan admitted.

Stefan posted 20 wins in 1986-87, leading the team in that department for the fourth straight season, as Detroit reached the Stanley Cup semi-finals for the first time since 1965-66.

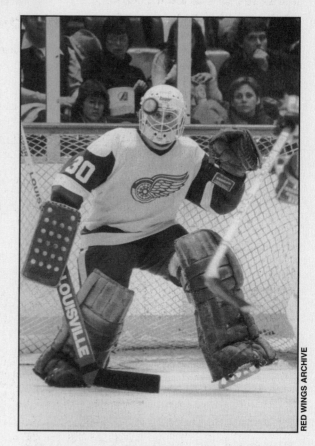

RED WINGS ARCHIVE

New coach Jacques Demers liked what he saw in his goalie. "There's no question in my mind that Greg is one of the best in hockey," Demers said. "He hates to lose and I like that in a player."

Splitting the goaltending chores with Glen Hanlon in 1987-88, Stefan posted a team-best 3.11 goals-against average and equaled his career high with 21 wins in 1988-89. But back and knee injuries scuttled his career in 1989-90 and Stefan played only seven more games in a Detroit uniform, winning just once.

After his playing days ended, Stefan worked as a goalie consultant in the junior ranks.

- **BORN:**
  Brantford, Ontario, February 11, 1961
- **ACQUIRED:**
  Selected 128th overall in the June 10, 1981 NHL entry draft
- **BEST SEASON WITH RED WINGS:**
  1987-88 (17-9-5, 1 SO, 3.11 GAA)

- **TOTALS WITH RED WINGS:**
  GP-299, W-115, L-127, T-30, SO-5, GAA-3.92
- **HONORS:**
  Led team in wins six times; Led team in shutouts three times; Led team in GAA four times

MOTOWN Classic

Hometown boy Cichocki makes debut

RED WINGS ARCHIVE

No Red Wing ever launched his career as effectively as right-winger Chris Cichocki, a free-agent acquisition from the Michigan Tech Huskies.

Born in Detroit, that's also where Cichocki played his first NHL game on October 10, 1985, scoring two goals in a 6-6 tie with the Minnesota North Stars at Joe Louis Arena.

"Not many people can live a dream," said Cichocki, a Wings fan his whole life. "Not a day went by when I didn't think what a great, wonderful thing it was to be playing at home."

Cichocki remains the only Red Wing to score twice in his NHL debut. He finished the season with 10 goals and also displayed a pretty fair sense of humor. Clipped in the mouth by the stick of Washington's Bengt Gustafsson, Cichocki suffered multiple cuts to his cheek, upper lip, tongue and inside his throat near his tonsils.

"Tell Thomas Hearns I won't be able to spar with him this week," Cichocki said after being stitched up.

ASSEMBLY LINE

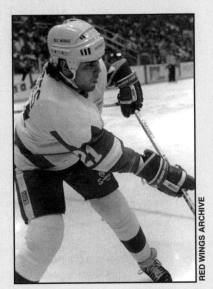

RED WINGS ARCHIVE

Adam Oates

Wholesale changes were made in an effort to shake Detroit from its doldrums. Ron Duguay was dealt to Pittsburgh for center Doug Shedden. John Barrett and Greg Smith went to Washington for defenseman Darren Veitch. Bruce Eakin was traded to Edmonton for center Billy Carroll. Reed Larson was traded to Boston for defenseman Mike O'Connell. Free agents were signed in abundance. From the college ranks, Detroit inked defenseman Tim Friday, center Adam Oates and right-wingers Ted Speers, Chris Cichocki and Ray Staszak. Defensemen Jim Leavins, Mike McEwen and Harold Snepsts, left-wingers Basil McRae and Warren Young, center Glenn Merkosky and goalie Mark Laforest were pro free-agent pickups. McEwen was later dealt to the New York Rangers for defenseman Steve Richmond. NHL draftees earning shots included left-wingers Petr Klima and Bob Probert, goalie Chris Pusey and defenseman Doug Houda.

Red Wings Facts

Longest Individual Point-Scoring Streaks

Steve Yzerman - 28 Games
November 1, 1988 to January 4, 1989

Steve Yzerman - 22 Games
November 25, 1987 to January 10, 1988

Gordie Howe - 18 Games
February 13, 1963 to March 23, 1963

Short Passes

The Wings surrendered double digits in goals in five 1985-86 games - losing 12-3 to Edmonton, 10-2 to Minnesota and the New York Rangers and 10-1 to Minnesota and Montreal.

265

THE BRUISE BROTHERS

In what can only be described as the toughest draft day in NHL history, the Detroit Red Wings tabbed Bob Probert, Joe Kocur and Stu Grimson during the selection process at the 1983 NHL entry draft.

Grimson went on to enforce the law in other cities, making a brief appearance in Detroit later in his career, but by then, Kocur and Probert had achieved cult status in Hockeytown as "The Bruise Brothers."

"They were the two toughest guys in the league," Detroit senior vice-president Jimmy Devellano said.

Many contenders challenged them for the crown and many contenders fell.

"I saw those guys seriously hurt people in fights," teammate John Ogrodnick said.

Kocur's strength was a devastating knockout punch. He once kayoed Winnipeg enforcer Jim Kyte with one blow. "Fighting is pretty much what got me to the league and it's what's kept me in the league," Kocur said.

Probert was known for his endurance and ability to take a punch, winning most of his bouts in the late stages, after his sparring partner grew tired.

"Fighting Bob Probert is not something you look forward to," confessed Toronto tough guy Tie Domi.

Kocur captured the NHL penalty title in 1985-86, garnering 377 minutes.

Two seasons later, Probert topped the NHL with a club-record 398 penalty minutes.

To classify either as a goon would be a misnomer, because both players were capable of using their hands for more than just rendering opponents unconscious. Probert had two 20-goal seasons for the Wings and his 21 points during the 1987-88 playoffs established a new team mark.

"From the blueline in, Bob Probert is as good with the puck as any player in the NHL," said former NHL coach Terry Crisp, who coached Probert in junior.

While not as offensively-skilled as Probert, Kocur chalked up 16-20-36 totals in 1989-90 and scored four goals during the 1997-98 playoffs, helping the Wings defend the Stanley Cup.

That was during Kocur's second stint as a Red Wing. Out of hockey, he was signed as a free agent in 1996 and provided a steady contribution on the

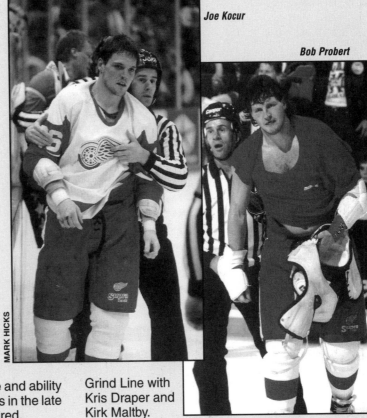

Joe Kocur

Bob Probert

MARK HICKS

MARK HICKS

Grind Line with Kris Draper and Kirk Maltby.

"I have to admit, when they told me Joe Kocur was going to be on my line, I didn't know what to expect," Draper said. "I knew he could fight. I found out he could play."

Off the ice, Probert battled substance-abuse problems and ran afoul of the law. "There was far too much social work with Probert, but we genuinely liked him," Devellano said. The club released Probert in 1994 and after a year out of the game in which he straightened out his life, Probert returned to the NHL wars with Chicago.

"It's been a complete turnaround," Probert said of sobriety. "It makes life definitely different."

Kocur retired in 2000 to take a position with the Wings breaking down video for the coaching staff, but Probert continues to patrol left wing for the Blackhawks and strike fear into opponents.

"The fact that he is still Probert is still true," Chicago vice-president Bob Pulford said.

BACK in TIME

- **December 30, 1986**
President Reagan admitted mistakes were made in his secret policy initiatives with Iran.

- **February 4, 1987**
Overriding President Reagan's veto, Congress passed a $20 billion Clean Water Act.

- **August 17, 1987**
Rudolf Hess, the last of Hitler's close colleagues, died by strangulating himself with an electric cord at West Berlin's Spandau prison; he was 93.

quick cuts

Most Goals
Brent Ashton: 40
Most Assists
Steve Yzerman: 59
Most Points
Steve Yzerman: 90
Most Penalty Minutes
Joe Kocur: 276
Most Wins, Goaltender
Greg Stefan: 20
Lowest Goals-Against Average
Glen Hanlon: 3.18
Most Shutouts
Glen Hanlon & Greg Stefan: 1 each
NHL Award Winners
Jacques Demers - Jack Adams Award

FINAL STANDINGS

Norris Division	W	L	T	PTS	GF	GA
St. Louis	32	33	15	79	281	293
DETROIT	34	36	10	78	260	274
Chicago	29	37	14	72	290	310
Toronto	32	42	6	70	286	319
Minnesota	30	40	10	70	296	314

OTHER DIVISION WINNERS
Smythe Division - Edmonton Oilers
Adams Division - Hartford Whalers
Patrick Division - Philadelphia Flyers

Playoff Results
Defeated the Chicago Blackhawks in Series "F" (3-0)
Defeated the Toronto Maple Leafs in Series "K" (4-3)
Lost to the Edmonton Oilers in Series "N" (4-1)
Leading Playoff Scorers
Steve Yzerman (18PTS) - Gerard Gallant (14PTS)
Stanley Cup Champion
Edmonton Oilers

He bubbled with enthusiasm and exuded infectious, positive energy. Lured away from the St. Louis Blues, new coach Jacques Demers quickly transformed the Wings from doormats into Detroit's darlings, a team which reached heights not scaled in these parts for more than two decades.

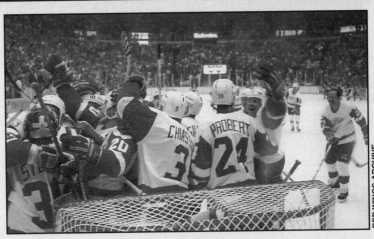

One of the first changes made after Demers came on board was to name Steve Yzerman, 21, as captain, succeeding the departed Danny Gare. "I was impressed by Yzerman the player and at a young age, he was a mature man," Demers said. "I really believed this was the guy that I wanted to build the club around.

"He was the leader. I knew we could go forward with a guy like Yzerman."

After a 40-point season, there was nowhere to go but up for Detroit and up is where they went – to second place in the Norris Division, just one point from earning a division title.

Adorned with the captaincy, Yzerman posted his best season as a pro, collecting 90 points. Newly-acquired left-winger Brent Ashton scored 40 goals, while "Bruise Brothers" Bob Probert and Joe Kocur patrolled the wings, forming the most feared 1-2 punch in hockey.

The first round of the playoffs saw Detroit sweep Chicago. In the second round, the Wings rallied from a 3-1 series deficit to take out Toronto in seven games.

Wayne Gretzky and the Edmonton Oilers were Detroit's first semi-final opponent since 1966 and were stunned 3-1 losers to the Wings in Game 1 at Edmonton's Northlands Coliseum. "We were big underdogs, but Edmonton found out they were going to get a game from us," Demers said.

The Oilers swept the next four games, but the Wings had put a scare into them.

"It was a great season," Yzerman said. "I'm proud to be a Red Wing again."

HOCKEYTOWN MOMENT
Wings turn to Demers

Aware that he needed to do something to give Wings fans hope for the future, Detroit GM Jimmy Devellano set out in search of a new coach. "We had to do something dynamic," Devellano said. "Not only to improve the team, but to sell tickets. We needed a coach with a lot of enthusiasm. Being good with the media was important."

He didn't have to look far, finding his solution working behind the bench of Norris Division rivals the St. Louis Blues. The charismatic Jacques Demers had taken the Blues to the Stanley Cup final four in 1985-86 and he would do the same for the Wings in 1986-87 and 1987-88.

"He was a great motivator," said right-winger Joe Kocur, who played for Demers. "For us young guys, he had us so excited to go out on the ice for every shift. He was a great coach to have."

After guiding the Wings to a second-place finish with a 34-36-10 mark, good for 78 points and a 38-point improvement on their dismal 1985-86 showing, Demers earned the Jack Adams Award as NHL coach of the year.

Gerard Gallant

One of the few positives to develop from Detroit's disastrous 1985-86 campaign was the emergence of left-winger Gerard Gallant.

"He hated to lose," coach Jacques Demers said of the determined Gallant. "He came to play every night. He was a spitting image of Brian Sutter."

A native of Summerside, P.E.I., "Spud," as he was known to his teammates, scored 20 goals in 1985-86, his first full NHL campaign, then rapped home 38 goals during the 1986-87 season, skating on Steve Yzerman's left wing.

The two linemates grew to be close friends, suiting up side-by-side in the Wings dressing room.

"The team had a lot of older players back then, so we were kind of thrown together by the fact we were the only young guys," Gallant said. "Then, we started playing on the same line and the friendship just continued to grow."

So did Gallant's stature in NHL circles. Overlooked on draft day, Detroit tabbed the 5-foot-10, 190-pound Gallant with the 107th pick in the 1981 draft.

"He was the type you had to go back and watch a few times to appreciate," remembered Jimmy Skinner, Detroit GM at the time. "He wasn't an exceptional skater, but he never backed down and that kind of thing always impresses you."

"The draft is overrated," Gallant said. "How many first-round picks never make it, or you never even hear of them again? "Look at (1981). After the Wings took me in the sixth round, they got (goalie) Greg Stefan in the seventh and (defenseman) Rick Zombo in the eighth."

All three were key players for the Detroit teams which earned Campbell Conference final appearances in 1986-87 and 1987-88.

Gallant's 38-goal performance in 1986-87 was the first of four straight 30-goal campaigns. He potted a personal-best 39 goals in 1988-89, earning selection to the NHL's Second All-Star Team. He also played for Canada at the World Championships that spring.

Yzerman, Gallant and right-winger Paul MacLean combined for 140 goals and 319 points in 1988-89, all club marks for a forward line.

JOHN HARTMAN

"He was one of the leaders of the club, but off the ice, he was an entirely different guy," MacLean said. Known as a prankster, one of Gallant's favorite tricks was to sneak under the table during a team dinner and cover the shoes of unsuspecting teammates with sour cream. "I've always been a practical joker," Gallant said. "You have to have a sense of humor in this game."

That ability to laugh kept Gallant going during the lean times early in his Detroit career.

"My first two years were really tough," he said. "You never want to be part of losing, but I think that made me a better person. You know what it's like to lose and you just don't want it to happen again."

Gallant's Red Wing days ended when he signed a free-agent deal with Tampa Bay in 1993, where he played the final two seasons of his NHL career.

- **BORN:**
  Summerside, P.E.I., September 2, 1963
- **ACQUIRED:**
  Selected 107th overall in the June 10, 1981 NHL entry draft
- **BEST SEASON WITH RED WINGS:**
  1988-89 (39-54-93)

- **TOTALS WITH RED WINGS:**
  GP-563, G-207, A-260, PTS-467
- **HONORS:**
  Selected to NHL Second All-Star Team, 1988-89; Led team in penalty minutes, 1988-89; Played for Canada, 1989 World Championships

MOTOWN Classic

Burr sets new rookie mark during playoffs

RED WINGS ARCHIVE

Center Shawn Burr fit the image of the Jacques Demers-coached Red Wings – feisty, pesky, emotional, determined never to give up.

Playing his first full NHL season in 1986-87, Burr skated as the Wings' checking-line center.

"He bothers people and he's got range," Detroit GM Jimmy Devellano said. "Shawn's got a very important role. I want him to play against (Denis) Savard, (Wayne) Gretzky and (Peter) Stastny."

Detroit's top pick in the 1984 NHL entry draft, Burr produced solid 22-25-47 totals, tying a club record with a three-goal third period November 13 during a 7-5 loss at Philadelphia.

"Philadelphia played my style of game – gritty and determined – so I always liked to play against them," said Burr, who tallied his first NHL goal January 23, 1986 at Philadelphia's Spectrum.

In the playoffs, Burr collected seven goals and nine points, setting team rookie marks.

ASSEMBLY LINE

The Wings got veteran goalie Glen Hanlon and third-round draft choices in 1987 (Dennis Holland) and 1988 (Guy Dupuis) from the New York Rangers for Jim Leavins, Kelly Kisio and Lane Lambert. John Ogrodnick, Doug Shedden and Basil McRae went to Quebec for left-winger Brent Ashton, right-winger Mark Kumpel and defenseman Gilbert Delorme. Defenseman Doug Halward came from Vancouver for a 1988 sixth-round draft pick (Phil Von Stefenelli). Claude Loiselle went to New Jersey for right-winger Tim Higgins. In separate deals

JOHN HARTMAN

Lee Norwood

with the Devils, the Wings also sent Chris Cichocki and a 1987 third round pick there for center Mel Bridgman and dealt Steve Richmond for goalie Sam St. Laurent. Randy Ladouceur was shipped to Hartford for right-winger Dave Barr. Defenseman Lee Norwood was acquired from St. Louis for Larry Trader and right-winger Ric Seiling was added from Buffalo for future considerations. Center Mark Lamb, defenseman Dave Lewis and left-winger Dale Krentz were free-agent additions. Right-winger Joe Murphy, the first player chosen in the 1986 NHL entry draft, was joined by fellow draftees defensemen Steve Chiasson, Doug Houda and Jeff Sharples in cracking the Wings roster.

Red Wings Facts

Most Playoff Points in a Career

Steve Yzerman - 175
Sergei Fedorov - 160
Gordie Howe - 158
Nicklas Lidstrom - 107
Alex Delvecchio - 104
Ted Lindsay - 88
Vyacheslav Kozlov -79
Norm Ullman - 74
Sid Abel - 58
Igor Larionov - 58
Brendan Shanahan - 58

Short Passes

Alex Delvecchio served as Detroit captain from 1962-73. Steve Yzerman has been Detroit captain since 1986. In between the two, 18 different men wore the "C" for the Red Wings.

BACK in TIME

• **December 8, 1987**

Soviet leader Mikhal Gorbachev and President Ronald Reagan signed the first treaty to reduce the size of their countries' nuclear arsenals.

• **February 24, 1988**

The Supreme Court ruled that Hustler magazine's satires of evangelist Jerry Falwell were protected as freedom of speech under the constitution.

• **June 27, 1988**

Michigan became the first state to outlaw surrogate mother contracts.

quick cuts

Most Goals
Steve Yzerman: 50
Most Assists
Steve Yzerman: 52
Most Points
Steve Yzerman: 102
Most Penalty Minutes
Bob Probert: 398
Most Wins, Goaltender
Glen Hanlon: 22
Lowest Goals-Against Average
Greg Stefan: 3.11
Most Shutouts
Glen Hanlon: 4
NHL Award Winners
Jacques Demers - Jack Adams Award

FINAL STANDINGS

Norris Division	W	L	T	PTS	GF	GA
DETROIT	41	28	11	93	322	269
St. Louis	34	38	8	76	278	294
Chicago	30	41	9	69	284	328
Toronto	21	49	10	52	273	345
Minnesota	19	48	13	51	242	349

OTHER CONFERENCE WINNERS:
Smythe Division - Calgary Flames
Adams Division - Montreal Canadiens
Patrick Division - NY Islanders

Playoff Results
Defeated the Toronto Maple Leafs in Series "E" (4-2)
Defeated the St. Louis Blues in Series "K" (4-1)
Lost to the Edmonton Oilers in Series "N" (4-1)
Leading Playoff Scorers
Bob Probert (21PTS) - Adam Oates (20PTS)
Stanley Cup Champion
Edmonton Oilers

1987-88 Season in Review

They weren't the most talented team in the NHL, but they certainly were the league's most determined squad.

Other than skilled captain Steve Yzerman, the Wings' persona was that of a no-nonsense, lunch-bucket bunch who got by on hard work.

Detroit's success story was fashioned around the grit of grinders like Shawn Burr, Dave Barr and Mel Bridgman; unforgiving defensemen Gilbert Delorme and Lee Norwood, affectionately known as "Hack and Whack;" and the brutal toughness of enforcers Joe Kocur and Bob Probert, who struck fear into the opposition. Probert led the NHL with a club-record 398 penalty minutes, recorded a club-record 21 points in the playoffs and joined Yzerman in the NHL All-Star Game.

The Wings displayed a knack for scoring quickly. Jeff Sharples and Brent Ashton scored seven seconds apart November 25 in a 10-8 win over Winnipeg, a game which saw the team net five goals in a span of 4:54. Tim Higgins and Yzerman tallied in the first 37 seconds of a 12-0 December 4 rout of Chicago. All were team records.

When the Wings finished the regular season with a Norris Division-leading 41-28-11 slate, it was their first winning season since 1972-73 and the first time they'd come out on top since 1964-65.

A downer came March 1 against Buffalo, when Yzerman crashed into a goal post and tore a ligament in his right knee. Earlier in the game, he'd scored his 50th goal of the season, but was now expected to miss the playoffs.

Bob Probert

Detroit took out Toronto with a six-game first-round verdict, whipping the Leafs 8-0 right at Maple Leaf Gardens in Game 4. St. Louis fell next in five games and the Wings moved on to another showdown with the Stanley Cup champion Edmonton Oilers.

Returning home down 2-0 in the series, Yzerman suited up, sparking the Wings to a 5-2 win in Game 3. The Oilers were 4-3 winners in Game 4 and wrapped the series up with an 8-4 decision on home ice.

It was learned six players were at an Edmonton bar called Goose Loonies past curfew the night before Game 5 and that discovery left a sour taste with many of the non-offending players. "Each player will be fined to the maximum," coach Jacques Demers indicated.

HOCKEYTOWN MOMENT
Two in a row for Jacques

Several team firsts led to a second straight Jack Adams Award as the NHL's top bench boss for Wings coach Jacques Demers.

For the first time since 1964-65, the team garnered a first-place finish. Detroit outscored the opposition 322-269, the first season the Wings had recorded a plus ratio in the goals column since 1972-73. The 322 goals were a club record.

Detroit's 93 points were the best output by the club since a 95-point performance in 1969-70. As well, the 41 wins posted in 1987-88 under Demers were the most recorded by a Detroit coach since Jimmy Skinner led the team to 42 victories in 1954-55.

"When Jacques came into Detroit, he was a perfect fit," remembered Dave Lewis, a Wings defenseman before becoming an assistant coach under Demers in 1987. "He was energetic, he was upbeat. There couldn't have been a better man to take over at that time."

Demers is the only coach in the history of the the Jack Adams Award to win it two years in succession.

Glen Hanlon

He was brought to Detroit to provide a calming influence and ended up backstopping the Wings to one of the most impressive comebacks in Stanley Cup history.

Glen Hanlon had nine years of NHL experience under his belt when the Wings shipped three players to the New York Rangers for him and two draft picks in the summer of 1986, seeking a veteran to tutor volatile, young No. 1 man Greg Stefan and to also ease Stefan's workload.

"He was a key component in the rise from the ashes," Detroit GM Jimmy Devellano said of Hanlon's contribution during the 1986-87 season, which saw the Wings show a 38-point improvement during the regular season. Things suddenly went awry in the post-season, as upset-minded Toronto gained a 3-1 advantage over Detroit in the second round. Facing elimination in Game 5, Wings coach Jacques Demers turned to the veteran and Hanlon came through, blocking 30 shots for a 3-0 shutout victory.

Demers stayed with his hot goalie for Game 6 at Maple Leaf Gardens and Hanlon delivered a 24-save performance and a 4-2 victory.

"Glen has been marvelous," Demers acknowledged before Game 7 at Joe Louis Arena, where Hanlon again shut the door, making 30 stops for another 3-0 win to take the series.

"Hanlon gave a great effort," Toronto coach John Brophy said. "He was phenomenal," Demers added. "They didn't beat us because they couldn't beat Hanlon at all."

Hanlon's two shutouts and 1.67 goals-against average led all netminders in the 1986-87 playoffs, as did his four shutouts during the 1987-88 regular season, but his main claim to hockey fame was that on October 14, 1979, while tending goal for the Vancouver Canucks, he allowed the first of Wayne Gretzky's NHL-record 894 goals.

The Wings welcomed Hanlon to the fold as much for his work in the dressing room as his work between the pipes. "When we became a competitive team, he was a major reason," Devellano said. "He was a popu-

RED WINGS ARCHIVE

lar player, the kind of guy you liked having around and that all added to his value."

Hanlon's sense of humor was subtle, but wicked. One night when the Wings had skated through a particularly lethargic period, Demers launched into a tirade in the dressing room during the intermission.

Seeking to emphasize his point, Demers grabbed Hanlon's goal stick and attempted to break it across a table, but the thick paddle refused to snap.

Hanlon jumped up from his stall, went around the corner to the stick rack and came back with a player's stick.

"Here Jacques, try this one," he said.

Even when it was over, Hanlon left them laughing. Assigned to San Diego of the IHL during the 1990-91 season, his last as a pro, Hanlon hung a message in his locker for everyone to see. "Gone fishing," was all it said.

After hanging up his pads, Hanlon worked as a goaltending instructor with the Canucks and is currently coach of the AHL's Portland Pirates.

- **BORN:**
  Brandon, Man., February 20, 1957
- **ACQUIRED:**
  July 29, 1986 trade with New York Rangers
- **BEST SEASON WITH RED WINGS:**
  1987-88 (22-17-5, 4 SO, 3.23 GAA)

- **TOTALS WITH RED WINGS:**
  GP-186, W-65, L-71, T-26, SO-7, GAA-3.47
- **HONORS:**
  Led goalies in shutouts and GAA, 1986-87 Stanley Cup playoffs; Led team in wins, 1987-88; Led team in shutouts four times; Led team in GAA twice

MOTOWN Classic

Klima finds his niche in Detroit

The Petr principle was a key factor in Detroit's successful run during the 1988 playoffs. Petr Klima, who scored a career-high 37 goals during the regular season added 10 more, including a pair of hat tricks, in 12 Stanley Cup games until he was sidelined with a fractured right thumb. The hat tricks tied Norm Ullman's single-season playoff mark and the 10 goals broke Gordie Howe's club record for a playoff

campaign. Klima also scored Detroit's first playoff penalty shot goal when he beat Toronto's Allan Bester on April 9.

It was an impressive performance, but certainly not the most courageous of Klima's career. Just to get to the Red Wings, the left-winger had to be smuggled out of Communist Czechoslovakia, a daring move engineered by Wings assistant GM Nick Polano and vice-president Jim Lites.

ASSEMBLY LINE

Right-winger Jim Nill, currently Detroit's assistant GM, was acquired from St. Louis for Mark Kumpel. John Barrett and Greg Smith went to Washington for defenseman Darren Veitch. Defenseman Jim Pavese was picked up from the New York Rangers for future considerations. Centers John Chabot and Murray Eaves, left-wingers Kris King and Steve Martinson and goalie Darren Eliot were signed as free agents, while

Jim Nill

draft picks who made the grade included center Adam Graves and left-winger Brent Fedyk. The NHL entry draft was held in Detroit for the first time and the Wings selected defenseman Yves Racine with their first pick.

Red Wings Facts

Most Goals By Position - One Season

Center
Steve Yzerman 65 (1988 - 89)

Right Wing
Mickey Redmond 52 (1972 - 73)

Left Wing
John Ogrodnick 55 (1984 - 85)

Defense
Reed Larson 27 (1980 - 81)

Goal
Chris Osgood 1 (1995 - 96)

Short Passes

The Wings were one of nine NHL teams left-winger Brent Ashton played for. On July 15, 1981, he was traded twice in a matter of hours while playing a round of golf at the Saskatoon Golf and Country Club. "I teed off a Vancouver Canuck, made the turn a Winnipeg Jet and putted out a Colorado Rockie," Ashton recalled.

BACK in TIME

• December 31, 1988

A Pan Am 747 plane exploded in midair over Lockerbie, Scotland, killing 259 persons on board and 11 people on the ground.

• March 24, 1989

240,000 barrels of oil from Exxon's tanker Valdez, spilled and spread over 500 square miles of Alaskan waters and coated huge stretches of coastline.

• May 11, 1989

Fearing the extinction of African elephants, Kenya called for a worldwide ban on the trade of ivory.

quick cuts

Most Goals
Steve Yzerman: 65

Most Assists
Steve Yzerman: 90

Most Points
Steve Yzerman: 155

Most Penalty Minutes
Gerard Gallant: 230

Most Wins, Goaltender
Greg Stefan: 21

Lowest Goals-Against Average
Glen Hanlon: 3.56

Most Shutouts
Glen Hanlon: 1

NHL Award Winners
Steve Yzerman - Lester B. Pearson Award
Gerard Gallant - 2nd Team All-Star

FINAL STANDINGS

Norris Division	W	L	T	PTS	GF	GA
DETROIT	34	34	12	80	313	316
St. Louis	33	35	12	78	275	285
Minnesota	27	37	16	70	258	278
Chicago	27	41	12	66	297	335
Toronto	28	46	6	62	259	342

OTHER CONFERENCE WINNERS
Smythe Division - Calgary Flames
Adams Division - Montreal Canadiens
Patrick Division - Washington Capitals

Playoff Results
Lost to the Chicago Blackhawks in Series "E" (4-2)
Leading Playoff Scorers
Steve Yzerman (10PTS) - Adam Oates (8PTS)
Stanley Cup Champion
Calgary Flames

1988-89 Season in Review

Some of the numbers the Wings put up in 1988-89 were impressive. Others, not so impressive.

At the top of those making impressions were the totals of Steve Yzerman. Any doubters who suggested that the captain's name shouldn't be uttered in the same breath with Wayne Gretzky and Mario Lemieux were silenced when Yzerman set Detroit records with 65 goals, 90 assists and 155 points, finishing third in NHL scoring and earning the Lester B. Pearson Award as the top player in the league according to the NHL Players' Association.

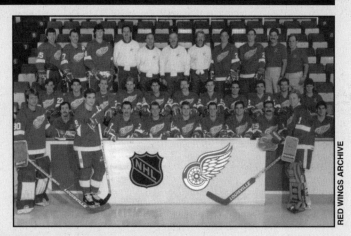

The forward line of Yzerman, left-winger Gerard Gallant and right-winger Paul MacLean, the latter acquired in the off-season from Winnipeg, combined for 140 goals and 319 points, both club marks for a forward unit.

Gallant potted a career-high 39 goals and earned selection to the NHL's Second All-Star Team, while MacLean scored 36 times. All three played for Canada at the 1989 World Championships.

As potent as that unit was, they weren't enough to offset the sudden defensive shortcomings of the Wings, who allowed 316 goals, three more than they scored. Those problems were evident in an 8-2 season-opening loss at Los Angeles and during an 8-8 tie in the home opener against St. Louis. The Wings surrendered six or more goals in 16 games, including a 10-5 loss Jan. 28 at Pittsburgh.

There were other concerns. Bob Probert was caught smuggling cocaine across the border through the Detroit-Windsor Tunnel, leading to jail time and NHL suspension for the Detroit left-winger.

The Wings held first place, but it was misleading, because they grabbed top spot in the weak Norris Division with a 34-34-12 record and their 80-point total was only good enough for 11th overall in the NHL.

"The Norris Division was a lot like puppy love," Wings GM Jimmy Devellano said. "From the outside, it might not have looked like much, but it meant a lot to the puppies."

The playoffs brought a first-round match-up with Chicago and sudden disappointment for Wings fans. After two straight years in the conference final, the Wings were ousted in the first round, losing in six games.

The Wings were whipped 7-1 in the decisive sixth game at Chicago Stadium.

HOCKEYTOWN MOMENT
Another first place finish for Detroit

The Wings couldn't put together back-to-back winning seasons, but they were able to assemble successive first-place finishes.

Even though they slipped from 93 to 80 points, at 34-34-12, the Wings still managed to hold off St. Louis for the Norris Division title.

Detroit hadn't captured two first-place finishes in as many seasons since 1953-54 and 1954-55, both campaigns which saw the Wings win the Stanley Cup.

They wouldn't get close to living that dream. Chicago doused Detroit's hopes quickly in the playoffs.

The Wings won the opener 3-2 on Dave Barr's goal, then lost the next three games. They staved off elimination with a 6-4 win at Joe Louis Arena in Game 5, before succumbing 7-1 at Chicago Stadium.

The 25 goals tied a mark for the most allowed by a Detroit team in a playoff series. Toronto scored 25 goals against the Wings in the 1942 finals, but needed seven games to do it.

Special teams really let the Wings down in post-season play. Chicago buried 10 power-play goals during the series and rubbed salt in Detroit's wounds by tallying four shorthanded markers.

Shawn Burr

Whether it involved checking or chuckling, you could usually find Shawn Burr playing a prominent role.

A junior sniper, Burr adapted to a new job description in the pro ranks, becoming a defensive forward, utilizing his speed on skates as a neutralizing force against enemy scorers.

"He was a relentless forechecker, who went fast and made things happen," said Nick Polano, Burr's first Detroit coach. "He was very clever." Burr also adapted to a new position, moving from center to left wing during his Detroit days. "Center, left wing, defense, it's all the same to me," Burr said. "Just don't put me in goal. I have a pretty weak five-hole."

Such sentiments were typical of Burr, who was quick with a quip. When it game to postgame quotes, Burr was a first team all-star in the eyes of the media. When the Wings blasted Montreal 9-0 on April 13, 1994, handing the Canadiens their worst shutout loss in 52 years, Burr, who scored two of the goals, stepped up to take the credit, pointing out he hadn't played earlier in the season, when Montreal hammered Detroit 8-1.

"Obviously, I was the difference," Burr said. "I'm a 17-goal swing." He kept his teammates in stitches and tied the opposition power play in knots. An outstanding penalty killer, Burr set a club record January 9, 1990 against Minnesota when he scored a pair of shorthanded goals, part of a three-goal, two assist performance on his part in a 9-0 rout of the North Stars.

"I think the last time I got five points was in junior with Kitchener," said Burr, Detroit's first-round draft pick in 1984, who had a 60-goal season for the OHL's Kitchener Rangers in 1985-86.

Certainly not as potent as an NHLer, Burr still knew where the net was. He posted three 20-goal seasons and in the 1986-87 playoffs, set team marks for rookies with seven goals and nine points. He tied a

RED WINGS ARCHIVE

club mark November 13, 1986 with three goals in the third period of a 7-5 loss at Philadelphia.

"I wasn't going to be a 50-goal scorer, but I still felt I could score my 25-30 goals and help out by bumping and grinding and checking," Burr said.

Burr played for Canada at the 1990 World Championships and was part of the Detroit team which reached the 1995 Stanley Cup final, but was traded to Tampa Bay in the summer of 1995.

He also played with the San Jose Sharks and retired as a player following the 1999-2000 season.

Burr sees the game from another side now. He and former Wings teammate Dino Ciccarelli are among the owners of the OHL's Sarnia Sting.

- **BORN:**
  Sarnia, Ontario, July 1, 1966
- **ACQUIRED:**
  Selected seventh overall in the June 9, 1984 NHL entry draft
- **BEST SEASON WITH RED WINGS:**
  1989-90 (24-32-56)
- **TOTALS WITH RED WINGS:**
  GP-659, G-148, A-214, PTS-362

- **HONORS:**
  Set club record for assists (seven) and points (nine) by a rookie in Stanley Cup playoffs; Shares team record for goals in a period (three); Played for Canada, 1990 World Championship

MOTOWN
Classic

Yzerman rewrites the record book

Putting together one of the finest individual seasons in NHL history told everyone that Steve Yzerman was the real deal.

His 65 goals shattered John Ogrodnick's 1984-85 club mark by 10 and with 90 assists and 155 points, Yzerman obliterated the Detroit standards of 74 assists and 121 points established by Marcel Dionne in 1974-75. His 388 shots on goal were also a new record for the Wings.

He had goals in each of the first six games of the season to set another team mark. Other record-setting performances by "Stevie Y" included a nine-game goal-scoring streak from November 18 to December 5 and a 28-game point-scoring streak from November 1 to January 4.

"He's the best player in the NHL," Minnesota coach Pierre Page said. "I truly believe that."

The Hockey News named Yzerman its player of the year and he skated for the Campbell Conference in the NHL All-Star Game.

ASSEMBLY LINE

Brent Ashton was dealt to Winnipeg for right-winger Paul MacLean, who skated on Detroit's record-setting top line with Steve Yzerman and Gerard Gallant. Darren Veitch was shipped to Toronto for right-winger Miroslav Frycer, who was traded to Edmonton during the season for a 1989 10th round draft pick (Rick Judson). Jim Pavese went to Hartford for left-winger Torrie Robertson. Left-wingers Jeff Brubaker and Miroslav Ihnacak, defenseman John Mokosak and Detroit-born defenseman John Blum were signed as free agents. The NHL entry draft supplied goalie Tim Cheveldae and right-winger Randy McKay.

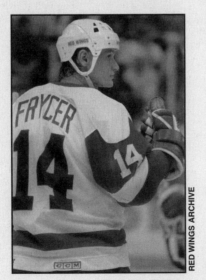

Miroslav Frycer

Red Wings Facts

Most Decisive Road Wins

11-1
at Montreal, December 2, 1995

11-2
at St. Louis, December 13, 1934

10-1
at Boston, December 11, 1952

10-3
at San Jose, January 6, 1994

10-6
at Chicago, March 16, 1947

Short Passes

Defenseman Lee Norwood, who posted career-high 10-32-42 totals in 1988-89, was the first product of the Little Caesars minor hockey system to play for the Wings.

- 1989 1990 -

BACK in TIME

- **December 21, 1989**

Following a year of increased interest rates, the prime rate reached 21.5 percent.

- **January 3, 1990**

Manuel Noriega surrendered following the U.S. invasion of Panama on December 20th and was extradited to the United States for trial on drug trafficking charges.

- **August 2, 1990**

At dawn, Iraqi troops and warfare aggressively crossed the Kuwait border and seized control of the tiny oil-rich state on the Persian Gulf.

quick cuts

Most Goals
Steve Yzerman: 62

Most Assists
Steve Yzerman: 65

Most Points
Steve Yzerman: 127

Most Penalty Minutes
Joe Kocur: 268

Most Wins, Goaltender
Glen Hanlon: 15

Lowest Goals-Against Average
Sam St. Laurent: 3.76

Most Shutouts
Glen Hanlon: 15

NHL Award Winners
None

FINAL STANDINGS

Norris Division	W	L	T	PTS	GF	GA
Chicago	41	33	6	88	316	294
St. Louis	37	34	9	83	295	279
Toronto	38	38	4	80	337	358
Minnesota	36	40	4	76	284	291
DETROIT	28	38	14	70	288	323

OTHER DIVISION WINNERS:
Smythe Division - Calgary Flames
Adams Division - Boston Bruins
Patrick Division - NY Rangers

Playoff Results
Did Not Qualify
Stanley Cup Champion
Edmonton Oilers

1989-90 Season in Review

It was a season of big trades and big-time disappointment in Hockeytown.

The promise of 1986-87, when the arrival of coach Jacques Demers sparked a renaissance in Red Wings hockey, was a balloon of hope that was quickly deflating.

An off-season deal which sent center Adam Oates and right-winger Paul MacLean to St. Louis for center Bernie Federko and left-winger Tony McKegney was the first indication of things to come.

Federko was a four-time 100-point scorer for the Blues, but his best years were behind him and he produced 57 points for Detroit in what would be his farewell NHL campaign. McKegney played only 14 games in a Wings uniform. Meanwhile, MacLean scored 36 goals for St. Louis and Oates became an NHL All-Star, garnering a pair of 90-assist seasons as Brett Hull's center.

The Wings were 10-7 losers in the season opener at Calgary and won only one of their first 11 road games.

Another deal was engineered in a bid to shake things up, a move which saw forwards Adam Graves, Petr Klima and Joe Murphy and defenseman Jeff Sharples go to Edmonton for center Jimmy Carson, a Detroit native and right-winger Kevin McClelland. Carson scored 21 goals, while Murphy, Klima and Graves played key roles as the Oilers won the Stanley Cup.

One of the few bright spots was a 9-0 shutout win January 9 over Minnesota which saw the Wings score a record three shorthanded goals. Shawn Burr netted

two of them, also setting a record. Captain Steve Yzerman registered 62-65-127 totals and played in the NHL All-Star Game.

Most nights it was the Wings who came up short handed. Left-winger Bob Probert missed all but the last four games of the season while serving a prison sentence for his 1988 drug arrest at the Detroit-Windsor tunnel. Down the stretch, the Wings closed 2-5-2 and a 6-5 home-ice loss to Buffalo sealed their fate. They were officially out of the playoffs.

"I don't think we played well all season," Yzerman said. "When you didn't make the playoffs and 16 of 21 teams make it, it's a bit of a joke."

HOCKEYTOWN MOMENT
Wings score big at the draft

The 1989-90 season didn't go so well for the Red Wings, but the 1989 NHL entry draft couldn't have gone much better.

The foundation for a powerhouse squad of the 1990s was assembled in the middle and late rounds, where the club landed defenseman Nicklas Lidstrom with the 43rd pick, center Sergei Fedorov at No. 74 and defenseman Vladimir Konstantinov with 221st selection.

Fedorov would win the Hart Trophy in 1993-94 and would become a two-time Selke Trophy winner, while Lidstrom would win the Norris Trophy in 2000-01. Konstantinov would finish as the Norris Trophy runner-up in 1996-97. Between them, they would earn six NHL All-Star Team selections and were all be key members of Detroit's 1996-97 Stanley Cup winner.

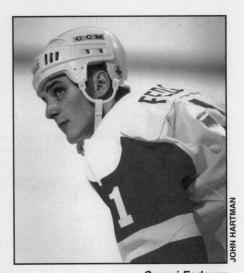

Sergei Fedorov

Center Mike Sillinger (11th) and right-winger Dallas Drake (116th) also played for the Wings, while defenseman Bob Boughner (32nd) went on to play with Buffalo, Nashville, Pittsburgh and Calgary.

Wings of Legend
Steve Chiasson

Steve Chiasson was a player who believed in the basic approach. "Steve was a simple guy," Wings captain Steve Yzerman said. "The thing I'll always remember about him was when things weren't going well, he wasn't one to analyze. He'd always say, 'Just shut up and play.' I've always carried that philosophy with me."

Taken with the 50th pick of the 1985 NHL entry draft, Chiasson, a six-foot, 205-pound defenseman, won a Memorial Cup with the Guelph Platers in 1985-86 and was named MVP of the tournament, cracking Detroit's lineup the following season at the age of 19.

The Wings allowed Chiasson to join the Canadian team for the World Junior Championships, but Canada was disqualified from the tournament after a bench-clearing brawl with Russia. Chiasson ended up paired off with Vladimir Konstantinov during the scrap, a fact the two men came to realize five seasons later when they were defense partners with the Red Wings.

"Steve was a big, strong kid, who might have lacked a little bit of mobility," Detroit GM Jimmy Devellano said. "But he was a pretty good competitor and a better than average player."

Chiasson's best season was the 1992-93 campaign, in which he garnered 10-52-62 numbers and selection to play in the NHL All-Star Game, the first Detroit defenseman picked to play in the mid-season classic since Willie Huber in 1982-83.

"It's a bonus, another jersey for my basement to go with the collection," Chiasson said.

An underrated offensive contributor, Chiasson hit the 40-point plateau four times and reached double digits in goals on five occasions, scoring a career-high 14 goals in 1989-90.

"He was a player that the other players liked and as a teammate, I think he was an under-appreciated player," Yzerman said. "He's a guy that played hard. He played through some pretty serious injuries, broken bones and such."

MARK HICKS

Chiasson played much of the 1990-91 season on a broken ankle, an injury he aggravated three times.

"He was always accountable," Yzerman said.

The Wings traded Chiasson to the Calgary Flames in 1994, getting in return goaltender Mike Vernon, who would backstop Detroit to the Stanley Cup in 1996-97.

"It's part of the business and you accept that it could happen," Chiasson said after the trade. "You just never think you'll be the one until it happens to you."

After three seasons in Calgary, Chiasson was dealt to Hartford, a franchise which relocated to become the Carolina Hurricanes in 1997. Driving home from a team party following the conclusion of the 1998-99 season, Chiasson was killed in a single-car accident. He was 32 years old.

- **BORN:**
  Barrie, Ontario, April 14, 1967
- **ACQUIRED:**
  Selected 50th overall in the June 15, 1985 NHL entry draft
- **BEST SEASON WITH RED WINGS:**
  1992-93 (10-52-62)

- **TOTALS WITH RED WINGS:**
  GP-471, G-67, A-200, PTS-267
- **HONORS:**
  Played in NHL All-Star Game, 1992-93; Played for Canada, 1986 World Junior Championships

MOTOWN Classic

Chevy drives the Wings

With Greg Stefan injured and Glen Hanlon wearing down, the Wings recalled Tim Cheveldae from their Adirondack AHL farm club on February 9 and the move paid immediate dividends.

Cheveldae assumed the No. 1 goaltender's role and blossomed, going 6-0-4 in his first 10 starts, falling two short of Terry Sawchuk's club-record unbeaten streak of 12 games.

"Sometimes, it's hard to believe all this is happening," admitted Cheveldae, who was 8-2-7 in his first 17 decisions. "You kind of look around and say, 'Yeah, I'm a Detroit Red Wing and I'm playing in the NHL.'"

Cheveldae finished 10-9-8 in 27 games, the only Detroit goalie to post a winning slate, but that held no solace for him when the club missed the playoffs.

"It's like a nightmare, except it's real," Cheveldae said. "At least in a nightmare, you get to wake up."

ASSEMBLY LINE

Jimmy Carson

In a pair of blockbuster moves, Adam Oates and Paul MacLean were dealt to St. Louis for center Bernie Federko and left-winger Tony McKegney, while Adam Graves, Petr Klima, Joe Murphy and Jeff Sharples switched to Edmonton in exchange for center Jimmy Carson and right-winger Kevin McClelland. McKegney was then dealt to Quebec early in the season for defenseman Robert Picard and left-winger Greg C. Adams. Kris King was shipped to the New York Rangers for left-winger Chris McRae and a 1990 fifth-round draft pick (Tony Burns). Defensemen Borje Salming, Chris Kotsopoulos and Peter Dineen, right-winger Daniel Shank and center/right-winger Marc Habscheid were signed as free agents. Defenseman Dean Morton, who later became an NHL referee and right-winger Sheldon Kennedy were products of the NHL entry draft.

Red Wings Facts

Most Assists by a Goaltender
(game & season)

Game
2
Jimmy Rutherford
February 18, 1979 vs Pittsburgh
1
Numerous Occasions

Season
5
Tim Cheveldae 1990-91

Short Passes

Right-winger Gordie Howe (1965) and left-winger Frank Mahovlich (1969) are the only Red Wings to be named MVP of the NHL All-Star Game.

JIMMY DEVELLANO

In an era of constant change in professional sport, where loyalty to one team seems to have gone the way of the maskless netminder, Jimmy Devellano has been an ever-present part of the Detroit Red Wings' success story.

The first move Mike Ilitch made when he purchased the team in 1982 was to hire Devellano as GM. Ilitch has completed many successful transactions since then, but it's hard to argue he's made a better one.

"Jimmy D," as he's known, took an NHL doormat and built them to where they were the envy of all others. And he started where every successful structure begins — with a sturdy foundation.

His plan was to build through the draft and develop a solid farm system.

"It means we're going to have to suffer a little longer," he told Wings fans, seeking their patience. "It will take five or six years of solid drafting to build this team to where it should be."

Devellano's first draft in 1983 brought Steve Yzerman, Bob Probert, Petr Klima and Joe Kocur to the team and over the years, his strategy added the likes of Shawn Burr, Steve Chiasson, Adam Graves, Nicklas Lidstrom, Sergei Fedorov, Dallas Drake and Vladimir Konstantinov.

He hired Jacques Demers as coach in 1986 and the following season, Demers guided Detroit to first place for the first time since the 1964-65 season.

Destined to be a talent spotter, Devellano's best scouting report was perhaps the one he wrote about himself. "I was a terrible player," he said. "I couldn't skate and I wasn't very big."

He could spot others who had ability and earned a scouting position with the St. Louis Blues in 1967, moving to the New York Islanders in 1972, where he helped assemble the nucleus of their four Stanley Cup winners.

By 1991-92, when the Wings launched their first of 10 consecutive winning seasons, Devellano had been promoted to senior vice-president, with Bryan Murray in place as coach-GM. Scotty Bowman came aboard as coach in 1993 and Murray was out as GM a year later, with Bowman, assistant GM Ken Holland and Devellano working together to run the front office.

RED WINGS ARCHIVE

That triumvirate led Detroit to its first Stanley Cup in 42 seasons in 1996-97.

A solid hockey man who turned the Wings into champions, Devellano is also to be admired for his candor. The first to call his own number when he makes mistakes, Devellano still describes his 1989 move which sent Adam Oates and Paul MacLean to St. Louis for Tony McKegney and Bernie Federko as, "The worst trade I ever made."

Devellano doesn't like to dwell on the past, but looking back at the words Devellano uttered when he was hired shows the man delivered on his promise.

"I really think I can turn things around," Devellano said at the time.

"If we can put a quality product on the ice, tremendous things could happen at Joe Louis Arena."

He turned it around. And tremendous things certainly happened.

- 1990   1991 -

BACK in TIME

• October 3, 1990
After 45 years of division, East and West Germany were reunited under one government known as the Federal Republic of Germany, headed by Chancellor Helmut Kohl.

• February 1, 1991
President De Klerk announced the abolition of the last remaining apartheid laws in Africa.

• February 28, 1991
Six weeks after the launch of Desert Storm, the Gulf War ended with the liberation of Kuwait and defeat of Iraq's army.

quick cuts

Most Goals
Steve Yzerman: 51
Most Assists
Steve Yzerman: 57
Most Points
Steve Yzerman: 108
Most Penalty Minutes
Bob Probert: 315
Most Wins, Goaltender
Tim Cheveldae: 30
Lowest Goals-Against Average
Glen Hanlon: 3.20
Most Shutouts
Tim Cheveldae: 2
NHL Award Winners
Mike Ilitch - Lester Patrick Trophy

FINAL STANDINGS

Norris Division	W	L	T	PTS	GF	GA
Chicago	49	23	8	106	284	211
St. Louis	47	22	11	105	310	250
DETROIT	34	38	8	76	273	298
Minnesota	27	39	14	68	256	266
Toronto	23	46	11	57	241	318

OTHER CONFERENCE WINNERS
Smythe Division - Los Angeles Kings
Adams Division - Boston Bruins
Patrick Division - Pittsburgh Penguins

Playoff Results
Lost to the St. Louis Blues in Series "F" (4-3)
Leading Playoff Scorers
Steve Yzerman & Sergei Fedorov (6PTS each)
Stanley Cup Champion
Pittsburgh Penguins

1990-91 Season in Review

Change was on the agenda as the Wings embarked on a new decade. Jacques Demers was out as coach, replaced by Bryan Murray, who also took over Jimmy Devellano's GM portfolio. Devellano assumed the role of senior vice-president.

"Near the end of the eighties, we had a good team, but we had a lot of off-ice problems," Devellano said. "We didn't slip horribly, but we did slip out of the the playoffs (in 1989-90), so there was a feeling we needed some change."

The retooling was obvious on the ice, where the Wings employed a club-record 45 players in search of the right mix. Among the newcomers were center Keith Primeau, Detroit's 1990 first-round draft pick and center Sergei Fedorov, who slipped away from the Russian team at the Goodwill Games in Seattle during the summer, seeking political asylum.

A solid start at Joe Louis Arena featured six straight home-ice wins to open the season, tying a team mark. Captain Steve Yzerman posted his third straight 50-goal season, equaling team records for goals (three) and points (four) in a period November 17 during the opening frame of an 8-4 win over Toronto. Six days later, rookie left-winger Johan Garpenlov scored four goals in a 5-3 victory over St. Louis. Goalie Tim Cheveldae also contributed to the offense, setting a team mark for netminders by collecting five assists.

1990-91 DETROIT RED WINGS

RED WINGS ARCHIVE

The Wings finished 34-38-8, third in the Norris Division. Fedorov registered 31-48-79 totals, finished as runner-up to Chicago goalie Ed Belfour in the Calder Trophy voting and was named to the NHL All-Rookie Team. Yzerman represented Detroit in the NHL All-Star Game.

St. Louis, 105-point producers during the regular-season, provided playoff opposition and Detroit surprisingly raced to a 3-1 series lead. The St. Louis turnaround began with a 6-1 win in Game 5, a slugfest which saw the Wings establish Stanley Cup records for the most penalties (33) and penalty minutes (152) in a game.

The Blues were 3-0 winners in Game 6 and took the set with a 3-2 margin in Game 7. Fedorov tied a team playoff record for rookies, acquiring five assists.

"Winning would have done wonders for some of our guys," Murray said. "But losing gives you a message that something has to be done."

HOCKEYTOWN MOMENT

Wings hire Bryan Murray as new coach-GM

JOHN HARTMAN

Friday, June 13, 1990 proved to an unlucky day for Jacques Demers, who was fired as coach of the Red Wings.

Bryan Murray, who had posted six winning seasons in eight as coach of the Washington Capitals and the seventh-best (.572) winning percentage in NHL history, was hired as coach and GM of the club, with GM Jimmy Devellano promoted to senior vice-president.

"In the NHL, this is as good as it gets," Murray said of coming to Detroit. Murray indicated he would have happily settled for just the coaching position with the Wings, but welcomed the opportunity to wear both hats.

"I think in this case, the coach and the general manager will agree most of the time," Murray said.

Steve Yzerman

In Detroit sporting circles during the 1980s and 1990s, the greatest players were recognized by simple terms. "Isiah" was all you had to say and people knew you meant Detroit Pistons captain Isiah Thomas. Likewise, "Barry" could be none other than Detroit Lions running back Barry Sanders, while "Tram and Lou" were Alan Trammell and Lou Whitaker, the sensational double-play combination of the Detroit Tigers.

On the ice, Wings center Steve Yzerman also carried a straightforward handle. He was - and still is - "The Captain."

It's a handle he wears with pride.

"When I was looking for a captain, I wanted a guy with the Red Wings crest tattooed on his chest," said former Detroit coach Jacques Demers, who named Yzerman captain in 1986. "Steve Yzerman was that guy."

He set Wings rookie standards with 39-48-87 totals in 1983-84 and continued his assault on the record book ever since. Yzerman's 1988-89 numbers of 65-90-155 remain single-season club production standards. He's posted two 60-goal and three 50-goal seasons, collecting 100 points on six occasions.

Lately, he's been knocking off some of the all-time greats, as Yzerman ascends to the elite class of NHL stars. He's a member of the NHL's 600-goal, 1,000-assist club, a group whose membership also includes Gordie Howe, Wayne Gretzky, Mario Lemieux, Mark Messier and Marcel Dionne.

"These guys I'm moving up amongst, these are the guys who were the heroes of my era," Yzerman said. "It's great to be mentioned in the same sentence with them, but I certainly don't consider myself their equal."

That task is happily filled by others.

Danny Gare was the man who surrendered the "C" to Yzerman and the former Wing has followed his successor's career with great delight.

"He was doing the job then and he's still doing it today," Gare said. "When that team needs a lift, he's still the one they turn to, the one who gets them going."

KRISTY WILLS

For all his accomplishments, the one Yzerman cherishes most is that moment when he lifted the Stanley Cup in 1997, ending Detroit's 42-season title blight.

"For as long as I can remember, I dreamed of lifting the Stanley Cup," Yzerman said. "I watched the presentation every year. I watched the dressing-room celebration and I dreamed of the day it would be me."

He's a hero of Hockeytown and also back home in Nepean, Ontario, where Yzerman grew up. "I played for the same Tier II junior team that he did," former Wings defenseman Aaron Ward said. "In the Steve Yzerman Sportsplex.

"As soon as you walk in the rink, his pictures are everywhere. He's a legend."

Perhaps Philadelphia Flyers winger Rick Tocchet, a career opponent of Yzerman's, summed it up best.

"The game is a better place with Steve Yzerman in it," Tocchet said.

- **BORN:**
  Cranbrook, British Columbia, May 9, 1965
- **ACQUIRED:**
  Selected fourth overall in the June 8, 1983 NHL entry draft
- **BEST SEASON WITH RED WINGS:**
  1988-89 (65-90-155)
- **TOTALS WITH RED WINGS:**
  GP-1,362, G-658, A-1,004, PTS-1,662

- **HONORS:**
  Won Conn Smythe Trophy, 1997-98; Won Selke Trophy, 1999-2000; Won Lester B. Pearson Award, 1988-89; Selected to NHL First All-Star Team, 1999-2000; Selected to NHL All-Rookie Team, 1983-84; Played in nine NHL All-Star Games; Named team captain in 1986; Played for Canada in 1989 and 1990 World Championship, 1996 World Cup and 1998 Winter Olympics; Won Olympic Gold Medal for Canada, 2002 Winter Olympics

MOTOWN Classic

Ilitch receives Lester Patrick Trophy

From rags to riches. From worst to first. The turnaround in the fortunes of the Red Wings since Mike Ilitch purchased the team in 1982 was noticed by everyone, including the presenters of the Lester Patrick Trophy, who in 1991 honored Ilitch with the award for outstanding service to hockey in the United States.

"It's been particularly gratifying for me to see the Red Wings grow into the successful team they've become," Ilitch said. "In the beginning, the team was struggling. We worked hard to build up the fans' confidence in the team and put together a team that worked."

Ilitch joined a list of Red Wings luminaries who'd won the award, such as Jack Adams (1966), Gordie Howe and James Norris Sr. (1967), Terry Sawchuk (1971), Alex Delvecchio (1974) and Tommy Ivan (1975).

ASSEMBLY LINE

New faces were abundant as the Wings sought a different look. Center Kevin Miller, left-winger Jim Cummins and defenseman Dennis Vial came from the New York Rangers for Joe Kocur and Per Djoos. Lee Norwood went to New Jersey for left-winger Paul Ysebaert. Doug Houda was dealt to Hartford for defenseman Doug Crossman. A 1990 second round draft pick went to Calgary for defenseman Brad McCrimmon, 1991 sixth (Alexander Kuzminsky) and eighth (Robb McIntyre) round draft choices were shipped to

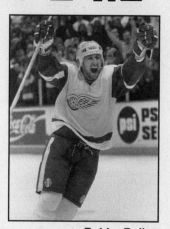

Bobby Dollas

Toronto for goalie Allan Bester and defenseman Brad Marsh in separate deals, while a 1991 fifth round pick was sent to Montreal for defenseman Rick Green. Defenseman Bobby Dollas, center Bill McDougall and goalies Alain Chevrier and Dave Gagnon were free-agent additions. Centers Sergei Fedorov, Keith Primeau, Tom Bissett and Mike Sillinger, right-winger Randy McKay, goalie Scott King, defensemen Chris Luongo, Bob Wilkie and Gord Kruppke and left-wingers Marc Potvin and Johan Garpenlov were NHL entry draft picks, while right-winger Gary Shuchuk came through the NHL supplemental draft.

Red Wings Facts

Most Goals One Season

65
Steve Yzerman 1988-89
62
Steve Yzerman 1989-90
58
Steve Yzerman 1992-93
56
Sergei Fedorov 1993-94
55
John Ogrodnick 1984-85
52
Mickey Redmond 1972-73
52
Ray Sheppard 1993-94
51
Mickey Redmond 1973-74
51
Steve Yzerman 1990-91

Short Passes

The Murrays were Detroit's only brother combination in which one brother wasn't a player. Bryan Murray was coach of the Wings from 1990-93 and GM from 1990-94. Terry Murray played defense for the Wings in 1976-77.

- 1991 1992 -

BACK in TIME

- **December 25, 1991**

The Soviet Union was officially abolished with the resignation of President Mikhal Gorbachev following the formation of the Commonwealth of Independent States four days earlier.

- **February 24, 1992**

General Motors announced a world record deficit of $4.5 billion, following Ford's announcement of its biggest loss ever 10 days earlier.

- **August 12, 1992**

The United States, Canada and Mexico agreed to the North American Free Trade Agreement (NAFTA), aimed at creating the world's largest and wealthiest trading bloc.

quick cuts

Most Goals
Steve Yzerman: 45

Most Assists
Steve Yzerman: 58

Most Points
Steve Yzerman: 103

Most Penalty Minutes
Bob Probert: 276

Most Wins, Goaltender
Tim Cheveldae: 38

Lowest Goals-Against Average
Greg Millen: 2.71

Most Shutouts
Tim Cheveldae: 2

NHL Award Winners
Paul Ysebaert - Plus Minus Award

FINAL STANDINGS

Norris Division	W	L	T	PTS	GF	GA
DETROIT	43	25	12	98	320	256
Chicago	36	29	15	87	257	236
St. Louis	36	33	11	83	279	266
Minnesota	32	42	6	70	246	278
Toronto	30	43	7	67	234	294

OTHER DIVISION WINNERS
Smythe Division - Vancouver Canucks
Adams Division - Montreal Canadiens
Patrick Division - NY Rangers

Playoff Results
Defeated the Minnesota North Stars in Series "E" (4-3)
Lost to the Chicago Blackhawks in Series "K" (4-0)
Leading Playoff Scorers
Sergei Fedorov (10PTS) Steve Yzerman & Ray Sheppard (8PTS each)
Stanley Cup Champion
Pittsburgh Penguins

1991-92 Season in Review

One of the most impressive regular seasons in Red Wings history commenced in rather unimpressive fashion. The Wings were winless through their first four games and an unspectacular 6-8-1 through 15 contests.

A 5-4 victory November 8 over Washington launched a nine-game unbeaten string and Detroit lost only four times in its next 28 games.

Captain Steve Yzerman was his usual self, which is to say he was outstanding. Leading the team with 45-58-103 totals, Yzerman tied his own club mark with a nine-game goal-scoring streak from January 29 to February 12 and equaled Shawn Burr's 1989-90 achievement of scoring two shorthanded goals in the same game, turning the trick April 14 in a 7-4 decision over Minnesota.

Goalie Tim Cheveldae set club standards with 72 games played and 4,236 minutes logged between the pipes. Center Sergei Fedorov tied the team mark for points in a period, garnering four January 21 during the second stanza of a 7-3 triumph over Philadelphia. Left-winger Paul Ysebaert led the NHL with a plus-44 rating.

Cheveldae, Fedorov and Yzerman all appeared in the NHL All-Star Game, the first time three Wings had participated in the mid-season affair since the 1969-70 season.

Detroit finished first in the Norris Division with 98 points, the third first-place showing by the club in five

1991-92 DETROIT RED WINGS
Norris Division Champions

RED WINGS ARCHIVE

seasons. The Wings opened the playoffs against Minnesota in a series which was the reversal of Detroit's 1991 set with St. Louis.

The North Stars took three of the first four games, then Cheveldae took over, posting back-to-back shutouts to force a decisive seventh game. Game 6 was a 1-0 Detroit victory in which Sergei Fedorov's goal at 16:13 of overtime was detected by video replay, the first time a Stanley Cup OT game had been decided by a video replay official.

Game 7 belonged to the Wings by a 5-2 count, with right-winger Ray Sheppard burying a hat trick.

Unfortunately, the comeback took the wind out of Detroit's sails and the Wings had little left in the tank for Chicago. The Blackhawks took the second-round series between the two teams in the minimum four games.

HOCKEYTOWN MOMENT
Wings bounce back

Detroit's second season under the Bryan Murray regime was among the most successful in franchise history.

Capturing the Norris Division title by 11 points over Chicago, the Wing posted 43 victories, second only to the 44 victories garnered by the 1951-52 Wings. Detroit's 43-25-12 record produced 98 points, third-best in club history.

Even a 10-day players' strike April 1-10 couldn't slow the Wings, who returned from the layoff to go 2-0-1 in their final three regular-season games.

"We've got some people who can play this year," Murray said.

With captain Steve Yzerman and second-year center Sergei Fedorov joined by rookie defensemen Vladimir Konstantinov and Nicklas Lidstrom, it was clearly evident Detroit's skill level had risen significantly.

"Things are starting to look really good," Yzerman said. "Nik and Vladdy look really solid on the points."

RED WINGS ARCHIVE

291

Vladimir Konstantinov

Red Wings scouts Neil Smith and Christer Rockstrom were assigned to cover the 1986-87 World Junior Championships in Czechoslovakia and they certainly got an eyeful when Canada and Russia staged a bench-clearing brawl.

During the fisticuffs, one Russian player stood out, because he was the only one standing up to the aggressive Canadians.

That youngster was Vladimir Konstantinov.

"He was the only one of the Russians who fought back," Smith recalled.

They made note and in 1989, the Wings made Konstantinov the 221st pick of the NHL entry draft. The changing political climate in the former Soviet Union soon made it possible for hockey players to come to North America and Konstantinov joined the Wings in 1991-92.

Konstantinov was paired with Steve Chiasson during his rookie season and Chiasson thought he saw something familiar about his new partner. As Konstantinov's English improved, Chiasson and Konstantinov figured out they were also paired off in that infamous 1987 brawl.

"Now I know why everyone in the league thinks you're such a pain in the neck," Chiasson told Konstantinov.

The "Vladinator" delivered pain to anyone foolish enough to venture into his area. "He's one of the few Russians who didn't get credit for his tremendous skills, but he was an outstanding hockey player," former Wings goalie Tim Cheveldae said.

"For my game, I don't need to score the goal," Konstantinov once explained. "I need someone to start thinking about me and forgetting about scoring goals."

Konstantinov's game was to get others off theirs and he did it better than anyone. "He was just a great competitor," St. Louis forward Keith Tkachuk remembered of Konstantinov. "He never let up. He was always looking to hit you."

But Konstantinov was far more than just a pest. He led the NHL in plus-minus with a plus-60 rating in 1995-96. Konstantinov was selected to the NHL

RED WINGS ARCHIVE

Second All-Star Team that season and finished as runner-up in the Norris Trophy voting in 1996-97. He was an NHL All-Rookie Team choice in 1983-84.

"As a young boy, he played center," Wings center Igor Larionov said of Konstantinov. "So what you had was a player with great skill, who was also the toughest defenseman in the NHL."

A fun-loving man who always called it as he saw it, Konstantinov's career was ended and his life forever altered when he suffered debilitating brain injuries in a limousine crash six days after Detroit's 1996-97 Stanley Cup win.

The following spring, moments after the Wings won the title, Konstantinov was wheeled to the ice and fellow countrymen Larionov and Slava Fetisov helped him tour the Cup around the rink.

"Vladdy's spirit was with us in the room all season," Fetisov said. The finest tribute to Konstantinov's unwavering competitiveness came from Tkachuk, so often his bitter foe on the ice.

"If you had 20 guys like him, you'd win the Stanley Cup every year," Tkachuk said of Konstantinov.

- **BORN:**
  Murmansk, Russia, March 19, 1967
- **ACQUIRED:**
  Selected 221st overall in the June 17, 1989 NHL entry draft
- **BEST SEASON WITH RED WINGS:**
  1996-97 (5-33-38)
- **TOTALS WITH RED WINGS:**
  GP-446, G-47, A-128, PTS-175

- **HONORS:**
  Selected to NHL Second All-Star Team, 1995-96; Won Alka-Seltzer Plus Award, 1995-96; Runner-up in Norris Trophy voting, 1996-97; Selected to NHL All-Rookie Team, 1991-92

MOTOWN Classic

Lidstrom and Konstantinov make "All-Rookie" team

Nicklas Lidstrom and Vladimir Konstantinov wasted little time showing the rest of the NHL they were going to be impact performers.

A slick, skilled defenseman from Sweden, Lidstrom collected 49 assists and 60 points to equal the rookie marks for Detroit defenders set in 1977-78 by Reed Larson and finished the season a plus-36. He was second in the Calder Trophy voting behind Vancouver's Pavel Bure and Lidstrom earned one of two defense positions on the NHL All-Rookie Team.

The other was filled by teammate Konstantinov, a former captain of the Russian national team, who also had skill in abundance, but became quickly recognized around the league for his abrasive, intimidating style of patrolling the blueline. Konstantinov collected 24 points and 172 penalty minutes in 79 games and was plus-25.

ASSEMBLY LINE

Signed as a free agent, right-winger Ray Sheppard potted 36 goals. Right-winger Troy Crowder was another free-agent addition from New Jersey, costing Dave Barr and Randy McKay in compensation. Marc Habscheid was dealt to Calgary for left-winger Brian MacLellan. Defenseman Bob McGill and a 1992 eighth round draft pick (C.J. Denomme) came from San Jose for Johan Garpenlov. Right-winger Alan Kerr was acquired from the New

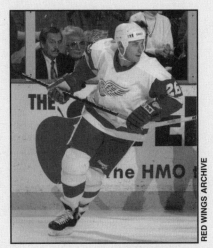

Ray Sheppard

York Islanders for Rick Green and goalie Greg Millen was picked up from the New York Rangers for future considerations. Rick Zombo went to St. Louis in exchange for Vincent Riendeau, the goalie who beat the Wings out of the 1991 playoffs. Center Chris Tancill was picked up from Hartford for Daniel Shank. Bengt Gustafsson was lost to San Jose in the NHL expansion draft. The NHL entry draft brought defensemen Vladimir Konstantinov and Nicklas Lidstrom, right-winger Martin Lapointe and center Vyacheslav Kozlov.

Red Wings Facts

Most Power-Play Goals one season

21
Mickey Redmond 1973-74

21
Dino Ciccarelli 1992-93

20
Brendan Shanahan 1996-97

19
Danny Grant 1974-75

19
John Ogrodnick 1983-84

19
Ray Sheppard 1993-94

17
Gerard Gallant 1986-87

17
Steve Yzerman 1988-89

Short Passes

Detroit goalie Tim Cheveldae appeared in an NHL-leading 72 games in 1991-92, yet the Wings shared the NHL lead in goaltenders used, employing five different netminders. Besides Cheveldae, Greg Millen (10 games), Vincent Riendeau (two), Scott King (one), Allan Bester (one) also played.

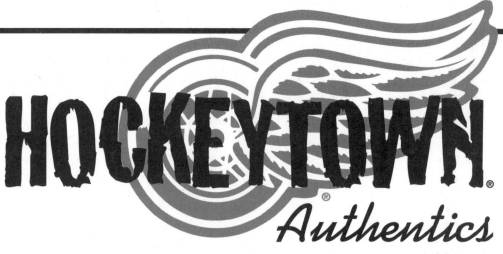

Being a native of Latvia, Arturs Irbe was never schooled in the ways of the projectile mollusk.

During Game 1 of the 1993-94 Stanley Cup series between the Detroit Red Wings and Irbe's San Jose Sharks, the goalie was mortified as one octopus after another rained down from the Joe Louis Arena rafters.

"I am not laughing, but I am thinking that this felt like a joke," Irbe said. "These people, they are throwing seafood on the ice."

Please Arturs, allow us to explain.

As Detroit proceeded to sweep to the 1951-52 Stanley Cup championship in the minimum eight games, it set off a light bulb over the heads of Red Wings season-tickets holders Jerry and Pete Cusimano.

"My dad was in the fish and poultry business," Pete said. "Anyway, my brother said, 'Why don't we throw an octopus on the ice for good luck? It's got eight legs and that might be a good omen for eight straight wins.'"

When the final series with Montreal returned to the Olympia, Pete launched an octopus onto the ice during the Cup-clinching game and a Detroit playoff tradition was born, though not without some suffering.

"You ever smelled a half-boiled octopus?" he asked. "It ain't exactly Chanel No. 5. But you should have seen how the ref jumped."

At first, the officials weren't the only ones who were not amused.

"Octopi shall not occupy the ice," broadcast the Olympia public-address announcer. "Please refrain from throwing same."

Eventually, people came to accept and cherish this quaint, yet odd practice. Even the referees didn't mind too much.

"The squids in Detroit were a piece of cake," Hall of Fame arbiter Bill Chadwick insisted. "They were inert. You just loaded them onto a shovel and off they went."

The tradition continued and Red Wings officials went from trying to put a stop to it to marketing its uniqueness. In recent years, a giant purple octopus — nicknamed Al by the Red Wings players, after Joe

RED WINGS ARCHIVE

Louis Arena Zamboni driver Al Sobotka — fell to ice level before every Detroit playoff game.

During lean times from the late 1960s through the early 1980s, few octopi were required. After a three-year absence, Detroit qualified for the 1969-70 play-offs and defenseman Bob Baun dealt with the first octopus by stickhandling the monster of the deep into the corner, picking it up barehanded and tossing it over the glass.

Another eight years would pass until Bobby Kromm coached the Wings into the post-season. Kromm insisted that one of the things which made hockey at the Olympia great was that, "You might go home with a bag of fish at playoff time."

Don't think it hasn't been considered.

Devils defenseman Ken Daneyko, who owned a seafood restaurant back in New Jersey, rolled his eyes as he watched rink attendants gather up the octopi for disposal during the 1995 Cup finals.

"Don't these people realize how much I pay for calamari by the pound?" Daneyko asked incredulously.

- 1992 1993 -

BACK in TIME

• **August 15, 1992**

The world was appalled to see shocking images of emaciated prisoners held in Serbian prison camps in Bosnia and learn of the brutality, murder and rape that took place against innocent civilians.

• **January 1, 1993**

In a peaceful split, Czechoslovakia ceased to exist and its 15.6 million inhabitants became citizens of either Slovakia or the Czech Republic.

• **August 24, 1993**

The $1 billion spacecraft Mars Observer was to begin orbiting Mars this date, but NASA reported it had lost contact 72 hours earlier.

quick cuts

Most Goals
Steve Yzerman: 58
Most Assists
Steve Yzerman: 79
Most Points
Steve Yzerman: 137
Most Penalty Minutes
Bob Probert: 292
Most Wins, Goaltender
Tim Cheveldae: 34
Lowest Goals-Against Average
Vincent Riendeau: 3.22
Most Shutouts
Tim Cheveldae: 4
NHL Award Winners
None

FINAL STANDINGS

Norris Division	W	L	T	PTS	GF	GA
Chicago	47	25	12	106	279	230
DETROIT	47	28	9	103	396	280
Toronto	44	29	11	99	288	241
St. Louis	37	36	11	85	282	278
Minnesota	36	38	10	82	272	293
Tampa Bay	23	54	7	53	245	332

OTHER CONFERENCE WINNERS
Smythe Division - Vancouver Canucks
Adams Division - Boston Bruins
Patrick Division - Pittsburgh Penguins

Playoff Results
Lost to the Toronto Maple Leafs in Series "F" (4-3)
Leading Playoff Scorers
Paul Coffey (11PTS) & Sergei Fedorov (9PTS each)
Stanley Cup Champion
Montreal Canadiens

296

1992-93 Season in Review

It didn't start out like a record-setting season and it certainly didn't end like one. But in between, the Red Wings put on quite a show.

Sitting with a 15-15-1 record in December, the Wings turned on the power, losing just five of their next 30 contests.

The rally wasn't enough to retain first place. At 47-28-9, Detroit came home second, three points behind Norris Division winners Chicago, but the 103 points collected established a new club record.

The Wings also lit the red light at record pace, scoring 369 times to lead the NHL and obliterate the old team standard of 322, set in 1987-88. Of those goals, 113 came on the power play, another Detroit record. Newly-acquired right-winger Dino Ciccarelli tallied 21 of his 41 goals when Detroit held the man advantage, tying the team mark set by Mickey Redmond in 1973-74.

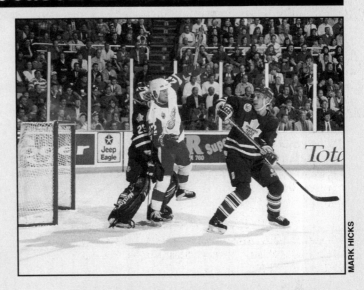

MARK HICKS

Captain Steve Yzerman equaled a Wings standard by scoring two shorthanded goals April 8 in a 9-1 win over Tampa Bay and collected his 1,000th NHL point with an assist February 24 in a 10-7 loss at Buffalo.

Yzerman paced the attack with 58-79-137 numbers, appearing in the NHL All-Star Game along with defensemen Steve Chiasson and Paul Coffey. The latter produced 87 points after being picked up in a blockbuster trade with Los Angeles. The Wings also added another famous name when defenseman Mark Howe, son of Wings legend Gordie Howe, was signed as a free agent.

Toronto would be Detroit's playoff foe and the Wings looked set to make short work of the Leafs, opening the series with 6-3 and 6-2 wins at Joe Louis Arena. Toronto battled back to take two games at Maple Leaf Gardens and posted a 6-5 verdict in Game 5 on an overtime goal by former Wing Mike Foligno.

Detroit whipped the Leafs 7-3 in Game 6, but Nikolai Borschevsky's overtime goal gave Toronto a 4-3 verdict in Game 7 and the set.

"People were expecting great things from this hockey club," Wings forward Dallas Drake said. "We were expecting those things, too and for it to end this way is a tremendous letdown."

HOCKEYTOWN MOMENT

Wings bolster defense with famous names

MARK HICKS

Paul Coffey

The Wings added a link to the past July 7, 1992 when they signed free-agent defenseman Mark Howe.

"I'm back," the Detroit-born son of Wings legend Gordie Howe said. "It took me 20 years, but I'm back."

Mark Howe played with the Detroit Junior Red Wings from 1970-72 and he brought more than a famous name to Hockeytown. Howe was a three-time NHL First All-Star Team selection with Philadelphia and led the NHL in plus-minus in 1985-86.

Meanwhile, the Wings unleashed a blockbuster move on January 29, 1993, acquiring defenseman Paul Coffey in a six-player trade with Los Angeles.

At the time of the trade, Coffey was the NHL career leader in goals (326), assists (845) and points (1,171) by a defenseman and held the single-season mark for goals by a rearguard, netting 48 times in 1985-86.

"This is such a great hockey town," Coffey said upon arrival. "You can feel the tradition when you step out on the ice."

Wings of Legend

Slava Kozlov

Slava Kozlov was the first to admit that his adjustment to the NHL and the North American lifestyle was not an easy one.

"My first two years here, I was very homesick," Kozlov recalled. "A couple of times, I nearly went home."

Red Wings fans were glad he didn't.

The least-discussed member of Detroit's Russian Five unit, Kozlov was an outstanding playoff performer for the Wings' powerhouse clubs of the mid-to-late 1990s.

He fired 34 goals and 73 points in 1993-94, then potted 36 goals in 1995-96, equaling his career-high with another 73-point performance. Four other times, Kozlov ascended to the 20-goal plateau. But it was in post-season play that his star shone the brightest.

Between 1993-94 and 1997-98, Kozlov registered 30 goals in Stanley Cup play, trailing only Claude Lemieux (41), Joe Sakic (32) and Jaromir Jagr (31) during that span. Kozlov's 11 game-winning goals in those five Stanley Cup tournaments led all players.

Many of those game winners were huge. It was Kozlov's tally after 22:25 of overtime in Game 5 of the 1995 Western Conference final against Chicago – one of a club-record four winners he scored that spring – which gave the Wings a 2-1 victory and their first Stanley Cup final appearance in 29 seasons. He scored in triple OT against Anaheim in the second round of the 1997 playoffs, the spring which saw Detroit capture the Stanley Cup for the first time since 1955. The following season, his four playoff game-winning tallies tied his team mark and helped the Wings successfully defend their title.

His 12 career playoff game winners are a team record, as are Kozlov's two career Stanley Cup OT goals. "The playoffs are Kozzy's time," Detroit assistant coach Dave Lewis said. "He loves to play at that time of year."

Kozlov gave credit for these developments to teammate Igor Larionov, who helped Kozlov adapt to his new surroundings.

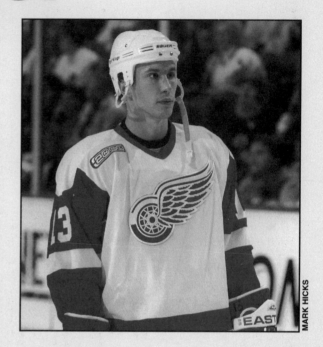

MARK HICKS

"Igor knew the American system very well," Kozlov said. "He taught me what I should do."

Despite his success, the soft-spoken Kozlov was often overlooked amongst his compatriots – the legendary Larionov and Slava Fetisov, the flashy Sergei Fedorov and the irascible Vladimir Konstantinov – and that was just fine with him.

"I'm a quiet guy," Kozlov said. "I don't like to get a lot of attention. I don't like being in big crowds."

The numbers posted by this quiet man who collects fine China as a hobby and loves to read Russian literature made him stand out in the crowd just the same.

"He was a low-maintenance player, who turned out to be an above-average player for our hockey club," Detroit senior vice-president Jimmy Devellano said.

Kozlov's Detroit days ended July 1, 2001, when he was traded to Buffalo as part of a package which landed six-time Vezina Trophy winner Dominik Hasek.

- **BORN:**
  Voskresensk, Russia, May 3, 1972
- **ACQUIRED:**
  Selected 45th overall in the June 16, 1990 NHL entry draft
- **BEST SEASON WITH RED WINGS:**
  1995-96 (36-37-73)
- **TOTALS WITH RED WINGS:**
  GP-607, G-202, A-213, PTS-415

- **HONORS:**
  Shares team record for most Stanley Cup overtime goals; Holds team record for most Stanley Cup game-winning goals; Shares team record for game-winning goals in a playoff season; Played for Russia, 1994 World Championship, 1996 World Cup

MOTOWN Classic

Ciccarelli powers Wings' power play

Dino Ciccarelli's office was not a place for the faint of heart. Ciccarelli made a career of parking his stocky frame in front of the opposition net, defying defenders to keep him from knocking in goals from their doorstep.

Detroit picked up the two-time 50-goal scorer from Washington in the summer of 1992 and he scored 41 times during the 1992-93 campaign, netting 21 of them on the power play to tie the club record Mickey Redmond established in 1973-74. Ciccarelli tallied a hat trick of power-play markers April 29 in Detroit's 7-1 playoff win over Toronto.

"Anyone who's willing to take that constant pounding to score goals, you've got to admire their courage," Detroit goalie Tim Cheveldae said.

Ciccarelli wasn't nearly as impressed. "That's my game, I'm not going to change," he said. "People talk about 35-40 goals as being high expectations, but to me, I'd be disappointed if I didn't put up those numbers."

ASSEMBLY LINE

A major move at mid-season saw the Wings pick up Norris Trophy-winning defenseman Paul Coffey and left-winger Jim Hiller from Los Angeles for Jimmy Carson, Gary Shuchuk and Marc Potvin. Kevin Miller went to Washington for right-winger Dino Ciccarelli. Defenseman Mark Howe, the son of Gordie Howe, was signed as a free agent from Philadelphia. Left-winger John Ogrodnick returned to the Wings as a free agent from the New York

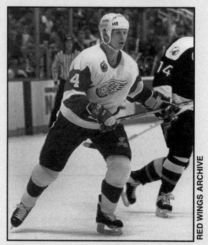

Mark Howe

Rangers and defenseman Steve Konroyd was picked up from Hartford for a 1993 sixth round draft pick. Lonnie Loach (Ottawa) and Bob McGill (Tampa Bay) were NHL expansion-draft losses. Defenseman Jason York and center/left-winger Dallas Drake arrived via the NHL entry draft.

Red Wings Facts

Most Goals by a Rookie

39
Steve Yzerman 1983-84

36
Mike Foligno 1979-80

33
Dale McCourt 1977-78

32
Petr Klima 1985-86

31
Sergei Fedorov 1990-91

30
Tom Webster 1970-71

Short Passes

A 10-5 win November 23, 1992 over Tampa Bay, followed by an 11-6 rout of the St. Louis Blues November 25, 1992 marked the first time in Wings history the club registered double digits on the scoreboard in successive games.

SCOTTY BOWMAN

After a 5-1 win over the St. Louis Blues on March 9, 1972, the Montreal Canadiens were slumbering at the St. Louis Hilton Inn, when the shrill sounds of the fire alarm awoke them.

Fire engulfing his room, Montreal coach Scotty Bowman sought refuge on his fourth-floor balcony. "I was getting ready to jump," said Bowman, the second-last person to be rescued. "I wasn't going to burn to death up there."

He wasn't panicking, simply weighing his options.

This episode, as much as any, explains why Bowman, coach of the Detroit Red Wings since 1993, has handled more games (2,058) and posted more victories (1,193) than any coach in NHL history. Bowman's eight Stanley Cups as a coach — the last two coming in Detroit — are matched only by his mentor, former Montreal coach Toe Blake.

The man who ended Detroit's 42-year Stanley Cup drought in 1997 never stops thinking, never believes he's figured it all out, that there isn't another avenue which can give him an edge.

This old dog isn't afraid to learn a new trick.

"He knows more about the game and more about the players in this league than anybody," said Larry Murphy, who won Cups with Bowman in Detroit and Pittsburgh. "He's not afraid to experiment or to try new innovations." When Bowman made his NHL debut behind the Blues' bench on Nov. 22, 1967, Vince Lombardi was still coaching the Green Bay Packers. "He's an old-school guy who's adjusted to new-school personalities," Dallas coach Ken Hitch-cock said.

Bowman lives by a simple philosophy. The comfort zone is not a place where anyone around him should reside. Contentment breeds complacency.

This theory was easy to maintain in St. Louis, during an era when coaches held complete control. Bowman once came upon a group of Blues enjoying a night out. He didn't say a word, just sauntered over to the juke box, made a selection and left.

Fats Domino singing, "I'm Going to Kansas City," soon filled the room.

The Blues' minor-league affiliate was located in Kansas City.

RED WINGS ARCHIVE

In today's era of free agency and no-trade contracts, Bowman's options are limited, but he finds methods to keep players on their toes.

Bowman often calls players into his office, grilling them on the state of the NHL. "He's always thinking hockey," Murphy said. "And he makes sure you are, too."

Bowman will leave a stick with the hotel front desk at curfew time, asking the clerk to get any players who come by to sign it. Those who do have obviously broken curfew. "If anybody asks me for an autograph late at night, I always sign Darren McCarty," Detroit's Brendan Shanahan joked.

Bowman's lasting recollection of that St. Louis fire is the 18-stitch cut defenseman Serge Savard suffered while kicking out the window of his smoke-filled room. "We lost him for the playoffs because of that," Bowman said.

With Scotty, everything comes back to the game. Always has. Always will.

- 1993 1994 -

BACK in TIME

• September 13, 1993

Chairman of the PLO, Yasser Arafat, and Israel's prime minister, Yitzhak Rabin, shook hands on the White House lawn following an agreement to provide for limited Palestinian autonomy in the Gaza Strip and the West Bank.

• February 28, 1994

In its first offensive action in a 45 year history, NATO planes shot down four Bosnian Serb war planes when the aircraft ignored warnings to leave the United Nations no fly zone.

• May 10, 1994

Nelson Mandela, who had spent 27 years in jail as a prisoner of the apartheid regime, was inaugurated as South Africa's first black president.

quick cuts

Most Goals
Segei Fedorov: 56
Most Assists
Segei Fedorov: 64
Most Points
Segei Fedorov: 120
Most Penalty Minutes
Bob Probert: 275
Most Wins, Goaltender
Chris Osgood: 23
Lowest Goals-Against Average
Chris Osgood: 2.86
Most Shutouts
Chris Osgood: 2
NHL Award Winners
Segei Fedorov - Hart Trophy
1st Team All-Star, Frank Selke Trophy
& Lester Pearson Trophy

FINAL STANDINGS

Central Division	W	L	T	PTS	GF	GA
DETROIT	46	30	8	100	356	275
Toronto	43	29	12	98	280	243
Dallas	42	29	13	97	286	265
St. Louis	40	33	11	91	270	283

OTHER DIVISION WINNER:
Pacific Division - Calgary Flames
Northeast Division - Pittsburgh Penguins
Atlantic Division - NY Rangers

Playoff Results
Lost to the San Jose Sharks in Series "E" (4-3)
Leading Playoff Scorers
Sergei Fedorov (8PTS)
Dino Ciccarelli, Slava Kozlov & Paul Coffey (7PTS each)
Stanley Cup Champion
New York Rangers

1993-94 Season in Review

The season commenced with a new man behind the bench and a series of calamities.

Scotty Bowman, who'd coached six Stanley Cup winners, took the reins, leaving Bryan Murray to focus solely on his duties as GM.

Right off the bat, there were problems. A back injury sidelined captain Steve Yzerman. Goalie Tim Cheveldae hurt his knee in a season-opening 6-4 loss at Dallas. By the sixth game of the season, the Wings were 1-5 and had gone through four goalies, with Vince Riendeau, Peter Ing and Chris Osgood all getting opportunities to fill Cheveldae's skates. Late in the season, Cheveldae and Winnipeg goalie Bob Essensa changed sweaters as part of a four-player deal.

With Yzerman sidelined for 26 games, others picked up the offensive slack, as the Wings led the NHL with 356 goals. Ray Sheppard scored 52 times, tying Mickey Redmond's club record for right-wingers. Paul Coffey set team marks for defensemen with 63 assists and 77 points. Center Slava Kozlov (34 goals) and center/left-winger Keith Primeau (31) arrived as productive offensive players. Dino Ciccarelli scored 28 times, four coming April 5 in an 8-3 verdict over Vancouver. Yzerman gathered 82 points in 58 games, but the star of the show was Sergei Fedorov.

The fourth-year center produced team-leading 56-64-120 totals, a performance that earned Fedorov the Hart and Selke Trophies and selection to the NHL's

1993-94 DETROIT RED WINGS
Central Division Champions

RED WINGS ARCHIVE

First All-Star Team. Fedorov and Coffey played in the NHL All-Star Game.

An NHL switch of divisional names and alignment saw the Wings situated in the Central Division with Toronto, Chicago, St. Louis, Winnipeg and Dallas. The Wings proved to be the best of this new bunch, garnering first place with 100 points. In the seats, the team set an NHL attendance record of 812,640, the seventh straight season that Detroit's gate showed an increase.

In their first playoff series, upstart San Jose met the Wings and were 5-4 victors in Game 1. Turning to the rookie Osgood, the Wings won 4-0 in Game 2 and he joined Normie Smith (1935-36) as the only Detroit goalies to post shutouts in their playoff debut.

The series went back and forth right until the final period of Game 7, when Jamie Baker's goal gave San Jose a 3-2 win and one of the biggest upsets in Stanley Cup history.

HOCKEYTOWN MOMENT
Scotty Bowman hired as Head Coach

Hired to coach the Wings, Scotty Bowman quickly discovered the passion of Hockeytown. "I never realized how much hockey means to Detroit," Bowman said. "You can't go anywhere in the city without people saying, 'You've got to do it this year.'"

It was a good marriage, because no one loved winning more than Bowman, who coached five Stanley Cup winners in Montreal and one in Pittsburgh. "I'm not a good loser," Bowman cautioned. "I'm not a lot of fun to be around when I lose."

Seeking answers to Detroit's perplexingly poor playoff performances, owner Mike Ilitch asked senior vice-president Jimmy Devellano to name the game's best bench bosses. Devellano presented a short list of two candidates - Al Arbour and Scotty Bowman.

MARK HICKS

Arbour was reluctant to leave the New York Islanders, where he'd won four titles, but Bowman was open to a new opportunity.

The NHL's winningest coach, Bowman owned 834 victories and six Stanley Cup rings from a coaching career which started with St. Louis in 1967-68.

Wings of Legend
Sergei Fedorov

If Steve Yzerman is the heart and soul of the Detroit Red Wings, then Sergei Fedorov is the blood that pumps life into the team. He can electrify a crowd with an end-to-end rush, or defend a lead with his tenacious checking skills.

"He's a gamebreaker," Detroit center Kris Draper said of Fedorov. The Red Wings record book is filled with marks etched by Fedorov. He established a team record for game-winning goals with 11 in 1995-96 and shares the club standard for points in a period, garnering four in one frame January 21, 1992 against Philadelphia. He led all scorers during the 1995 Stanley Cup playoffs with a Detroit-record 24 points.

Only Gordie Howe, Yzerman and Alex Delvecchio have accumulated more points in a Detroit uniform than the 803 produced by Fedorov.

Some nights, Fedorov has picked the Wings up and carried them on his back. He scored all four Detroit goals February 12, 1995 in a 4-4 tie with Los Angeles and netted five goals December 26, 1996 in a 5-4 victory over Washington.

The Wings experimented briefly with Fedorov on defense during the 1995-96 season and again during the 1996-97 playoffs. "I'm convinced if we left him there, he'd have won a Norris Trophy," Wings senior vice-president Jimmy Devellano said.

Fedorov came to the Wings in intriguing fashion, walking away from the Russian national team during the 1990 Goodwill Games in Seattle. Fedorov informed the Wings he was ready to defect and told them to meet him in the lobby of the team hotel after a game. With Wings vice-president Jim Lites waiting calmly in the hotel lobby, Fedorov, the last player off the team bus, walked up to him and said, "Hi Jim, it's time to go."

Seven years later, he walked away from Detroit in a contract holdout, but when the Carolina Hurricanes presented Fedorov with a six-year, $28-million offer sheet in February of 1998, Wings owner Mike Ilitch didn't hesitate to match, even though it meant paying Fedorov a $12 million bonus if Detroit reached the conference finals.

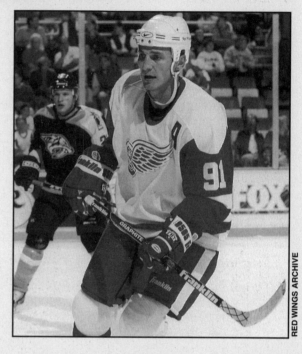

RED WINGS ARCHIVE

The Wings went all the way that spring, defending their Stanley Cup title and Fedorov played a key role, matching a club playoff mark with 10 goals. One of those, a spectacular, highlight-reel tally in Game 3 of the finals against Washington, gave Detroit a 2-1 win.

Fedorov beat Capitals defenseman Calle Johansson with an inside-out fake, then rifled a shot past goalie Olaf Kolzig.

"He turned nothing into a game-winning goal," Draper said. The victory came on the one-year anniversary of the limousine crash which left Wings defenseman Vladimir Konstantinov and team masseur Sergei Mnatsakanov with brain injuries. "I will take the puck and give it to them, in memory of what they meant to the team," Fedorov said.

Fedorov can be an enigmatic player, but there's no doubt that without him, the Stanley Cup might never have come to town.

- **BORN:**
  Pskov, Russia, December 13, 1969
- **ACQUIRED:**
  Selected 74th overall in the June 17, 1989 NHL entry draft
- **BEST SEASON WITH RED WINGS:**
  1993-94 (56-64-120)
- **TOTALS WITH RED WINGS:**
  GP-828, G-364, A-507, PTS-871

- **HONORS:**
  Won Hart Trophy, 1993-94; Won Selke Trophy, 1993-94, 1995-96; Won Lester B. Pearson Award, 1993-94; Selected to NHL First All-Star Team, 1993-94; Selected to NHL All-Rookie Team, 1990-91; Played in five NHL All-Star Games; Played for Russia, 1991 Canada Cup, 1996 World Cup, 1998 and 2002 Winter Olympics

MOTOWN Classic

Fedorov wins Hart Trophy

Stepping to the fore with captain Steve Yzerman idled by injury, center Sergei Fedorov took the NHL by storm. He collected 56 goals and 120 points, good for second in NHL scoring, the highest finish by a Red Wing since Norm Ullman also placed second in 1964-65. Fedorov tallied 10 game-winning goals and his four shorthanded markers were part of the team's club-record 22.

"That is just an exceptional hockey player," Detroit coach Scotty Bowman said of Fedorov, a fact recognized at NHL awards time. Fedorov won the Hart Trophy as the league's MVP, the first Red Wing to be so honored since Gordie Howe in 1962-63. Fedorov also received the Selke Trophy as the NHL's top defensive player and the NHLPA presented him with the Lester B. Pearson Award as the players' choice for top player in the league.

Fedorov appeared unfazed by the accumulating accolades.

"Everybody wants to talk about my points, but I do not worry about points," Fedorov said. "What matters is winning."

ASSEMBLY LINE

Aaron Ward

The Wings and Winnipeg Jets were busy trading partners. Detroit sent Tim Cheveldae and Dallas Drake to Winnipeg for defenseman Sergei Bautin and former Michigan State goalie Bob Essensa. Paul Ysebaert and Alan Kerr were dealt to Winnipeg for the rights to Michigan Wolverines defenseman Aaron Ward, Sheldon Kennedy went to the Jets for a 1995 third round draft pick (Darryl Laplante) and center Kris Draper's contract was purchased from Winnipeg. Jim Cummins and a 1994 fifth round draft pick went to Philadelphia for Greg Johnson and a 1994 fourth round choice and Yves Racine and a 1994 fourth round draft choice went to the Flyers for defenseman Terry Carkner. A 1994 seventh round draft pick was shipped to Edmonton for goalie Peter Ing. Dennis Vial was traded to Tampa Bay for left-winger Steve Maltais. Free-agent signees included defenseman Bob Halkidis, center/left-winger Tim Taylor, left-winger Mark Pederson and center Micah Aivazoff. Pete Stauber (Florida) and Bobby Dollas (Anaheim) were NHL expansion-draft losses.

Red Wings Facts

Most Wins By A Detroit Coach

Jack Adams – 413

Scotty Bowman – 410

Sid Abel – 340

Tommy Ivan – 262

Jacques Demers – 137

Bryan Murray – 124

Jimmy Skinner – 123

Bobby Kromm – 79

Nick Polano – 79

Short Passes

On June 30, 1993, the Wings purchased the contract of checking center Kris Draper from the Winnipeg Jets for one dollar. "The worst part is, I think it was a Canadian dollar," Draper said.

- 1994 1995 -

BACK in TIME

- **November 9, 1994**
The Republicans took control of both houses of Congress for the first time in 40 years.

- **January 24, 1995**
The trial of O.J. Simpson for the murder of his ex-wife and her male friend started in Los Angeles; more than eight months later, he was found innocent.

- **April 19, 1995**
The Federal Building in Oklahoma City was blasted by a huge car bomb killing hundreds of innocent people and children from the on-site child care center.

quick cuts

Most Goals
Ray Sheppard: 30
Most Assists
Paul Coffey: 44
Most Points
Paul Coffey: 58
Most Penalty Minutes
Stu Grimson: 147
Most Wins, Goaltender
Mike Vernon: 19
Lowest Goals-Against Average
Chris Osgood: 2.26
Most Shutouts
Chris Osgood & Mike Vernon: 1 each
NHL Award Winners
Paul Coffey - Norris Trophy
& 1st Team All-Star

FINAL STANDINGS

Central Division	W	L	T	PTS	GF	GA
DETROIT	33	11	4	70	180	117
St. Louis	28	15	5	61	178	135
Chicago	24	19	5	53	156	115
Toronto	21	19	8	50	135	146
Dallas	17	23	8	42	136	135
Winnipeg	16	25	7	39	157	177

OTHER DIVISION WINNERS
Pacific Division - Calgary Flames
Northeast Division - Quebec Nordiques
Atlantic Division - Philadelphia Flyers

Playoff Results
Defeated the Dallas Stars in Series "E" (4-1)
Defeated the San Jose Sharks in Series "K" (4-0)
Defeated the Chicago Blackhawks in Series "N" (4-1)
Lost to the New Jersey Devils in Series "O" (4-0)
Leading Playoff Scorers
Sergei Fedorov (24PTS) - Paul Coffey (18PTS)
Stanley Cup Champion
New Jersey Devils

1994-95 Season in Review

The new campaign began with more changes in Detroit and without the NHL.

A second straight first-round playoff exit cost GM Bryan Murray his job. The Wings opted to fill the position with a three-person committee – senior vice-president Jimmy Devellano, assistant GM Ken Holland and coach Scotty Bowman, with the added title of director of player personnel, would consult on player changes.

One of the first moves they made was to acquire goalie Mike Vernon from Calgary, where he'd won a Stanley Cup, but the triumvirate would be forced to wait some time for the opportunity to see what effect Vernon's addition would have. An owners' lockout put the NHL season on ice until Jan. 20. A shortened, 48-game season, featuring only intra-conference play, saw Detroit open with a 4-1 win over Chicago.

Once the season commenced, it was evident the Wings were a cut above the rest of the Western Conference. A new checking system installed by Bowman, the left-wing lock, solidified Detroit's defense and the Wings rolled to a 33-11-4 record, earning the President's Trophy as the NHL's best regular-season club.

The 11 losses were a team low and the Wings posted a club-record seven straight road wins from March 25 to April 14. Center Sergei Fedorov scored all four goals February 12 in a 4-4 tie with Los Angeles and was thwarted by Kings goalie Kelly Hrudey on a penalty shot in overtime.

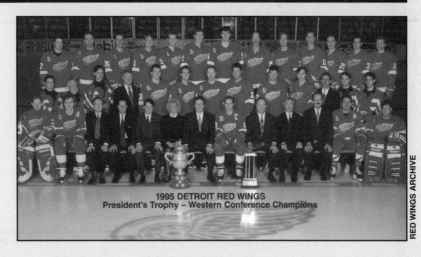

1995 DETROIT RED WINGS
President's Trophy – Western Conference Champions

RED WINGS ARCHIVE

Records were also set in abundance. The Wings collected a club-record eight straight wins in the process of taking the first three playoff rounds with a combined mark of 12-2. Slava Kozlov collected a playoff-record four game-winning goals and tied another club record May 21 with three assists in the third period of a 6-0 win over San Jose. The Wings scored 22 power-play goals in the playoffs, which was a record, as were the six power-play markers potted by Dino Ciccarelli, who tied another mark by scoring three times with the man advantage in that May 11 victory at Dallas.

Fedorov's 24 points were a new Detroit playoff record, as were the six goals scored by defenseman Paul Coffey.

One mark eluded the Wings, though. Swept by New Jersey in the Stanley Cup final, Detroit's title drought was extended to 40 years.

HOCKEYTOWN MOMENT

Wings reach first Stanley Cup final in 29 years

Back in the Stanley Cup for the first time since the Roger Crozier-led Wings in 1966, it would be a short, disappointing stay for the Wings, who were swept aside by the New Jersey Devils.

The Devils came into Joe Louis Arena and grabbed hard-fought 2-1 and 4-2 victories, then turned on the jets to roll to back-to-back 5-2 decisions in New Jersey.

Just like that, a season of hope was shattered.

"I don't think we had time to get frustrated," captain Steve Yzerman said. "It all happened so quickly."

Amidst the stunned silence of the losing dressing-room, winger Dino Ciccarelli summed up the devastation.

"Maybe there will be people saying things went pretty good this year," Ciccarelli said. "But for me, anything short of the Stanley Cup was short of the goal."

Mike Vernon

He arrived with a Stanley Cup on his resume and a chip on his shoulder. Mike Vernon was the goalie brought to Hockeytown for the sole purpose of acquiring a championship and he nearly delivered the goods during his first season as a Wing.

Vernon backstopped the Wings to the Stanley Cup final, where they were shunted aside by the New Jersey Devils in the minimum four games. Like everything else, Vernon took the letdown in stride. "I've been booed by fans and I've been cheered by them," Vernon said. "I've been praised and crapped on in the papers. You have to learn to live with it, because it's all part of the game."

With five NHL All-Star Game appearances and two Stanley Cup final appearances before coming to Detroit, Vernon knew exactly why he'd been acquired by the Wings. And he was prepared for those high expectations. "I know there's going to be a lot of pressure placed upon me, but my experience will help me get by in Detroit," he said. "I'm looking forward to the challenge."

It looked as if Vernon had lost his No. 1 job to Chris Osgood through the 1995-96 and 1996-97 seasons, when Osgood was the goalie called upon to play the most games. But when the 1996-97 playoffs commenced, Vernon was the go-to guy for the Wings.

"When Mike Vernon was available, I talked to (Hall of Fame netminder) Glenn Hall, who was the goalie coach in Calgary," Detroit coach Scotty Bowman said. "He told me, 'You'll like him. He plays big in big games. He's a winner.'

"That was good enough for me."

Vernon started all 20 games that spring, posting a 1.76 goals-against average and winning the Conn Smythe Trophy as playoff MVP, leading the Wings to their first Stanley Cup in 42 seasons.

When it was over, Vernon puffed on a victory cigar while touring Lord Stanley's mug around the Joe Louis Arena ice.

"If you had asked me at Christmas, I would have thought for sure that I'd be traded by the deadline," said

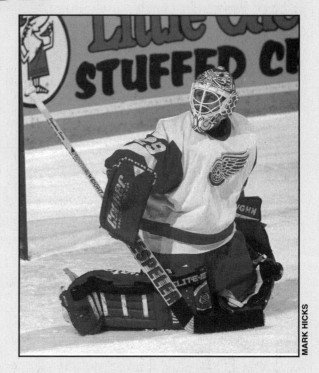

MARK HICKS

Vernon, who started just 11 of Detroit's first 41 games in 1996-97. "Towards the end of February, Scotty called me into his office and said he was going to get me some chances to play, that he was going to go with me."

As soon as he'd brought home the treasure, Vernon was cast adrift, traded to San Jose for draft picks two months after the Cup triumph.

"He did everything for us that we possibly could have asked of him in his three years here," Detroit GM Ken Holland said at the time of the trade, an assessment Vernon wasn't about to dispute.

"I was brought in here for a couple of things," Vernon said. "To win a Stanley Cup and to help Chris Osgood develop into a front-line NHL goalie.

"I think I did my job in those respects."

- **BORN:**
  Calgary, Alberta, February 24, 1963
- **ACQUIRED:**
  June 29, 1994 trade with Calgary
- **BEST SEASON WITH RED WINGS:**
  1995-96 (21-7-2, 3 SO, 2.26 GAA)
- **TOTALS WITH RED WINGS:**
  GP-95, W-53, L-24, T-14, SO-4, GAA-2.40

- **HONORS:**
  Won Conn Smythe Trophy, 1996-97; Won William Jennings Trophy, 1995-96; Led team in wins and shutouts, 1994-95

MOTOWN Classic

Coffey takes home Norris Trophy

The Norris Trophy, which goes to the NHL's top defenseman, was initiated to honor the memory of Red Wings owner James Norris Sr. and its first winner was Detroit's Red Kelly in 1953-54. Kelly was also Detroit's last winner of the award until Paul Coffey came along.

Possessor of virtually every offensive mark ever posted by an NHL defenseman, Coffey wrote a few new chapters during the lockout-shortened 1994-95 campaign. With 14-44-58 totals, Coffey became the first defenseman to lead the Red Wings in scoring and his six playoff goals established a new post-season standard for Detroit rearguards.

Coffey finished seventh in NHL scoring, earning a place on the NHL's First All-Star Team and picking up the Norris Trophy for the third time in his career. Coffey won the award twice while playing for the Edmonton Oilers.

"Explosive offense, night in and night out," Wayne Gretzky said of Coffey. "He has uncanny ability."

ASSEMBLY LINE

Steve Chiasson was traded to Calgary for goalie Mike Vernon, while defensemen Mike Ramsey and Bob Rouse, center/left-winger Mike Krushelnyski and center Andrew McKim were signed as free agents. Jason York and Mike Sillinger were dealt to Anaheim for defenseman Mark Ferner, left-winger Stu Grimson and a 1996 sixth round draft choice (Magnus Nilsson). Winger Doug Brown was claimed from Pittsburgh in the NHL waiver draft and a 1995 fifth round draft pick (Michal Bros) went to San Jose for left-winger Bob Errey. Defenseman Viacheslav Fetisov came from New Jersey for a 1995 third round draft choice (David Gosselin).

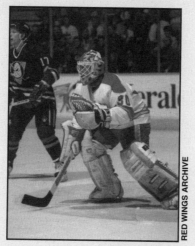

Mike Vernon

Red Wings Facts

Most Assists One Season

Steve Yzerman **90** (1988-89)
Steve Yzerman **79** (1992-93)
Marcel Dionne **74** (1974-75)
Sergei Fedorov **68** (1995-96)
Steve Yzerman **65** (1989-90)
Sergei Fedorov **64** (1993-94)

Short Passes

Smith is the most common surname among Red Wings players. There have been 11 in the lineup - Normie, Floyd, Al, Alex, Brad, Carl, Brian, Rick, Greg, Derek and Nakina Dalton. Brown is next in line, with eight representatives.

THE GRIND LINE

MARK HICKS

They might appear to be no more than spare parts. The fourth line. The scrubs. The guys who fill out the roster. But to Red Wings fans, they were so much more than that.

Detroit's Grind Line — center Kris Draper, left-winger Kirk Maltby and right-winger Joe Kocur — played as large a role in Detroit's back-to-back Stanley Cup victories in 1996-97 and 1997-98 as Steve Yzerman, Brendan Shanahan and Sergei Fedorov. Coach Scotty Bowman started virtually every period with the Grind Line taking the faceoff at center. Draper and Maltby were key contributors as penalty killers.

While the part they played in Detroit's championship runs is obvious, the assembly of the parts of this line wasn't exactly front-page news.

Draper's contract was purchased June 30, 1993 from the Winnipeg Jets. The price? One dollar. "I think it was even a Canadian dollar," Draper said with a shrug.

Maltby, another speed merchant, was acquired March 20, 1996 from the Edmonton Oilers for defenseman Dan McGillis. "I'm not going to score 40 or 50 goals," Maltby said. "I know my job. I muck it up and take the body."

A second coming completed this trio December 27, 1996, when Kocur was signed as a free agent. A former NHL penalty-minute king who toiled for the Wings from 1984-91, Kocur was out of the NHL and playing in a beer league in Lakeland, Mich. "One of the first things Scotty told me was that he didn't want me going out there and fighting all the time," Kocur said. "It was the first time I could recall a coach demanding that of me."

Kocur served as lord protector for his linemates, both acid-tongued agitators. "There was always something going on when those two were on the ice and usually it was their mouths," Kocur said.

Increasing their value exponentially was the way they produced in the playoffs. "I'm not a guy who cares much about regular-season numbers," Draper said. "When playoff time comes, it's such an emotional game and I'm an emotional guy."

The Wings were 2-0 shutout losers to St. Louis in the opening game of the 1996-97 playoffs. Trailing 1-0 in the third period of Game 2, Draper burst into the clear while Detroit was playing shorthanded and squirted a wrist shot past Blues goalie Grant Fuhr, sparking Detroit's 2-1 victory. "It's such an emotional lift when a third or fourth-line guy can get a goal for the team," Draper said.

In Game 2 of the 1998 final against Washington, Draper's overtime goal earned Detroit a 5-4 win, completing a comeback from a 4-2 third-period deficit. "That was my biggest goal ever," Draper said. "That's what you dream about, putting it in for your team in the Stanley Cup final."

Maltby scored twice in the 1997 final with Philadelphia, netting the winner in Game 2. Kocur tallied four times in the 1998 post-season. "We'd roll four lines and everybody would contribute," Shanahan said. "We'd really discourage other teams when we'd do that."

The Grind Line was an essential element in that equation. They did the dirty work, often logging ice time against the other team's big shooters.

In the process, these fourth-liners evolved into first-rate Hockeytown heroes.

THE RUSSIAN FIVE

MARK HICKS

When Detroit coach Scotty Bowman assembled a five-man unit of Russian players during the 1995-96 season, critics chuckled.

Slick passing and fancy skating were no longer in vogue, they noted, suggesting the game had finally passed Bowman by.

Guess who had the last laugh?

Labeled the "Russian Five," this quintet turned a very good Detroit team into an NHL powerhouse.

Sergei Fedorov was the first to arrive, establishing his credentials by winning the Hart Trophy as MVP of the NHL in 1993-94.

"He's Mr. Impact," was how teammate Larry Murphy described Fedorov.

Vladimir Konstantinov came next and was unlike any Russian player ever seen — tough, unyielding, an absolute warrior, until a 1997 limousine crash left him with career-ending brain injuries.

"Vladdy's game never changed," Detroit associate coach Dave Lewis said.

"He forced the other team to change their game in order to deal with him."

There was the quiet, often overshadowed Slava Kozlov, who delivered big goals at huge times, including a pair of playoff overtime winners. "The playoffs are Kozzy's time of year," Lewis said.

The courage of Fetisov and Larionov, the final pieces of this puzzle, allowed them to stand out in the crowd. Or, in Fetisov's case, amidst the crowd which gathered at the Kremlin in front of Russian tanks, thwarting a 1991 coup attempt staged by old-guard Communists in a bid to to overthrow the country's new democratic system.

"It was a very scary moment, but we didn't think the soldiers would shoot their own people," Fetisov recalled.

"Papa Bear" and "The Professor," as Fetisov and Larionov are known, battled to gain freedom for Russian players to skate in the NHL and their Olympic and World Championship experience brought a steadying influence to the Wings.

Members of Detroit's 1996-97 championship club feel a night out on the Russian Five at a Russian restaurant in Los Angeles was key towards melding the team into title-winners. "We ask them to assimilate into our culture so much, I think it meant a lot to them that we wanted to share a night of their culture," goalie Kevin Hodson remembered. "It showed everyone that we're all in this together."

During the Cup celebration, captain Steve Yzerman handed Lord Stanley's mug to Fetisov and Larionov. "I wanted Igor and I to carry the Cup together," Fetisov said. "We fought the Soviet system to get here and came over together."

"This is the only trophy that was missing from our collection," Larionov added.

A year later, Larionov wheeled the injured Konstantinov around Washington's MCI Center with the Cup they'd retained to honor their fallen comrade.

Taking the NHL by storm, they dispelled the foolish myth which suggested Russian players found the Stanley Cup meaningless.

"They don't play for themselves," Lewis said. "They play for the crest on the front of their jersey."

- 1995 1996 -

BACK in TIME

• October 16, 1995

Following the lead of Louis Farrakhan, more than one half a million African American men gathered in the Mall in Washington D.C.

• January 6, 1996

President Clinton signed a stop gap spending measure that authorized the federal government to resume full operations, ending the longest government shutdown in U.S. history.

• July 27, 1996

A homemade pipe bomb went off at the Olympic games held in Atlanta, Georgia, killing one person and injuring eleven.

quick cuts

Most Goals
Sergei Fedorov: 39
Most Assists
Sergei Fedorov: 68
Most Points
Sergei Fedorov: 107
Most Penalty Minutes
Keith Primeau: 168
Most Wins, Goaltender
Chris Osgood: 39
Lowest Goals-Against Average
Chris Osgood: 2.17
Most Shutouts
Chris Osgood: 5
NHL Award Winners
Chris Osgood & Mike Vernon - Willam M. Jennings Trophy
Sergei Fedorov - Frank J. Selke Trophy
Scotty Bowman - Jack Adams Trophy
Vladimir Konstantinov - Plus/Minus Award
Chris Osgood & Vladimir Konstantinov
2nd Team All-Star

FINAL STANDINGS

Central Division	W	L	T	PTS	GF	GA
DETROIT	62	13	7	131	325	181
Chicago	40	28	14	94	273	220
Toronto	34	36	12	80	247	252
St. Louis	32	34	16	80	219	248
Winnipeg	36	40	6	78	275	291
Dallas	26	42	14	66	227	280

OTHER DIVISION WINNERS
Northeast Division - Pittsburgh Penguins
Atlantic Division - Philadelphia Flyers
Pacific Division - Colorado Avalanche

Playoff Results
Defeated the Winnipeg Jets in Series "E" (4-2)
Defeated the St. Louis Blues in Series "K" (4-3)
Lost to the Colorado Avalanche in Series "N" (4-2)
Leading Playoff Scorers
Steve Yzerman & Sergei Fedorov (20PTS each)
Stanley Cup Champion
Colorado Avalanche

1995-96 Season in Review

Coming off their first Stanley Cup final appearance in nearly three decades, the Red Wings posted the greatest regular season in NHL history.

A mediocre 5-5-2 after 12 games, the Wings lost only eight of their remaining 70 games, winning an NHL-record 62 times.

Outstanding performances abounded. Steve Yzerman scored his 500th NHL goal January 17 against Colorado's Patrick Roy and tied two playoff marks May 5, with three points in the first period and five in the game during an 8-3 win over St. Louis. Scotty Bowman worked his 1,607th game behind the bench, becoming the NHL's career leader in games coached. Dino Ciccarelli tied a club mark with six playoff power-play tallies. Igor Larionov was acquired from San Jose and an all-Russian unit of Larionov, Sergei Fedorov, Vladimir Konstantinov, Slava Kozlov and Viacheslav Fetisov made its mark around the league. Konstantinov led the NHL with a plus-minus rating of plus-60. Fedorov tallied a team-record 11 game-winning goals and a club-record 18 assists in the playoffs. Kozlov scored four goals December 2 in an 11-1 win at Montreal.

Honors were also plentiful. Goalies Chris Osgood and Mike Vernon shared the Jennings Trophy, Fedorov took home the Selke Trophy and Bowman captured the Jack Adams Award. Osgood and Konstantinov were NHL Second All-Star Team selections. Bowman, Fedorov, Osgood, defensemen Paul Coffey and

RED WINGS ARCHIVE

Nicklas Lidstrom were all part of the NHL All-Star Game.

As smooth as the regular-season was, the playoffs provided pitfalls. It took six games to oust first-round opponent Winnipeg, then Detroit rallied from a 3-2 series deficit to beat St. Louis 1-0 on Yzerman's Game 7 tally in double overtime.

Colorado opened the Western Conference final with two wins at Detroit and took out the Wings in six games. A nasty incident in Game 6 saw Colorado's Claude Lemieux drill Detroit center Kris Draper into the boards with a check from behind, leaving Draper with severe facial injuries.

Hockeytown was heartbroken again. For all the accomplishments, the most significant achievement remained elusive.

"We've had two great seasons and two pretty good playoff years," Bowman said. "But we still have a lot of unfinished business to do."

HOCKEYTOWN MOMENT

Wings post NHL-record 62-win season

The 1976-77 Montreal Canadiens, who won 60 games and the 1995-96 Wings, who broke that NHL mark with 62 wins, possessed a common trait. Both were coached by Scotty Bowman.

"(Montreal) had four lines, just like we have here," Bowman said. "But that team didn't play a seven-man defensive unit like this team does."

Detroit's 131 points were second only to the 132 garnered by that Montreal club and along with the 62 victories, were among many team marks established.

Detroit's 36 home victories equaled the NHL record established by Philadelphia in 1975-76. Detroit also finished 28 points ahead of its nearest rival, the Flyers, the widest margin ever to lead the NHL. Twenty-six road wins was a new team mark and a pair of nine-game winning streaks, as well as a seven-game road winning stretch, tied club standards.

The 1995-96 Red Wings posted at least one victory against all 25 other NHL teams.

Chris Osgood

Starting goalie for the defending Stanley Cup champions?

No big deal.

Star of the school play?

Major perspiration.

"That, more than anything, was nerve-wracking," Chris Osgood recalled of the time he forgot his lines during a sixth-grade school show growing up in Medicine Hat, Alta.

Uncomfortable in the spotlight, Osgood nonetheless thrived on the pressure of performing in the red-light district in front of an NHL net. "I love going out there and playing in the big game," Osgood said. "That's what's fun to me. That's when I'm in my element."

Osgood's first opportunity to play a starring role was panned when San Jose's Jamie Baker deposited an errant clearing pass by the rookie netminder into the Wings net for the deciding goal in Game 7 of the playoff series between the two teams.

"I just hope I can get over this and not let it ruin my career," a weeping Osgood said afterwards.

He got over it and then some, displaying a character and determination which defied his boyish appearance. "I don't think I have a nice-guy persona," Osgood said. "I'm not nice at all when I play."

In 1995-96, Osgood led the NHL with 39 wins, setting Wings marks for the longest winning streak (13 games) and unbeaten run (21 games), sharing the Jennings Trophy for the NHL's best goals-against average with goaltending partner Mike Vernon. He earned selection to the NHL's Second All-Star Team and made his first of three successive appearances in the NHL All-Star Game.

In Red Wings history, only Terry Sawchuk has posted more wins and shutouts than the 221 victories and 30 shutouts registered by the poised Osgood, who became an NHL regular at the league's toughest position when he was 20.

"The guy has no pulse," teammate Darren McCarty suggested, but Osgood insisted this calm exterior was an extension of his inner peace.

MARK HICKS

"I don't worry about things," Osgood said. "I'm just not the worrying sort."

Osgood took a seat on the bench while Vernon backstopped Detroit to the Stanley Cup final in 1995 and to the club's first Cup in 42 seasons in 1996-97, but was the man between the pipes when the Wings sought to defend that crown the following spring - Conn Smythe Trophy winner Vernon having been traded to San Jose.

Osgood played a club-record 22 games and 1,361 minutes as the Wings retained their crown.

"The day the playoffs started, nobody in the league faced any of the pressure or scrutiny that Chris Osgood had," Detroit GM Ken Holland said after the club defended its title. "He was replacing the Conn Smythe Trophy winner in the hockey-crazy city of the defending Stanley Cup champs."

Vindication was his, but Osgood sought no apologies from those who doubted him.

"I didn't play for that," he said. "I played for my teammates. I played for me.

"I played to win the Stanley Cup."

- **BORN:**
  Peace River, Alberta, November 26, 1972
- **ACQUIRED:**
  Selected 54th overall in the June 9, 1991 NHL entry draft
- **BEST SEASON WITH RED WINGS:**
  1995-96 (39-6-5, 5 SO, 2.17 GAA)
- **TOTALS WITH RED WINGS:**
  GP-389, W-221, L-110, T-46, SO-30, GAA-2.40

- **HONORS:**
  Won William Jennings Trophy, 1995-96; Named to NHL Second All-Star Team, 1995-96; Played in NHL All-Star Game, 1995-96, 1996-97, 1997-98; Led team in wins seven times; Led team in shutouts eight times; Led team in GAA seven times

MOTOWN Classic

Coffey reaches 1,000-point plateau

The thought of becoming the first NHL defenseman to ascend to the 1,000-assist plateau did not weigh heavily on Paul Coffey's mind. "It's not like 50 goals in 50 games, or a point-scoring streak," Coffey said. "It's going to happen. It's inevitable."

The inevitable arrived December 13, 1995 at Joe Louis Arena, when Igor Larionov converted Coffey's drop pass for Detroit's first goal of a 3-1 win over Chicago.

"I was hoping it would be a nice play, or a big goal and I got both of them," said Coffey, who joined Wayne Gretzky, Gordie Howe and Marcel Dionne in the NHL's 1,000-assist club.

"He's probably the best all-time offensive defenseman," Chicago coach Craig Hartsburg said. "I don't think anyone will come close to achieving what Paul Coffey has accomplished in this league."

RED WINGS ARCHIVE

ASSEMBLY LINE

Restructuring the 1995 Stanley Cup finalist team, the Wings traded Shawn Burr to Tampa Bay for defenseman Marc Bergevin and right-winger Ben Hankinson and shipped Ray Sheppard to San Jose for center Igor Larionov. Dan McGillis went to Edmonton for left-winger Kirk Maltby, while goalie Kevin Hodson and center Wes Walz were signed as free agents. Defensemen Jamie Pushor and Anders Eriksson and right-winger/defenseman Mathieu Dandenault were NHL entry draft selections who made the grade.

Igor Larionov

RED WINGS ARCHIVE

Red Wings Facts

Two Hat-Tricks In One Game

March 16, 1947
Roy Conacher (4) & Ted Lindsay (3)

February 11, 1950
Gerry Couture (4) & Gordie Howe (3)

October 29, 1981
Mike Foligno & John Ogrodnick

December 23, 1983
Steve Yzerman & John Ogrodnick

February 27, 1985
Danny Gare & Reed Larson

January 6, 1994
Ray Sheppard & Vyacheslav Kozlov

Short Passes

Lofting a shot towards the empty Hartford Whalers net in the closing seconds of a March 6, 1996 game, Chris Osgood became the first Red Wings netminder to score a goal, clinching a 4-2 victory with his tally at 19:49 of the third period.

- 1996 1997 -

BACK in TIME

- ### November 5, 1996
  After major defeats in the past, 52 percent of Detroit voters approved legislation to bring casino gambling to their city.

- ### February 19, 1997
  The longest newspaper strike in U.S. history came to an end when managers from the two Detroit newspapers accepted the strikers unconditional offer to return to work.

- ### August 31, 1997
  Britain's Diana, Princess of Wales, was killed in a car crash in Paris along with her companion Emad Mohamed (Dodi) al Fayed, an Egyptian born film producer with whom she was romantically linked.

quick cuts

Most Goals
Brendan Shanahan: 47
Most Assists
Steve Yzerman: 63
Most Points
Brendan Shanahan: 88
Most Penalty Minutes
Martin Lapointe: 167
Most Wins, Goaltender
Chris Osgood: 23
Lowest Goals-Against Average
Chris Osgood: 2.30
Most Shutouts
Chris Osgood: 6
NHL Award Winners
Mike Vernon - Conn Smythe Trophy

FINAL STANDINGS

Central Division	W	L	T	PTS	GF	GA
Dallas	48	26	8	104	252	198
DETROIT	38	26	18	94	253	197
Phoenix	38	37	7	83	240	243
St. Louis	36	35	11	83	236	239
Chicago	34	35	13	81	223	210
Toronto	30	44	8	68	230	273

OTHER DIVISION WINNERS:
Pacific Division: Colorado Avalanche
Northeast Division: Buffalo Sabres
Atlantic Division: New Jersey Devils

Playoff Results
Defeated the St. Louis Blues in Series "G" (4-2)
Defeated the Anaheim Mighty Ducks in Series "L" (4-0)
Defeated the Colorado Avalanche in Series "N" (4-2)
Defeated the Philadelphia Flyers in Series "O" (4-0)
Leading Playoff Scorers
Sergei Fedorov (20PTS) & Brendan Shanahan (17PTS)
Stanley Cup Champion
Detroit Red Wings

1996-97 Season in Review

It was the year the ultimate prize finally came back to Detroit, but it was a season which concluded under tragic circumstances.

Nine Wings – Canada's Steve Yzerman, Paul Coffey and Keith Primeau, Russia's Vyacheslav Kozlov, Igor Larionov, Sergei Fedorov and Viacheslav Fetisov and Sweden's Nicklas Lidstrom and Tomas Holmstrom – participated in the pre-season World Cup, along with Detroit assistant coach Barry Smith, who worked with the Swedes and trainer John Wharton, who served with the Russians.

An October trade brought left-winger Brendan Shanahan to Detroit and hope to Hockeytown. Shanahan led the club with 47 goals and 88 points and was aware of his status. "I'm not saying I'm the missing piece of the (Stanley Cup) puzzle," Shanahan said. "But I definitely think I can be a big piece in that puzzle."

Shanahan, Yzerman and Fetisov played in the NHL All-Star Game and Shanahan tied a club record February 12 with three goals in one period of a 7-1 win against San Jose. Sergei Fedorov scored all five goals December 26 as the Wings edged Washington 5-4. A scoreless tie December 10 with Edmonton was Detroit's first 0-0 game since 1976-77.

Before the playoffs commenced, a score was settled. Colorado came to town March 26 and a brawl saw Detroit's Darren McCarty pummel Colorado's Claude Lemieux, exacting revenge for Lemieux's cheap shot on Kris Draper in the 1996 playoffs. McCarty scored the game-winner after 39 seconds of overtime to give Detroit a 6-5 win and much more.

"Detroit won the Stanley Cup that night," confessed Colorado goalie Patrick Roy.

Officially, the inscriptions on Lord Stanley's mug weren't earned until a sweep of Philadelphia in the final series, following series wins over St. Louis, Anaheim and Colorado en route to Detroit's date with destiny. The party was sweet and sadly, short. Less than a week after their first Cup triumph in 42 seasons, Fetisov, Konstantinov and team masseur Sergei Mnatsakanov were injured in a limousine crash, the latter two suffering career-ending closed-head injuries.

"For a team as close as us, for this to finish it off, it's the worst thing that could ever happen," forward Mathieu Dandenault said.

HOCKEYTOWN MOMENT
Wings celebrate eighth Stanley Cup

Forty-two years of frustration seeped out in a tumultuous ovation from a capacity Joe Louis Arena crowd as the last seconds ticked off the clock in Detroit's 2-1 Stanley Cup-clinching victory over the Philadelphia Flyers.

"I said we'd get it here," noted Wings senior vice-president Jimmy Devellano, who promised to deliver a Stanley Cup when hired as GM in 1982. "It took us a long time, but we got it here."

The roar reached its peak when captain Steve Yzerman hoisted the shiny, silver mug aloft.

"The majority of this team played in the Stanley Cup final two years ago," Yzerman said. "You realize that finishing second means absolutely nothing."

Scotty Bowman, who coached his seventh Cup winner, praised the determination of his team.

"This team went through a lot of agony the last two years and sometimes I think you have to take that pill to learn what you have to do to win," Bowman said.

Kris Draper & Steve Yzerman

MARK HICKS

317

Wings of Legend
Darren McCarty

The hero of Detroit's Stanley Cup-clinching victory, the man who netted the first Stanley Cup-winning goal scored by a Red Wing in 42 seasons, Darren McCarty found his reception during the summer of 1997 to be somewhat different than he had anticipated.

"When people would come up to me, they'd say, 'What you did to (Claude) Lemieux, that was awesome, man,'" McCarty recollected. "'And oh yeah, nice goal, too.'"

The goal came in the decisive fourth game of the 1997 Stanley Cup final. McCarty beat Philadelphia defenseman Janne Niinimaa one-on-one, then deked around goalie Ron Hextall before depositing the puck into the net for what proved to be the title-clinching goal in Detroit's 2-1 triumph.

"Even a blind squirrel sometimes finds a nut," McCarty said of his highlight-reel goal.

The fight came a few months earlier. McCarty punished Colorado's Claude Lemieux for his sneak attack on Detroit's Kris Draper in the 1996 playoffs, a cheap shot which left Draper with multiple facial fractures.

"The big thing you learn in this league is that if you retaliate, you get caught," McCarty said. "But if you put it in the bank, the opportunity will come to settle the score."

In McCarty's world, fighting Lemieux meant as much as the goal, because he was standing up for a teammate. "To me, team accomplishments always overshadow individual awards," said McCarty, who insists that their coming together during a line brawl between the two clubs in that March 26, 1997 game was mere coincidence.

"There was no premeditation," McCarty said. "It must have been God's will.

"I didn't feel bad about it, though."

Family is another McCarty priority and after the 1997 Cup victory, he established the McCarty Cancer Foundation for his father Craig, who was battling multiple myeloma, a rare form of bone cancer.

Craig even wrote a book – Rinkside: A Family's Story of Courage and iInspiration – about their life experiences to aid fund-raising for the cause. "For one of the first times in my life, I don't have anything to say,

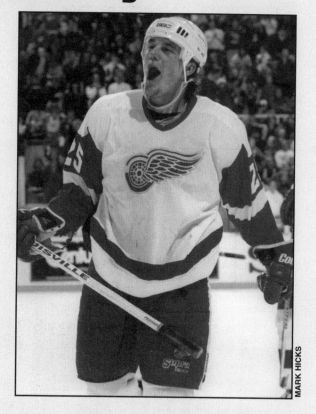

MARK HICKS

other to tell everyone how proud I am of him," Darren remarked after reading his dad's book."

The illness claimed Craig's life in November of 1999. Darren, out with a groin injury which limited his season to 24 games, was able to be at his father's side during those final days.

"It was a difficult period, but being able to spend that time with my dad, I wouldn't change a thing about the way it worked out," he said.

Drawing inspiration from the way his dad thrived during his life, Darren also chooses to live life to the fullest. He's donned a kilt to compete in the highland games and even drove a racehorse.

"That's what life is all about," Darren said. "Having a good time."

- **BORN:**
  Burnaby, B.C., April 1, 1972
- **ACQUIRED:**
  Selected 46th overall in the June 20, 1992 NHL entry draft
- **BEST SEASON WITH RED WINGS:**
  1996-97 (19-30-49)

- **TOTALS WITH RED WINGS:**
  GP-527, G-100, A-140, PTS-240
- **HONORS:**
  Scored Stanley Cup winning goal, 1996-97; Led team in penalty minutes, 1997-98

MOTOWN Classic

Vernon captures Conn Smythe Trophy

Chris Osgood was Detroit's No. 1 goalie during the regular season, playing 47 of 82 games, but Mike Vernon was the man in the playoffs.

"You start with goaltending and he got hot at the right time," Detroit coach Scotty Bowman said of Vernon, who backstopped the Wings to their first Stanley Cup in 42 seasons.

Vernon posted a 16-4 record and a 1.76 goals-against average during the playoffs, earning the Conn Smythe Trophy as Stanley Cup MVP.

"You don't get many opportunities like this and I'm enjoying it," Vernon said, puffing on a victory cigar after the Cup was secured, while sharing the credit for his individual honor with his teammates. "We gained a lot of experience and a lot of knowledge over the past few years. This hockey club was well focused."

Vernon achieved another personal milestone earlier in the season. A 6-5 verdict March 26 over the Colorado Avalanche was his 300th win as an NHLer.

MARK HICKS

ASSEMBLY LINE

Looking to make their team grittier and more difficult to play against, the Wings pulled off several moves designed to toughen up their roster. They traded Paul Coffey, Keith Primeau and a 1997 first round draft pick (Nikos Tselios) to Hartford for left-winger Brendan Shanahan and defenseman Brian Glynn. Greg Johnson went to Pittsburgh for irascible right-winger Tomas Sandstrom. Defenseman Larry Murphy, with two Stanley Cups to his credit, was picked up from Toronto for future considerations. Right-winger Joe Kocur, a former Wing who was playing senior hockey in Lakeland, Mich., was signed as a free agent, as was left-winger Mark Major. The NHL entry draft supplied left-winger Tomas Holmstrom and right-winger Mike Knuble. Bob Errey (San Jose) and Stu Grimson (Hartford) were both lost on waiver claims and Dino Ciccarelli went to Tampa Bay for future considerations.

MARK HICKS

Brendan Shanahan

Red Wings Facts

Most Appearances in an NHL All-Star Game

Gordie Howe **22**
Alex Delvecchio **13**
Ted Lindsay **10**
Steve Yzerman **10**
Red Kelly **9**
Marcel Provonost **9**
Norm Ullman **8**
Nicklas Lidstrom **6**
John Ogrodnick **5**
Sergei Fedorov **5**
Brendan Shanahan **5**

Short Passes

Right-winger Joe Kocur played for the 1993-94 New York Rangers team which ended that club's 54-year Stanley Cup drought and for the 1996-97 Red Wings team, Detroit's first Stanley Cup winner in 42 years.

- 1997  1998 -

BACK in TIME

- **November 29, 1997**

Coleman A. Young, Detroit's first African American mayor, as well as its longest serving mayor, died of respiratory failure.

- **January 1, 1998**

The University of Michigan won the Rose Bowl, defeating Washington State University by a score of 21-16, but it only brought a share of the national title with Nebraska.

- **May 7, 1998**

In the biggest industrial merger in history, German luxury carmaker Daimler-Benz announced it was buying Chrysler Corporation.

quick cuts

Most Goals
Brendan Shanahan: 28
Most Assists
Steve Yzerman: 45
Most Points
Steve Yzerman: 69
Most Penalty Minutes
Darren McCarty: 157
Most Wins, Goaltender
Chris Osgood: 33
Lowest Goals-Against Average
Chris Osgood: 2.21
Most Shutouts
Chris Osgood: 6
NHL Award Winners
Steve Yzerman - Conn Smythe Trophy
Nicklas Lidstrom - 1st Team All-Star

FINAL STANDINGS

Centrtal Division	W	L	T	PTS	GF	GA
Dallas	49	22	11	109	242	167
DETROIT	44	23	15	103	250	196
St. Louis	45	29	8	96	256	204
Phoenix	35	35	12	82	224	227
Chicago	30	39	13	73	192	199
Toronto	30	43	9	69	194	237

OTHER DIVISION WINNERS:
Pacific Division - Colorado Avalanche
Northeast Division - Pittsburgh Penguins
Atlantic Division - New Jersey Devils

Playoff Results
Defeated the Phoenix Coyotes in Series "G" (4-2)
Defeated the St. Louis Blues in Series "L" (4-2)
Defeated the Dallas Stars in Series "N" (4-2)
Defeated the Washington Capitals in Series "O" (4-0)
Leading Playoff Scorers
Steve Yzerman (24PTS) - Sergei Fedorov (20PTS)
Stanley Cup Champion
Detroit Red Wings

1997-98 Season in Review

The campaign commenced with heavy hearts and a specific goal in mind, a sentiment expressed on the shoulders of every Red Wings jersey.

"Believe," said the crest in Russian and English. While defenseman Vladimir Konstantinov and team masseur Sergei Mnatsakanov fought the battle of their lives to overcome brain injuries suffered in an off-season limousine accident, the Wings set about on their mission to retain Lord Stanley's mug without their fallen comrades.

They'd also have to start the season without center Sergei Fedorov, holding out in a contract dispute with the team.

A 10-1-2 start to the season got the Wings rolling, but there would be periods of struggle - enough to allow Dallas to claim first place in the Central Division, three points ahead of Detroit, which finished 44-23-15.

Captain Steve Yzerman led the club with 69 points, the first time he'd been Detroit's leading scorer since 1992-93. Brendan Shanahan's 28 goals were the lowest total to top the team in 21 seasons. Winger Doug Brown tied two club marks December 19 with three goals and four points in one period of a 5-4 victory over New Jersey.

The return of Fedorov to the lineup came February 3, when he signed a six-year, $38-million deal, which included a $14-million signing bonus and a $12-million bonus if the Wings advanced to the final four.

The NHL went to the Winter Olympics for the first time and the Wings were well represented. Yzerman and Shanahan (Canada), Fedorov (Russia) and

MARK HICKS

defenseman Nicklas Lidstrom (Sweden) all participated. Shanahan, Lidstrom, center Igor Larionov and defenseman Slava Fetisov performed in the NHL All-Star Game.

In the playoffs, winger Slava Kozlov scored a record-tying four game winners, while the club set records with 75 goals and six shorthanded markers. Fedorov's 10 goals during the playoffs and three points May 3 in the second period of a 5-2 series-clinching win over Phoenix tied team marks.

After rallying from a 2-1 series deficit to oust Phoenix in six games, St. Louis won the first game of the second round, but Detroit again came back to win in six. The Wings never trailed the Western Conference final against Dallas, taking another six-game verdict. Only Washington stood in the way of a repeat. The Capitals were swept aside in the minimum four games and Stanley stayed put in Hockeytown.

HOCKEYTOWN MOMENT
Wings win two Cups in a row

As emotional as Detroit's 1996-97 Stanley Cup victory was for long-suffering Wings fans, the 1997-98 triumph melted even the coldest of hearts.

When injured defenseman Vladimir Konstantinov was wheeled onto the ice after Detroit's 4-1 Cup-winning verdict at Washington's MCI Center, the sentiment of the moment took over. "This is so emotional, it's great," Igor Larionov said as he helped Konstantinov take a victory lap in his wheelchair with the Stanley Cup. "This is for Vladdy and Sergei (Mnatsakanov)."

Scotty Bowman won his eighth Cup as a coach, tying the record of Toe Blake, his mentor. Captain Steve Yzerman set a club record with 18 assists and 24 points and was presented the Conn Smythe Trophy as playoff MVP.

"We found a lot of ways to play," Bowman said. "We found a lot of ways to win. This team was totally focused on the mission." And they never stopped believing.

Igor Larionov

The secret to eternal youth?

"Two glasses of wine every day," insists center Igor Larionov, still playing brilliant hockey for the Wings past his 40th birthday.

Larionov's acquisition from San Jose early in the 1995-96 season allowed the Wings to assemble an all-Russian unit and it added tremendous character to the Detroit dressing room. Larionov and Detroit teammate Viacheslav Fetisov challenged the Soviet sports system in the late 1980s, eventually winning the freedom for Russian players to skate in the NHL.

A two-time Olympic gold medalist, Larionov risked everything by criticizing the Soviet system in letters and magazine articles. "We decided to fight for freedom for Russian players to choose their own path," Larionov said.

It was not a battle that was won easily.

"Igor is a very brave man," Fetisov said. "We were in the army, so they could have sent us anywhere, anytime. It was a critical moment in our lives."

Columbus Blue Jackets coach Dave King was in charge of the Canadian Olympic team at the time and he marveled at Larionov's courage.

"He went against the Soviet system, because he wanted time for his family," King said. "He was principled. We should all be so strong."

This combination of character and skill made Larionov an ideal fit with the talent-rich Red Wings. He was a key component on the Cup-winning squads of 1996-97, 1997-98 and 2001-02.

"He does so many little things well," Detroit captain Steve Yzerman said of Larionov. "The way he makes those little passes, those little moves with the puck. He's just a pleasure to watch and a very smart hockey player."

Off the ice, Larionov hones his hockey skills by playing chess. "In chess, you're always in attacking mode, thinking two or three steps ahead," Larionov said. "That's the way hockey should be played." Larionov's dedication to defense definitely has kept him from putting up even more dominant totals. "He's always on the defensive side of the man he's covering," King said. "He doesn't get beat."

MARK HICKS

No matter who the opponent might be.

When you've wrestled the mighty Soviet bear into submission, little else will faze you.

"Our careers would have been unfulfilled if we couldn't play in the National Hockey League," Larionov said, speaking on behalf of Russian hockey players.

Allowed to leave for Florida via free agency after the 1999-2000 season, the struggling Wings moved to reacquire Larionov during the 2000-01 season and his return sparked Detroit's second-half revival.

"I have dedicated my life to hockey," Larionov said. "To be honest, when I was a kid from six to 18, I never missed a practice.

"I love the game and try to share my experiences with the young guys and try to be useful for any team I play for and give as much as I can."

Few have given more to the game than Larionov.

- **BORN:**
  Voskresensk, Russia, December 3, 1960
- **ACQUIRED:**
  October 24, 1995 trade with San Jose
- **BEST SEASON WITH RED WINGS:**
  1995-96 (22-51-73)

- **TOTALS WITH RED WINGS:**
  GP-465, G-79, A-275, PTS-354
- **HONORS:**
  Played in NHL All-Star Game, 1997-98; Led team in assists, 1998-99; Played for Russia, 1996 World Cup, 2002 Winter Olympics

MOTOWN Classic

Lidstrom leads all defenseman in points

RED WINGS ARCHIVE

Performing effectively ever since he first joined the Red Wings to start the 1991-92 season, the 1997-98 campaign brought an element to Nicklas Lidstrom's game not seen before.

It was called recognition and it was long overdue.

Lidstrom led all NHL blueliners with 59 points, one shy of the career-high points total he assembled during his rookie season. Lidstrom also tallied a personal-best 17 goals. The result was selection to the NHL's First All-Star Team and runner-up status behind Rob Blake of Los Angeles in the voting for the Norris Trophy.

"It has been a long time coming," teammate Darren McCarty said. "He's always been the most underrated player in the league – our little secret."

In the playoffs, Lidstrom established new Wings standards for defensemen with 13 assists and 19 points, while tying Paul Coffey's club mark for goals with six.

ASSEMBLY LINE

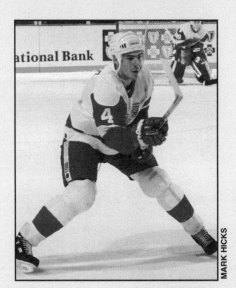

MARK HICKS

Jamie Pushor

Two months after he'd won the Conn Smythe Trophy as Stanley Cup MVP, Mike Vernon was dealt to San Jose with a 1999 fifth round draft pick for second round picks in 1998 and 1999. Left-winger Brent Gilchrist was signed as a free agent and Tim Taylor was lost to Boston in the NHL waiver draft. Jamie Pushor was dealt to Anaheim for defenseman Dmitri Mironov and a 1998 fourth round draft choice went to Toronto for defenseman Jamie Macoun. The NHL entry draft supplied center Darryl Laplante, defenseman Yan Golubovsky and goalie Norm Maracle.

Red Wings Facts

Red Wings Selected First-overall in NHL Draft:

1964 - Claude Gauthier

1977 - Dale McCourt

1986 - Joe Murphy

Short Passes

Forwards Pavel Datsyuk (2001-02), Vyacheslav Kozlov (1991-2001) and Gizzy Hart (1926-27) are the only Wings players to wear No. 13 on their jersey.

VLADIMIR KONSTANTINOV:
THE AFTERMATH OF THE ACCIDENT

MARK HICKS

What if he had been more convincing? What if he had been more forceful? If only they had listened.

For years, such thoughts have haunted Brendan Shanahan.

The date unnerved him even before it turned out to be fateful.

Friday, June 13, 1997. Six days after their Stanley Cup win, the Detroit Red Wings planned a golf outing, a farewell before players headed their separate ways for summer.

"I'm a superstitious guy," said left-winger Shanahan. "I remember thinking, 'I'm glad we all got limos, because it's Friday the 13th.'"

Shanahan eschewed golf that day, but arrived at the course later in the evening, spotting a limousine getting ready to leave. Inside were defensemen Slava Fetisov and Vladimir Konstantinov and team masseur Sergei Mnatsakanov.

"I poked my head in the window and said, 'Stay and play cards.' "They said, 'No, we're tired' and they drove off."

The call came a couple of hours later. There had been an accident. The limousine had veered off Woodward Ave. in Birmingham, Mich. and slammed into a tree at an estimated 50 m.p.h.

Konstantinov and Mnatsakanov were both comatose after suffering closed head injuries. Konstantinov also suffered severe nerve and muscle damage to one arm. Mnatsakanov was left paralyzed in both legs and one arm.

There has been improvement since, although both men are nowhere near the people they used to be.

Fetisov suffered bruises to his chest and lungs and cracked ribs. He was back in the Detroit lineup in 1997-98, helping defend the Stanley Cup, left to wonder why he was spared.

"What I must deal with doesn't compare to the pain Vladimir and Sergei must go through," Fetisov said.

Konstantinov's locker in the Red Wings dressing room remained a shrine to the man they called "The Vladinator" during the 1997 Cup run.

The locker included a Curious George doll in a Red Wings sweater. That was Konstantinov's nickname because, like the cartoon monkey, he stuck his nose in where it didn't belong.

A pet rock inscribed with the word "Believe," rested on the shelf.

The Konstantinov who patrolled the blueline for Detroit was a contradiction in terms. On the ice, unyielding, a warrior. Someone who asked no quarter and gave none. Away from the rink, as warm and as friendly as a man could be.

"Vladdy liked everybody," Detroit senior vice-president Jimmy Devellano said. "And he had time for everyone."

"Great guy," Fetisov said, recalling his friend and teammate. "Big heart. Easy going.

"Sometimes, I'd look at Vladdy's locker and I wanted to cry. But you couldn't cry. You had to stand up and play your best again and again — like Vladimir did."

The players also wore their hearts on their sleeves. A patch with both men's initials and the word believe, in English and Russian, adorned each Detroit sweater.

The Red Wings believe. They retain hope. And they never forget.

"How could you every forget a guy like Vladdy?" asked goalie Chris Osgood.

BACK-TO-BACK CUPS

Detroit winger Joe Kocur, a member of the 1993-94 New York Ranger club which ended that franchise's 54-year Stanley Cup drought, pondered how such a celebration would unfold in Detroit.

"In New York, it was big, but they win lots of championships," Kocur said. "Winning it here, I think it would be a non-stop party for about three months."

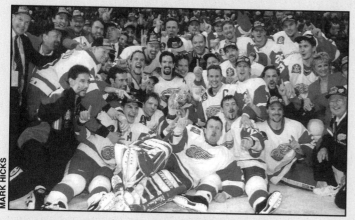

MARK HICKS

Hockey experts made other suggestions as the 1996-97 commenced — that the window of Stanley Cup opportunity had closed on the Wings, who were swept by New Jersey in the 1995 final and beaten by Colorado in the 1995-96 Western Conference final, despite winning an NHL-record 62 games that season.

Without a Stanley Cup since 1954-55, Detroit simply wasn't destiny's darling, the thinking went.

On second thought . . .

The Wings slumped to fifth overall in 1996-97, but captain Steve Yzerman cautioned people to be wary of the winged wheelers. "I still think this team will win a Stanley Cup," he said at mid-season.

Defenseman Vladimir Konstantinov agreed, feeling the club had a better mix of talent than previous teams which failed. "We used to be all skill," Konstantinov said. "Now we run at guys, we get in your face."

A slow start to the playoffs saw the Wings struggle for four games in the first round against St. Louis. Then it all seemed to click. They dumped the Blues in six games, swept Anaheim, downed arch-rival Colorado in a six-game Western Conference final, then broomed Philadelphia in the final, winning Game 4 before a frenzied, sellout crowd at Joe Louis Arena.

For the first time in 42 years, Stanley was back in the house.

"As the playoffs went on, it became more apparent that we were the best team," Detroit defenseman Larry Murphy said. "Nobody could touch us." Coach Scotty Bowman let his emotions rule in the post-game celebration, donning his skates to tour the rink holding the Cup aloft. "I always felt like doing it and this time, I decided to go for it," Bowman said.

Yzerman, who had endured much playoff heartbreak, savored the final triumph. "For as long as I can remember, I've dreamed of lifting the Stanley Cup," he said. "I don't know if you can ever equal a dream, but this is pretty close."

The celebration lasted six days, until Konstantinov and team masseur Sergei Mnatsakanov were critically injured in a limousine crash. With both left wheelchair-bound, retaining the Cup for their fallen teammates became Detroit's mission in 1997-98.

Again there were early difficulties, this time against first-round opponent Phoenix, but once Detroit got into gear, no team could stop them.

Sweeping Washington in the final, the Wings wheeled Konstantinov onto the ice and helped him carry the Cup around the rink. "Win No. 16 is for No. 16," said defenseman Slava Fetisov, noting the victories required to keep the Cup and Konstantinov's jersey number were identical.

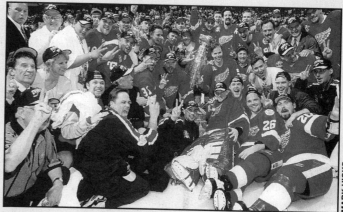

MARK HICKS

Two seasons. Two Cups. So many memories.

"We owed it to this town to bring them a Stanley Cup," Kocur said.

BACK in TIME

- **September 30, 1998**

President Clinton announced a $70 million U.S. budget surplus, the first surplus since 1969.

- **November 3, 1998**

Former wrestler Jessie Ventura was elected governor of Minnesota, the first member of the Reform Party to be elected governor.

- **November 25, 1998**

Dr. Jack Kervorkian, an advocate of the right to physician-assisted suicide, was charged with first degree murder for the televised death of a terminally ill man.

- **December 5, 1998**

James Hoffa, son of the former Teamster president who disappeared in 1975, was elected president of the union.

King Hussein of Jordan died at age 63 after ruling his kingdom for 46 years.

quick cuts

Most Goals
Wendel Clark: 32

Most Assists
Igor Larionov: 49

Most Points
Steve Yzerman: 74

Most Penalty Minutes
Martin Lapointe: 141

Most Wins, Goaltender
Chris Osgood: 34

Lowest Goals-Against Average
Norm Maracle: 2.27

Most Shutouts
Chris Osgood: 3

NHL Award Winners
Nicklas Lidstrom - 1st Team All-Star

FINAL STANDINGS

Central Division	W	L	T	PTS	GF	GA
DETROIT	43	32	7	93	245	202
St. Louis	37	32	13	87	237	209
Chicago	29	41	12	70	202	248
Nashville	28	47	7	63	190	261

Western Conference Winner - Dallas Stars

Playoff Results
Defeated Anaheim 4 Games to None
Lost to Colorado 4 Games to 2
Stanley Cup Champion
Dallas Stars

1998-99 Season in Review

MARK HICKS

Off-season surgery left the two-time defending Stanley Cup champions without a coach to commence the campaign.

Scotty Bowman underwent a balloon angioplasty treatment on his heart and had his arthritic left knee replaced with a titanium artificial knee, leaving the bench duties in the hands of associate coaches Dave Lewis and Barry Smith.

"It's a unique situation," said Ken Holland, promoted from assistant GM to general manager in the summer. And a positive situation. The Wings got off to a 4-1 start under their interim bosses before Bowman returned to work.

Detroit stumbled to a 4-8-2 mark in December, which included a five-game losing streak. Winning once in eight games from February 21 through March 12, it was clear drastic measures were required - especially considering defenseman Uwe Krupp, an off-season free-agent addition from Colorado, was done for the year with a back injury.

On March 23, NHL trade deadline day, Detroit added goalie Bill Ranford, defensemen Chris Chelios and Ulf Samuelsson and left-winger Wendel Clark in a series of blockbuster trades.

A 2-1 win over Buffalo the next night launched a nine-game unbeaten run and the Wings entered the post-season on a 9-2-1 tear.

They swept Anaheim aside in the opening round of the playoffs. In Game 1 of the series, captain Steve Yzerman tallied his club-record fourth playoff hat trick. Left-winger Brendan Shanahan tied a team mark with three points in the first period of Detroit's 5-1 Game 2 rout.

Goalie Chris Osgood went down with a knee injury, but Ranford stepped in and the winning continued in the second round against Colorado, Detroit taking the first two games, both played at Denver. Going back to last season, the Wings had set club playoff records for the most consecutive wins (11) and the most consecutive road wins (six).

Coming home, the bubble burst. Colorado won twice in Detroit. Bowman turned to third stringer Norm Maracle, then to the injured Osgood, but neither goalie could stop the slide. The Avalanche captured the series in six games.

The Stanley Cup champs had been dethroned.

"It hurts," Shanahan said. "Once you win the Stanley Cup, you feel a sense of ownership. You don't ever want to see anyone else touching it."

"Usually, we're the team that gets stronger as the series goes on," Yzerman said. "That didn't happen this time."

HOCKEYTOWN MOMENT
Murphy tops defensemen in games played

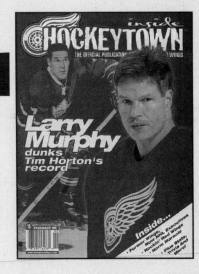

Growing up in the Toronto suburb of Scarborough, Larry Murphy worshipped the Toronto Maple Leafs. "I was a diehard Leaf fan as a kid," Murphy recalled. "I remember when the Leafs won the Stanley Cup in 1967. I knew everybody on the team.

"I remember Tim Horton well off that team."

Nearly 32 years later, on February 5, 1999, Murphy was making everyone remember Horton when the Wings rearguard played his 1,447th NHL game, passing Hall of Famer Horton to become the NHL defenseman with the most career games played.

"It's something I don't think a lot about, but it is something I take pride in," Murphy said of the achievement. "Being able to last a lot longer than a number of other players, I take pride in that accomplishment."

Murphy was picked to play in the 1998-99 NHL All-Star Game, where he was joined by Detroit teammates Nicklas Lidstrom and Brendan Shanahan.

Wings of Legend

Larry Murphy

Larry Murphy was such a poor skater as a youngster, he was the last player chosen in a player draft for the house league in his hometown, the Toronto suburb of Scarborough. His coach wouldn't let Murphy stray past his own blueline, afraid Murphy wouldn't be able to get back if there was a sudden turnover.

People mocked Murphy's lack of footspeed for years, as he steadily ascended to honor after honor during an impressive NHL career.

He played for the Canadian midget champion Don Mills Flyers. He won a Memorial Cup with the Peterborough Petes.

In his first NHL season, playing for the Los Angeles Kings, Murphy established NHL rookie records for defensemen with 60 assists and 76 points, marks which still stand today.

By the time he arrived in Detroit late in the 1996-97 campaign, Murphy owned two Stanley Cup rings, three Canada Cup titles and was a three-time NHL All-Star selection.

The guy without the wheels was on quite a roll. But people still chose to underestimate him.

Before the 1997 Stanley Cup final, Philadelphia's Legion Of Doom – Eric Lindros, John LeClair and Mikael Renberg – salivated at the opportunity to go up against Murphy.

"We looked at the pairings, looked at what he could do and couldn't do and thought we had an advantage," LeClair said. "But it turned out very badly for us."

Detroit swept the series, as Murphy and partner Nicklas Lidstrom held Philly's big guns to three goals in four games.

"Murphy and Lidstrom made a joke out of that forward line," Hall of Fame defenseman Denis Potvin said. "They were three steps ahead of them, four games in a row."

Those who have enjoyed the pleasure of playing alongside Murphy are never surprised to hear such tales. "He's the smartest player I've ever seen," said Pittsburgh's Jaromir Jagr, Murphy's teammate on two Cup winners with the Penguins.

MARK HICKS

Clearly the tortoise in the old fable of the tortoise and the hare, Murphy's guile kept him going as an NHLer for two decades. "His game is so steady," Lidstrom said. "He's so smart with the puck. He seldom makes mistakes and his positioning is perfect."

Murphy surpassed Tim Horton (1,446 games) as the NHL's all-time leader in games played by a defenseman in 1998-99 and by the end of the 2000-01 season, Murphy's career totals of 1,615 games played stood second on the overall NHL list, behind only former Red Wing Gordie Howe (1,767).

"We can't all skate like Howie Morenz," Hall of Fame defenseman Harry Howell said. "Some of us had to find other methods to be successful.

"Larry Murphy is a perfect example of someone who found those methods."

- **BORN:**
  Scarborough, Ontario, March 8, 1961
- **ACQUIRED:**
  March 18, 1997 trade with Toronto
- **BEST SEASON WITH RED WINGS:**
  1996-97 (11-41-52)
- **TOTALS WITH RED WINGS:**
  GP-312, G-35, A-136, PTS-171

- **HONORS:**
  NHL career leader in games played by a defenseman; Played in 1998-99 NHL All-Star Game; Led team in plus-minus, 1998-99

MOTOWN Classic

Wings reshaped at trade deadline

MARK HICKS

Wendel Clark

It played like the opening scene from the Magnificent Seven.

One by one, the hired guns entered the Detroit dressing room. First came ex-Toronto left-winger Wendel Clark, a five-time 30-goal scorer and runner-up in the 1985-86 Calder Trophy voting. Next to arrive was former Chicago Blackhawks defenseman Chris Chelios, a three-time Norris Trophy winner. Following close behind was goalie Bill Ranford, 1989-90 winner of the Conn Smythe Trophy as Stanley Cup MVP. Finally, there was irascible defenseman Ulf Samuelsson, a two-time Stanley Cup winner.

All acquired at the NHL trade deadline, the fantastic four had the Wings thinking threepeat. "There are only certain opportunities a team has to win," Detroit coach Scotty Bowman said after the moves, handing the credit to GM Ken Holland. "He worked the phones as well as I've ever seen anyone work them."

ASSEMBLY LINE

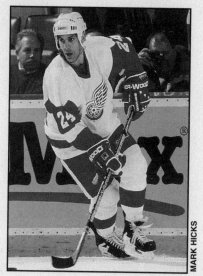

MARK HICKS

Chris Chelios

The boldest day in the history of the NHL trade deadline saw the Wings acquire defenseman Chris Chelios from Chicago for Anders Eriksson and first round draft picks in 1999 and 2001; left-winger Wendel Clark from Tampa Bay for Kevin Hodson and a 1999 second round draft pick; defenseman Ulf Samuelsson from the New York Rangers for another 1999 second round draft pick; and goalie Bill Ranford from Tampa Bay for future considerations. Right winger Doug Brown was lost to Nashville in the NHL expansion draft, then reacquired in exchange for Petr Sykora and a 1999 third round draft choice. Future considerations were dealt to Tampa Bay to regain left-winger Brent Gilchrist, claimed by the Lightning in the NHL waiver draft. Future considerations also went to Anaheim for former Wings defenseman Doug Houda. Defenseman Uwe Krupp was signed as a free agent. Defenseman Todd Gill was claimed on waivers from St. Louis. Left-winger Petr Klima, another ex-Wing, was signed as a free agent, as was center Stacy Roest. Left-winger Philippe Audet was a product of the NHL entry draft.

Red Wings Facts

Red Wing Playoff Hat Tricks

Syd Howe - Mar. 23, 1939 vs. Montreal Canadiens
Mud Bruneteau - Apr. 1, 1943 vs. Boston Bruins
Don Grosso - Apr 7, 1943 vs. Boston Bruins
Carl Liscombe - Apr. 3, 1945 vs. Boston Bruins
Ted Lindsay - Apr. 5 , 1955 vs. Montreal Canadiens
Gordie Howe - Apr. 10, 1955 vs. Montreal Canadiens
Norm Ullman - Mar. 29, 1964 vs. Chicago Blackhawks
Norm Ullman - Apr. 7, 1964 vs. Chicago Blackhawks
Norm Ullman - Apr. 11, 1965 vs. Chicago Blackhawks
Petr Klima - Apr. 7, 1988 vs. Toronto Maple Leafs
Petr Klima - Apr. 21, 1988 vs. St. Louis Blues
Steve Yzerman - Apr. 6, 1989 vs. Chicago Blackhawks
Steve Yzerman - Apr. 4, 1991 vs. St. Louis Blues
Ray Sheppard - Apr. 24, 1992 vs. Minnesota North Stars
Dino Ciccarelli - Apr. 29, 1993 vs. Toronto Maple Leafs
Dino Ciccarelli - May 11, 1995 vs. Dallas Stars
Steve Yzerman - May 8, 1996 vs. St. Louis Blues
Steve Yzerman - Apr. 21, 1999 vs. Anaheim Mighty Ducks
Martin Lapointe - Apr. 15, 2000 vs. Los Angeles Kings
Brett Hull - Apr. 27, 2002 vs Vancouver Canucks
Darren McCarty - May 18, 2002 vs Colorado Avalanche

Short Passes

Detroit's Bill Ranford is the only goalie to backstop teams to Stanley Cup, Canada Cup and World Championship titles.

BACK in TIME

- **July 16, 1999**

John F. Kennedy, Jr. and his wife and sister-in-law were killed when his private plane crashed into the Atlantic Ocean.

- **February 6, 2000**

First Lady Hillary Clinton officially declared her candidacy for the U.S. Senate seat from the state of New York.

- **April 11, 2000**

After playing baseball at the corner of Michigan and Trumbull for over one hundred years, the Detroit Tigers played their first game at the new Comerica Park, located in downtown Detroit.

quick cuts

Most Goals
Brendan Shanahan: 41

Most Assists
Nicklas Lidstrom: 53

Most Points
Steve Yzerman: 79

Most Penalty Minutes
Martin Lapointe: 121

Most Wins, Goaltender
Chris Osgood: 30

Lowest Goals-Against Average
Chris Osgood: 2.40

Most Shutouts
Chris Osgood: 6

NHL Award Winners
Steve Yzerman - Frank J. Selke Trophy
Steve Yzerman, Brendan Shanahan
& Nicklas Lidstrom - 1st Team All Stars

FINAL STANDINGS

Central Division	W	L	T	RT	PTS	GF	GA
St. Louis	51	20	11	1	114	248	165
DETROIT	48	24	10	2	108	278	210
Chicago	33	39	10	2	78	242	245
Nashville	28	47	7	7	70	199	240

Western Conference Winner - Dallas Stars

Playoff Results
Defeated Los Angeles Kings 4 games to 0
Lost to Colorado Avalanche 4 games to 1
Stanley Cup Champion
New Jersey Devils

1999-2000 Season in Review

The dawning of a new millennium brought many milestone moments to Hockeytown.

Left-winger Brendan Shanahan got the ball rolling. His goal November 13 at Toronto gained the Wings a 1-1 tie with the Leafs and was the 400th goal of Shanahan's NHL career.

Captain Steve Yzerman collected three historic pucks. He tallied his 900th NHL assist November 17 at Vancouver. Yzerman garnered his 1,500th NHL point November 20 at Edmonton, setting up Mathieu Dandenault's goal. Back at Joe Louis Arena November 26 for a rematch with the Oilers, Yzerman stuffed a loose puck past Edmonton's Tommy Salo for his 600th NHL goal.

That same night, defenseman Larry Murphy became the fourth NHLer to perform in 1,500 games. But the milestone mania was far from finished.

Right-winger Pat Verbeek, signed as a free agent in November after playing for the Stanley Cup champion Dallas Stars in 1998-99, reached the 1,000-point plateau February 27 with an assist against Tampa Bay. Verbeek beat Calgary's Fred Brathwaite March 22 to gain membership in the 500-goal fraternity.

Center Sergei Fedorov potted his 300th NHL goal March 29. Vancouver's Felix Potvin was the victim. Fedorov also gained his 400th assist and 700th point during the season.

A club record for the fastest four goals was established December 28 in a 7-2 victory at Buffalo when Igor Larionov, Nicklas Lidstrom, Aaron Ward and Verbeek scored in a span of 1:55.

Yzerman won the Selke Trophy and Lidstrom was runner-up in the Norris Trophy voting. Yzerman, Shanahan and Lidstrom were named to the NHL's First All-Star Team and Shanahan, Yzerman, Lidstrom, defenseman Chris Chelios and coach Scotty Bowman all participated in the NHL All-Star Game.

Detroit finished second to St. Louis in the Central Division and second overall in the league with 108 points.

Los Angeles met Detroit in the opening round of the playoffs. It was the first post-season meeting between the Wings and Kings and it was over quickly, Detroit sweeping the best-of-seven set.

The second-round foe was more familiar, as was the result. Colorado shunted aside the Wings in five games, the third time in the last five seasons that the Avalanche had ended Detroit's season.

HOCKEYTOWN MOMENT
Yzerman scores 600th goal

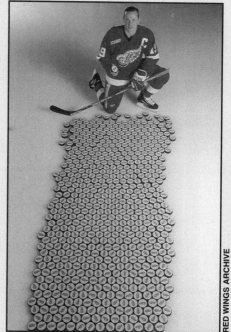

Two magical moments were part of Detroit's 4-2 victory over the Edmonton Oilers on November 26 at Joe Louis Arena. Defenseman Larry Murphy joined the NHL's 1,500-game fraternity and Steve Yzerman shot his way into the 600-goal club.

The 11th member of this select group, Yzerman beat Tommy Salo for this historic tally. Only Gordie Howe (786 goals) has tallied more often in a Detroit uniform than "The Captain."

"He has given this organization hope and fulfilled it beyond anyone's wildest expectations," Wings GM Ken Holland said of Yzerman.

Six days earlier at Edmonton, Yzerman assisted on a Mathieu Dandenault goal for his 1,500th NHL point. He and Howe, along with Wayne Gretzky, Marcel Dionne, Mark Messier and Mario Lemieux are the only NHLers to accumulate 600 goals and 900 assists during their NHL careers.

Yzerman also skated in his 1,200th NHL contest, a 4-2 home-ice win over St. Louis on November 24, 1999.

Brendan Shanahan

The moment he arrived in Detroit, Brendan Shanahan knew he'd found what he was looking for.

"You quickly get a sense of the passion here, of how much the people in this city care about their hockey team," Shanahan said after being acquired in a 1996 trade with Hartford. "There's a mandate from the fans to win a Stanley Cup. I like that."

Red Wings fans liked the goods delivered by Shanahan, who proved to be a key component in answering that mandate.

Shanahan led the club with 47 goals as Detroit won the Stanley Cup in 1996-97 and was also the club's goal-scoring leader when the Wings defended their title in 1997-98. "I like being in the big games and I like being out there during the big moments of those games," he said.

Many looked upon the acquisition of Shanahan as giving Detroit the final push to climb to the top of the mountain. "He's the type of player we didn't have," GM Ken Holland said.

Coach Scotty Bowman was more elaborate in explaining the elements Shanahan added to the Detroit mix. "He's a winger, a power winger who can score," Bowman said. "I don't know another player like him in the league."

He's produced two 40-goal seasons in a Detroit uniform and was selected to the NHL's First All-Star Team in 1999-2000, tallying his 400th career goal that season. Shanahan and Vaclav Nedomansky are the only players in Red Wings history to register hat tricks in consecutive games.

Shanahan's winters are the stuff of legend, but Shanny's summers tend to take on a more mythic tone.

According to his bio, Shanahan's off-seasons have seen him serve as Ireland's second-string goalkeeper in soccer's 1994 World Cup; play saxophone during the Canadian Jazz Festival; appear in the film Forrest Gump and fail a screen test for the role of Dino in the movie version of The Flintstones.

None of it is true. "I saw some of the exciting stuff some of the other guys were doing in the summer and figured I ought to liven up my life a little bit," Shanahan

MARK HICKS

said. "I don't want to be a movie star. I want to be a hockey star. "

Shanahan's quick wit can enliven the Red Wings dressing room as often as his quick release of his powerful shot can illuminate the goal light.

During the 2000-01 season, when he was presented with an NHL Milestone Award for playing his 1,000th game, Shanahan left a box of Kleenex at the Wings bench before accepting the honor.

"I knew the players and the coaching staff would be overcome with emotion," he joked.

When it comes time to drop the puck, this prankster is all business.

"I can be a happy-go-lucky guy, but I'm very serious about my hockey," Shanahan said. "My whole life, all I wanted to be was a hockey player."

Wings fans are delighted he became one of their hockey players.

- **BORN:**
  Mimico, Ontario, January 23, 1969
- **ACQUIRED:**
  October 9, 1996 trade with Hartford
- **BEST SEASON WITH RED WINGS:**
  1996-97 (47-41-88)
- **TOTALS WITH RED WINGS:**
  GP-474, G-214, A-217, PTS-431

- **HONORS:**
  Selected to NHL First All-Star Team, 1999-2000; Selected to NHL Second All-Star Team, 2001-02; Played in five NHL All-Star Games; Led team in goals six times; Led team in points, 1996-97, 2000-01, 2001-02; Played for Canada, 1998 Winter Olympics; Won Gold Medal for Canada, 2002 Winter Olympics

MOTOWN Classic

Murphy plays in 1500th game

MARK HICKS

Stepping on the ice for his first shift of a 4-2 win November 26, 1999 over the Edmonton Oilers at Joe Louis Arena, Larry Murphy logged the 1,500th game of his NHL career.

By the end of the season, Murphy's total of 1,558 games had surpassed former Red Wings captain Alex Delvecchio (1,549 games) and only the most famous Red Wing of them all - Gordie Howe, with 1,767 games - stood ahead of Murphy on the NHL's all-time games played list.

"It does overwhelm you, when you sit down and think about it and say, 'Wow, these are great players in the game,'" the modest Murphy said, almost embarrassed to be mentioned in the same sentence with such Hall-of-Fame talent.

Another astounding Murphy milestone - he's played a game in 54 different NHL arenas during his career - from his NHL debut for L.A. against the Wings October, 11, 1980 at the Los Angeles Forum, through his appearance March 11, 2001 at Minnesota's Xcel Energy Center.

ASSEMBLY LINE

Trades were few, but moves were still plentiful for the Wings, who used their checkbook instead of the barter system as the No. 1 method of change. Defenseman Steve Duchesne, goalies Manny Legace and Ken Wregget, right-winger Pat Verbeek and right-winger Marc Rodgers were signed as free agents. Philippe Audet was traded to Phoenix for defenseman Todd Gill, who was making his second tour as a Red Wing. Defensemen Jiri Fischer and Jesse Wallin, center Yuri Butsayev and right-winger B.J. Young, the first Alaskan-born Red Wing, were acquired through the NHL entry draft. Norm Maracle was lost to Atlanta in the NHL expansion draft.

MARK HICKS

Todd Gill

Red Wings Facts

Most Career Hat Tricks By A Detroit Player
(Regular-Season Only)

Gordie Howe - 19
Steve Yzerman - 18
Norm Ullman - 11
Brendan Shanahan - 8
Syd Howe - 7
Dale McCourt - 7
John Ogrodnick - 6
Frank Mahovlich - 5
Mickey Redmond - 5
Sergei Fedorov - 4
Vaclav Nedomansky - 4
Marcel Dionne - 4
Jimmy Carson - 4
Ray Sheppard - 4
Ron Duguay - 4

Short Passes

Versatile Doug Brown could play either left or right wing and he was also the definition of a quietly consistent producer. Through the 2000-01 season, Brown had tallied 160 NHL goals without ever scoring more than 19 in a campaign.

STEVE YZERMAN

Forget the 600 goals, the 900 assists and the record book filled with his name.

The memories Steve Yzerman will cherish from his Red Wings days speak more to what the man is all about than any crooked number.

Lifting two Stanley Cups are the moments he finds worth remembering.

"It's the only accomplishment that really matters," said the man who has captained the Wings since 1986 and is beloved by Detroit fans on a scale with Gordie Howe.

"He's the ultimate captain," teammate Chris Chelios said of Yzerman. "No one competes more than him. He's been like that ever since I've known him." Yzerman's career offensive totals rank second to Howe and his 65-90-155 numbers in 1988-89 remain club single-season marks.

Arriving as Detroit's top draft pick in 1983, Yzerman evolved from a skilled, point-scoring superstar to rate among the game's best two-way players. He's the only player in NHL history to record a 150-point season and also win the Selke Trophy as the league's top defensive forward during his career.

MARK HICKS

"When you first come into the league, you want to make your mark individually," Detroit associate coach Dave Lewis said. "Stevie did that.

"Through the years, you learn that to win and be successful, you have to be a more all-around player. He saw that and now Stevie is the complete package." Detroit coach Scotty Bowman has coached and opposed many great players in more than three decades working behind NHL benches and puts Yzerman right up there with the all-time greats.

"He doesn't take a second off," Bowman said. "There's a select few players that show up for every game and every practice and that's why they get to where they are.

"Wayne Gretzky was like that. Bobby Orr was like that. Guy Lafleur was like that in Montreal. And so is Stevie." Like Howe, Yzerman's charity work in the community has made him a larger Detroit icon. Another trait he shares with Howe is an on-ice soul-less ambivalence towards the opposition. Stand in his way of success and you'll regret it.

"Stevie Y" isn't a touchy-feely captain. He leads by example.

"He's always been a quiet leader, but now, he steps up a little more and says his piece," noted Joe Kocur, Yzerman's teammate when he was named captain in 1986-87 and when he led the team to Stanley Cups in 1996-97 and 1997-98.

"If he sees something wrong, or somebody acting up, he's the first to step in." For nearly two decades, he's been stepping up for the Wings, filling Hockeytown with fond recollections, but there will always be three at the top of Yzerman's list.

"By far, the most rewarding thing is going through four rounds of the playoffs and winning the Cup," Yzerman said.

- 2000   2001 -

BACK in TIME

- **January 1, 2001**

Shortly after midnight, Mayor Dennis Archer opened the 19th-century time capsule sealed January 1, 1901 to kick off the Detroit Tricentennial year-long celebration.

- **January 20, 2001**

George W. Bush, only the second son to follow his father into the White House, was sworn in as the 43rd President of the United States.

- **June 11, 2001**

Oklahoma City Bomber Timothy McVeigh is put to death by lethal injection, marking the first Federal execution in 38 years.

quick cuts

Most Goals
Sergei Fedorov: 32
Most Assists
Nicklas Lidstrom: 56
Most Points
Brendan Shanahan: 76
Most Penalty Minutes
Martin Lapointe: 127
Most Wins, Goaltender
Chris Osgood: 25
Lowest Goals-Against Average
Manny Legace: 2.05
Most Shutouts
Manny Legace: 2
NHL Award Winners
Nicklas Lidstrom - Norris Trophy
& 1st Team All-Star

FINAL STANDINGS

Central Division	W	L	T	OTL	PTS	GF	GA
DETROIT	49	20	9	4	111	253	202
St. Louis	43	22	12	5	103	249	195
Nashville	34	36	9	3	80	186	200
Chicago	29	40	8	5	71	210	246
Columbus	28	39	9	6	71	190	233

Western Conference Winner - Colorado Avalanche

Playoff Results
Lost to Los Angeles Kings in Series "F" 4-2
Stanley Cup Champion
Colorado Avalanche

2000-01 Season in Review

MARK HICKS

Detroit's dominance over the last half of the previous decade could be easily calculated. From the start of the 1995-96 season through the end of the 1999-2000 campaign, the Wings posted a .645 winning percentage, the best in the NHL.

Another strong season was about to commence, though it didn't start smoothly. Captain Steve Yzerman and defenseman Chris Chelios both went out with knee injuries and the Wings were just 12-8-1-1 through 22 games.

There would be only 12 more losses the rest of the way. Commencing with a 2-1 New Year's Eve victory over Los Angeles, Detroit would run the rest of the regular-season table at Joe Louis Arena without tasting defeat, posting a club-record 19-game unbeaten streak on home ice.

A 9-0-2 slate in February marked the first unbeaten month in franchise history. Overcoming their slow start, the Wings eclipsed St. Louis to take the Central Division title with 111 points. It was the 11th first-place finish in team history.

Defenseman Nicklas Lidstrom won the Norris Trophy and was selected to the NHL's First All-Star Team. Lidstrom and center Sergei Fedorov skated in the NHL All-Star Game.

Left-winger Brendan Shanahan led the team with 31-45-76 totals, including a four-goal performance March 15 in a 5-2 win over Calgary. Fedorov recorded his 800th NHL point, joining Gordie Howe, Steve Yzerman and Alex Delvecchio as the only players to reach that number in a Detroit uniform. A 5-4 win over Buffalo was posted October 21 in Detroit's 5,000th NHL game and a 3-2 victory November 24 over Vancouver saw Detroit's Scotty Bowman become the first NHL coach to work 2,000 games behind the bench.

Los Angeles was the playoff opponent for the second straight year and Detroit opened with two straight home-ice victories, despite losing Shanahan (broken foot) and Yzerman (broken ankle) to fractures. The Kings took Game 3, then rallied for a stunning, 4-3 overtime win in Game 4, a contest the Wings led 3-0 with 6:07 left in regulation time.

Shaken, the Wings fell 3-2 in Game 5, their first loss in 22 games at the JLA. Los Angeles completed the comeback with a 3-2 OT decision in Game 6.

For the first time since 1993-94, Detroit was eliminated in the first round of the playoffs.

HOCKEYTOWN MOMENT
Yzerman joins the 1,600 club

MARK HICKS

It's an exclusive group and Steve Yzerman joined the club February 23 when he beat St. Louis goalie Brent Johnson - the grandson of Wings legend Sid Abel - for a goal which was his 1,600th NHL point.

By the conclusion of the 2000-01 season, only Wayne Gretzky (2,857), Gordie Howe (1,850), Marcel Dionne (1,771), Mark Messier (1,781) and Ron Francis (1,624) had accumulated more points in NHL history than the 1,614 produced by Yzerman.

Eighteen years in the league brought Yzerman accolades, fame and fortune, but ESPN analyst and former NHL goalie Darren Pang, Yzerman's close friend, reminded everyone the spoils of success were not what drove "Stevie Y."

"He doesn't play for the Porsche, he doesn't play for the big house," Pang said. "He plays because he wants to be a winner."

Wings of Legend

Nicklas Lidstrom

Each spring, the day after the NHL tabulated its awards ballots, Red Wings players would glance at the results with puzzled stares.

"We'd look at the Norris (Trophy) voting every year and we'd think, 'Why hasn't he won it?'" Detroit left-winger Brendan Shanahan said of teammate Nicklas Lidstrom. "We didn't know what else they were looking for. The guy does it all - plays the power play, kills penalties, is always out against the other team's best players and he puts up numbers.

"He's one of the most talented players I've ever seen."

After the 2000-01 season, such questions no longer required posing. Lidstrom was presented with the honor as the NHL's best defenseman. He'd finished as Norris Trophy runner-up the three previous seasons. Displaying an amazing ability to perform his defensive tasks within the framework of the rules, Lidstrom was also runner-up in the Lady Byng Trophy voting for three campaigns in a row commencing with 1998-99.

"Usually, when defensemen get penalties, it's because of their stick - they cross-check someone at the net, or get beat and give the guy a tug," said Detroit associate coach Dave Lewis, a former NHL defenseman. "Nick's such a good positional player, he doesn't have to rely on that."

Lidstrom won his second straight Norris in 2001-02, along with the Conn Smythe Trophy as Stanley Cup MVP.

A five-time NHL First All-Star Team selection, Lidstrom has also performed with remarkable resiliency, missing just 21 games in 12 seasons with the Wings.

"He makes your game a lot easier," longtime defense partner Larry Murphy said of Lidstrom. "He likes to play the control game and likes to make the play with the puck."

If anything held Lidstrom back, it was his quiet nature and quietly effective game. Spectacular end-to-end rushes and bone-jarring hits aren't his style, but neither are miscues.

"Nick doesn't seek out the spotlight and the spotlight usually doesn't shine on guys like him," Murphy

MARK HICKS

said. "Guys who can go end-to-end with the puck, like Brian Leetch (of the New York Rangers), or big hitters like Scott Stevens (of New Jersey), they get noticed.

"Nick isn't flashy, just effective. He always makes the right play. He makes himself available so he can receive the pass."

Lidstrom footage won't make for play-of-the-day highlights, but he will make the plays that pay off at the end of the day.

Night after night, year after year.

"He's so steady, so reliable," former Detroit defenseman Todd Gill said. "He reminds me of Ray Bourque in his heyday - not flashy, but a true superstar in every sense of the word."

Detroit captain Steve Yzerman, the greatest Red Wing of the current era, took the superlatives one step further.

"Lidstrom's the best player I've ever played with," Yzerman said.

- **BORN:**
  Vasteras, Sweden, April 28, 1970
- **ACQUIRED:**
  Selected 53rd overall by Detroit in the June 17, 1989 NHL entry draft
- **BEST SEASON WITH RED WINGS:**
  1999-2000 (20-53-73)
- **TOTALS WITH RED WINGS:**
  GP-853, G-145, A-481, PTS-626

- **HONORS:**
  Won Norris Trophy, 2000-01 and 2001-02; Won Conn Smythe Trophy, 2001-02; Named to NHL First All-Star team, 1997-98, 1998-99, 1999-2000, 2000-01 and 2001-02; Played in six NHL All-Star Games; Named to NHL All-Rookie Team, 1991-92; Played for Sweden, 1994 World Championship, 1996 World Cup, 1998 and 2002 Winter Olympics; All-time scoring leader among Detroit defensemen

MOTOWN Classic

Lidstrom wins Norris Trophy

MARK HICKS

Three times in a row, Nicklas Lidstrom came second when the Norris Trophy votes were counted, but a landslide victory was his following the 2000-01 season.

Lidstrom joined Paul Coffey and Red Kelly as the only Detroit defensemen to win the award as the NHL's best rearguard, also earning selection to the NHL's First All-Star Team while collecting a career-high 56 assists.

"The general consensus around the league was that it was his time," Detroit coach Scotty Bowman said of Lidstrom. "I think he's had his best year and this is a guy who's had some great years. He has all the attributes you need to win. Every aspect of his game is top-notch."

Some players might have griped about always being a bridesmaid. Lidstrom appreciated it. "It's an honor just to be a finalist," he said. "The guys who won the Norris the three years before me (Rob Blake, Al MacInnis, Chris Pronger) all had outstanding seasons and deserved it."

ASSEMBLY LINE

Dismayed by their first-round playoff exit, the Wings went on a summer spending spree which stocked their 2001-02 lineup with three of the most accomplished performers in the NHL. Six-time Vezina Trophy-winning goalie Dominik Hasek, also with two Hart Trophies on his resume, was acquired from Buffalo for Slava Kozlov and a 2002 first round draft pick. Left-winger Luc Robitaille, a five-time NHL First All-Star Team selection and a member of the NHL's 600-goal club, was signed as a free agent from Los Angeles.

Boyd Devereaux

MARK HICKS

Brett Hull, past winner of the Hart and Lady Byng Trophies and author of more than 600 NHL goals, including 87 in 1990-91, an NHL record for goals by a right-winger, was a free-agent addition from Dallas. Defenseman Fredrik Olausson was another free-agent acquisition. During the season, centers Boyd Devereaux and Jason Williams were free-agent additions, while the NHL entry draft supplied defenseman Maxim Kuznetsov. Yan Golubovsky was dealt to Florida to reacquire former Wings center Igor Larionov. Centers Stacy Roest and Darryl Laplante were lost to Minnesota in the NHL expansion draft.

Red Wings Facts

Detroit's All Time Record vs. Other Teams from the "Original Six"

	W	L	T
Boston	243	231	95
Chicago	329	249	84
Montreal	197	267	96
New York	255	209	103
Toronto	271	271	94

Short Passes

For the first time in club history, Detroit's 2000-01 lineup included two 40-year-old players - center Igor Larionov, who turned 40 on December 3 and defenseman Larry Murphy, who reached 40 on March 8.

inside

HOCKEYTOWN

THE OFFICIAL PUBLICATION OF THE DETROIT RED WINGS

October 200

$5

THE ALL-TIME RED WINGS TEAM: THIRD ERA (1976-Present)

CENTER — STEVE YZERMAN

Just 21 when he became the youngest captain in team history in 1986-87, "Stevie Y" has reigned as Detroit's ultimate leader ever since. His 39 goals and 87 points were Red Wings rookie marks in 1983-84 and his 65-90-155 totals in 1988-89 established club single-season standards in all three categories. He led the Wings to back-to-back Cups in 1996-97 and 1997-98, winning the Conn Smythe Trophy as playoff MVP the latter year. He also won the Selke Trophy as the NHL's top defensive forward in 1999-2000 and was winner of the Lester B. Pearson Trophy, which goes to the NHLPA's choice for NHL player of the year, in 1988-89.

LEFT WING — JOHN OGRODNICK

Armed with a powerful shot, Ogrodnick set a club record for his position when he rattled home 55 goals in 1984-85, a performance which earned him selection to the NHL's First All-Star Team. His 105 points that season were also a club mark for left-wingers. A sleeper in his draft year of 1979, Ogrodnick was the 66th player chosen, but blossomed to lead the Wings in goal scoring for six straight seasons from 1980-81 through 1985-86. He was club points leader in 1981-82 and 1984-85. Ogrodnick was selected to play in five NHL All-Star Games and represented Canada at the 1981 World Championships.

RIGHT WING — SERGEI FEDOROV

Fedorov boldly walked away from the Soviet national team at the 1990 Goodwill Games in Seattle and into the Wings lineup, quickly establishing credentials as an NHL superstar. He won the Hart Trophy as NHL MVP in 1993-94, finishing second in league scoring with 120 points and also winning the Pearson Award as the NHLPA's top player. Fedorov has excelled in the post-season, where he shares club marks for goals (10), assists (18) and points (24) in a Stanley Cup campaign. Fedorov's versatility has allowed him to twice win the Selke Award as the NHL's top defensive forward and to perform at center, defense and right wing during his Detroit days.

DEFENSEMAN — NICKLAS LIDSTROM

Lidstrom's outstanding play was recognized when he was awarded the Norris Trophy as the NHL's best defender in 2000-01. Three times, he'd been runner-up for the award. Playing solid defense within the framework of the rules, Lidstrom has also been a finalist for the Lady Byng Trophy as the NHL's most gentlemanly player on three occasions.

Lidstrom equaled Reed Larson's club record for rookie defensemen by registering 49 assists and 60 points in 1991-92 and was named to the NHL's All-Rookie Team. He led the team with 53 assists in 1999-2000 and became Detroit's career scoring leader among defensemen early in the 2001-02 season.

Four times, Lidstrom's been named to the NHL's First All-Star Team.

DEFENSEMAN — REED LARSON

The owner of a wicked slapshot and virtually every offensive record for Detroit rear-guards, Larson is the club's second all-time scoring leader at the position with 570 points. His 27 goals in 1980-81 remain a club record and Larson's 74 points in 1982-83 stood as the team standard for 11 seasons. He led the Wings in assists three times and the Minneapolis-born Larson was the first American NHLer to accumulate 500 NHL points. Larson won an NCAA title at the University of Minnesota in 1975-76, played in three NHL All-Star Games and was enshrined in the U.S. Hockey Hall of Fame in 1996.

GOALTENDER — CHRIS OSGOOD

The pressure was squarely on Osgood's shoulders when the defending Stanley Cup champion Wings traded Conn Smythe Trophy-winning goalie Mike Vernon to San Jose in the summer of 1997. Osgood responded by leading the team to the title once again. Osgood and Vernon combined to win the Jennings Trophy with the NHL's best goals-against average in 1995-96, a season in which Osgood led the NHL with 39 wins and posted two club-records — a 13-game winning streak and a 21-game unbeaten run.

Named to the NHL's Second All-Star Team in 1995-96, Osgood has appeared in three NHL All-Star Games and is one of the few NHL netminders to score a goal, tallying March 6, 1996 against Hartford.

KEN HOLLAND

When Ken Holland was blocking pucks in the youth leagues of Vernon, British Columbia, he dreamed the same dream as every Canadian kid. When he was pushing across miles of barren prairie highway between outposts like Prince Albert, Saskatchewan and Medicine Hat, Alberta, he dreamed the same dream of every hockey man.

Both of his dreams came true.

"I think back to being 17 or 18, playing Tier II junior in Vernon, B.C., wondering what I would be doing in a few years," Holland said. "And look at where I am today."

Now he serves as general manager of the Detroit Red Wings, overseeing the day-to-day operations of the No. 1 franchise in the National Hockey League. A positively-charged, tireless worker with a keen sense for the game and a wickedly dry sense of humor, Holland was named GM of the Wings in 1998, shortly after they'd won their first Stanley Cup in 42 seasons, more than a decade after he'd given up his job as a professional netminder to become the club's Western amateur scout.

"I remember the day I got hired, I was on a conference call with Jimmy Devellano and Neil Smith," Holland recalled, naming two other men who, like him, worked their way up from scouting positions to win Stanley Cups as a GM. "They told me to get my foot in the business, work hard, try and do the best job you can and you never know where it can take you.

"At the time, I can't say I was thinking that someday, I wanted to be an NHL GM. I just wanted to stay in the game.

"Today, to be an NHL GM of an Original Six team, – the Stanley Cup champions – is a truly like a dream come true."

Holland's first hockey dream, to perform in the NHL as a goalie, also came true, albeit briefly. He was an NHL netminder for four games - one with the Hartford Whalers and three with the Red Wings, who signed him as a free agent in 1983. "I had two three-week stints in the NHL and I've

STEVE KOVICH

worked those for a lot of material over the years," Holland joked, before getting serious. "I lived every kid's dream. It might have only been for six weeks, but I got there and they can't take that away from me."

Holland worked his way up to assistant GM of the Wings for three years prior to ascending to the GM's chair in 1997, where he's displayed a bold flair for making franchise-shaping moves. His acquisitions of goalie Dominik Hasek, defenseman Fredrik Olausson and wingers Brett Hull and Luc Robitaille in the summer of 2001 propelled the Red Wings back to Stanley Cup glory at the end of the 2001-02 season, allowing him to relive another dream.

"To have a chance to hold up the Stanley Cup after your team has won it is something I'll never forget," Holland said.

BACK in TIME

- **September 11, 2001**

The United States was attacked by terrorists organized by Osama bin Laden when highjacked commercial planes crashed into the World Trade Center towers in New York City and the Pentagon in Washington, D.C.

- **January 1, 2002**

Detroit's youngest mayor, Kwame Kilpatrick at age 31, took office and was officially sworn in on Friday, January 4 at the historic Fox Theatre.

- **January 22, 2002**

K Mart Corporation, with roots dating back to 1897, filled for Chapter 11 protection, making it the largest such filing by a retailer in U.S. history.

quick cuts

Most Goals
Brendan Shanahan: 38
Most Assists
Nicklas Lidstrom: 50
Most Points
Brendan Shanahan: 75
Most Penalty Minutes
Chris Chelios: 126
Most Wins, Goaltender
Dominik Hasek: 41
Lowest Goals-Against Average
Dominik Hasek: 2.17
Most Shutouts
Dominik Hasek: 5
NHL Award Winners
Chris Chelios - Bud Light Plus-Minus Award
& 1st Team All-Star
Nicklas Lidstrom - Norris Trophy
& 1st Team All-Star
Brendan Shanahan - 2nd Team All-Star

FINAL STANDINGS

Central Division	W	L	T	OTL	PTS	GF	GA
DETROIT	51	17	10	4	116	251	187
St. Louis	43	27	8	4	98	227	188
Chicago	41	27	13	1	96	216	207
Nashville	28	41	13	0	69	196	230
Columbus	22	47	8	5	57	164	255

Western Conference Winner - Detroit Red Wings

Playoff Results
Defeated the Vancouver Canucks in Series "E" 4-2
Defeated the St. Louis Blues in Series "K" 4-1
Defeated the Colorado Avalanche in Series "N" 4-3
Defeated the Carolina Hurricanes in Series "O" 4-1

Stanley Cup Champion
Detroit Red Wings

2001-02 Season in Review

STEVE KOVICH

In the spring of 2001, for the first time in seven years, the Stanley Cup had been decided without a single round being decided in Detroit's favor. You didn't need to be a member of the Red Wings organization to know that such failure wouldn't fly. Within days of their first-round upset at the hands of the Los Angeles Kings, the wheels of change were set in motion, with six-time Vezina Trophy-winning goalie Dominik Hasek arriving from Buffalo. Hasek would handle the stopping and free agents Luc Robitaille and Brett Hull were signed to beef up the club's goal-scoring potency. The Wings jumped from the gate like Secretariat in the Belmont, leaving all challengers behind. Rolling to a 28-12-6-3 start, they were the talk of the hockey world, winning the President's Trophy as NHL regular-season champions with 116 points.

As befitting a team of great legends, milestone performances abounded. Reigning Norris Trophy holder Nicklas Lidstrom garnered two assists Oct. 12 in a 4-2 win over Buffalo to surpass Reed Larson (570 points) as Detroit's all-time top-scoring defenseman. Brendan Shanahan beat Colorado's Patrick Roy March 23 to record his 500th NHL goal. He also garnered his 1,000th NHL point. Scotty Bowman coached his NHL-record 1,200th game and joined Jack Adams as the only men to post 400 wins as Wings coach. When Steve Yzerman set up Mathieu Dandenault's overtime winner Jan. 20 against Ottawa, it gave the Detroit captain 1,000 NHL assists. Robitaille joined Yzerman and Hull in the NHL's exclusive 600-goal club Nov. 9 at Anaheim, but didn't stop there. Jan. 18 against Washington, Robitaille scored his 612th career goal, to surpass Brett's dad Bobby Hull as the all-time leading goal scorer among left wingers in NHL history. Lidstrom won the Norris Trophy as the NHL's top defenseman, but for all the history they made, only one bauble interested this group – Lord Stanley's mug. The Cup would make a comeback to Detroit, but not without first providing a couple of frightening moments. The Wings dropped their first two games of their first-round series on home ice against Vancouver, then rallied to win the set in six. St. Louis fell easily in five games in the second round, leaving Colorado the last team in the way of a return trip to the Stanley Cup Finals.

When the Avalanche grabbed a 3-2 series lead, things looked grim. But Hasek delivered back-to-back shutouts, the second coming in a memorable 7-0 Game 7 rout in which the Wings chased long-time nemesis Roy to the bench. The upstart Carolina Hurricanes upset the applecart with a Game 1 OT win at the JLA, but the Wings persevered once more and ultimately prevailed in a five-game final series. This golden team had provided Hockeytown another silver lining.

HOCKEYTOWN MOMENT
Wings' Cup Triumph a Perfect 10

Lord Stanley's mug came back to Hockeytown for the 10th time, but it didn't come easily, making its arrival all the more sweeter. Detroit trailed in three of its four playoff rounds and faced elimination twice, but never surrendered. That perseverance paid off when Brendan Shanahan scored twice in the Cup-clinching 3-1 win over the Carolina Hurricanes. Nicklas Lidstrom won the Conn Smythe Trophy as playoff MVP, but any number of players could have taken the honor. There was captain Steve Yzerman, gamely playing on a knee in dire need of surgical repair; Dominik Hasek, posting a Stanley Cup-record six shutouts; Brett Hull, firing a team-leading 10 goals; Sergei Fedorov, who made the puck his own personal plaything; and Igor Larionov, 41, who became the oldest player to score in a Cup final game, netting the winner in triple overtime in Game 3 against Carolina. That so many contributed was the perfect finish for a club which was a team in every sense of the word.

Nicklas Lidstrom

STEVE KOVICH

Dominik Hasek

From the moment he first donned a Red Wings jersey, Dominik Hasek set the agenda, the reason why his desire led him to Hockeytown.

"In Buffalo, I felt there was nothing more I could do," Hasek said at the press conference to announce his acquisition from the Sabres. "I just want to win the Cup."

He'd already won everything else. Two Hart Trophies as the NHL's most valuable player. Six Vezina Trophies as the league's top netminder. An Olympic gold medal with the Czech Republic in 1998.

"He's put our little country on the map. He is our Michael Jordan, our Muhammad Ali," Wings teammate and countryman Jiri Fischer said, explaining the aura of Hasek in his homeland.

Hasek's aura among NHL shooters required no explanation. "We won't take shots against him that we'll take against every other goalie in the league," Carolina Hurricanes coach Paul Maurice said.

With his unique puckstopping ability - part butterfly, part Baryshnikov, part Gumby - watching Hasek stop the puck is like an evening at the improv. Watching him perform in practice is to understand why he is simply known as "The Dominator."

"Dominik Hasek's work habits are legendary," Detroit goaltending consultant Jim Bedard said.

"He's very focused," added Wings coach Scotty Bowman. "He has got his own structured workout."

Hasek will holler at players if he thinks they are not trying hard enough to beat him. "I went a week into training camp before I scored on him," Detroit winger Tomas Holmstrom complained. Hasek's zero tolerance when it comes to surrendering goals only helped make the Wings a better team.

Especially when it mattered most.

Down 2-0 to Vancouver in the first round of the playoffs, Hasek blocked 23 shots for a 3-1 verdict in Game 3 at GM Place. Trailing 3-2 to Colorado in the Western Conference final, Hasek posted successive shutouts to send the Avalanche to the sidelines. Hasek garnered six shutouts during the playoffs, a new Stanley Cup record. His 41-regular-season wins were also a personal best,

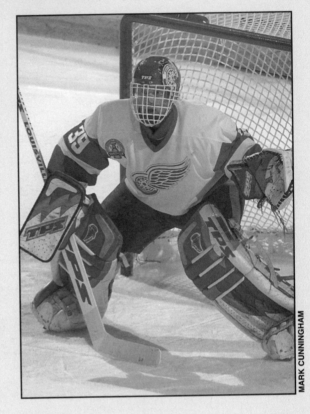

MARK CUNNINGHAM

but it was the honor he received at season's end which provided Hasek the most satisfaction.

The opportunity to lift the Stanley Cup.

"This was my dream," he said. "And now it is a dream come true."

Cup in hand and career complete, Hasek decided that his one season in Detroit would be his last. On June 25, 2002, Hasek retired from the NHL.

"I am not truly American like my teammates Chris Chelios and Brett Hull, but I love this city and I am and I will be a Red Wing forever."

- **BORN:**
  Pardubice, Czechoslovakia,
  Jan. 29, 1965
- **ACQUIRED:**
  July 1, 2001 trade with Buffalo
- **BEST SEASON WITH RED WINGS:**
  2001-02 (65-140-5-2.17)
- **TOTALS WITH RED WINGS:**
  GP: 65 GA: 140 SO: 5 GAA: 2.17

- **HONORS:**
  Posted a Stanley Cup-record record six shutouts, 2001-02; Led team in wins, shutouts and goals-against average, 2001-02; Played in NHL All-Star Game, 2001-02

MOTOWN Classic

Scotty calls it a day

The Stanley Cup captured, Detroit coach Scotty Bowman donned his skates to tour Lord Stanley's mug around the Joe Louis Arena ice surface.

Then he hung them up for good.

"I just coached my last game," Bowman told Wings GM Ken Holland moments after the Cup was acquired.

"I made my mind up in February," Bowman, 68, said later. "I know it's time now."

Bowman finished his career with an NHL-record 1,244 regular-season wins. His playoff (227) and Cup final (36) wins totals are also league marks. The Cup triumph, Bowman's third with Detroit, was his record ninth as a coach, shattering the mark he shared with his mentor, long-time Montreal coach Toe Blake. Blake, who imparted his hockey wisdom upon a young Bowman when the latter coached Montreal's junior squad in the early 1960s, retired in 1968 after winning his eighth Cup at the expense of the St. Louis Blues and their rookie coach Bowman.

ASSEMBLY LINE

Brett Hull

Three future Hall of Famers joined the fold when goalie Dominik Hasek was added from Buffalo and right-winger Brett Hull and left-winger Luc Robitaille were signed as free agents. Defenseman Fredrik Olausson was another free-agent addition, as were center Sean Avery and right-winger Ladislav Kohn. Yuri Butsayev and a 2002 third-round draft pick were dealt to Atlanta for defenseman Jiri Slegr. Center Pavel Datsyuk was suppled by the NHL entry draft. Goalie Chris Osgood was lost to the New York Islanders in the NHL waiver draft, right-winger Martin Lapointe was signed as a free agent by Boston and center/winger Brent Gilchrist was lost on waivers to Dallas.

Red Wings Facts

Most Shutouts, One Playoff Year

Dominik Hasek	6	2001-02
Terry Sawchuk	4	1951-52
Harry Lumley	3	1949-50

*Ten others tied with two apiece

Short Passes

Detroit's Steve Yzerman and Brendan Shanahan also helped Canada to the gold medal at the 2002 Winter Olympics, joining Ken Morrow (USA, New York Islanders – 1980) as the only players to win a Stanley Cup and an Olympic gold medal in the same year.

WHAT IS HOCKEYTOWN?

Don't believe that Detroit is Hockeytown?

Then take a look around the next time you're in Joe Louis Arena.

Where else could you find, amidst the sea of red-and-white, a guy wearing a Perry Miller Red Wings jersey, sitting next to a woman in a Sergei Fedorov sweater, just a few rows up from the fellow in the Dale Krentz jersey?

Call it a passion, an unwavering love bordering on obsession, but such a scene isn't likely to be witnessed in many other NHL arenas.

Certainly, you'll find this level of involvement in traditional centers like Toronto and Montreal, but those people were weaned on hockey. It's their national game. What makes Detroiters unique is that they reside in an American city, yet embrace Canada's game as if it were their own child.

"Hockey gets in your blood, how can you not love it?" said Colleen Howe, who admits she never watched a game before meeting her future husband, Wings legend Gordie Howe.

The proximity to Canada, with Windsor, Ontario across the Detroit River, is certainly a factor in this love affair with pucks and skates. Perhaps when Detroit played its first NHL season in 1926-27 with Windsor's Border Cities Arena as home, Detroit fans got hooked on hockey.

"Detroit was a hockey town when I played," said Carl Liscombe, a Wing from 1937-46.

It's certainly Hockeytown today.

"There's no greater hockey-crazed area than the Detroit area," said Tom Anastos, president of the Central Collegiate Hockey Association. "In Detroit, the community supports so many different levels of hockey, from the NHL right on down to the midget programs and they all continue to grow every year."

Approximately 40 per cent of senior hockey players in the United States are registered in Michigan.

"After we won the Stanley Cup (in 1997), you couldn't go anywhere in the state and not be recognized," former Wings goalie Kevin Hodson said.

Michigan is a hotbed for NHL scouts. Besides the Red Wings, these bird dogs can also get an eyeful of minor pro, junior, college and high school hockey, all within a short drive of Joe Louis Arena.

"I think it's the best hockey area in North America," said NHLPA executive director Bob Goodenow, a native of Detroit.

Don Cherry, star of Hockey Night In Canada's Coach's Corner, feels Detroit's hockey worship is on par with any NHL city.

"The reason I call Detroit, 'Hockey City, U.S.A.,' is because even when the Wings were not the top dog in the NHL, the community still supported them," Cherry said.

When the Wings ended a 42-year title drought by capturing the Stanley Cup in 1996-97, NHL commissioner Gary Bettman handed the storied mug to Detroit captain Steve Yzerman, uttering the words, "Everyone knows Detroit is truly Hockeytown."

Yzerman, a Wing since 1983, couldn't agree more.

"I don't know who came up with the term, 'Hockeytown,'" Yzerman said, "but to me, Detroit is Hockeytown.

"Period."

SOURCES

Alberta On Ice, by Gary Zeman

Crunch, by Kevin Allen

Detroit Red Wings Media Guide

Gordie Howe®, No. 9, by Jim Vipond

Great Book Of Hockey, by Stan and Shirley Fischler

Heroes Of Hockeytown From A–Z, by Paul Harris

Hockey All-Stars, by Chris McDonell

Hockey Hall Of Fame Legends, by Michael McKinley

Hockey Hall Of Fame Registry, edited by Dan Diamond

Hockey's Greatest Stars, by Chris McDonell

Hockey's 100, by Stan Fischler

Inside Hockey **Magazine**

Inside Hockeytown **Magazine**

It's Easy: All You Have To Do Is Win, by Trent Frayne

NHL Official Guide and Record Book, edited by Dan Diamond

NHL 75th Anniversary Commemorative Book, edited by Dan Diamond

NHL Stanley Cup Centennial Book, edited by Dan Diamond

NHL: The World Of Professional Hockey, by Jay Greenberg, Frank Orr and Gary Ronberg

100 Greatest Moments In Hockey, by Brian Kendall

Personal archives of Bob Duff

The Complete Encyclopedia Of Hockey, edited by Zander Hollander

The Detroit *News*

The Detroit *Free Press*

The Red Wings Book, by Andrew Podnieks

The Hockey Encyclopedia (1983), by Stan and Shirley Fischler

The Hockey Encyclopedia (1974), by Gary Ronberg

The *Hockey News*

The *Hockey News:* **A Century Of Hockey**, edited by Steve Dryden

The Mad Men Of Hockey, by Trent Frayne

The Patricks: Hockey's Royal Family, by Eric Whitehead

The Windsor *Star*

Total Hockey, edited by Dan Diamond

Years Of Glory, The Six-Team Era, edited by Dan Diamond

Detroit
Red Wings

YEARS

DETROIT RED WINGS
ALL-TIME GOALTENDING RECORDS

PLAYER	YRS	GP	WON	LOST	TIED	GA	SO	AVG
Terry Sawchuk	14	734	352	244	130	1782	85	2.46
Chris Osgood	8	389	221	110	46	900	30	2.40
Harry Lumley	7	324	163	107	54	885	26	2.73
Roger Crozier	7	310	130	119	43	853	20	2.94
Tim Cheveldae	6	264	128	93	30	851	9	3.39
Greg Stefan	9	299	115	127	30	1068	5	3.92
Jim Rutherford	10	314	97	165	43	1112	10	3.68
Roy Edwards	6	221	95	74	34	601	14	2.94
Norm Smith	7	178	76	68	34	417	17	2.34
Glenn Hall	4	148	74	45	29	317	17	2.14
John Mowers	4	152	65	61	26	399	13	2.63
Glen Hanlon	5	186	65	71	26	569	7	3.47
Mike Vernon	3	95	53	24	14	225	4	2.40
Dominik Hasek	1	65	41	15	8	140	5	2.17
John Ross Roach	3	89	41	37	11	201	11	2.26
MANNY LEGACE	**3**	**63**	**38**	**11**	**7**	**129**	**3**	**2.22**
Clarence Dolson	3	93	35	41	17	192	17	2.06
Hank Bassen	6	99	34	39	19	274	3	2.99
Cecil Thompson	2	85	32	41	12	225	7	2.65
Harry Holmes	2	85	30	46	9	179	17	2.11
Rogie Vachon	2	109	30	57	19	398	4	3.74
Corrado Micalef	5	113	26	59	15	409	2	4.23
Connie Dion	2	38	23	11	4	119	1	3.13
Eddie Giacomin	3	71	23	37	7	234	6	3.47
Gilles Gilbert	3	95	21	48	16	365	0	4.18
Alex Connell	1	48	18	20	10	108	6	2.25
Al Smith	1	43	18	20	4	135	4	3.24
Doug Grant	3	46	17	22	2	182	1	4.33
Vince Riendeau	3	32	17	8	2	89	0	3.28
Wilf Cude	1	29	15	6	8	47	4	1.62
Bill Beveridge	1	39	14	20	5	109	2	2.79
Ken Wregget	1	29	14	10	2	70	0	2.66
Kevin Hodson	4	35	13	7	4	64	4	2.37
Joe Daley	1	29	11	10	5	85	0	3.15
Bob Sauve	1	41	11	25	4	165	0	4.19
Norm Maracle	2	20	10	7	2	37	0	2.22
Ed Mio	3	49	10	20	5	205	1	5.00

Ron Low	1	32	9	12	9	102	1	3.37
Denis DeJordy	2	25	8	12	3	87	1	3.86
George Gardner	3	24	7	7	3	69	0	3.59
Jim Franks	2	18	7	8	3	72	1	4.00
Andy Brown	2	17	6	6	3	57	0	3.80
Mark Laforest	2	33	6	22	0	126	1	4.71
Larry Lozinski	1	30	6	11	7	105	0	4.32
Sam St. Laurent	4	30	5	11	4	79	0	3.76
Dennis Riggin	2	18	5	9	2	54	1	3.27
Bill McKenzie	2	26	5	13	6	101	1	4.16
Bob Essensa	1	13	4	7	2	34	1	2.62
Bill Ranford	1	4	3	0	1	8	0	1.97
Terry Richardson	4	19	3	10	0	75	0	5.31
Don McLeod	1	14	3	7	0	60	0	5.15
Greg Millen	1	10	3	2	3	22	0	2.71
Dave Gatherum	1	3	2	1	0	3	1	1.00
Bob Perreault	1	3	2	1	0	9	1	3.00
Harvey Teno	1	5	2	3	0	15	0	3.00
Herb Stuart	1	3	1	2	0	5	0	1.60
Gerry Gray	1	7	1	4	1	30	0	4.73
Peter Ing	1	3	1	2	0	15	0	5.29
Abbie Cox	1	1	0	0	1	4	0	4.00
Joe Turner	1	1	0	0	1	3	0	3.00
Ralph Almas	2	2	0	1	1	8	0	4.00
Ken Holland	1	3	0	1	1	11	0	4.11
Claude Legris	2	4	0	1	1	4	0	2.66
Pete McDuffe	1	4	0	3	1	22	0	5.50
Allan Bester	2	4	0	3	0	15	0	4.31
Darren Eliot	1	3	0	0	1	9	0	5.57
Alain Chevrier	1	3	0	3	0	11	0	6.11
Carl Wetzel	1	2	0	1	0	4	0	8.00
Claude Bourque	1	1	0	1	0	3	0	3.00
Alfie Moore	1	1	0	1	0	3	0	3.00
Pat Rupp	1	1	0	1	0	4	0	4.00
Harrison Gray	1	1	0	1	0	5	0	7.50
Al Jensen	1	1	0	1	0	7	0	7.00
Gillies Boisvert	1	3	0	3	0	9	0	3.00
Dave Gagnon	1	2	0	1	0	6	0	10.29
Scott King	2	2	0	0	0	3	0	2.95
Chris Pusey	1	1	0	0	0	3	0	4.50
Tom McGrattan	1	1	0	0	0	1	0	7.50
Lefty Wilson	1	1	0	0	0	0	0	0.00

ACTIVE PLAYERS IN BOLD CAPITALS

DETROIT RED WINGS CAREER SCORING LEADERS
(Minimum 100 points)

RANK	PLAYER	YEARS	GP	G	A	PTS
1.	Gordie Howe	25	1687	786	1023	1809
2.	**STEVE YZERMAN**	**19**	**1362**	**658**	**1004**	**1662**
3.	Alex Delvecchio	24	1549	456	825	1281
4.	**SERGEI FEDOROV**	**12**	**828**	**364**	**507**	**871**
5.	Norm Ullman	13	875	324	434	758
6.	Ted Lindsay	14	862	335	393	728
7.	**NICKLAS LIDSTROM**	**11**	**853**	**145**	**481**	**626**
8.	Reed Larson	10	708	188	382	570
9.	John Ogrodnick	9	558	265	281	546
10.	Red Kelly	13	846	162	310	472
11.	Gerard Gallant	9	563	207	260	467
	Nick Libett	12	861	217	250	467
13.	Sid Abel	12	571	184	279	463
14.	Syd Howe	12	513	188	247	435
15.	**BRENDAN SHANAHAN**	**6**	**474**	**214**	**217**	**431**
16.	Vyacheslav Kozlov	10	607	202	213	415
17.	Marcel Dionne	4	309	139	227	366
18.	Shawn Burr	11	659	148	214	362
19.	**IGOR LARIONOV**	**7**	**465**	**79**	**275**	**354**
20.	Dale McCourt	5	341	134	203	337
21.	Ebbie Goodfellow	14	557	134	190	324
22.	Mickey Redmond	6	317	177	133	310
23.	Herbie Lewis	11	483	148	161	309
24.	Gary Bergman	11	706	60	243	303
25.	Marcel Pronovost	15	983	80	217	297
26.	Mud Bruneteau	11	411	139	138	277
27.	Carl Liscombe	9	373	137	140	277
28.	Larry Aurie	12	489	147	129	276
29.	Steve Chiasson	8	471	67	200	267
30.	Ray Sheppard	5	274	152	113	265
31.	Bob Probert	9	474	114	145	259
32.	Walt McKechnie	5	321	89	167	256
33.	Marty Pavelich	10	634	93	159	252
34.	Vaclav Nedomansky	5	364	108	139	247
35.	**DARREN McCARTY**	**9**	**527**	**100**	**140**	**240**
	Dino Ciccarelli	4	254	107	133	240
37.	Paul Coffey	4	231	46	193	239
38.	Joe Carveth	8	325	104	132	236
39.	Martin Lapointe	10	552	108	122	230
	Keith Primeau	6	363	97	133	230
41.	Petr Klima	6	306	130	93	223
42.	Ron Duguay	3	227	90	127	217
43.	Parker MacDonald	7	361	94	122	216
44.	Floyd Smith	6	347	93	122	215
	Earl (Dutch) Reibel	5	306	74	141	215
46.	Metro Prystai	8	431	91	123	214
47.	Willie Huber	5	372	68	140	208
48.	Jimmy Carson	4	240	100	102	202
49.	Red Berenson	5	283	73	128	201
50.	Dave Barr	5	293	82	118	200

RANK	PLAYER	YEARS	GP	G	A	PTS
51.	Adam Oates	4	246	54	145	199
52.	Kelly Kisio	4	236	68	129	197
53.	Frank Mahovlich	4	198	108	88	196
54.	Paul Woods	7	501	72	124	196
55.	John Sorrell	8	347	96	86	182
56.	Danny Gare	5	306	86	95	181
57.	Johnny Wilson	8	379	79	100	179
58.	Vladimir Konstantinov	6	446	47	128	175
59.	Larry Murphy	5	312	35	136	171
	Doug Brown	7	427	74	97	171
61.	Don Grosso	7	235	71	99	170
	Paul Ysebaert	3	210	84	86	170
63.	**TOMAS HOLMSTROM**	**6**	**400**	**61**	**105**	**166**
64.	Ivan Boldirev	3	183	67	95	162
65.	Mike Foligno	3	186	77	83	160
66.	**KRIS DRAPER**	**9**	**555**	**67**	**91**	**158**
67.	Marty Barry	4	192	60	94	154
68.	Garry Unger	4	216	84	68	152
69.	Dean Prentice	4	230	60	89	149
70.	Paul Henderson	6	269	67	79	146
71.	Bill Hogaboam	6	221	61	84	145
72.	Jim McFadden	4	253	64	78	142
73.	Dennis Polonich	8	390	59	82	141
74.	Guy Charron	5	265	61	78	139
75.	Dan Maloney	3	177	56	81	137
76.	Vic Stasiuk	8	330	52	84	136
77.	Errol Thompson	4	200	76	58	134
	Eddie Wares	6	216	50	84	134
79.	Joe Kocur	10	535	66	66	132
	Lee Norwood	5	259	36	96	132
81.	Bill Collins	4	239	54	77	131
82.	Bill Quackenbush	7	313	40	89	129
	Greg Smith	5	352	24	105	129
84.	John Chabot	4	226	29	99	128
85.	Danny Grant	4	174	64	62	126
86.	Bill Lochead	5	296	65	60	125
87.	Yves Racine	4	231	22	102	124
88.	Glen Skov	6	301	62	61	123
	Andre St. Laurent	3	172	50	73	123
90.	Dennis Hextall	4	193	39	82	121
91.	Tim Ecclestone	4	191	40	80	120
92.	**MATHIEU DANDENAULT**	**7**	**477**	**41**	**77**	**118**
93.	Carson Cooper	5	222	68	48	116
94.	Pete Stemkowski	4	170	51	63	114
95.	George Hay	6	204	60	52	112
	Bill Gadsby	5	323	18	94	112
97.	Michel Bergeron	4	174	64	46	110
	Dwight Foster	4	215	48	62	110
	Mark Osborne	2	160	45	65	110
100.	Jack Stewart	10	503	30	79	109
101.	Gerry Couture	7	266	61	46	107
102.	Dan Labraaten	3	198	52	54	106
103.	Mike Blaisdell	3	192	44	61	105
104.	Doug Barkley	4	247	24	80	104
105.	**KIRK MALTBY**	**7**	**392**	**53**	**50**	**103**
	Bob Goldham	6	406	11	92	103
	Darren Veitch	3	153	20	83	103
108.	Brad Park	2	147	18	83	101
	Adam Brown	5	148	58	43	101
110.	Tony Leswick	5	302	41	59	100
	Warren Godfrey	12	528	23	77	100

ACTIVE PLAYERS IN BOLD CAPITALS

DETROIT RED WINGS ALL-TIME SEASON RECORDS

Season	GP	W	L	T	PTS	GF	GA	Position	Coach
1926-27	44	12	28	4	28	76	105	5th✗	Art Duncan/ Duke Keats*
1927-28	44	19	19	6	44	88	79	4th✗	Jack Adams
1928-29	44	19	16	9	47	72	63	3rd	Adams
1929-30	44	14	24	6	34	117	133	4th✗	Adams
1930-31	44	16	21	7	39	102	105	4th✗	Adams
1931-32	48	18	20	10	46	95	108	3rd	Adams
1932-33	48	25	15	8	58	111	93	2nd	Adams
1933-34	48	24	14	10	58	113	98	1st	Adams
1934-35	48	19	22	7	45	127	114	4th✗	Adams
1935-36	48	24	16	8	56	124	103	1st-**SC**	Adams
1936-37	48	25	14	9	59	128	102	1st-**SC**	Adams
1937-38	48	12	25	11	35	99	133	4th✗	Adams
1938-39	48	18	24	6	42	107	128	5th	Adams
1939-40	48	16	26	6	38	90	126	5th	Adams
1940-41	48	21	16	11	53	112	102	3rd	Adams
1941-42	48	19	25	4	42	140	147	5th	Adams
1942-43	50	25	14	11	61	169	124	1st-**SC**	Adams
1943-44	50	26	18	6	58	214	177	2nd	Adams
1944-45	50	31	14	5	67	218	161	2nd	Adams
1945-46	50	20	20	10	50	146	159	4th	Adams
1946-47	60	22	27	11	55	190	193	4th	Adams
1947-48	60	30	18	12	72	187	148	2nd	Tommy Ivan
1948-49	60	34	19	7	75	195	145	1st	Ivan
1949-50	70	37	19	14	88	229	164	1st-**SC**	Ivan
1950-51	70	44	13	13	101	236	139	1st	Ivan
1951-52	70	44	14	12	100	215	133	1st-**SC**	Ivan
1952-53	70	36	16	18	90	222	133	1st	Ivan
1953-54	70	37	19	14	88	191	132	1st-**SC**	Ivan
1954-55	70	42	17	11	95	204	134	1st-**SC**	Jimmy Skinner
1955-56	70	30	24	16	76	183	148	2nd	Skinner
1956-57	70	38	20	12	88	198	157	1st	Skinner
1957-58	70	29	29	12	70	176	207	3rd	Skinner/ Sid Abel
1958-59	70	25	37	8	58	167	218	6th✗	Abel
1959-60	70	26	29	15	67	186	197	4th	Abel
1960-61	70	25	29	16	66	195	215	4th	Abel
1961-62	70	23	33	14	60	184	219	5th✗	Abel
1962-63	70	32	25	13	77	200	194	4th	Abel
1963-64	70	30	29	11	71	191	204	4th	Abel
1964-65	70	40	23	7	87	224	175	1st	Abel
1965-66	70	31	27	12	74	221	194	4th	Abel
1966-67	70	27	39	4	58	212	241	5th✗	Abel

Season	GP	W	L	T	Pts	GF	GA	Finish	Coach
1967-68	74	27	35	12	66	245	257	6th✗	Abel
1968-69	76	33	31	12	78	239	221	5th✗	Bill Gadsby
1969-70	76	40	21	15	95	246	199	3rd	Gadsby/ Abel
1970-71	78	22	45	11	55	209	308	7th✗	Ned Harkness/ Doug Barkley
1971-72	78	33	35	10	76	261	262	5th✗	Barkley/ Johnny Wilson
1972-73	78	37	29	12	86	265	243	5th✗	Wilson
1973-74	78	29	39	10	68	255	319	6th✗	Ted Garvin/ Alex Delvecchio
1974-75	80	23	45	12	58	259	335	4th✗	Delvecchio
1975-76	80	26	44	10	62	226	300	4th✗	Barkley/ Delvecchio/ Billy Dea*
1976-77	80	16	55	9	41	183	309	5th✗	Dea*/ Larry Wilson
1977-78	80	32	34	14	78	252	266	2nd	Bobby Kromm
1978-79	80	23	41	16	62	252	295	5th✗	Kromm
1979-80	80	26	43	11	63	268	306	5th✗	Kromm/ Marcel Pronovost*
1980-81	80	19	43	18	56	252	339	5th✗	Ted Lindsay/ Wayne Maxner
1981-82	80	21	47	12	54	270	351	6th✗	Maxner/ Dea
1982-83	80	21	44	15	57	263	344	5th✗	Nick Polano
1983-84	80	31	42	7	69	298	323	3rd	Polano
1984-85	80	27	41	12	66	313	357	3rd	Polano
1985-86	80	17	57	6	40	266	415	5th✗	Harry Neale/ Brad Park
1986-87	80	34	36	10	78	260	274	2nd	Jacques Demers
1987-88	80	41	28	11	93	322	269	1st	Demers
1988-89	80	34	34	12	80	313	316	1st	Demers
1989-90	80	28	38	14	70	288	323	5th✗	Demers
1990-91	80	34	38	8	76	273	298	3rd	Bryan Murray
1991-92	80	43	25	12	98	320	256	1st	Murray
1992-93	84	47	28	9	103	369	280	2nd	Murray
1993-94	84	46	30	8	100	356	275	1st	Scotty Bowman
1995	48	33	11	4	70	180	117	1st	Bowman
1995-96	82	62	13	7	131	325	181	1st	Bowman
1996-97	82	38	26	18	94	253	197	3rd-SC	Bowman
1997-98	82	44	23	15	103	250	196	3rd-SC	Bowman
1998-99	82	43	32	7	93	245	202	3rd	Bowman+
1999-00	82	48	#24	10	108	278	210	4th	Bowman
2000-01	82	49	●24	9	111	253	202	2nd	Bowman
2001-02	82	51	●21	10	116	251	187	1st-SC	Bowman
TOTALS	5156	2263	2099	794	5330	15922	15582		

✗-Out of playoffs

\# - A loss in overtime was counted as a regulation tie and a loss but given a point. (2 RT)

● - A loss in overtime is now counted as an overtime loss, not a loss and given a point. (4 OTL)

SC- Won Stanley Cup

*-Interim coach

+-Scotty Bowman missed first five games of regular season.

1st-20   2nd-9   3rd-9   4th-14   5th-16   6th-4   7th-1

DETROIT RED WINGS ALL-TIME SEASON LEADERS

Season	GOALS Player	Total	ASSISTS Player	Total	POINTS Player	G	A	TP	PENALTIES Player	TPM
1926-27	J. Sheppard	13	J. Sheppard	8	J. Sheppard	13	8	21	J. Sheppard	60
1927-28	Hay	22	Hay	13	Hay	22	13	35	Traub	78
1928-29	Cooper	18	Cooper	9	Cooper	18	9	27	Connors	68
1929-30	H. Lewis	20	Cooper	18	Cooper	18	18	36	Rockburn	97
1930-31	Goodfellow	25	Goodfellow	23	Goodfellow	25	23	48	Rockburn	118*
1931-32	Goodfellow	14	Goodfellow	16	Goodfellow	14	16	30	Noble	72
1932-33	H. Lewis	20	H. Lewis	14	H. Lewis	20	14	34	Evans	74
1933-34	Sorrell	21	Aurie	19	Aurie	16	19	35	Emms	51
1934-35	S. Howe	22	Aurie	29	S. Howe	22	25	47	Goodfellow	44
1935-36	Barry	21	H. Lewis	23	Barry	21	19	40	Goodfellow	69
1936-37	Aurie	23*	Barry	27	Barry	17	27	44	Goodfellow	43
1937-38	Liscombe	14	Barry	20	H. Lewis	13	18	31	Barry	34
1938-39	S. Howe	16	Barry	28	Barry	13	28	41	C. Conacher	39
1939-40	S. Howe	14	S. Howe	23	S. Howe	14	23	37	Orlando	54
1940-41	S. Howe	20	S. Howe	24	S. Howe	20	24	44	Orlando	99*
1941-42	Grosso	23	S. Abel	31	Grosso	23	30	53	Orlando	111*
1942-43	Bruneteau	23	S. Howe	35	S. Howe	20	35	55	Orlando	99*
1943-44	Liscombe	36	Liscombe	37	Liscombe	36	37	73	Jackson	76
1944-45	Carveth	26	S. Howe	36	Carveth	26	28	54	Jackson	45
1945-46	A. Brown	20	Carveth / Armstrong	18 / 18	Carveth	17	18	35	J. Stewart	73*
1946-47	R. Conacher	30	B. Taylor	46*	B. Taylor	17	46	63	J. Stewart	83
1947-48	Lindsay	33*	S. Abel	30	Lindsay	33	19	52	Lindsay	95
1948-49	S. Abel	28*	Lindsay	28	S. Abel / Lindsay	28 / 26	26 / 28	54 / 54	Lindsay	97
1949-50	G. Howe	35	Lindsay	55*	Lindsay	23	55	78*	Lindsay	141
1950-51	G. Howe	43*	G. Howe	43*	G. Howe	43	43	86*	Lindsay	110
1951-52	G. Howe	47*	G. Howe/ Lindsay	39*	G. Howe	47	39	86*	Lindsay	123
1952-53	G. Howe	49*	G. Howe	46*	G. Howe	49	46	95*	Lindsay	111
1953-54	G. Howe	33	G. Howe	48*	G. Howe	33	48	81*	Lindsay	112
1954-55	G. Howe	29	Reibel	41	Reibel	25	41	66	Leswick	137
1955-56	G. Howe	38	G. Howe	41	G. Howe	38	41	79	Lindsay	161
1956-57	G. Howe	44*	Lindsay	55*	G. Howe	44	45	89*	Lindsay / Godfrey	103 / 103
1957-58	G. Howe	33	G. Howe	44	G. Howe	33	44	77	F. Kennedy	135
1958-59	G. Howe	32	G. Howe	46	G. Howe	32	46	78	Goegan	111
1959-60	G. Howe	28	G. Howe	45	G. Howe	28	45	73	Morrison	62

Season	GOALS Player	Total	ASSISTS Player	Total	POINTS Player	G	A	TP	PENALTIES Player	TPM
1959-60	G. Howe	28	G. Howe	45	G. Howe	28	45	73	Morrison	62
1960-61	Ullman	28	G. Howe	49	G. Howe	23	49	72	H. Young	108
1961-62	G. Howe	33	G. Howe	44	G. Howe	33	44	77	Gadsby	88
1962-63	G. Howe	38*	G. Howe	48	G. Howe	38	48	86*	H. Young	273*
1963-64	G. Howe	26	G. Howe	47	G. Howe	26	47	73	Barkley	115
1964-65	Ullman	42	G. Howe	47	Ullman	42	41	83	Lindsay	173
1965-66	Ullman	31	G. Howe	46	G. Howe	29	46	75	B. Watson	133
	Delvecchio	31								
1966-67	MacGregor	28	Ullman	44	Ullman	26	44	70	G. Bergman	129
1967-68	G. Howe	39	Delvecchio	48	G. Howe	39	43	82	K. Douglas	126
1968-69	F. Mahovlich	49	G. Howe	59	G. Howe	44	59	103	Baun	121
1969-70	Unger	42	Delvecchio	47	G. Howe	31	40	71	G. Bergman	122
1970-71	Webster	30	Webster	37	Webster	30	37	67	G. Bergman	149
1971-72	Redmond	42	Dionne	49	Dionne	28	49	77	G. Bergman	138
1972-73	Redmond	52	Delvecchio	53	Redmond	52	41	93	Johnston	169
1973-74	Redmond	51	Dionne	54	Dionne	24	53	78	Johnston	139
1974-75	Grant	50	Dionne	74	Dionne	47	74	121	B. Watson	238
1975-76	Bergeron	32	McKechnie	56	McKechnie	26	56	82	B. Watson	322
1976-77	McKechnie	25	McKechnie	34	McKechnie	24	34	59	Polonich	274
1977-78	McCourt	33	Larson	41	McCourt	33	39	72	Polonich	254
1978-79	Nedomansky	38	Larson	49	Nedomansky	38	35	73	Polonich	208
1979-80	Foligno	36	McCourt	51	McCourt	30	51	81	Huber	164
1980-81	Ogrodnick	35	McCourt	56	McCourt	30	56	86	Korn	246
1981-82	Ogrodnick	28	Osborne	41	Osborne	26	41	67	Larson	112
1982-83	Ogrodnick	41	Larson	52	Ogrodnick	41	44	85	Gare	107
1983-84	Ogrodnick	42	Park	53	Yzerman	39	48	87	Paterson	148
1984-85	Ogrodnick	55	Yzerman	59	Ogrodnick	55	50	105	Gare	163
1985-86	Ogrodnick	38	Kisio	48	Shedden	34	37	71	Kocur	377*
1986-87	Ashton	40	Yzerman	59	Yzerman	31	59	90	Kocur	276
1987-88	Yzerman	50	Yzerman	52	Yzerman	50	52	102	Probert	398*
1988-89	Yzerman	65	Yzerman	90	Yzerman	65	90	155	Gallant	230
1989-90	Yzerman	62	Yzerman	65	Yzerman	62	65	127	Kocur	268
1990-91	Yzerman	51	Yzerman	57	Yzerman	51	57	108	Probert	315
1991-92	Yzerman	45	Yzerman	58	Yzerman	45	58	103	Probert	276
1992-93	Yzerman	58	Yzerman	79	Yzerman	58	79	137	Probert	292
1993-94	Fedorov	56	Fedorov	64	Fedorov	56	64	120	Probert	275
1995	R. Sheppard	30	Coffey	44	Coffey	14	44	58	Grimson	147
1995-96	Fedorov	39	Fedorov	68	Fedorov	39	68	107	Primeau	168
1996-97	Shanahan	47	Yzerman	63	Shanahan	47	41	88	Lapointe	167
1997-98	Shanahan	28	Yzerman	45	Yzerman	24	45	69	McCarty	157
1998-99	Shanahan	31	Larionov	49	Yzerman	29	45	74	Lapointe	141
1999-00	Shanahan	41	Lidstrom	53	Yzerman	35	44	79	Lapointe	121
2000-01	Fedorov	32	Lidstrom	56	Shanahan	31	45	76	Lapointe	127
2001-02	Shanahan	37	Lidstrom	50	Shanahan	37	38	75	Chelios	126

*-League leader

DETROIT RED WINGS TOP-SCORING SEASONS

GOALS

Total	Player	Season		Total	Player	Season
65	**STEVE YZERMAN**	**88-89**		35	Mud Bruneteau	43-44
62	**STEVE YZERMAN**	**89-90**			Gordie Howe	49-50
58	**STEVE YZERMAN**	**92-93**			Vaclav Nedomansky	79-80
56	**SERGEI FEDOROV**	**93-94**			John Ogrodnick	80-81
55	John Ogrodnick	84-85			Ivan Boldirev	83-84
52	Mickey Redmond	72-73			Errol Thompson	79-80
	Ray Sheppard	93-94			Paul Ysebaert	91-92
51	Mickey Redmond	73-74			**STEVE YZERMAN**	**99-00**
	STEVE YZERMAN	**90-91**		34	Gerard Gallant	87-88
50	Danny Grant	74-75			Jimmy Carson	91-92
	STEVE YZERMAN	**87-88**			Paul Ysebaert	92-93
49	Gordie Howe	52-53			Vyacheslav Kozlov	93-94
	Frank Mahovlich	68-69		33	Ted Lindsay	47-48
47	Gordie Howe	51-52			Gordie Howe (3)	53-54
	Marcel Dionne	74-75				57-58
47	**BRENDAN SHANAHAN**	**96-97**				61-62
45	**STEVE YZERMAN**	**91-92**			Parker MacDonald	62-63
44	Gordie Howe (2)	56-57			Dale McCourt	77-78
		68-69			Ron Duguay	83-84
43	Gordie Howe	50-51		32	Syd Howe	43-44
42	Norm Ullman	64-65			Ted Lindsay	52-53
	Garry Unger	69-70			Gordie Howe	58-59
	Mickey Redmond	71-72			Michel Bergeron	75-76
	John Ogrodnick	83-84			Petr Klima	85-86
41	John Ogrodnick	82-83			**SERGEI FEDOROV (2)**	**91-92**
	Dino Ciccarelli	92-93				**2000-01**
	BRENDAN SHANAHAN	**99-00**			Ray Sheppard	92-93
40	Marcel Dionne	72-73		31	Norm Ullman	65-66
39	Gordie Howe	67-68			Alex Delvecchio	65-66
	STEVE YZERMAN	**83-84**			Gordie Howe	69-70
	Gerard Gallant	88-89			Nick Libett	71-72
	SERGEI FEDOROV	**95-96**			Andre St. Laurent	77-78
38	Gordie Howe (2)	55-56			**STEVE YZERMAN**	**86-87**
		66-63			**SERGEI FEDOROV**	**90-91**
	Frank Mahovlich	69-70				**2001-02**
	Vaclav Nedomansky	78-79			Keith Primeau	93-94
	Ron Duguay	84-85			**BRENDAN SHANAHAN (2)**	**98-99**
	John Ogrodnick	85-86				**2000-01**
	Gerard Gallant	86-87		30	Roy Conacher	46-47
37	Petr Klima	87-88			Ted Lindsay (2)	51-52
	BRENDAN SHANAHAN	**2001-02**				56-57
36	Carl Liscombe	43-44			Norm Ullman	67-68
	Mike Foligno	79-80			Tom Webster	70-71
	Paul MacLean	88-89			Dale McCourt	79-80
	Gerard Gallant	89-90			Dan Labraaten	79-80
	Ray Sheppard	91-92			Dale McCourt	80-81
	STEVE YZERMAN	**95-96**			**STEVE YZERMAN**	**84-85**
	Vyacheslav Kozlov	95-96			Petr Klima	86-87
					Ray Sheppard	95-96
					SERGEI FEDOROV	**96-97**
					BRETT HULL	**2001-02**
					LUC ROBITAILLE	**2001-02**

ASSISTS

Total	Player	Season
90	**STEVE YZERMAN**	**88-89**
79	**STEVE YZERMAN**	**92-93**
74	Marcel Dionne	74-75
68	**SERGEI FEDOROV**	**95-96**
65	**STEVE YZERMAN**	**89-90**
64	**SERGEI FEDOROV**	**93-94**
63	**STEVE YZERMAN**	**96-97**
	Paul Coffey	93-94
62	Adam Oates	88-89
60	Paul Coffey	95-96
59	Gordie Howe	68-69
	STEVE YZERMAN (3)	**84-85**
		86-87
		95-96
58	Alex Delvecchio	68-69
	STEVE YZERMAN (2)	**91-92**
		93-94
57	**STEVE YZERMAN**	**90-91**
56	Walt McKechnie	75-76
	Dale McCourt	80-81
	Dino Ciccarelli	92-93
	NICKLAS LIDSTROM	**2000-01**
55	Ted Lindsay (2)	49-50
		56-57
54	Marcel Dionne	73-74
	Gerard Gallant	88-89
	SERGEI FEDOROV	**91-92**
53	Alex Delvecchio	72-73
	Brad Park	83-84
	SERGEI FEDOROV	**92-93**
	NICKLAS LIDSTROM	**99-00**
52	Reed Larson	82-83
	STEVE YZERMAN	**87-88**
51	Dale McCourt	79-89
	Ron Duguay	84-85
	IGOR LARIONOV	**95-96**
50	Marcel Dionne	72-73
	John Ogrodnick	84-85
	Steve Chiasson	92-93
	NICKLAS LIDSTROM	**95-96**
		2001-02
49	Gordie Howe	60-61
	Marcel Dionne	71-72
	Reed Larson	78-79
	Peter Mahovlich	79-80
	NICKLAS LIDSTROM	**91-92**
	IGOR LARIONOV	**98-99**
48	Gordie Howe (2)	53-54
		62-63
	Alex Delvecchio	67-68
	STEVE YZERMAN	**83-84**
	Ivan Boldirev	83-84
	Kelly Kisio	85-86
	SERGEI FEDOROV	**90-91**
47	Gordie Howe (2)	63-64
		64-65
	Alex Delvecchio	69-70
	Ron Duguay	83-84

Total	Player	Season
	Alex Delvecchio	69-70
46	Billy Taylor	46-47
	Gordie Howe (3)	52-53
		58-59
		65-66
	NICKLAS LIDSTROM	**93-94**
45	Gordie Howe (2)	56-57
		59-60
	Alex Delvecchio	71-72
	Reed Larson	84-85
	BRENDAN SHANAHAN	**2000-01**
	Darren Veitch	86-87
	STEVE YZERMAN (2)	**97-98**
		98-99
44	Gordie Howe (2)	57-58
		61-62
	Alex Delvecchio	62-63
	Norm Ullman	66-67
	Reed Larson	79-80
	John Ogrondick	82-83
	John Chabot	87-88
	Gerard Gallant	89-90
	Paul Coffey	95
	STEVE YZERMAN	**99-00**
43	Gordie Howe (2)	50-51
		67-68
	Alex Delvecchio (2)	52-53
		61-62
	Dale McCourt	78-79
	Mickey Redmond	72-73
	Red Berenson	71-72
	Reed Larson	77-78
	Mark Osborne	81-82
	Kelly Kisio	84-85
	NICKLAS LIDSTROM	**98-99**
42	Norm Ullman	60-61
	Alex Delvecchio	64-65
	Red Berenson	73-74
	Keith Primeau	93-94
	IGOR LARIONOV	**96-97**
	NICKLAS LIDSTROM (2)	**96-97**
		97-98
	Larry Murphy	98-99
41	Dutch Reibel	54-55
	Gordie Howe	55-56
	Norm Ullman (2)	60-61
		65-66
	Ray Sheppard	93-94
	BRENDAN SHANAHAN	**96-97**
	Larry Murphy	97-98
40	Gordie Howe (2)	66-67
		69-70
	Adam Oates	87-88
	Bernie Federko	89-90
	John Chabot	89-90
	Yves Racine	90-91
	Paul Ysebaert	91-92

POINTS

Total	Player	Season
155	**STEVE YZERMAN**	**88-89**
137	**STEVE YZERMAN**	**92-93**
127	**STEVE YZERMAN**	**89-90**
120	**SERGEI FEDOROV**	**93-94**
121	Marcel Dionne	74-75
108	**STEVE YZERMAN**	**90-91**
107	**SERGEI FEDOROV**	**95-96**
105	John Ogrodnick	84-85
103	Gordie Howe	68-69
	STEVE YZERMAN	**91-92**
102	**STEVE YZERMAN**	**87-88**
97	Dino Ciccarelli	92-93
95	Gordie Howe	52-53
	STEVE YZERMAN	**95-96**
93	Mickey Redmond	72-73
	Gerard Gallant	88-89
	Ray Sheppard	93-94
90	Marcel Dionne	72-73
	STEVE YZERMAN	**86-87**
89	Gordie Howe	56-57
	Ron Duguay	84-85
	STEVE YZERMAN	**84-85**
87	**STEVE YZERMAN**	**83-84**
	SERGEI FEDOROV	**92-93**
	BRENDAN SHANAHAN	**96-97**
86	Gordie Howe (3)	50-51
		51-52
		62-63
	Danny Grant	74-75
	Dale McCourt	80-81
	SERGEI FEDOROV	**91-92**
85	Ted Lindsay	56-57
	John Ogrodnick	82-83
	STEVE YZERMAN	**96-97**
83	Norm Ullman	64-65
	Alex Delvecchio	68-69
	Ivan Boldirev	83-84
82	Gordie Howe	67-68
	Walt McKechnie	75-76
	STEVE YZERMAN	**93-94**
81	Gordie Howe	53-54
	Dale McCourt	79-80
80	Ron Duguay	83-84
	Gerard Gallant	89-90
79	Gordie Howe	55-56
	SERGEI FEDOROV	**90-91**
	STEVE YZERMAN	**99-00**
78	Ted Lindsay	49-50
	Gordie Howe	58-59
	Frank Mahovlich	68-69
	Marcel Dionne	73-74
	John Ogrodnick	83-84
	Adam Oates	88-89
	BRENDAN SHANAHAN	**99-00**

Total	Player	Season
77	Gordie Howe (2)	57-58
		61-62
	Marcel Dionne	71-72
	Mickey Redmond	73-74
	Paul Coffey	93-94
76	Gordie Howe	64-65
	BRENDAN SHANAHAN	**2000-01**
75	Gordie Howe	65-66
	Paul Ysebaert	91-92
	BRENDAN SHANAHAN	**2001-02**
74	Vaclav Nedomansky	79-80
	Reed Larson	82-83
	STEVE YZERMAN	**98-99**
	Paul Coffey	95-96
73	Carl Liscombe	43-44
	Gordie Howe (2)	59-60
		63-64
	Vaclav Nedomansky	78-79
	Gerard Gallant	87-88
	Vyacheslav Kozlov	93-94
	Keith Primeau	93-94
	Vyacheslav Kozlov	95-96
	Igor Iarionov	95-96
	NICKLAS LIDSTROM	**99-00**
72	Gordie Howe	60-61
	Norm Ullman	65-66
	Dale McCourt	77-78
	Gerard Gallant	86-87
71	Ted Lindsay	52-53
	Gordie Howe	69-70
	Mickey Redmond	71-72
	Alex Delvecchio	72-73
	Dale McCourt	78-79
	Mike Foligno	79-80
	Paul MacLean	88-89
	NICKLAS LIDSTROM	**2000-01**
70	Norm Ullman (2)	60-61
		66-67
	Alex Delvecchio	67-68
	Frank Mahovlich	69-70
	Andre St. Laurent	77-78
	John Ogrodnick (2)	80-81
		85-86

ACTIVE PLAYERS IN BOLD CAPITALS

DETROIT RED WINGS IN HOCKEY HALL OF FAME

Sid Abel 1969	Red Kelly 1969
Jack Adams 1959	Herbie Lewis 1989
Al Arbour 1996	Ted Lindsay 1966
Marty Barry 1965	Harry Lumley 1980
Andy Bathgate 1978	Budd Lynch 1985
Leo Boivin 1986	Frank Mahovlich 1981
Scotty Bowman 1991	Bruce Martyn 1991
John Bucyk 1981	Reg Noble 1962
Charlie Conacher 1961	Bruce A. Norris 1969
Roy Conacher 1998	James Norris 1958
Alex Connell 1958	James D. Norris 1962
Alex Delvecchio 1977	Brad Park 1988
Marcel Dionne 1992	Bud Poile 1990
Bernie Federko 2002	Marcel Pronovost 1978
Frank Foyston 1958	Bill Quackenbush 1976
Frank Fredrickson 1958	Borje Salming 1996
Bill Gadsby 1970	Terry Sawchuk 1971
Ed Giacomin 1987	Earl Seibert 1964
Ebbie Goodfellow 1963	Darryl Sittler 1989
Glenn Hall 1975	Jack Stewart 1964
Doug Harvey 1973	Cecil "Tiny" Thompson 1959
George Hay 1958	Norm Ullman 1982
Hap Holmes 1972	Carl Voss 1974
Gordie Howe 1972	Jack Walker 1960
Syd Howe 1965	Harry Watson 1994
Tommy Ivan 1974	Cooney Weiland 1971
Duke Keats 1958	John A. Ziegler Jr. 1987

DETROIT RED WINGS NHL TROPHY WINNERS

ART ROSS TROPHY
(Leading Point-scorer)
Ted Lindsay 1949-50
Gordie Howe 1950-51
Gordie Howe 1951-52
Gordie Howe 1952-53
Gordie Howe 1953-54
Gordie Howe 1956-57
Gordie Howe 1962-63

HART TROPHY
(Most Valuable Player)
Ebbie Goodfellow.........................1939-40
Sid Abel......................................1948-49
Gordie Howe 1951-52
Gordie Howe 1952-53
Gordie Howe 1956-57
Gordie Howe 1957-58
Gordie Howe 1959-60
Gordie Howe 1962-63
SERGEI FEDOROV....................1993-94

VEZINA TROPHY
(Best Goalie)
Norm Smith. 1936-37
John Mowers...............................1942-43
Terry Sawchuk 1951-52
Terry Sawchuk 1952-53
Terry Sawchuk 1954-55

NORRIS TROPHY
(Best Defenseman)
Red Kelly....................................1953-54
Paul Coffey......................................1995
NICKLAS LIDSTROM 2000-01
NICKLAS LIDSTROM 2001-02

CALDER TROPHY
(Rookie of the Year)
Carl Voss 1932-33
Jim McFadden 1947-48
Terry Sawchuk 1950-51
Glenn Hall 1955-56
Roger Crozier..............................1964-65

FRANK J. SELKE TROPHY
(Best Defensive Forward)
SERGEI FEDOROV....................1993-94
SERGEI FEDOROV....................1995-96
STEVE YZERMAN 1999-2000

WILLIAM M. JENNINGS TROPHY
(Goaltenders on Team with Fewest Regular Season Goals Against)
Chris Osgood & Mike Vernon........1995-96

LADY BYNG TROPHY
(Sportsmanship & Ability)
Marty Barry 1936-37
Bill Quackenbush 1948-49
Red Kelly....................................1950-51
Red Kelly....................................1952-53
Red Kelly....................................1953-54
Dutch Reibel 1955-56
Alex Delvecchio 1958-59
Alex Delvecchio 1965-66
Alex Delvecchio 1968-69
Marcel Dionne.............................1974-75

LESTER B. PEARSON AWARD
(Oustanding Performer Selected by Players' Assn.)
STEVE YZERMAN 1988-89
SERGEI FEDOROV....................1993-94

PLUS-MINUS AWARD
(Plus-Minus Leader)
Paul Ysebaert 1991-92
Vladimir Konstantinov 1995-96

CONN SMYTHE TROPHY
(Playoff MVP)
Roger Crozier.....................................1966
Mike Vernon 1997
STEVE YZERMAN.............................1998
NICKLAS LIDSTROM 2002

JACK ADAMS AWARD
(Coach of the Year)
Bobby Kromm 1977-78
Jacques Demers 1986-87
Jacques Demers 1987-88
SCOTTY BOWMAN 1995-96

BILL MASTERTON TROPHY
(Perseverance, Sportsmanship and Dedication to Hockey)
Brad Park 1983-84

LESTER PATRICK TROPHY
(Outstanding Service to U.S. Hockey)
Jack Adams 1965-66
Gordie Howe 1966-67
Alex Delvecchio 1973-74
Bruce A. Norris............................1974-75
MIKE ILITCH 1990-91

ACTIVE PLAYER/OWNER/COACH IN BOLD CAPITALS

	GC	W	L	T	OTL
ART DUNCAN, 1926-27 (First 33 games)	33	10	21	2	
* DUKE KEATS, 1926-27 (Final 11 games)	11	2	7	2	
JACK ADAMS, 1927-28 through 1946-47	964	413	390	161	
TOMMY IVAN, 1947-48 through 1953-54	470	262	118	90	
JIMMY SKINNER, 1954-55 to 1957-58 (First 38 games)	247	123	78	46	
SID ABEL, 1957-58 (Final 32 games) through 1967-68 & 1969-70 (Final 74 games)	811	340	339	132	
BILL GADSBY, 1968-69 to1969-70 (First 2 games)	78	35	31	12	
NED HARKNESS, 1970-71 (First 38 games)	38	12	22	4	
DOUG BARKLEY, 1970-71 (Final 40 games), 1971-72 (First 11 games) & 1975-76 (First 26 games)	77	20	46	11	
JOHNNY WILSON, 1971-72 (Final 67 games) through 1972-73	145	67	56	22	
TED GARVIN, 1973-74 (First 11 games)	11	2	8	1	
ALEX DELVECCHIO, 1973-74 (Final 67 games) through 1974-75 & 1975-76 (9 games)	156	53	82	21	
**BILLY DEA, 1975-76 (Final 45 games), 1976-77 (First 44 games) & 1981-82 (Final 11 games)	100	32	57	11	
LARRY WILSON, 1976-77 (Final 36 games)	36	3	29	4	
BOBBY KROMM, 1977-78 through 1978-79, & 1979-80 (First 71 games)	231	79	111	41	
***MARCEL PRONOVOST, 1979-80 (Final 9 games)	9	2	7	0	
TED LINDSAY, 1980-81 (First 20 games)	20	3	14	3	
WAYNE MAXNER, 1980-81 (Final 60 games) & 1981-82 (First 69 games)	129	34	68	27	
NICK POLANO, 1982-83 through 1984-85	240	79	127	34	
HARRY NEALE, 1985-86 (First 35 games)	35	8	23	4	
BRAD PARK, 1985-86 (45 games)	45	9	34	2	
JACQUES DEMERS, 1986-87 to 1989-90	320	137	136	47	
BRYAN MURRAY, 1990-91 to 1992-93	244	124	91	29	
SCOTTY BOWMAN, 1993-94 to 1997-98; 1999-2002	624	371	164	81	8
1998-99 (Final 77 games)	77	39	31	7	
BOWMAN'S DETROIT TOTALS	(701	410	203	88	8)
1998-99 (First 5 games)+	5	4	1	0	
FRANCHISE TOTALS	5156	2263	2095	794	8

*-Art Duncan remained general manager/player but gave coaching duties to Duke Keats.

**-Alex Delvecchio officially was head coach late in 75-76 season and early 76-77, but Billy Dea worked behind bench. In 81-82, Dea replaced the fired Wayne Maxner late in season.

***-Ted Lindsay officially was head coach but Marcel Pronovost worked behind bench.

+- Associate Coaches Dave Lewis and Barry Smith shared head coaching duties for the first five games of the 1998-99 regular season while Scotty Bowman convalesced.

ART DUNCAN
1926-27

JACK ADAMS
1927-28 through 1962-63

SID ABEL
1963-64 to 1970-71 (First 38 games)

NED HARKNESS
1970-71 (Final 40 games) through 1973-74

ALEX DELVECCHIO
1974-75 to 1976-77 (First 70 games)

TED LINDSAY
1976-77 (Final 10 games) through 1979-80

JIMMY SKINNER
1980-81 through 1981-82

JIM DEVELLANO
1982-83 to 1989-90

BRYAN MURRAY
1990-91 to 1993-94

JIM DEVELLANO
1994-95 to 1996-97
(Senior Vice-President/Hockey Operations)

KEN HOLLAND
1997-98 to present

DETROIT RED WINGS ENTRY DRAFT SELECTIONS
(Since inception in 1963)

Round	Overall	Round	Overall	Round	Overall
1963		**1971**		**1974**	
1 Pete Mahovlich	2	1 Marcel Dionne	2	1 Bill Lochead	9
2 Bill Cosburn	8	2 Henry Boucha	16	3 Dan Mandryk	44
		3 Ralph Hopiavouri	30	3 Bill Evo	45
1964		4 George Hulme	44	4 Michel Bergeron	63
1 Claude Gauthier	1	5 Earl Anderson	58	5 John Taft	81
2 Brian Watts	7	6 Charlie Shaw	72	6 Don Dufek	99
3 Ralph Buchanan	13	7 Jim Nahrgang	86	7 Jack Carlson	117
4 Ronald LeClerc	19	8 Bob Boyd	100	8 Gregg Steele	134
				9 Glen McLeod	151
1965		**1972**			
1 George Forge	3	2 Pierre Guite	26	**1975**	
2 Bob Birdsell	8	3 Bob Kreiger	42	1 Rick Lapointe	5
		4 Danny Gruen	68	2 Jerry Rollins	23
1966		5 Dennis Johnson	74	3 Al Cameron	37
1 Steve Atkinson	6	6 Bill Miller	90	3 Blair Davidson	45
2 Jim Whitaker	12	7 Glen Seperich	106	3 Clarke Hamilton	50
3 Lee Carpenter	18	8 Mike Ford	122	4 Mike Wirachowski	59
4 Grant Cole	24	9 George Kuzmicz	138	5 Mike Wong	77
		12 Dave Arundel	150	6 Mike Harazny	95
1967				7 Jean-Luc Phaneuf	113
1 Ron Barkwell	9	**1973**		8 Steve Carlson	131
2 Al Karlander	17	1 Terry Richardson	11	9 Gary Vaughn	148
		3 Nelson Pyatt	39	10 Jean Thibodeau	164
1968		3 Robbie Neale	43	11 Dave Hanson	176
1 Steve Adrascik	11	4 Mike Korney	59	11 Robin Larson	178
2 Herb Boxer	17	5 Blair Stewart	75		
		6 Glen Cikello	91	**1976**	
1969		7 Brian Middleton	107	1 Fred Williams	4
1 Jim Rutherford	10	8 Dennis Polonich	123	2 Reed Larson	22
2 Ron Garwasiuk	21	9 Dennis O'Brien	135	3 Fred Berry	40
3 Wayne Hawrysh	33	9 Tom Newman	138	4 Kevin Schamehorn	58
4 Warren Chernecki	45	9 Ray Bibeau	139	5 Dwight Schofield	76
5 Wally Olds	57	10 Kevin Neville	151	6 Tony Horvath	94
		10 Ken Gibb	154	7 Fern LeBlanc	111
1970		10 Mitch Brandt	155	8 Claude Legris	120
1 Serge Lajeunesse	12				
2 Bob Guindon	26				
3 Yvon Lambert	40				
4 Tom Johnstone	54				
5 Tom Mellor	68				
6 Bernard McNeil	82				
7 Ed Hays	95				

Round		Overall	Round		Overall	Round		Overall
1977			**1980**			**1984**		
1	Dale McCourt	1	1	Mike Blaisdell	11	1	Shawn Burr	7
3	Rick Vasko	37	3	Mark Osborne	46	2	Doug Houda	28
4	John Hilworth	55	5	Mike Corrigan	88	3	Milan Chalupa	49
5	Jim Korn	73	6	Wayne Crawford	109	5	Mats Lundstrom	91
6	Jim Baxter	91	7	Mike Braun	130	6	Randy Hansch	112
7	Randy Wilson	109	8	John Beukeboom	151	7	Stefan Larsson	133
8	Ray Roy	125	9	Dave Miles	172	8	Lars Karlsson	152
9	Kip Churchill	141	10	Brian Rorabeck	193	8	Urban Nordin	154
10	Lance Gatoni	155				9	Bill Shibicky	175
11	Rob Plumb	163	**1981**			10	Jay Rose	195
12	Alain Belanger	170	2	Claude Loiselle	23	11	Tim Kaiser	216
13	Dean Willers	175	3	Corrado Micalef	44	12	Tom Nickolau	236
14	Roland Cloutier	178	5	Larry Trader	86			
15	Ed Hill	181	6	Gerard Gallant	107	**1985**		
16	Val James	184	7	Greg Stefan	128	1	Brent Fedyk	8
17	Grant Morin	185	8	Rick Zombo	149	2	Jeff Sharples	29
			9	Don LeBlanc	170	3	Steve Chiasson	50
1978			10	Robert Nordmark	191	4	Mark Gowans	71
1	Willie Huber	9				5	Chris Luongo	92
1	Brent Peterson	12	**1982**			6	Randy McKay	113
2	Glen Hicks	28	1	Murray Craven	17	7	Thomas Bjuhr	134
2	Al Jensen	31	2	Yves Courteau	23	8	Mike Luckraft	155
3	Doug Derkson	53	3	Carmine Vani	44	9	Rob Schenna	176
4	Bjorn Skaare	62	4	Craig Coxe	66	10	Eerik Hamalainen	197
5	Ted Nolan	78	5	Brad Shaw	86	11	Bo Svanberg	218
6	Sylvain Locas	95	6	Claude Vilgrain	107	12	Mikael Lindman	239
7	Wes George	112	7	Greg Hudas	128			
8	John Barrett	129	8	Pat Lahey	149	**1986**		
9	Jim Malazdrewicz	146	9	Gary Cullen	170	1	Joe Murphy	1
10	Geoff Shaw	163	10	Brent Meckling	191	2	Adam Graves	22
11	Carl VanHarrewyn	178	11	Mike Stern	212	3	Derek Mayer	43
12	Ladislav Svozil	194	12	Shaun Reagan	233	4	Tim Cheveldae	64
13	Tom Bailey	208				5	Johan Garpenlov	85
14	Larry Lozinski	219	**1983**			6	Jay Stark	106
15	Randy Betty	224	1	Steve Yzerman	4	7	Per Djoos	127
16	Brian Crawley	226	2	Lane Lambert	25	8	Dean Morton	148
17	Doug Feasby	228	3	Bob Probert	46	9	Marc Potvin	169
			4	Dave Korol	70	10	Scott King	190
1979			5	Petr Klima	88	11	Tom Bissett	211
1	Mike Foligno	3	5	Joe Kocur	91	12	Peter Ekroth	232
3	Jody Gage	45	6	Chris Pusey	109			
3	Boris Fistric	46	7	Bob Pierson	130	**1987**		
4	John Ogrodnick	66	8	Craig Butz	151	1	Yves Racine	11
5	Joe Paterson	87	9	Dave Sikorski	172	2	Gord Kruppke	32
6	Carmine Cirella	108	10	Stu Grimson	193	2	Bob Wilkie	41
			11	Jeff Frank	214	3	Dennis Holland	52
			12	Chuck Chiatto	235	4	Mark Reimer	74
						5	Radomir Brazda	95
						6	Sean Clifford	116
						7	Mike Gober	137
						8	Kevin Scott	158
						9	Mikko Haapakoski	179
						10	Darin Bannister	200
						11	Craig Quinlan	221
						12	Tomas Jansson	242

Round	Overall
1988	
1 Kory Kocur	17
2 Serge Anglehart	38
3 Guy Dupuis	47
3 Petr Hrbek	59
4 Sheldon Kennedy	80
7 Kelly Hurd	143
8 Brian McCormack	164
9 Jody Praznik	185
10 Glenn Goodall	206
11 Darren Colbourne	227
12 Don Stone	248
1989	
1 Mike Sillinger	11
2 Bob Boughner	32
3 Nicklas Lidstrom	53
4 Sergei Fedorov	74
5 Shawn McCosh	95
6 Dallas Drake	116
7 Scott Zygulski	137
8 Andy Suhy	158
9 Bob Jones	179
10 Greg Bignell	200
10 Rick Judson	204
11 Vladimir Konstantinov	221
12 Joseph Frederick	242
12 Jason Glickman	246
1990	
1 Keith Primeau	3
3 Vyacheslav Kozlov	45
4 Stewart Malgunas	66
5 Tony Burns	87
6 Claude Barthe	108
7 Jason York	129
8 Wes McCauley	150
9 Anthony Gruba	171
10 Travis Tucker	192
11 Brett Larson	213
12 John Hendry	234
1991	
1 Martin Lapointe	10
2 Jamie Pushor	32
3 Chris Osgood	54
4 Mike Knuble	76
5 Dimitri Motkov	98
7 Igor Malykhin	142
9 Jim Bermingham	186
10 Jason Firth	208
11 Bart Turner	230
12 Andrew Miller	252

Round	Overall
1992	
1 Curtis Bowen	22
2 Darren McCarty	46
3 Sylvain Cloutier	70
5 Mike Sullivan	118
6 Jason MacDonald	142
7 Greg Scott	166
8 Justin Krall	183
8 C.J. Denomme	189
9 Jeff Walker	214
10 Dan McGillis	238
11 Ryan Bach	262
1993	
1 Anders Eriksson	22
2 Jon Coleman	48
3 Kevin Hilton	74
4 John Jakopin	97
4 Benoit Larose	100
5 Norm Maracle	126
6 Tim Spitzig	152
7 Yuri Yeresko	178
8 Viteslav Skuta	204
9 Ryan Shanahan	230
10 Jim Kosecki	256
11 Gord Hunt	282
1994	
1 Yan Golubovsky	23
2 Mathieu Dandenault	49
3 Sean Gilliam	75
5 Frederic Deschenes	114
5 Doug Battaglia	127
6 Paval Agarkov	153
8 Jason Elliott	205
9 Jeff Mikesch	231
10 Tomas Holmstrom	257
11 Toivo Suursoo	283
1995	
1 Maxim Kuznetsov	26
2 Philippe Audet	52
3 Darryl Laplante	58
4 Anatoly Ustugov	104
5 Chad Wilchynski	125
5 David Arsenault	126
6 Tyler Perry	156
7 Per Eklund	182
8 Andrei Samokvalov	208
9 David Engblom	234
1996	
1 Jesse Wallin	26
2 Aren Miller	52
4 Johan Forsander	108
5 Michal Podolka	135
6 Magnus Nilsson	144
6 Alexandre Jacques	162
7 Colin Beardsmore	189
8 Craig Stahl	215
9 Eugeniy Afanasiev	241

Round	Overall
1997	
2 Yuri Butsayev	49
3 Petr Sykora	76
4 Quintin Lang	102
5 John Wikstrom	129
6 B.J. Young	157
7 Mike Laceby	186
8 Steve Wilejto	213
9 Greg Willers	239
1998	
1 Jiri Fischer	25
2 Ryan Barnes	55
2 Tomek Valtonen	56
3 Jake McCracken	84
4 Brent Hobday	111
5 Calle Steen	142
6 Adam Deleeuw	151
7 Pavel Datsyuk	171
7 Jeremy Goetzinger	198
8 David Petrasek	226
9 Petja Pietilainen	256
1999	
4 Jari Toulsa	120
5 Andrei Maximenko	149
6 Kent McDonell	181
7 Henrik Zetterberg	210
8 Anton Borodkin	238
9 Ken Davis	266
2000	
1 Niklas Kronvall	29
2 Tomas Kopecky	38
4 Stefan Liv	102
4 Dmitri Semyenov	127
4 Alexander Seluyanov	128
4 Aaron Van Leusen	130
6 Per Backer	187
6 Paul Ballantyne	196
7 Jimmie Svensson	228
8 Todd Jackson	251
8 Evgeni Bumagin	260
2001	
2 Igor Grigorenko	62
4 Drew MacIntyre	121
4 Miloslav Blatak	129
5 Andreas Jämtin	157
6 Nick Pannoni	195
8 Dimitri Bykov	258
9 François Senez	288

SUPPLEMENTAL DRAFT
1987 — Mike LaMoine
1988 — Gary Shuchuk
1989 — Brad Kreick
1990 — Mike Casselman;
         Don Oliver
1991 — Kelly Sorensen

DETROIT RED WINGS vs. ALL NHL TEAMS

SINCE 1926-27 SEASON

Detroit Red Wings vs.	GP	W	L	T	OTL	PTS
Chicago Blackhawks	762	329	247	84	2	744
Toronto Maple Leafs	635	271	270	93	2	637
New York Rangers	567	255	209	103	0	613
Boston Bruins	569	243	231	95	0	581
Montréal Canadiens	560	197	267	96	0	203
❶ Dallas Stars	204	87	88	29	2	192
St. Louis Blues	209	77	95	36	0	146
Vancouver Canucks	123	64	41	18	1	135
Los Angeles Kings	151	54	70	26	0	126
Pittsburgh Penguins	127	55	56	16	0	107
Philadelphia Flyers	115	43	51	21	0	106
❷ Calgary Flames	111	45	50	16	0	98
❸ Phoenix Coyotes	92	39	33	20	0	95
Buffalo Sabres	105	41	51	13	0	94
Washington Capitals	90	39	35	16	0	91
New York Islanders	88	43	40	5	0	82
Edmonton Oilers	80	36	34	10	0	79
❹ Colorado Avalanche	74	37	32	5	0	77
❺ New Jersey Devils	77	33	33	11	0	66
San Jose Sharks	43	31	8	4	0	63
❻ Carolina Hurricanes	58	28	23	7	0	52
Anaheim Mighty Ducks	36	23	7	6	0	37
Tampa Bay Lightning	23	18	4	1	2	33
Nashville Predators	22	14	3	3	0	21
Ottawa Senators	16	10	5	1	0	20
Florida Panthers	14	8	2	4	0	16
Columbus Blue Jackets	10	8	2	0	0	12
Minnesota Wild	8	5	1	1	1	10
Atlanta Thrashers	5	5	0	0	0	304
(a) Defunct Teams	282	125	103	54	0	304
TOTALS	**5156**	**2263**	**2095**	**794**	**8**	**5330**

HOME

Detroit Red Wings vs.	GP	W	L	T	OTL	PTS
Chicago Blackhawks	330	199	97	33	1	432
Toronto Maple Leafs	321	167	106	46	2	382
New York Rangers	284	163	76	45	0	371
Boston Bruins	283	153	78	52	0	358
Montréal Canadiens	279	130	96	53	0	313
❶ Dallas Stars	102	51	37	14	0	116
St. Louis Blues	104	47	40	17	0	111
Pittsburgh Penguins	64	39	13	12	0	90
Vancouver Canucks	62	39	15	8	0	86
Los Angeles Kings	75	33	30	12	0	78
Philadelphia Flyers	58	30	18	10	0	70
Buffalo Sabres	54	31	18	5	0	67
❷ Calgary Flames	55	28	17	10	0	66
❸ Phoenix Coyotes	47	23	17	7	0	53
Washington Capitals	46	21	14	11	0	53
New York Islanders	43	24	17	2	0	50

HOME (continued)

Detroit Red Wings vs.	GP	W	L	T	OTL	PTS
❺ New Jersey Devils	38	23	13	2	0	48
Edmonton Oilers	40	22	15	3	0	47
❹ Colorado Avalanche	36	22	13	1	0	45
❻ Carolina Hurricanes	30	17	7	6	0	40
San Jose Sharks	21	18	2	1	0	37
Anaheim Mighty Ducks	18	13	2	3	0	29
Nashville Predators	12	10	0	1	1	22
Tampa Bay Lightning	10	9	1	0	0	18
Ottawa Senators	8	5	3	0	0	10
Columbus Blue Jackets	5	4	1	0	0	8
Florida Panthers	6	3	1	2	0	8
Atlanta Thrashers	3	3	0	0	0	6
Minnesota Wild	4	3	1	0	0	6
(a) Defunct Teams	141	76	40	25	0	177
TOTALS	**2578**	**1405**	**788**	**381**	**4**	**3195**

ROAD

Detroit Red Wings vs.	GP	W	L	T	OTL	PTS
Chicago Blackhawks	332	130	150	51	1	312
Toronto Maple Leafs	314	104	163	47	0	255
New York Rangers	283	92	133	58	0	242
Boston Bruins	286	90	153	43	0	223
Montréal Canadiens	281	67	171	43	0	177
❶ Dallas Stars	102	36	51	15	0	87
St. Louis Blues	105	30	54	19	2	81
Vancouver Canucks	61	25	26	10	0	60
Los Angeles Kings	76	21	40	14	1	57
❸ Phoenix Coyotes	45	16	16	13	0	45
New York Islanders	45	19	23	3	0	41
Washington Capitals	44	18	21	5	0	41
❷ Calgary Flames	56	17	33	6	0	40
Philadelphia Flyers	57	13	33	11	0	37
Pittsburgh Penguins	63	16	43	4	0	36
Edmonton Oilers	40	14	19	7	0	35
❹ Colorado Avalanche	38	15	19	4	0	34
❺ New Jersey Devils	39	10	20	9	0	29
San Jose Sharks	22	13	6	3	0	29
Buffalo Sabres	51	10	33	8	0	28
Anaheim Mighty Ducks	18	10	5	3	0	23
❻ Carolina Hurricanes	28	11	16	1	0	23
Tampa Bay Lightning	13	9	3	1	0	19
Florida Panthers	8	5	1	2	0	12
Nashville Predators	10	4	3	2	1	11
Ottawa Senators	8	5	2	1	0	11
Columbus Blue Jackets	5	4	1	0	0	8
Minnesota Wild	4	2	0	1	1	6
Atlanta Thrashers	2	2	0	0	0	4
(a) Defunct Teams	141	49	63	29	0	127
TOTALS	**2578**	**858**	**1301**	**413**	**6**	**2135**

❶-Formerly Minnesota North Stars.
❷-Formerly Atlanta Flames.
❸-Formerly Winnipeg Jets.
❹-Formerly Québec Nordiques.
❺-Formerly Kansas City Scouts, Colorado Rockies.
❻-Formerly Hartford Whalers.

(a)- Includes records vs. Montréal Maroons, New York Americans, Ottawa Senators (1917-31), Pittsburgh Pirates, Philadelphia Quakers, St. Louis Eagles, California Golden Seals and Cleveland Barons.

DETROIT RED WINGS
NHL GOALTENDING LEADERS

REGULAR SEASON
(Minimum 30 Wins)

SHUTOUTS

T. Sawchuk – 12.51-52, 53-54, 54-55
G. Hall – 12 55-56
H. Holmes – 11 27-28
T. Sawchuk – 11 50-51
J. R. Roach – 10 32-33
C. Dolson – 10 28-29
T. Sawchuk – 9 52-53
H. Lumley – 7..................47-48,49-50
R. Crozier – 7...........................65-66
H. Holmes – 6 26-27
C. Dolson – 6 30-31
A. Connell – 6 31-32
N. Smith – 6...................35-36, *36-37
H. Lumley – 6...........................48-49
R. Crozier – 6...........................64-65
R. Edwards – 6 ....*72-73
C. Osgood – 6 ....96-97, 97-98, 99-00
D. Hasek – 5 2001-02
C. Osgood – 5..........................95-96
G. Hanlon – 4 ....*87-88
T. Cheveldae – 4.....................92-93
C. Osgood – 3..........................98-99

*-Shared lead
+-1st in NHL

WINS

T. Sawchuk – 44 ....50-51, 51-52
+ D. Hasek – 41 2001-02
T. Sawchuk – 40 54-55
R. Crozier – 40.........................64-65
+ C. Osgood – 39........................95-96
G. Hall – 38..............................56-57
T. Cheveldae – 38 91-92
T. Sawchuk – 35 53-54
H. Lumley – 34.........................48-49
C. Osgood – 34.........................98-99
H. Lumley – 33.........................49-50
C. Osgood – 33.........................97-98
T. Sawchuk – 32 52-53
H. Lumley – 30.........................47-48
G. Hall – 30..............................55-56
C. Osgood – 30.........................99-00

DETROIT RED WINGS SEASON-BY-SEASON GOALTENDING LEADERS

SEASON	GAMES		WINS		SHUT-OUTS		G.A.A.	
1926-27	Holmes	43	Holmes	12	Holmes	6	Holmes	2.33
1927-28	Holmes	44	Holmes	19	Holmes	11	Holmes	1.80
1928-29	Dolson	44	Dolson	19	Dolson	10	Dolson	1.43
1929-30	Beveridge	39	Beveridge	14	Beveridge	2	Beveridge	2.79
1930-31	Dolson	44	Dolson	16	Dolson	6	Dolson	2.39
1931-32	Connell	48	Connell	18	Connell	6	Connell	2.25
1932-33	Roach	48	Roach	25	Roach	10	Roach	1.94
1933-34	Cude	29	Cude	15	Cude	4	Cude	1.62
1934-35	N. Smith	25	N. Smith	12	Roach	4	N. Smith	2.08
1935-36	N. Smith	48	N. Smith	24	N. Smith	6	N. Smith	2.15
1936-37	N. Smith	48	N. Smith	25	N. Smith	6	N. Smith	2.13
1937-38	N. Smith	47	N. Smith	11	N. Smith	3	N. Smith	2.77
1938-39	Thompson	39	Thompson	16	Thompson	4	Thompson	2.59
1939-40	Thompson	46	Thompson	16	Thompson	3	Thompson	2.61
1940-41	Mowers	48	Mowers	21	Mowers	4	Mowers	2.13
1941-42	Mowers	47	Mowers	19	Mowers	5	Mowers	3.06
1942-43	Mowers	50	Mowers	25	Mowers	6	Mowers	2.47
1943-44	Dion	26	Dion	17	Dion/Franks	1	Dion	3.08
1944-45	Lumley	37	Lumley	24	Lumley	1	Lumley	3.22
1945-46	Lumley	50	Lumley	20	Lumley	2	Lumley	3.18
1946-47	Lumley	52	Lumley	22	Lumley	3	Lumley	3.06
1947-48	Lumley	60	Lumley	30	Lumley	7	Lumley	2.46
1948-49	Lumley	60	Lumley	34	Lumley	6	Lumley	2.42
1949-50	Lumley	63	Lumley	33	Lumley	7	Lumley	2.35
1950-51	Sawchuk	70	Sawchuk	44	Sawchuk	11	Sawchuk	1.99
1951-52	Sawchuk	70	Sawchuk	44	Sawchuk	12	Sawchuk	1.90
1952-53	Sawchuk	63	Sawchuk	32	Sawchuk	9	Sawchuk	1.90
1953-54	Sawchuk	67	Sawchuk	35	Sawchuk	12	Sawchuk	1.94
1954-55	Sawchuk	68	Sawchuk	40	Sawchuk	12	Sawchuk	1.96
1955-56	Hall	70	Hall	30	Hall	12	Hall	2.11
1956-57	Hall	70	Hall	38	Hall	4	Hall	2.24
1957-58	Sawchuk	70	Sawchuk	29	Sawchuk	3	Sawchuk	2.96
1958-59	Sawchuk	67	Sawchuk	23	Sawchuk	5	Sawchuk	3.12
1959-60	Sawchuk	58	Sawchuk	24	Sawchuk	5	Sawchuk	2.69

SEASON	GAMES		WINS		SHUT-OUTS		G.A.A.	
1960-61	Sawchuk	37	Bassen	13	Sawchuk	2	Bassen	2.89
1961-62	Sawchuk	43	Sawchuk	14	Sawchuk	5	Bassen	2.81
1962-63	Sawchuk	48	Sawchuk	23	Sawchuk	3	Sawchuk	2.48
1963-64	Sawchuk	53	Sawchuk	24	Sawchuk	5	Sawchuk	2.60
1964-65	Crozier	70	Crozier	40	Crozier	6	Crozier	2.42
1965-66	Crozier	64	Crozier	28	Crozier	7	Crozier	2.78
1966-67	Crozier	58	Crozier	22	Crozier	4	Crozier	3.35
1967-68	Edwards	41	Edwards	15	Crozier	1	Crozier	3.30
1968-69	Edwards	40	Edwards	18	Edwards	4	Edwards	2.54
1969-70	Edwards	47	Edwards	24	Edwards	2	Edwards	2.59
1970-71	Edwards	37	Edwards	11	Rutherford	1	Edwards	3.39
1971-72	A. Smith	43	A. Smith	18	A. Smith	4	Daley	3.15
1972-73	Edwards	52	Edwards	27	Edwards	6	Edwards	2.63
1973-74	Grant	37	Grant	15	McKenzie/ Grant	1	Rutherford	3.63
1974-75	Rutherford	59	Rutherford	20	Rutherford	2	Rutherford	3.74
1975-76	Rutherford	44	Rutherford	13	Rutherford	4	Giacomin	3.45
1976-77	Rutherford	48	Giacomin	8	Giacomin	3	Giacomin	3.58
1977-78	Rutherford	43	Rutherford	20	Rutherford/ Low	1	Rutherford	3.26
1978-79	Vachon	50	Rutherford	13	Rutherford	1	Rutherford	3.27
1979-80	Vachon	59	Vachon	20	Vachon	4	Vachon	3.61
1980-81	Gilbert	48	Gilbert	11			Gilbert	4.01
1981-82	Sauve	41	Sauve	11			Sauve	4.19
1982-83	Stefan	35	Micalef	11	Micalef	2	Micalef	3.62
1983-84	Stefan	50	Stefan	19	Stefan	2	Stefan	3.51
1984-85	Stefan	46	Stefan	21			Stefan	4.33
1985-86	Stefan	37	Stefan	10	Stefan/ Laforest	1	Stefan	4.50
1986-87	Stefan	43	Stefan	20	Hanlon/ Stefan	1	Hanlon	3.18
1987-88	Hanlon	47	Hanlon	22	Hanlon	4	Stefan	3.11
1988-89	Stefan	46	Stefan	21	Hanlon	1	Hanlon	3.56
1989-90	Hanlon	45	Hanlon	15	Hanlon	3	Cheveldae	3.79
1990-91	Cheveldae	65	Cheveldae	30	Cheveldae	2	Cheveldae	3.55
1991-92	Cheveldae	72	Cheveldae	38	Cheveldae	2	Cheveldae	3.20
1992-93	Cheveldae	67	Cheveldae	34	Cheveldae	4	Cheveldae	3.25
1993-94	Osgood	41	Osgood	23	Osgood	2	Osgood	2.86
1994-95	Vernon	30	Vernon	19	Osgood/ Vernon	1	Osgood	2.26
1995-96	Osgood	50	Osgood	39	Osgood	5	Osgood	2.17
1996-97	Osgood	47	Osgood	23	Osgood	6	Osgood	2.30
1997-98	Osgood	64	Osgood	33	Osgood	6	Osgood	2.21
1998-99	Osgood	63	Osgood	34	Osgood	3	Osgood	2.42
1999-00	Osgood	53	Osgood	30	Osgood	6	Osgood	2.40
2000-01	Osgood	52	Osgood	25	Legace	2	Legace	2.05
2001-02	Hasek	65	Hasek	41	Hasek	5	Hasek	2.17